# TextGraphs-15: Graph-based Methods for Natural Language Processing



Online
11 June 2021

ISBN: 978-1-7138-9158-1

**Printed from e-media with permission by:**

Curran Associates, Inc.
57 Morehouse Lane
Red Hook, NY 12571

**Some format issues inherent in the e-media version may also appear in this print version.**



Printed with permission by Curran Associates, Inc. (2024)



Association for Computational Linguistics
209 N. Eighth Street
Stroudsburg, Pennsylvania 18360

Phone: 1-570-476-8006
Fax: 1-570-476-0860

acl@aclweb.org

**Additional copies of this publication are available from:**

Curran Associates, Inc.
57 Morehouse Lane
Red Hook, NY 12571 USA
Phone: 845-758-0400
Fax: 845-758-2633
Email: curran@proceedings.com
Web: www.proceedings.com

NAACL-HLT 2021

# Graph-Based Methods for Natural Language Processing

## Proceedings of the Fifteenth Workshop

June 11, 2021

# Introduction

Welcome to TextGraphs, the Workshop on Graph-Based Methods for Natural Language Processing. The fifteenth edition of our workshop is being organized online on June 11, 2021, in conjunction with the 2021 Annual Conference of the North American Chapter of the Association for Computational Linguistics (NAACL-2021).

The workshops in the TextGraphs series have published and promoted the synergy between the field of Graph Theory (GT) and Natural Language Processing (NLP). The mix between the two started small, with graph theoretical frameworks providing efficient and elegant solutions for NLP applications. Graph-based solutions initially focused on single-document part-of-speech tagging, word sense disambiguation, and semantic role labeling, and became progressively larger to include ontology learning and information extraction from large text collections. Nowadays, graph-based solutions also target on Web-scale applications such as information propagation in social networks, rumor proliferation, e-reputation, multiple entity detection, language dynamics learning, and future events prediction, to name a few.

The target audience comprises researchers working on problems related to either Graph Theory or graph-based algorithms applied to Natural Language Processing, Social Media, and the Semantic Web.

This year, we received 22 submissions and accepted 17 of them for oral presentation (12 long papers and 5 short papers). Similarly to the last year, we organized a shared task on Multi-Hop Inference for Explanation Regeneration. The goal of the task was to provide detailed gold explanations for standardized elementary science exam questions by selecting facts from a knowledge base. This year's shared task on multi-hop explanation regeneration attracted four teams. Three participants' reports along with the shared task overview by its organizers are also presented at the workshop.

We would like to thank our invited speakers Laura Dietz (University of New Hampshire) and Jure Leskovec (Stanford University) for their talks. We are also thankful to the members of the program committee for their valuable and high-quality reviews. All submissions have benefited from their expert feedback. Their timely contribution was the basis for accepting an excellent list of papers and making the fourteenth edition of TextGraphs a success.

Alexander Panchenko, Fragkiskos D. Malliaros, Varvara Logacheva, Abhik Jana, Dmitry Ustalov, Peter Jansen.

TextGraphs-15 Organizers

June 2021

## Program Committee

Željko Agić, Unity Technologies, Denmark
Ilseyar Alimova, Kazan Federal University, Russian Federation
Martin Andrews, Red Dragon AI, Singapore
Amir Bakarov, Behavox, Russian Federation
Tomáš Brychcín, University of West Bohemia, Czech Republic
Ruben Cartuyvels, Catholic University of Leuven, Belgium
Flavio Massimiliano Cecchini, Università Cattolica del Sacro Cuore, Italy
Mihail Chernoskutov, IMM UB RAS, Russian Federation
Yew Ken Chia, Singapore University of Technology and Design, Singapore
Rajarshi Das, University of Massachusetts, Amherst, USA
Stefano Faralli, University of Rome Unitelma Sapienza, Italy
Deborah Ferreira, University of Manchester, UK
Michael Flor, Educational Testing Service, USA
Debanjan Ghosh, Educational Testing Service, USA
Goran Glavaš, University of Mannheim, Germany
Natalia Grabar, CNRS STL UMR8163, Université de Lille, France
Aayushee Gupta, International Institute of Information Technology, Bangalore, India
Binod Gyawali, Educational Testing Service, USA
Carlos Gómez-Rodríguez, Universidade da Coruña, Spain
Rima Hazra, Indian Institute of Technology, Kharagpur, India
Tomáš Hercig, University of West Bohemia, Czech Republic
Dmitry Ilvovsky, National Research University Higher School of Economics, Russian Federation
Mohammad Javad Hosseini, University of Edinburgh, Informatics, UK
Abhik Jana, Universität Hamburg, Germany
Ming Jiang, University of Illinois at Urbana-Champaign, USA
Sammy Khalife, Ecole Polytechnique, France
Fragkiskos Malliaros, CentraleSupélec, University of Paris-Saclay, France
Valentin Malykh, Huawei Noah's Ark Lab / Kazan Federal University, Russian Federation
Gabor Melli, OpenGov, USA
Alireza Mohammadshahi, IDIAP, Switzerland
Clayton Morrison, University of Arizona, USA
Matthew Mulholland, Educational Testing Service, USA
Giannis Nikolentzos, Ecole Polytechnique, France
Enrique Noriega-Atala, The University of Arizona, USA
Damien Nouvel, INALCO ERTIM, France
Chunguang Pan, DeepBlue Technology (Shanghai) Co., Ltd, China
Aditya Girish Pawate, Indian Institute of Technology, Kharagpur, India
Jan Wira Gotama Putra, Tokyo Institute of Technology, Japan
Zimeng Qiu, Amazon Alexa AI, USA
Leonardo F. R. Ribeiro, TU Darmstadt, Germany
Michael Richter, Leipzig University, Germany
Stephen Roller, Facebook AI Research, USA
Minoru Sasaki, Ibaraki University, Japan
Viktor Schlegel, University of Manchester, UK
Rebecca Sharp, University of Arizona, USA
Artem Shelmanov, Skolkovo Institute of Science and Technology, Russian Federation
Konstantinos Skianis, BLUAI, Greece
Mark Steedman, University of Edinburgh, UK
Mokanarangan Thayaparan, University of Manchester, UK

Antoine Tixier, Ecole Polytechnique, Palaiseau, France, France
Nicolas Turenne, BNU HKBU United International College (UIC), China
Adrian Ulges, RheinMain University of Applied Sciences, Germany
Vaibhav Vaibhav, Apple, USA
Anssi Yli-Jyrä, University of Helsinki, Finland
Xiang Zhao, National University of Defense Technology, China

## Organizing Committee

Alexander Panchenko, Skoltech
Fragkiskos D. Malliaros, CentraleSupélec, University of Paris-Saclay
Varvara Logacheva, Skoltech
Abhik Jana, University of Hamburg
Dmitry Ustalov, Yandex
Peter Jansen, School of Information, University of Arizona

# Table of Contents

# Workshop Program

**Friday, June 11, 2021**

**10:00–10:15 Opening Session**

**10:15–11:15 Invited Talk by Prof. Jure Leskovec (Stanford University)**

**11:15–11:30** ***Break***

**11:30–13:10 Oral Presentation Session - 1**

11:30–11:50 *Bootstrapping Large-Scale Fine-Grained Contextual Advertising Classifier from Wikipedia*
Yiping Jin, Vishakha Kadam and Dittaya Wanvarie

11:50–12:10 *Modeling Graph Structure via Relative Position for Text Generation from Knowledge Graphs*
Martin Schmitt, Leonardo F. R. Ribeiro, Philipp Dufter, Iryna Gurevych and Hinrich Schütze

12:10–12:30 *Entity Prediction in Knowledge Graphs with Joint Embeddings*
Matthias Baumgartner, Daniele Dell'Aglio and Abraham Bernstein

12:30–12:50 *Hierarchical Graph Convolutional Networks for Jointly Resolving Cross-document Coreference of Entity and Event Mentions*
Duy Phung, Tuan Ngo Nguyen and Thien Huu Nguyen

12:50–13:10 *GENE: Global Event Network Embedding*
Qi Zeng, Manling Li, Tuan Lai, Heng Ji, Mohit Bansal and Hanghang Tong

**13:10–13:25** ***Break***

**13:25–15:25 Oral Presentation Session - 2**

13:25–13:45 *Learning Clause Representation from Dependency-Anchor Graph for Connective Prediction*
Yanjun Gao, Ting-Hao Huang and Rebecca J. Passonneau

13:45–14:05 *WikiGraphs: A Wikipedia Text - Knowledge Graph Paired Dataset*
Luyu Wang, Yujia Li, Ozlem Aslan and Oriol Vinyals

14:05–14:20 *Selective Attention Based Graph Convolutional Networks for Aspect-Level Sentiment Classification*
Xiaochen Hou, Jing Huang, Guangtao Wang, Peng Qi, Xiaodong He and Bowen Zhou

14:20–14:45 *Keyword Extraction Using Unsupervised Learning on the Document's Adjacency Matrix*
Eirini Papagiannopoulou, Grigorios Tsoumakas and Apostolos Papadopoulos

14:45–15:05 *Improving Human Text Simplification with Sentence Fusion*
Max Schwarzer, Teerapaun Tanprasert and David Kauchak

15:05–15:25 *Structural Realization with GGNNs*
Jinman Zhao, Gerald Penn and huan ling

**15:25–15:40** ***Break***

**Friday, June 11, 2021 (continued)**

**15:40–16:40 Invited Talk by Prof. Laura Dietz (University of New Hampshire)**

**16:40–16:50** ***Break***

**16:50–18:05 Oral Presentation Session - 3**

16:50–17:05 *MG-BERT: Multi-Graph Augmented BERT for Masked Language Modeling*
Parishad BehnamGhader, Hossein Zakerinia and Mahdieh Soleymani Baghshah

17:05–17:20 *GTN-ED: Event Detection Using Graph Transformer Networks*
Sanghamitra Dutta, Liang Ma, Tanay Kumar Saha, Di Liu, Joel Tetreault and Alejandro Jaimes

17:20–17:35 *Fine-grained General Entity Typing in German using GermaNet*
Sabine Weber and Mark Steedman

17:35–17:50 *On Geodesic Distances and Contextual Embedding Compression for Text Classification*
Rishi Jha and Kai Mihata

17:50–18:05 *Semi-Supervised Joint Estimation of Word and Document Readability*
Yoshinari Fujinuma and Masato Hagiwara

**18:05–18:10** ***Break***

**Friday, June 11, 2021 (continued)**

**18:10–18:50 Poster Session**

18:10–18:50 *TextGraphs 2021 Shared Task on Multi-Hop Inference for Explanation Regeneration*
Peter Jansen, Mokanarangan Thayaparan, Marco Valentino and Dmitry Ustalov

18:10–18:50 *DeepBlueAI at TextGraphs 2021 Shared Task: Treating Multi-Hop Inference Explanation Regeneration as A Ranking Problem*
Chunguang Pan, Bingyan Song and Zhipeng Luo

18:10–18:50 *A Three-step Method for Multi-Hop Inference Explanation Regeneration*
Yuejia Xiang, Yunyan Zhang, Xiaoming Shi, Bo Liu, Wandi Xu and Xi Chen

18:10–18:50 *Textgraphs-15 Shared Task System Description : Multi-Hop Inference Explanation Regeneration by Matching Expert Ratings*
Sureshkumar Vivek Kalyan, Sam Witteveen and Martin Andrews

**18:50–19:00 Closing Remarks**

# Bootstrapping Large-Scale Fine-Grained Contextual Advertising Classifier from Wikipedia

**Yiping Jin**[1,2], **Vishakha Kadam**[1], **Dittaya Wanvarie**[2]
[1]Knorex, 140 Robinson Road, 14-16 Crown @ Robinson, Singapore
[2]Department of Mathematics & Computer Science, Chulalongkorn University, Thailand
`{jinyiping, vishakha.kadam@}@knorex.com`
`Dittaya.W@chula.ac.th`

## Abstract

Contextual advertising provides advertisers with the opportunity to target the context which is most relevant to their ads. The large variety of potential topics makes it very challenging to collect training documents to build a supervised classification model or compose expert-written rules in a rule-based classification system. Besides, in fine-grained classification, different categories often overlap or cooccur, making it harder to classify accurately.

In this work, we propose *wiki2cat*, a method to tackle large-scaled fine-grained text classification by tapping on the Wikipedia category graph. The categories in the IAB taxonomy are first mapped to category nodes in the graph. Then the label is propagated across the graph to obtain a list of labeled Wikipedia documents to induce text classifiers. The method is ideal for large-scale classification problems since it does not require any manually-labeled document or hand-curated rules or keywords. The proposed method is benchmarked with various learning-based and keyword-based baselines and yields competitive performance on publicly available datasets and a new dataset containing more than 300 fine-grained categories.

## 1 Introduction

Despite the fast advancement of text classification technologies, most text classification models are trained and applied to a relatively small number of categories. Popular benchmark datasets contain from two up to tens of categories, such as SST2 dataset for sentiment classification (2 categories) (Socher et al., 2013), AG news dataset (4 categories) (Zhang et al., 2015) and 20 Newsgroups dataset (Lang, 1995) for topic classification.

In the meantime, industrial applications often involve fine-grained classification with a large number of categories. For example, Walmart built a hybrid classifier to categorize products into 5000+ product categories (Sun et al., 2014), and Yahoo built a contextual advertising classifier with a taxonomy of around 6000 categories (Broder et al., 2007). Unfortunately, both systems require a huge human effort in composing and maintaining rules and keywords. Readers can neither reproduce their system nor is the system or data available for comparison.

In this work, we focus on the application of contextual advertising (Jin et al., 2017), which allows advertisers to target the context most relevant to their ads. However, we cannot fully utilize its power unless we can target the page content using fine-grained categories, e.g., "coupé" vs. "hatchback" instead of "automotive" vs. "sport". This motivates a classification taxonomy with both high coverage and high granularity. The commonly used contextual taxonomy introduced by Interactive Advertising Bureau (IAB) contains 23 coarse-grained categories and 355 fine-grained categories [1]. Figure 1 shows a snippet of the taxonomy.

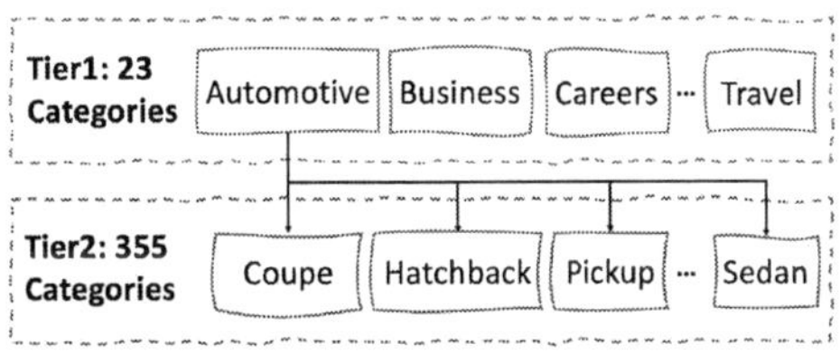


Figure 1: Snippet of IAB Content Categorization Taxonomy.

Large online encyclopedias, such as Wikipedia, contain an updated account of almost all topics. Therefore, we ask an essential question: **can we bootstrap a text classifier with hundreds of categories from Wikipedia without any manual labeling**?

We tap on and extend previous work on Wikipedia content analysis (Kittur et al., 2009) to automatically label Wikipedia articles related to

[1]`https://www.iab.com/guidelines/taxonomy/`



*Proceedings of the Fifteenth Workshop on Graph-Based Methods for Natural Language Processing (TextGraphs-15)*, pages 1–9
June 11, 2021. ©2021 Association for Computational Linguistics

each category in our taxonomy by Wikipedia category graph traversal. We then train classification models with the labeled Wikipedia articles. We compare our method with various learning-based and keyword-based baselines and obtain a competitive performance.

## 2 Related Work

### 2.1 Text Classification Using Knowledge Base

Large knowledge bases like Wikipedia or DMOZ content directory cover a wide range of topics. They also have a category hierarchy in either tree or graph structure, which provides a useful resource for building text classification models. Text classification using knowledge bases can be broadly categorized into two main approaches: vector space model and semantic model.

Vector space model aims to learn a category vector by aggregating the descendant pages and perform nearest neighbor search during classification. A pruning is usually performed first based on the depth from the root node or the number of child pages to reduce the number of categories. Subsequently, each document forms a document vector, which is aggregated to form the category vector. Lee et al. (2013) used tf-idf representation of the document, while Kim et al. (2018) combined word embeddings and tf-idf representations to obtain a better performance.

In semantic models, the input document is mapped explicitly to concepts in the knowledge base. The concepts are used either in conjunction with bag-of-words representation (Gabrilovich and Markovitch, 2006) or stand-alone (Chang et al., 2008) to assign categories to the document.

Gabrilovich and Markovitch (2006) used a feature generator to predict relevant Wikipedia concepts (articles) related to the input document. These concepts are orthogonal to the labels in specific text classification tasks and are used to enrich the representation of the input document. Experiments on multiple datasets demonstrated that the additional concepts helped improve the performance. Similarly, Zhang et al. (2013) enriched the document representation with both concepts and categories from Wikipedia.

Chang et al. (2008) proposed Dataless classification that maps both input documents and category names into Wikipedia concepts using Explicit Semantic Analysis (Gabrilovich et al., 2007). The idea is similar to Gabrilovich and Markovitch (2006), except (1) the input is mapped to a real-valued concept vector instead of a discrete list of related categories, and (2) the category name is mapped into the same semantic space, which removes the need for labeled documents.

Most recently, Chu et al. (2020) improved text classification by utilizing naturally labeled documents such as Wikipedia, Stack Exchange subareas, and Reddit subreddits. Instead of training a traditional supervised classifier, they concatenate the category name and the document and train a binary classifier, determining whether the document is related to the category. They benchmarked their proposed method extensively on 11 datasets covering topical and sentiment classification.

Our work is most similar to Lee et al. (2013). However, they only evaluated on random-split Wikipedia documents, while we apply the model to a real-world large-scale text classification problem. We also employed a graph traversal algorithm to label the documents instead of labeling all descendant documents.

### 2.2 Wikipedia Content Analysis

Some previous work tried to understand the distribution of topics in Wikipedia for data analysis and visualization (Mesgari et al., 2015). Kittur et al. (2009) calculated the distance between each page to top-level category nodes. They then assigned the category with the shortest distance to the page. With this approach, they provided the first quantitative analysis of the distribution of topics in Wikipedia.

Farina et al. (2011) extended the method by allowing traversing upward in the category graph and assigning categories proportional to the distance instead of assigning the category with the shortest-path only. More recently, Bekkerman and Donin (2017) visualized Wikipedia by building a two-level coarse-grained/fine-grained graph representation. The edges between categories capture the co-occurrence of categories on the same page. They further pruned edges between categories that rarely appear together. The resulting graph contains 441 largest categories and 4815 edges connecting them.

## 3 Method

We propose *wiki2cat*, a simple framework using **Wiki**pedia to bootstrap text **cat**egorizers. We first map the target taxonomy to correspond-

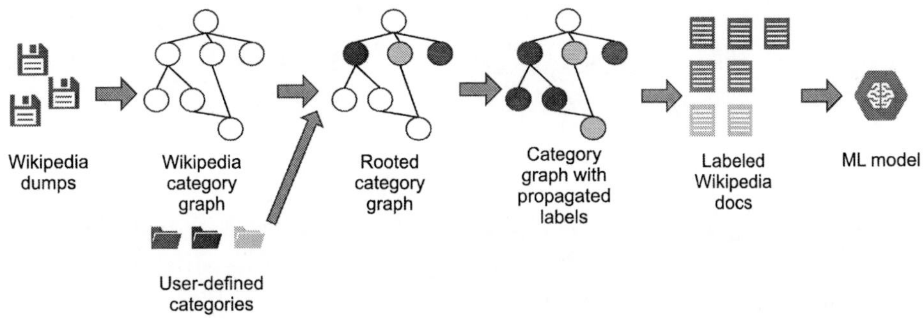


Figure 2: Overview of wiki2cat, a framework to bootstrap large-scale text classifiers from Wikipedia. We first map user-defined categories to category nodes in the Wikipedia category graph. Then, we traverse the category graph to label documents automatically. Lastly, we use the labeled documents to train a supervised classifier.

ing Wikipedia categories (briefed in Section 3.1). We then traverse the Wikipedia category graph to automatically label Wikipedia articles (Section 3.2). Finally, we induce a classifier from the labeled Wikipedia articles (Section 3.3). Figure 2 overviews the end-to-end process of building classifiers under the wiki2cat framework.

### 3.1 Mapping the Target Taxonomy to Wikipedia Categories

Wikipedia contains 2 million categories, which is 4 orders of magnitude larger than IAB taxonomy. We index all Wikipedia category names in Apache Lucene [2] and use the IAB category names to query the closest matches. We perform the following: 1) lemmatize the category names in both taxonomies, 2) index both Wikipedia category names and their alternative names from redirect links (e.g., "A.D.D." and "Attention deficit disorder"), 3) split conjunction category names and query separately (e.g., "Arts & Entertainment" $\rightarrow$ "Arts", "Entertainment"), and 4) capture small spelling variations with string similarity [3].

Out of all 23 coarse-grained and 355 fine-grained categories in IAB taxonomy, 311 categories (82%) can be mapped trivially. Their category names either match exactly or contain only small variations. E.g., the IAB category "Pagan/Wiccan" is matched to three Wikipedia categories "Paganism", "Pagans", and "Wiccans". One author of this paper took roughly 2 hours to curate the remaining 67 categories manually and provided the mapping to Wikipedia categories. Out of the 67 categories, 23 are categories that cannot be matched automatically because the category names look very different, e.g., "Road-Side Assistance" and "Emergency road services". The rest are categories where the system can find a match, but the string similarity is below the threshold (e.g., correct: "Chronic Pain" and "Chronic Pain Syndromes"; incorrect: "College Administration" and "Court Administration"). We use the curated mapping in subsequent sections.

### 3.2 Labeling Wikipedia Articles by Category Graph Traversal

With the mapping between IAB and Wikipedia categories, we can anchor each IAB category as nodes in the Wikipedia category graph [4], referred to as the *root category nodes*. Our task then becomes to obtain a set of labeled Wikipedia articles by performing graph traversal from the root category nodes. From each root category node, the category graph can be traversed using the breadth-first search algorithm to obtain a list of all descendant categories and pages.

One may argue that we can take all descendant pages of a Wikipedia category to form the labeled set. However, in Wikipedia page $A$ belongs to category $B$ does not imply a hypernym relation. In fact, some pages have a long list of categories, most of which are at their best remotely related to the main content of the page. E.g., the page "Truck Stop Women" [5] is a descendant page of the category "Trucks". However, it is a 1974 film, and

[2] https://lucene.apache.org

[3] We use Jaro-Winkler string similarity with a threshold of 0.9 to automatically map IAB categories to Wikipedia categories.

[4] We construct the category graph using the "subcat" (subcategory) relation in the Wikipedia dump. The graph contains both category nodes and page nodes. Pages all appear as leaf nodes while category nodes can be either internal or leaf nodes.

[5] https://en.wikipedia.org/wiki/Truck_Stop_Women

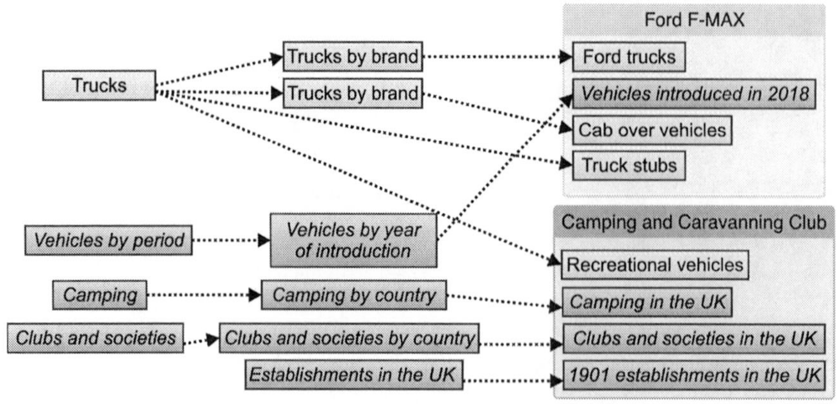


Figure 3: Intuition of the pruning for the category "Trucks". The page "Ford F-Max" belongs to four categories. Three of which can be traversed from "Trucks" and one cannot (marked in red and italic).

the main content of the page is about the plot and the cast.

We label Wikipedia pages using a competition-based algorithm following Kittur et al. (2009) and Farina et al. (2011). We treat each category node from which a page can be traversed as a candidate category and evaluate across all candidate categories to determine the final category(s) for the page.

Firstly, all pages are pruned based on the percentage of their parent categories that can be traversed from the root category. Figure 3 shows two Wikipedia pages with a snippet of their ancestor categories. Both pages have a shortest distance of 2 to the category "Trucks". However, the page "Ford F-Max" is likely more related to "Trucks" than the page "Camping and Caravanning Club" because most of its parent categories can be traversed from "Trucks". We empirically set the threshold that we will prune a page with respect to a root category if less than 30% of its parent categories can be traversed from the root category.

While the categories in IAB taxonomy occur in parallel, the corresponding categories in Wikipedia may occur in a hierarchy. For example, the category "SUVs" and "Trucks" are in parallel in IAB taxonomy but "SUVs" is a descendant category of "Trucks" in Wikipedia (Trucks ›Trucks by type ›Light trucks ›Sport utility vehicles). While traversing from the root category node, we prune all the branches corresponding to a competing category.

Pruning alone will not altogether remove the irrelevant content, because the degree of semantic relatedness is not considered. We measure the semantic relatedness between a page and a category based on two factors, namely the shortest path distance and the number of unique paths between them. Previous work depends only on the shortest path distance (Kittur et al., 2009; Farina et al., 2011). We observe that if a page is densely connected to a category via many unique paths, it is often an indication of a strong association. We calculate the weight $w$ of a page with respect to a category as follows:

$$w = \sum_{i=0}^{k} \frac{1}{2^{d_i}} \tag{1}$$

where $k$ is the number of unique paths between the page and the category node, and $d_i$ is the distance between the two in the $i$th path. To calculate the final list of categories, the weights for all competing categories are normalized to 1 by summing over each candidate category $j$ and the categories which have a weight higher than 0.3 are returned as the final assigned categories.

$$w_j = \sum_{i=0}^{k_j} \frac{1}{2^{d_{ij}}} / (\sum_{j} \sum_{i=0}^{k_j} \frac{1}{2^{d_{ij}}}) \tag{2}$$

The labeling process labeled in total 1.16 million Wikipedia articles. The blue scattered plot in Figure 4 plots the number of labeled training articles per fine-grained category in log-10 scale. We can see that the majority of the categories have between 100 to 10k articles.

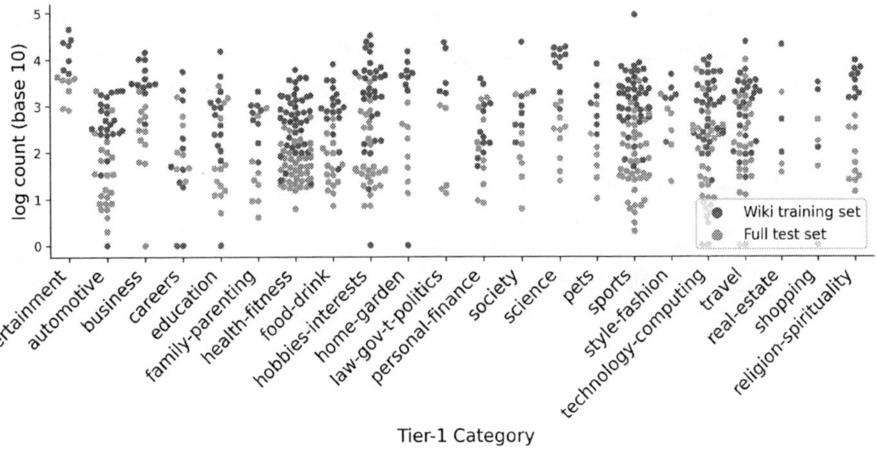


Figure 4: Blue: # of automatically labeled Wikipedia articles per fine-grained category in log-10 scale. (mean=2.95, std=0.86). Orange: # of articles per fine-grained category in the full test set in log-10 scale (mean=1.94, std=0.78).

### 3.3 Training Contextual Classifiers

The output of the algorithm described in Section 3.2 is a set of labeled Wikipedia pages. In theory, we can apply any supervised learning method to induce classifiers from the labeled dataset. The focus of this work is not to introduce a novel model architecture, but to demonstrate the effectiveness of the framework to bootstrap classifiers without manual labeling. We experiment with three simple and representative classification models. The first model is a linear SVM with tf-idf features, which is a competitive baseline for many NLP tasks (Wang and Manning, 2012). The second model is a centroid classifier, which is commonly used in large-scale text classification (Lee et al., 2013). It averages the tf-idf vectors of all documents belonging to each category and classifies by searching for the nearest category vector. The third model uses BERT (Devlin et al., 2019) to generate the semantic representation from the text and uses a single-layer feed-forward classification head on top. We freeze the pre-trained BERT model and train only the classification head for efficient training.

The number of labeled Wikipedia documents for each category is highly imbalanced. Minority categories contain only a handful of pages, while some categories have hundreds of thousands of pages. We perform random over- and downsampling to keep 1k documents for each fine-grained category and 20k documents for each coarse-grained category to form the training set. [6]

[6]We use the original dataset without sampling for the centroid classifier since it is not affected by label imbalance.

## 4 Experiments

### 4.1 Evaluation Datasets

We evaluated our method using three contextual classification datasets. The first two are coarse-grained evaluation datasets published by Jin et al. (2020) covering all IAB tier-1 categories except for "News" (totaling 22 categories). The datasets are collected using different methods (news-crawl-v2 dataset (nc-v2) by mapping from news categories; browsing dataset by manual labelling) and contain 2,127 and 1,501 documents separately [7].

We compiled another dataset for fine-grained classification comprising of documents labeled with one of the IAB tier-2 categories. The full dataset consists of 134k documents and took an effort of multiple person-year to collect. The sources of the dataset are news websites, URLs occurring in the online advertising traffic and URLs crawled with keywords using Google Custom Search [8].

The number of documents per category can be overviewed in Figure 4 (the orange scatter plot). 23 out of 355 IAB tier-2 categories are not included in the dataset because they are too rare and are not present in our data source. So there are in total 332 fine-grained categories in the datasets. Due to company policy, we can publish only a random sample of the dataset with ten documents per category [9]. We report the performance on both datasets

[7]https://github.com/YipingNUS/nle-supplementary-dataset

[8]https://developers.google.com/custom-search/

[9]https://github.com/YipingNUS/

for future work to reproduce our result. To our best knowledge, this dataset will be the only publicly available dataset for fine-grained contextual classification.

We focus on classifying among fine-grained categories under the same parent category. Figure 5 shows the number of fine-grained categories under each coarse category. While the median number of categories is 10, the classification is challenging because categories are similar to each other.

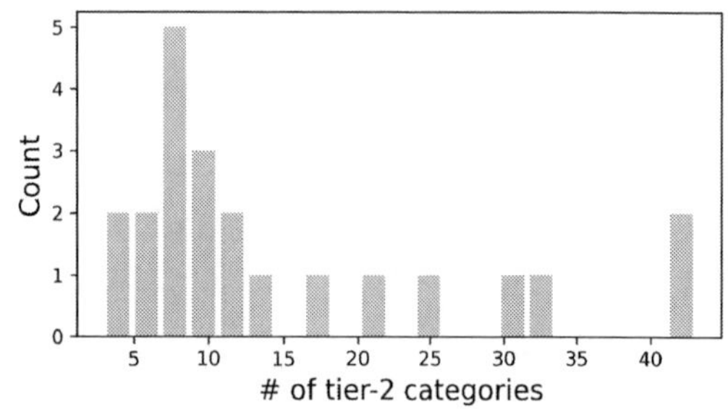


Figure 5: Number of fine-grained categories per coarse-grained category in our fine-grained contextual classification evaluation dataset.

### 4.2 Experimental Settings

Throughout this paper, we use the Wikipedia dump downloaded on 10 December 2019. After removing hidden categories and list pages, the final category graph contains 14.9 million articles, 1.9 million categories and 37.9 million links. The graph is stored in Neo4J database [10] and occupies 4.7GB disk space (not including the page content).

We use the SGD classifier implementation in scikit-learn [11] with default hyperparameters for linear SVM. Words are weighted using tf-idf with a minimum term frequency cutoff of 3. We implement the centroid classifier using TfidfVectorizer in scikit-learn and use numpy to implement the nearest neighbor classification.

For BERT, we use DistilBERT implementation by HuggingFace [12], a model which is both smaller and faster than the original BERT-base model. We use a single hidden layer with 256 units for the feed-forward classification head. The model is implemented in PyTorch and optimized with Adam optimizer with a learning rate of 0.01.

contextual-eval-dataset

[10] https://neo4j.com

[11] https://scikit-learn.org

[12] https://huggingface.co/transformers/model_doc/distilbert.html

We compare wiki2cat with the following baselines:

- **Keyword voting** (kw voting): predicts the category whose name occurs most frequently in the input document. If none of the category names is present, the model predicts a random label.
- **Dataless** (Chang et al., 2008): maps the input document and the category name into the same semantic space representing Wikipedia concepts using Explicit Semantic Analysis (ESA) (Gabrilovich et al., 2007).
- **Doc2vec** (Le and Mikolov, 2014): similar to the Dataless model. Instead of using ESA, it uses doc2vec to generate the document and category vector.
- **STM** (Li et al., 2018): seed-guided topic model. The state-of-the-art model on coarse-grained contextual classification. Underlying, STM calculates each word's co-occurrence and uses it to "expand" the knowledge beyond the given seed words. For coarse-grained classification, STM used hand-curated seed words while STM,$S_{label}$ used category names as seed words. Both were trained by Jin et al. (2020) on a private in-domain dataset. We also trained STM using our Wikipedia dataset, referred to as STM,$D_{wiki}$. For fine-grained classification, we report only the result of STM,$S_{label}$ since no previously published seed words are available.

Keyword voting and Dataless do not require any training document. Both Doc2vec and STM require unlabeled training corpus. We copy the coarse-grained classification result for Doc2vec, STM, and STM,$S_{label}$ from Jin et al. (2020). For fine-grained classification, we train Doc2vec and STM,$S_{label}$ using the same set of Wikipedia documents as in wiki2cat.

### 4.3 Result of Coarse-Grained Contextual Classification

We present the performance of various models on nc-v2 and browsing dataset in Table 1.

We can observe that wiki2cat using SVM as the learning algorithm outperformed Dataless and Doc2vec baseline. However, it did not perform as well as STM. The STM model was trained using a list of around 30 carefully chosen keywords for each category. It also used in-domain unlabeled documents during training, which we do not

| Model | nc-v2 | | browsing | |
|---|---|---|---|---|
| | acc | ma$F_1$ | acc$^+$ | ma$F_1$ |
| kw voting | .196 | .180 | .251 | .189 |
| Dataless | .412 | .377 | .536 | .392 |
| Doc2vec | .480 | .461 | .557 | .424 |
| STM | **.623** | **.607** | **.794** | **.625** |
| STM,$S_{label}$ | .332 | .259 | .405 | .340 |
| STM,$D_{wiki}$ | .556 | .533 | .780 | .595 |
| w2c$_{svm}$ | .563 | .539 | .659 | .523 |
| w2c$_{centroid}$ | .471 | .426 | .675 | .523 |
| w2c$_{bert}$ | .440 | .403 | .621 | .482 |

Table 1: Performance of various models on IAB coarse-grained classification datasets. The best performance is highlighted in bold.

use. Jin et al. (2020) demonstrated that the choice of seed keywords has a significant impact on the model's accuracy. STM,$S_{label}$ is the result of STM using only unigrams in the category name as seed keywords. Despite using the same learning algorithm as STM, its performance was much worse than using hand-picked seed words.

To investigate the contribution of the in-domain unlabeled document to STM's superior performance, we trained an STM model with the manually-curated keywords in Jin et al. (2020) and the Wikipedia dataset we used to train wiki2cat (denoted as STM,$D_{wiki}$). There is a noticeable decrease in performance in STM,$D_{wiki}$ without in-domain unlabeled documents. It underperformed w2c$_{svm}$ on nc-v2 dataset and outperformed it on browsing dataset.

w2c$_{centroid}$ performed slightly better than w2c$_{svm}$ on the browsing dataset but worse on the nc-v2 dataset. Surprisingly, BERT did not perform as well as the other two much simpler models. We conjecture there are two possible causes. Firstly, BERT has a limitation of sequence length (maximum 512 words). The average sequence length of news-crawl-v2 and browsing datasets are 1,470 and 350 words. Incidentally, there was a more substantial performance gap between BERT and SVM on the news-crawl-v2 dataset. Secondly, our training corpus consists of only Wikipedia articles, while the model was applied to another domain. Therefore, the contextual information that BERT captured may be irrelevant or even counterproductive. We leave a more in-depth analysis to future work and adhere to the SVM and Centroid model hereafter.

### 4.4 Impact of Graph Labeling Algorithms

| Model | nc-v2 | | browsing | |
|---|---|---|---|---|
| | acc | ma$F_1$ | acc$^+$ | ma$F_1$ |
| w2c | **.563** | **.539** | **.659** | **.523** |
| w2c$_{child}$ | .325 | .289 | .340 | .322 |
| w2c$_{descendant}$ | .539 | .503 | .607 | .481 |
| w2c$_{min-dist}$ | .533 | .498 | .612 | .489 |
| w2c$_{no-pruning}$ | .488 | .466 | .608 | .491 |

Table 2: Performance of the SVM model trained with datasets labeled using different labeling algorithms.

We now turn our attention to the impact of different graph labeling algorithms on the final classification accuracy. We compare our graph labeling method introduced in Section 3.2 with three methods mentioned in previous work, namely labeling only immediate child pages (child), labeling all descendant pages (descendant), assigning the label with shortest distance (min-dist) as well as another baseline removing the pruning step from our method (no-pruning). We use an SVM model with the same hyperparameters as w2c$_{svm}$. Their performance is shown in Table 2.

Using only the immediate child pages led to poor performance. Firstly, it limited the number of training documents. Some categories have only a dozen of immediate child pages. Secondly, the authors of Wikipedia often prefer to assign pages to specific categories instead of general categories. They assign a page to a general category only when it is ambiguous. Despite previous work in Wikipedia content analysis advocated using shortest distance to assign the topic to articles (Kittur et al., 2009; Farina et al., 2011), we did not observe a substantial improvement using shortest distance over using all descendant pages. Our graph labeling method outperformed all baselines, including its modified version without pruning.

### 4.5 Result of Fine-Grained Contextual Classification

Table 3 presents the result on fine-grained classification. We notice a performance difference on the full and sample dataset. However, the relative performance of various models on the two datasets remains consistent.

A first observation is that the keyword voting baseline performed very poorly, having 7.5-10.8% accuracy. It shows that the category name itself is not enough to capture the semantics. E.g., the

| Model | Full dataset | | Sample dataset | |
|---|---|---|---|---|
| | acc | ma$F_1$ | acc | ma$F_1$ |
| kw voting | .108 | .018 | .075 | .025 |
| Dataless | .428 | .376 | .477 | .462 |
| Doc2vec | .246 | .152 | .253 | .211 |
| STM,$S_{label}$ | .493 | .370 | .533 | .464 |
| w2c$_{svm}$ | .542* | **.464*** | **.646*** | **.627*** |
| w2c$_{centroid}$ | **.548*** | .451* | .595* | .566* |

Table 3: Performance of various models on IAB fine-grained classification datasets. * indicates a statistically significant improvement from baselines with p-value<0.05 using single-sided sample T-test.

category "Travel > South America" does not match a document about traveling in Rio de Janeiro or Buenos Aires but will falsely match content about "*South* Korea" or "United States of *America*".

Dataless and STM outperformed the keyword voting baseline by a large margin. However, wiki2cat is clearly the winner, outperforming these baselines by 5-10%. It demonstrated that the automatically labeled documents are helpful for the more challenging fine-grained classification task where categories are more semantically similar and harder to be specified with a handful of keywords.

## 5 Conclusions and Future Work

We introduced *wiki2cat*, a simple framework to bootstrap large-scale fine-grained text classifiers from Wikipedia without having to label any document manually. The method was benchmarked on both coarse-grained and fine-grained contextual advertising datasets and achieved competitive performance against various baselines. It performed especially well on fine-grained classification, which both is more challenging and requires more manual labeling in a fully-supervised setting. As an ongoing effort, we are exploring using unlabeled in-domain documents for domain adaptation to achieve better accuracy.

## Acknowledgement

YJ was supported by the scholarship from 'The 100th Anniversary Chulalongkorn University Fund for Doctoral Scholarship'. We thank anonymous reviewers for their valuable feedback.

## References

Ron Bekkerman and Olga Donin. 2017. Visualizing wikipedia for interactive exploration. In *Proceedings of KDD 2017 Workshop on Interactive Data Exploration and Analytics (IDEA17)*, Halifax, Nova Scotia, Canada.

Andrei Broder, Marcus Fontoura, Vanja Josifovski, and Lance Riedel. 2007. A semantic approach to contextual advertising. In *Proceedings of the 30th International ACM SIGIR Conference on Research and Development in Information Retrieval*, pages 559–566.

Ming-Wei Chang, Lev-Arie Ratinov, Dan Roth, and Vivek Srikumar. 2008. Importance of semantic representation: Dataless classification. In *Proceedings of the AAAI Conference on Artificial Intelligence*, volume 2, pages 830–835.

Zewei Chu, Karl Stratos, and Kevin Gimpel. 2020. Natcat: Weakly supervised text classification with naturally annotated datasets. *arXiv preprint arXiv:2009.14335*.

Jacob Devlin, Ming-Wei Chang, Kenton Lee, and Kristina Toutanova. 2019. Bert: Pre-training of deep bidirectional transformers for language understanding. In *Proceedings of the Conference of the North American Chapter of the Association for Computational Linguistics: Human Language Technologies*, pages 4171–4186, Minneapolis, Minnesota.

Jacopo Farina, Riccardo Tasso, and David Laniado. 2011. Automatically assigning wikipedia articles to macrocategories. In *Proceedings of Hypertext*.

Evgeniy Gabrilovich and Shaul Markovitch. 2006. Overcoming the brittleness bottleneck using wikipedia: Enhancing text categorization with encyclopedic knowledge. In *Proceedings of the AAAI Conference on Artificial Intelligence*, volume 6, pages 1301–1306.

Evgeniy Gabrilovich, Shaul Markovitch, et al. 2007. Computing semantic relatedness using wikipedia-based explicit semantic analysis. In *Proceedings of the Twentieth International Joint Conference on Artificial Intelligence*, volume 7, pages 1606–1611.

Yiping Jin, Dittaya Wanvarie, and Phu Le. 2017. Combining lightly-supervised text classification models for accurate contextual advertising. In *Proceedings of the Eighth International Joint Conference on Natural Language Processing (Volume 1: Long Papers)*, pages 545–554.

Yiping Jin, Dittaya Wanvarie, and Phu T. V. Le. 2020. Learning from noisy out-of-domain corpus using dataless classification. *Natural Language Engineering*.

Kang-Min Kim, Aliyeva Dinara, Byung-Ju Choi, and SangKeun Lee. 2018. Incorporating word embeddings into open directory project based large-scale classification. In *Proceedings of the Pacific-Asia Conference on Knowledge Discovery and Data Mining*, pages 376–388. Springer.

Aniket Kittur, Ed H Chi, and Bongwon Suh. 2009. What's in wikipedia? mapping topics and conflict using socially annotated category structure. In *Proceedings of the SIGCHI Conference on Human Factors in Computing Systems*, pages 1509–1512.

Ken Lang. 1995. Newsweeder: Learning to filter netnews. In *Proceedings of the Twelfth International Conference on Machine Learning*, pages 331–339. Elsevier.

Quoc Le and Tomas Mikolov. 2014. Distributed representations of sentences and documents. In *Proceedings of the International Conference on Machine Learning*, pages 1188–1196.

Jung-Hyun Lee, Jongwoo Ha, Jin-Yong Jung, and Sangkeun Lee. 2013. Semantic contextual advertising based on the open directory project. *ACM Transactions on the Web (TWEB)*, 7(4):1–22.

Chenliang Li, Shiqian Chen, Jian Xing, Aixin Sun, and Zongyang Ma. 2018. Seed-guided topic model for document filtering and classification. *ACM Transactions on Information Systems*, 37(1):1–37.

Mostafa Mesgari, Chitu Okoli, Mohamad Mehdi, Finn Årup Nielsen, and Arto Lanamäki. 2015. The sum of all human knowledge: A systematic review of scholarly research on the content of wikipedia. *Journal of the Association for Information Science and Technology*, 66(2):219–245.

Richard Socher, Alex Perelygin, Jean Wu, Jason Chuang, Christopher D Manning, Andrew Y Ng, and Christopher Potts. 2013. Recursive deep models for semantic compositionality over a sentiment treebank. In *Proceedings of the 2013 Conference on Empirical Methods in Natural Language Processing*, pages 1631–1642.

Chong Sun, Narasimhan Rampalli, Frank Yang, and AnHai Doan. 2014. Chimera: Large-scale classification using machine learning, rules, and crowdsourcing. *Proceedings of the VLDB Endowment*, 7(13):1529–1540.

Sida Wang and Christopher D Manning. 2012. Baselines and bigrams: Simple, good sentiment and topic classification. In *Proceedings of the 50th Annual Meeting of the Association for Computational Linguistics: Short Papers-Volume 2*, pages 90–94. Association for Computational Linguistics.

Xiang Zhang, Junbo Zhao, and Yann LeCun. 2015. Character-level convolutional networks for text classification. In *Proceedings of Advances in Neural Information Processing Systems*, pages 649–657.

Zhilin Zhang, Huaizhong Lin, Pengfei Li, Huazhong Wang, and Dongming Lu. 2013. Improving semi-supervised text classification by using wikipedia knowledge. In *Proceedings of the International Conference on Web-Age Information Management*, pages 25–36. Springer.

# Modeling Graph Structure via Relative Position for Text Generation from Knowledge Graphs

**Martin Schmitt**[1] **Leonardo F. R. Ribeiro**[2] **Philipp Dufter**[1] **Iryna Gurevych**[2] **Hinrich Schütze**[1]

[1]Center for Information and Language Processing (CIS), LMU Munich
[2]Research Training Group AIPHES and UKP Lab, Technische Universität Darmstadt
martin@cis.lmu.de

## Abstract

We present *Graformer*, a novel Transformer-based encoder-decoder architecture for graph-to-text generation. With our novel graph self-attention, the encoding of a node relies on all nodes in the input graph – not only direct neighbors – facilitating the detection of global patterns. We represent the relation between two nodes as the length of the shortest path between them. Graformer learns to weight these node-node relations differently for different attention heads, thus virtually learning differently connected views of the input graph. We evaluate Graformer on two popular graph-to-text generation benchmarks, AGENDA and WebNLG, where it achieves strong performance while using many fewer parameters than other approaches.[1]

## 1 Introduction

A knowledge graph (KG) is a flexible data structure commonly used to store both general world knowledge (Auer et al., 2008) and specialized information, e.g., in biomedicine (Wishart et al., 2018) and computer vision (Krishna et al., 2017). Generating a natural language description of such a graph (KG→text) makes the stored information accessible to a broader audience of end users. It is therefore important for KG-based question answering (Bhowmik and de Melo, 2018), data-to-document generation (Moryossef et al., 2019; Koncel-Kedziorski et al., 2019) and interpretability of KGs in general (Schmitt et al., 2020).

Recent approaches to KG→text employ encoder-decoder architectures: the encoder first computes vector representations of the graph's nodes, the decoder then uses them to predict the text sequence. Typical encoder choices are graph neural networks based on message passing between direct neighbors in the graph (Kipf and Welling, 2017; Veličković et al., 2018) or variants of Transformer (Vaswani et al., 2017) that apply self-attention on all nodes together, including those that are not directly connected. To avoid losing information, the latter approaches use edge or node *labels* from the shortest path when computing the attention between two nodes (Zhu et al., 2019; Cai and Lam, 2020). Assuming the existence of a path between any two nodes is particularly problematic for KGs: a set of KG facts often does not form a connected graph.

We propose a flexible alternative that neither needs such an assumption nor uses label information to model graph structure: a Transformer-based encoder that interprets the *lengths* of shortest paths in a graph as relative position information and thus, by means of multi-head attention, dynamically learns different structural views of the input graph with differently weighted connection patterns. We call this new architecture *Graformer*.

Following previous work, we evaluate Graformer on two benchmarks: (i) the AGENDA dataset (Koncel-Kedziorski et al., 2019), i.e., the generation of scientific abstracts from automatically extracted entities and relations specific to scientific text, and (ii) the WebNLG challenge dataset (Gardent et al., 2017), i.e., the task of generating text from DBPedia subgraphs. On both datasets, Graformer achieves more than 96% of the state-of-the-art performance while using only about half as many parameters.

In summary, our contributions are as follows: (1) We develop *Graformer*, a novel graph-to-text architecture that interprets shortest path lengths as relative position information in a graph self-attention network. (2) Graformer achieves competitive performance on two popular KG-to-text generation benchmarks, showing that our architecture can learn about graph structure without any guidance other than its text generation objective. (3) To further investigate what Graformer learns about graph structure, we visualize the differently connected

[1]Our code is publicly available: https://github.com/mnschmit/graformer



*Proceedings of the Fifteenth Workshop on Graph-Based Methods for Natural Language Processing (TextGraphs-15)*, pages 10–21
June 11, 2021. 

graph views it has learned and indeed find different attention heads for more local and more global graph information. Interestingly, direct neighbors are considered particularly important even without any structural bias, such as introduced by a graph neural network. (4) Analyzing the performance w.r.t. different input graph properties, we find evidence that Graformer's more elaborate global view on the graph is an advantage when it is important to distinguish between distant but connected nodes and truly unreachable ones.

## 2 Related Work

Most recent approaches to graph-to-text generation employ a graph neural network (GNN) based on message passing through the input graph's topology as the encoder in their encoder-decoder architectures (Marcheggiani and Perez-Beltrachini, 2018; Koncel-Kedziorski et al., 2019; Ribeiro et al., 2019; Guo et al., 2019). As one layer of these encoders only considers immediate neighbors, a large number of stacked layers can be necessary to learn about distant nodes, which in turn also increases the risk of propagating noise (Li et al., 2018).

Other approaches (Zhu et al., 2019; Cai and Lam, 2020) base their encoder on the Transformer architecture (Vaswani et al., 2017) and thus, in each layer, compute self-attention on all nodes, not only direct neighbors, facilitating the information flow between distant nodes. Like Graformer, these approaches incorporate information about the graph topology with some variant of relative position embeddings (Shaw et al., 2018). They, however, assume that there is always a path between any pair of nodes, i.e., there are no unreachable nodes or disconnected subgraphs. Thus they use an LSTM (Hochreiter and Schmidhuber, 1997) to compute a relation embedding from the labels along this path. However, in contrast to the AMR[2] graphs used for their evaluation, KGs are frequently disconnected. Graformer is more flexible and makes no assumption about connectivity. Furthermore, its relative position embeddings only depend on the *lengths* of shortest paths i.e., purely structural information, not labels. It thus effectively learns *differently connected views* of its input graph.

Deficiencies in modeling long-range dependencies in GNNs have been considered a serious limitation before. Various solutions orthogonal to our approach have been proposed in recent work: By incorporating a connectivity score into their graph attention network, Zhang et al. (2020) manage to increase the attention span to k-hop neighborhoods but, finally, only experiment with $k = 2$. Our graph encoder efficiently handles dependencies between much more distant nodes. Pei et al. (2020) define an additional neighborhood based on Euclidean distance in a continuous node embedding space. Similar to our work, a node can thus receive information from distant nodes, given their embeddings are close enough. However, Pei et al. (2020) compute these embeddings only once before training whereas in our approach node similarity is based on the learned representation in each encoder layer. This allows Graformer to dynamically change node interaction patterns during training.

Recently, Ribeiro et al. (2020) use two GNN encoders – one using the original topology and one with a fully connected version of the graph – and combine their output in various ways for graph-to-text generation. This approach can only see two extreme versions of the graph: direct neighbors and full connection. Our approach is more flexible and dynamically learns a different structural view per attention head. It is also more parameter-efficient as our multi-view encoder does not need a separate set of parameters for each view.

## 3 The Graformer Model

Graformer follows the general multi-layer encoder-decoder pattern known from the original Transformer (Vaswani et al., 2017). In the following, we first describe our formalization of the KG input and then how it is processed by Graformer.

### 3.1 Graph data structure

**Knowledge graph.** We formalize a knowledge graph (KG) as a directed, labeled multigraph $G_{KG} = (V, A, s, t, l_V, l_A, \mathcal{E}, \mathcal{R})$ with $V$ a set of vertices (the KG entities), $A$ a set of arcs (the KG facts), $s, t : A \to V$ functions assigning to each arc its source/target node (the subject/object of a KG fact), and $l_V : V \to \mathcal{E}, l_A : A \to \mathcal{R}$ providing labels for vertices and arcs, where $\mathcal{R}$ is a set of KG-specific relations and $\mathcal{E}$ a set of entity names.

**Token graph.** Entity names usually consist of more than one token or subword unit. Hence, a tokenizer $tok : \mathcal{E} \to \Sigma_T^*$ is needed that splits an entity's label into its components from the vocabulary $\Sigma_T$ of text tokens. Following recent work (Ribeiro et al., 2020), we mimic this composition-

[2]abstract meaning representation

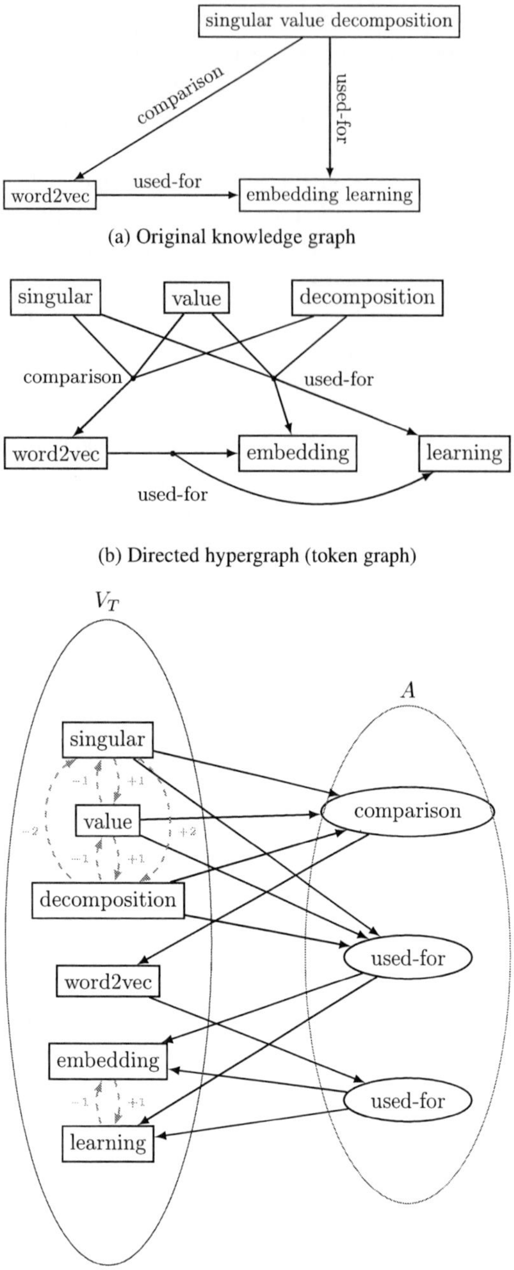


(a) Original knowledge graph

(b) Directed hypergraph (token graph)

(c) Incidence graph with $\textsc{same}_p$ edges (dashed green)

Figure 1: Different representations of the same KG (types are omitted for clarity).

ality of node labels in the graph structure by splitting each node into as many nodes as there are tokens in its label. We thus obtain a directed hypergraph $G_T = (V_T, A, s_T, t_T, l_T, l_A, \Sigma_T, \mathcal{R}, same)$, where $s_T, t_T : A \to \mathcal{P}(V_T)$ now assign a set of source (resp. target) nodes to each (hyper-) arc and all nodes are labeled with only one token, i.e., $l_T : V_T \to \Sigma_T$. Unlike Ribeiro et al. (2020), we additionally keep track of all token nodes' origins: $same : V_T \to \mathcal{P}(V_T \times \mathbb{Z})$ assigns to each node $n$ all other nodes $n'$ stemming from the same entity together with the relative position of $l_T(n)$ and $l_T(n')$ in the original tokenized entity name. Fig. 1b shows the token graph corresponding to the KG in Fig. 1a.

**Incidence graph.** For ease of implementation, our final data structure for the KG is the hypergraph's incidence graph, a bipartite graph where hyper-arcs are represented as nodes and edges are unlabeled: $G = (N, E, l, \Sigma, \{\textsc{same}_p \mid p \in \mathbb{Z}\})$ where $N = V_T \cup A$ is the set of nodes, $E = \{(n_1, n_2) \mid n_1 \in s_T(n_2) \vee n_2 \in t_T(n_1)\}$ the set of directed edges, $l : N \to \Sigma$ a label function, and $\Sigma = \Sigma_T \cup \mathcal{R}$ the vocabulary. We introduce $\textsc{same}_p$ edges to fully connect $same$ clusters: $\textsc{same}_p = \{(n_1, n_2) \mid (n_2, p) \in same(n_1)\}$ where $p$ differentiates between different relative positions in the original entity string, similar to (Shaw et al., 2018). See Fig. 1c for an example.

### 3.2 Graformer encoder

The initial graph representation $\boldsymbol{H}^{(0)} \in \mathbb{R}^{|N| \times d}$ is obtained by looking up embeddings for the node labels in the learned embedding matrix $\boldsymbol{E} \in \mathbb{R}^{|\Sigma| \times d}$, i.e., $\boldsymbol{H}_i^{(0)} = \boldsymbol{e}^{l(n_i)} \boldsymbol{E}$ where $\boldsymbol{e}^{l(n_i)}$ is the one-hot-encoding of the $i$th node's label.

To compute the node representation $\boldsymbol{H}^{(L)}$ in the $L$th layer, we follow Vaswani et al. (2017), i.e., we first normalize the input from the previous layer $\boldsymbol{H}^{(L-1)}$ via layer normalization $LN$, followed by multi-head graph self-attention $SelfAtt_g$ (see § 3.3 for details), which – after dropout regularization $Dr$ and a residual connection – yields the intermediate representation $\boldsymbol{\mathcal{I}}$ (cf. Eq. (1)). A feedforward layer $FF$ with one hidden layer and GeLU (Hendrycks and Gimpel, 2016) activation computes the final layer output (cf. Eq. (2)). As recommended by Chen et al. (2018), we apply an additional layer normalization step to the output $\boldsymbol{H}^{(L_E)}$ of the last encoder layer $L_E$.

$$\boldsymbol{\mathcal{I}}^{(L)} = Dr(SelfAtt_g(LN(\boldsymbol{H}^{(L-1)}))) + \boldsymbol{H}^{(L-1)} \tag{1}$$

$$\boldsymbol{H}^{(L)} = Dr(FF(LN(\boldsymbol{\mathcal{I}}^{(L)}))) + \boldsymbol{\mathcal{I}}^{(L)} \tag{2}$$

$SelfAtt_g$ computes a weighted sum of $\boldsymbol{H}^{(L-1)}$:

$$SelfAtt_g(\boldsymbol{H})_i = \sum_{j=1}^{|N|} \alpha_{ij}^g (\boldsymbol{H}_j \boldsymbol{W}^{V_g}) \tag{3}$$

where $\boldsymbol{W}^{V_g} \in \mathbb{R}^{d \times d}$ is a learned parameter matrix.

In the next section, we derive the definition of the graph-structure-informed attention weights $\alpha^g_{ij}$.

### 3.3 Self-attention for text and graphs with relative position embeddings

In this section, we describe the computation of attention weights for multi-head self-attention. Note that the formulas describe the computations for one head. The output of multiple heads is combined as in the original Transformer (Vaswani et al., 2017).

**Text self-attention.** Shaw et al. (2018) introduced position-aware self-attention in the Transformer by (i) adding a relative position embedding $\mathbf{A}^K \in \mathbb{R}^{M\times M\times d}$ to $\boldsymbol{X}$'s key representation, when computing the softmax-normalized attention scores $\boldsymbol{\alpha}_i$ between $\boldsymbol{X}_i \in \mathbb{R}^d$ and the complete input embedding matrix $\boldsymbol{X} \in \mathbb{R}^{M\times d}$ (cf. Eq. (4)), and (ii) adding a second type of position embedding $\mathbf{A}^V \in \mathbb{R}^{M\times M\times d}$ to $\boldsymbol{X}$'s value representation when computing the weighted sum (cf. Eq. (5)):

$$\boldsymbol{\alpha}_i = \sigma\left(\frac{\boldsymbol{X}_i \boldsymbol{W}^Q(\boldsymbol{X}\boldsymbol{W}^K + \mathbf{A}^K_i)^\top}{\sqrt{d}}\right) \quad (4)$$

$$\boldsymbol{V}_i = \sum_{j=1}^{n} \alpha_{ij}(\boldsymbol{X}_j \boldsymbol{W}^V + \mathbf{A}^V_{ij}) \quad (5)$$

where $\sigma(\cdot)$ denotes the softmax function, i.e.,

$$\sigma(\boldsymbol{b})_i = \frac{\exp(b_i)}{\sum_{j=1}^{J}\exp(b_j)}, \quad \text{for } \boldsymbol{b} \in \mathbb{R}^J.$$

Recent work (Raffel et al., 2019) has adopted a simplified form where value-modifying embeddings $\mathbf{A}^V$ are omitted and key-modifying embeddings $\mathbf{A}^K$ are replaced with learned scalar embeddings $\boldsymbol{S} \in \mathbb{R}^{M\times M}$ that – based on relative position – directly in- or decrease attention scores before normalization, i.e., Eq. (4) becomes Eq. (6).

$$\boldsymbol{\alpha}_i = \sigma\left(\frac{\boldsymbol{X}_i \boldsymbol{W}^Q(\boldsymbol{X}\boldsymbol{W}^K)^\top}{\sqrt{d}} + \boldsymbol{S}_i\right) \quad (6)$$

Shaw et al. (2018) share their position embeddings across attention heads but learn separate embeddings for each layer as word representations from different layers can vary a lot. Raffel et al. (2019) learn separate $\boldsymbol{S}$ matrices for each attention head but share them across layers. We use Raffel et al. (2019)'s form of relative position encoding for text self-attention in our decoder (§ 3.4).

**Graph self-attention.** Analogously to self-attention on text, we define our structural graph

| | $V_T$ | | | | | | $A$ | | |
|---|---|---|---|---|---|---|---|---|---|
| | s | v | d | w | e | l | c | u1 | u2 |
| s | 0 | 4 | 5 | 2 | 2 | 2 | 1 | 1 | 3 |
| v | -4 | 0 | 4 | 2 | 2 | 2 | 1 | 1 | 3 |
| d | -5 | -4 | 0 | 2 | 2 | 2 | 1 | 1 | 3 |
| w | -2 | -2 | -2 | 0 | 2 | 2 | -1 | ∞ | 1 |
| e | -2 | -2 | -2 | -2 | 0 | 4 | -3 | -1 | -1 |
| l | -2 | -2 | -2 | -2 | -4 | 0 | -3 | -1 | -1 |
| c | -1 | -1 | -1 | 1 | 3 | 3 | 0 | ∞ | 2 |
| u1 | -1 | -1 | -1 | ∞ | 1 | 1 | ∞ | 0 | ∞ |
| u2 | -3 | -3 | -3 | -1 | 1 | 1 | -2 | ∞ | 0 |

Figure 2: $\boldsymbol{R}$ matrix for the graph in Fig. 1c ($\delta_{max} = 3$).

self-attention as follows:

$$\boldsymbol{\alpha}^g_i = \sigma\left(\frac{\boldsymbol{H}_i \boldsymbol{W}^{Q_g}(\boldsymbol{H}\boldsymbol{W}^{K_g})^\top}{\sqrt{d}} + \gamma(\boldsymbol{R})_i\right) \quad (7)$$

$\boldsymbol{W}^{K_g}, \boldsymbol{W}^{Q_g} \in \mathbb{R}^{d\times d}$ are learned matrices and $\gamma : \mathbb{Z}\cup\{\infty\} \to \mathbb{R}$ looks up *learned scalar embeddings* for the relative graph positions in $\boldsymbol{R} \in \mathbb{R}^{N\times N}$.

We define the relative graph position $R_{ij}$ between the nodes $n_i$ and $n_j$ with respect to two factors: (i) the text relative position $p$ in the original entity name if $n_i$ and $n_j$ stem from the same original entity, i.e., $(n_i, n_j) \in \text{SAME}_p$ for some $p$ and (ii) shortest path lengths otherwise:

$$R_{ij} = \begin{cases} \infty, & \text{if } \delta(n_i,n_j) = \infty \\ & \text{and } \delta(n_j,n_i) = \infty \\ encode(p), & \text{if } (n_i,n_j) \in \text{SAME}_p \\ \delta(n_i,n_j), & \text{if } \delta(n_i,n_j) \le \delta(n_j,n_i) \\ -\delta(n_j,n_i), & \text{if } \delta(n_i,n_j) > \delta(n_j,n_i) \end{cases} \quad (8)$$

where $\delta(n_i, n_j)$ is the length of the shortest path from $n_i$ to $n_j$, which we define to be $\infty$ if and only if there is no such path. *encode* maps a text relative position $p \in \mathbb{Z}\setminus\{0\}$ to an integer outside $\delta$'s range to avoid clashes. Concretely, we use $encode(p) := sgn(p)\cdot\delta_{max} + p$ where $\delta_{max}$ is the maximum graph diameter, i.e., the maximum value of $\delta$ over all graphs under consideration.

Thus, we model graph relative position as the length of the shortest path using either only forward edges ($R_{ij} > 0$) or only backward edges ($R_{ij} < 0$). Additionally, two special cases are considered: (i) Nodes without any purely forward or purely backward path between them ($R_{ij} = \infty$) and (ii) token nodes from the same entity. Here the relative position in the original entity string $p$ is encoded outside the range of path length encodings (which are always in the interval $[-\delta_{max}, \delta_{max}]$).

In practice, we use two thresholds, $n_\delta$ and $n_p$. All values of $\delta$ exceeding $n_\delta$ are set to $n_\delta$ and analogously for $p$. This limits the number of different positions a model can distinguish.

**Intuition.** Our definition of relative position in graphs combines several advantages: (i) Any node can attend to any other node – even unreachable ones – while learning a suitable attention bias for different distances. (ii) $\text{SAME}_p$ edges are treated differently in the attention mechanism. Thus, entity representations can be learned like in a regular transformer encoder, given that tokens from the same entity are fully connected with $\text{SAME}_p$ edges with $p$ providing relative position information. (iii) The lengths of shortest paths often have an intuitively useful interpretation in our incidence graphs and the sign of the entries in $\boldsymbol{R}$ also captures the important distinction between incoming and outgoing paths. In this way, Graformer can, e.g., capture the difference between the subject and object of a fact, which is expressed as a relative position of $-1$ vs. 1. The subject and object nodes, in turn, see each other as 2 and $-2$, respectively.

Fig. 2 shows the $\boldsymbol{R}$ matrix corresponding to the graph from Fig. 1c. Note how token nodes from the same entity, e.g., `s`, `v`, and `d`, form clusters as they have the same distances to other nodes, and how the relations inside such a cluster are encoded outside the interval $[-3, 3]$, i.e., the range of shortest path lengths. It is also insightful to compare node pairs with the same value in $\boldsymbol{R}$. E.g., both `s` and `w` see `e` at a distance of 2 because the entities *SVD* and *word2vec* are both the subject of a fact with *embedding learning* as the object. Likewise, `s` sees both `c` and `u1` at a distance of 1 because its entity *SVD* is subject to both corresponding facts.

### 3.4 Graformer decoder

Our decoder follows closely the standard Transformer decoder (Vaswani et al., 2017), except for the modifications suggested by Chen et al. (2018).

**Hidden decoder representation.** The initial decoder representation $\boldsymbol{Z}^{(0)} \in \mathbb{R}^{M \times d}$ embeds the (partially generated) target text $\boldsymbol{T} \in \mathbb{R}^{M \times |\Sigma|}$, i.e., $\boldsymbol{Z}^{(0)} = \boldsymbol{TE}$. A decoder layer $L$ then obtains a contextualized representation via self-attention as in the encoder (§ 3.2):

$$\boldsymbol{C}^{(L)} = Dr(SelfAtt_t(LN(\boldsymbol{Z}^{(L-1)}))) + \boldsymbol{Z}^{(L-1)} \tag{9}$$

$SelfAtt_t$ differs from $SelfAtt_g$ by using different position embeddings in Eq. (7) and, obviously, $R_{ij}$ is defined in the usual way for text. $\boldsymbol{C}^{(L)}$ is then modified via multi-head attention $MHA$ on the output $\boldsymbol{H}^{(L_E)}$ of the last graph encoder layer $L_E$. As in § 3.2, we make use of residual connections, layer normalization $LN$, and dropout $Dr$:

$$\boldsymbol{U}^{(L)} = Dr(MHA(LN(\boldsymbol{C}^{(L)}), \boldsymbol{H}^{(L_E)})) + \boldsymbol{C}^{(L)} \tag{10}$$

$$\boldsymbol{Z}^{(L)} = Dr(FF(LN(\boldsymbol{U}^{(L)}))) + \boldsymbol{U}^{(L)} \tag{11}$$

where

$$MHA(\boldsymbol{C}, \boldsymbol{H})_i = \sum_{j=1}^{|N|} \alpha_{ij}(\boldsymbol{H}_j \boldsymbol{W}^{V_t}) \tag{12}$$

$$\boldsymbol{\alpha}_i = \sigma\left(\frac{\boldsymbol{C}_i \boldsymbol{W}^{Q_t}(\boldsymbol{H}\boldsymbol{W}^{K_t})^\top}{\sqrt{d}}\right) \tag{13}$$

**Generation probabilities.** The final representation $\boldsymbol{Z}^{(L_D)}$ of the last decoder layer $L_D$ is used to compute the probability distribution $\boldsymbol{P}_i \in [0,1]^{|\Sigma|}$ over all words in the vocabulary $\Sigma$ at time step $i$:

$$\boldsymbol{P}_i = \sigma\left(\boldsymbol{Z}_i^{(L_D)} \boldsymbol{E}^\top\right) \tag{14}$$

Note that $\boldsymbol{E} \in \mathbb{R}^{|\Sigma| \times d}$ is the same matrix that is also used to embed node labels and text tokens.

### 3.5 Training

We train Graformer by minimizing the standard negative log-likelihood loss based on the likelihood estimations described in the previous section.

## 4 Experiments

### 4.1 Datasets

We evaluate our new architecture on two popular benchmarks for KG-to-text generation, AGENDA (Koncel-Kedziorski et al., 2019) and WebNLG (Gardent et al., 2017). While the latter contains crowd-sourced texts corresponding to subgraphs from various DBPedia categories, the former was automatically created by applying an information extraction tool (Luan et al., 2018) on a corpus of scientific abstracts (Ammar et al., 2018). As this process is noisy, we corrected 7 train instances where an entity name was erroneously split on a special character and, for the same reason, deleted 1 train instance entirely. Otherwise, we use the data as is, including the train/dev/test split.

We list the number of instances per data split, as well as general statistics about the graphs in Table 1. Note that the graphs in WebNLG are human-authored subgraphs of DBpedia while the graphs

| | AGENDA | WebNLG |
|---|---|---|
| #instances in train | 38,719 | 18,102 |
| #instances in val | 1,000 | 872 |
| #instances in test | 1,000 | 971 |
| #relation types | 7 | 373 |
| avg #entities in KG | 13.4 | 4.0 |
| % connected graphs | 0.3 | 99.9 |
| avg #graph components | 8.4 | 1.0 |
| avg component size | 1.6 | 3.9 |
| avg #token nodes in graph | 98.0 | 36.0 |
| avg #tokens in text | 157.9 | 31.5 |
| avg % text tokens in graph | 42.7 | 56.1 |
| avg % graph tokens in text | 48.6 | 49.0 |
| Vocabulary size $\|\Sigma\|$ | 24,100 | 2,100 |
| Character coverage in % | 99.99 | 100.0 |

Table 1: Statistics of AGENDA and the dataset from the WebNLG challenge as used in our experiments. Upper part: data splits and original KGs. Lower part: token graphs and BPE settings.

in AGENDA were automatically extracted. This leads to a higher number of disconnected graph components. Nearly all WebNLG graphs consist of a single component, i.e., are connected graphs, whereas for AGENDA this is practically never the case. We also report statistics that depend on the tokenization (cf. § 4.2) as factors like the length of target texts and the percentage of tokens shared verbatim between input graph and target text largely impact the task difficulty.

### 4.2 Data preprocessing

Following previous work on AGENDA (Ribeiro et al., 2020), we put the paper title into the graph as another entity. In contrast to Ribeiro et al. (2020), we also link every node from a real entity to every node from the title by TITLE2TXT and TXT2TITLE edges. The type information provided by AGENDA is, as usual for KGs, expressed with one dedicated node per type and HAS-TYPE arcs that link entities to their types. We keep the original pretokenized texts but lowercase the title as both node labels and target texts are also lowercased.

For WebNLG, we follow previous work (Gardent et al., 2017) by replacing underscores in entity names with whitespace and breaking apart camel-cased relations. We furthermore follow the evaluation protocol of the original challenge by converting all characters to lowercased ASCII and separating all punctuation from alphanumeric characters during tokenization.

For both datasets, we train a BPE vocabulary using sentencepiece (Kudo and Richardson, 2018) on the train set, i.e., a concatenation of node labels and target texts. See Table 1 for vocabulary sizes. Note that for AGENDA, only 99.99% of the characters found in the train set are added to the vocabulary. This excludes exotic Unicode characters that occur in certain abstracts.

We prepend entity and relation labels with dedicated $\langle E \rangle$ and $\langle R \rangle$ tags.

### 4.3 Hyperparameters and training details

We train Graformer with the Adafactor optimizer (Shazeer and Stern, 2018) for 40 epochs on AGENDA and 200 epochs on WebNLG. We report test results for the model yielding the best validation performance measured in corpus-level BLEU (Papineni et al., 2002). For model selection, we decode greedily. The final results are generated by beam search. Following Ribeiro et al. (2020), we couple beam search with a length penalty (Wu et al., 2016) of 5.0. See Appendix A for more details and a full list of hyperparameters.

### 4.4 Epoch curriculum

We apply a data loading scheme inspired by the bucketing approach of Koncel-Kedziorski et al. (2019) and length-based curriculum learning (Platanios et al., 2019): We sort the train set by target text length and split it into four buckets of two times 40% and two times 10% of the data. After each training epoch, the buckets are shuffled internally but their global order stays the same from shorter target texts to longer ones. This reduces padding during batching as texts of similar lengths stay together and introduces a mini-curriculum from presumably easier examples (i.e., shorter targets) to more difficult ones for each epoch. This enables us to successfully train Graformer *even without a learning rate schedule*.

## 5 Results and Discussion

### 5.1 Overall performance

Table 2 shows the results of our evaluation on AGENDA in terms of BLEU (Papineni et al., 2002), METEOR (Banerjee and Lavie, 2005), and CHRF++ (Popović, 2017). Like the models we compare with, we report the average and standard deviation of 4 runs with different random seeds.

Our model outperforms previous Transformer-based models that only consider first-order neighborhoods per encoder layer (Koncel-Kedziorski et al., 2019; An et al., 2019). Compared to the very

| | BLEU | METEOR | CHRF++ | #P |
|---|---|---|---|---|
| Ours | 17.80 ±0.31 | 22.07 ±0.23 | 45.43 ±0.39 | 36.3 |
| GT | 14.30 ±1.01 | 18.80 ±0.28 | – | – |
| GT+RBS | 15.1 ±0.97 | 19.5 ±0.29 | – | – |
| CGE-LW | 18.01 ±0.14 | 22.34 ±0.07 | 46.69 ±0.17 | 69.8 |

Table 2: Experimental results on AGENDA. GT (Graph Transformer) from (Koncel-Kedziorski et al., 2019); GT+RBS from (An et al., 2019); CGE-LW from (Ribeiro et al., 2020). Number of parameters in millions.

| | BLEU | METEOR | CHRF++ | #P |
|---|---|---|---|---|
| Ours | 61.15 ±0.22 | 43.38 ±0.17 | 75.43 ±0.19 | 5.3 |
| UPF-FORGe | 40.88 | 40.00 | – | – |
| Melbourne | 54.52 | 41.00 | 70.72 | – |
| Adapt | 60.59 | 44.00 | 76.01 | – |
| Graph Conv. | 55.90 | 39.00 | – | 4.9 |
| GTR-LSTM | 58.60 | 40.60 | – | – |
| E2E GRU | 57.20 | 41.00 | – | – |
| CGE-LW-LG | 63.69 ±0.10 | 44.47 ±0.12 | 76.66 ±0.10 | 10.4 |

Table 3: Experimental results on the WebNLG test set with seen categories. CGE-LW-LG from (Ribeiro et al., 2020); Adapt, Melbourne and UPF-FORGe from (Gardent et al., 2017); Graph Conv. from (Marcheggiani and Perez-Beltrachini, 2018); GTR-LSTM from (Trisedya et al., 2018); E2E GRU from (Castro Ferreira et al., 2019). Number of parameters in millions.

| $\mu_c$ | | BLEU | METEOR | CHRF++ |
|---|---|---|---|---|
| < 1.25 | Ours | **15.44** | 20.59 | 43.23 |
| (213) | CGE-LW | 15.34 | **20.64** | **43.56** |
| < 1.5 | Ours | **17.45** | 22.03 | 45.67 |
| (338) | CGE-LW | 17.29 | **22.32** | **45.88** |
| < 2.0 | Ours | 18.94 | 22.86 | 46.49 |
| (294) | CGE-LW | **19.46** | **23.76** | **47.78** |
| ≥ 2.0 | Ours | **21.72** | 24.22 | 48.79 |
| (155) | CGE-LW | 20.97 | **24.98** | **49.83** |

(a) Average size $\mu_c$ of graph components.

| d | | BLEU | METEOR | CHRF++ |
|---|---|---|---|---|
| 1 | Ours | **16.48** | **21.16** | 43.94 |
| (368) | CGE-LW | 16.33 | **21.16** | **44.16** |
| 2 | Ours | **18.46** | 22.70 | 46.85 |
| (414) | CGE-LW | 18.20 | **23.14** | **47.28** |
| ≥ 3 | Ours | 19.44 | 23.17 | 47.29 |
| (218) | CGE-LW | **20.32** | **24.42** | **49.25** |

(b) Largest diameter d across all of a graph's components.

Table 4: Performance of a single run on the test split of AGENDA w.r.t. different input graph properties. The number of data points in each split is indicated in parentheses.

recent models by Ribeiro et al. (2020), Graformer performs very similarly. Using both a local and a global graph encoder, Ribeiro et al. (2020) combine information from very distant nodes but at the same time need extra parameters for the second encoder. Graformer is more efficient and still matches their best model's BLEU and METEOR scores within a standard deviation.

The results on the test set of seen categories of WebNLG (Table 3) look similar. Graformer outperforms most original challenge participants and more recent work. While not performing on par with CGE-LW on WebNLG, Graformer still achieves more than 96% of its performance while using only about half as many parameters.

## 5.2 Performance on different types of graphs

We investigate whether Graformer is more suitable for disconnected graphs by comparing its performance on different splits of the AGENDA test set according to two graph properties: (i) the average number of nodes per connected component ($\mu_c$) and (ii) the largest diameter across all of a graph's components (d).

We can see in Table 4 that the performance of both Graformer and CGE-LW (Ribeiro et al., 2020) increases with more graph structure (larger $\mu_c$ and d), i.e., more information leads to more accurate texts. Besides, Graformer outperforms CGE-LW on BLEU for graphs with smaller components ($0 < \mu_c < 1.5$) and smaller diameters (d < 3). Although METEOR and CHRF++ scores always favor CGE-LW, the performance difference is also smaller for cases where BLEU favors Graformer.

We conjecture that Graformer benefits from its more elaborate global view, i.e., its ability to distinguish between distant but connected nodes and unreachable ones. CGE-LW's global encoder cannot make this distinction because it only sees a fully connected version of the graph.

Curiously, Graformer's BLEU is also better for larger components ($\mu_c \geq 2.0$). With multiple larger components, Graformer might also better distinguish nodes that are part of the same component from those that belong to a different one.

Only for $1.5 < \mu_c < 2.0$, CGE-LW clearly outperforms Graformer in all metrics. It seems that Graformer is most helpful for extreme cases, i.e., when either most components are isolated nodes or when isolated nodes are the exception.

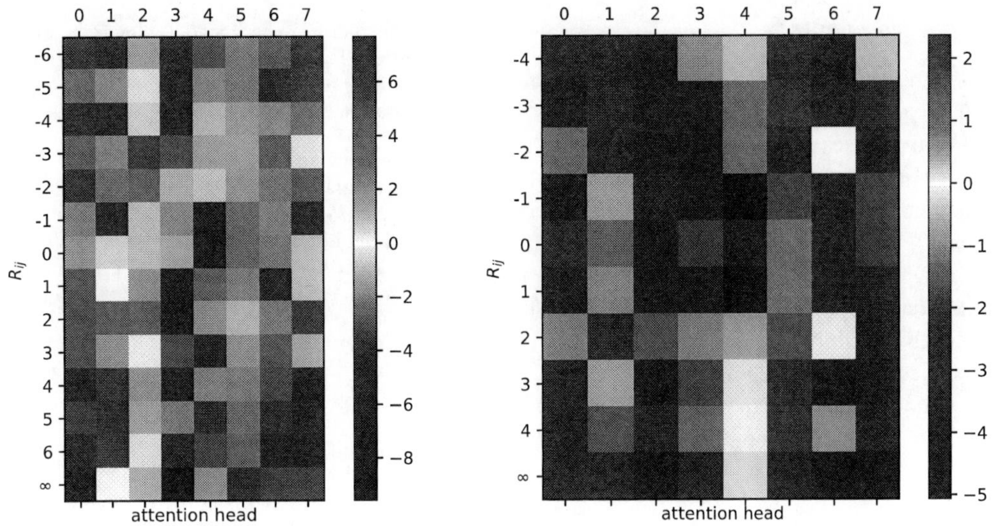


(a) AGENDA (b) WebNLG

Figure 3: Attention bias $\gamma$ learned by Graformer on the two datasets. $\text{SAME}_p$ edges are omitted.

| Model | BLEU | METEOR | CHRF++ |
|---|---|---|---|
| Graformer | 18.09 | 22.29 | 45.77 |
| -length penalty | 17.99 | 22.19 | 45.63 |
| -beam search | 17.33 | 21.74 | 44.87 |
| -epoch curriculum | 13.55 | 18.91 | 39.22 |

Table 5: Ablation study for a single run on the test portion of AGENDA.

### 5.3 Ablation study

In a small ablation study, we examine the impact of beam search, length penalty, and our new epoch curriculum training. We find that beam search and length penalty do contribute to the overall performance but to a relatively small extent. Training with our new epoch curriculum, however, proves crucial for good performance. Platanios et al. (2019) argue that curriculum learning can replace a learning rate schedule, which is usually essential to train a Transformer model. Indeed we successfully optimize Graformer without any learning rate schedule, when applying the epoch curriculum.

## 6 Learned graph structure

We visualize the learned attention bias $\gamma$ for different relative graph positions $R_{ij}$ (cf. § 3.3; esp. Eq. (7)) after training on AGENDA and WebNLG in Fig. 3. The eight attention heads (x-axis) have learned different weights for each graph position $R_{ij}$ (y-axis). Note that AGENDA has more possible $R_{ij}$ values because $n_\delta = 6$ whereas we set $n_\delta = 4$ for WebNLG.

For both datasets, we notice that one attention head primarily focuses on global information (5 for AGENDA, 4 for WebNLG). AGENDA even dedicates head 6 entirely to unreachable nodes, showing the importance of such nodes for this dataset. In contrast, most WebNLG heads suppress information from unreachable nodes.

For both datasets, we also observe that nearer nodes generally receive a high weight (focus on local information): In Fig. 3b, e.g., head 2 concentrates solely on direct incoming edges and head 0 on direct outgoing ones. Graformer can learn empirically based on its task where direct neighbors are most important and where they are not, showing that the strong bias from graph neural networks is not necessary to learn about graph structure.

## 7 Conclusion

We presented Graformer, a novel encoder-decoder architecture for graph-to-text generation based on Transformer. The Graformer encoder uses a novel type of self-attention for graphs based on shortest path lengths between nodes, allowing it to detect global patterns by automatically learning appropriate weights for higher-order neighborhoods. In our experiments on two popular benchmarks for text generation from knowledge graphs, Graformer achieved competitive results while using many fewer parameters than alternative models.

## Acknowledgments

This work was supported by the BMBF (first author) as part of the project MLWin (01IS18050), by the German Research Foundation (second author) as part of the Research Training Group "Adaptive Preparation of Information from Heterogeneous Sources" (AIPHES) under the grant No. GRK 1994/1, and by the Bavarian research institute for digital transformation (bidt) through their fellowship program (third author). We also gratefully acknowledge a Ph.D. scholarship awarded to the first author by the German Academic Scholarship Foundation (Studienstiftung des deutschen Volkes).

## References

Takuya Akiba, Shotaro Sano, Toshihiko Yanase, Takeru Ohta, and Masanori Koyama. 2019. Optuna: A next-generation hyperparameter optimization framework. In *Proceedings of the 25rd ACM SIGKDD International Conference on Knowledge Discovery and Data Mining*.

Waleed Ammar, Dirk Groeneveld, Chandra Bhagavatula, Iz Beltagy, Miles Crawford, Doug Downey, Jason Dunkelberger, Ahmed Elgohary, Sergey Feldman, Vu Ha, Rodney Kinney, Sebastian Kohlmeier, Kyle Lo, Tyler Murray, Hsu-Han Ooi, Matthew Peters, Joanna Power, Sam Skjonsberg, Lucy Wang, Chris Wilhelm, Zheng Yuan, Madeleine van Zuylen, and Oren Etzioni. 2018. Construction of the literature graph in semantic scholar. In *Proceedings of the 2018 Conference of the North American Chapter of the Association for Computational Linguistics: Human Language Technologies, Volume 3 (Industry Papers)*, pages 84–91, New Orleans - Louisiana. Association for Computational Linguistics.

Bang An, Xuannan Dong, and Changyou Chen. 2019. Repulsive bayesian sampling for diversified attention modeling. *4th workshop on Bayesian Deep Learning (NeurIPS 2019)*.

Sören Auer, Chris Bizer, Georgi Kobilarov, Jens Lehmann, Richard Cyganiak, and Zachary Ives. 2008. DBpedia: A nucleus for a web of open data. In *Proceedings of the 6th International Semantic Web Conference (ISWC)*, volume 4825 of *Lecture Notes in Computer Science*, pages 722–735. Springer.

Satanjeev Banerjee and Alon Lavie. 2005. METEOR: An automatic metric for MT evaluation with improved correlation with human judgments. In *Proceedings of the ACL Workshop on Intrinsic and Extrinsic Evaluation Measures for Machine Translation and/or Summarization*, pages 65–72, Ann Arbor, Michigan. Association for Computational Linguistics.

James S. Bergstra, Rémi Bardenet, Yoshua Bengio, and Balázs Kégl. 2011. Algorithms for hyper-parameter optimization. In J. Shawe-Taylor, R. S. Zemel, P. L. Bartlett, F. Pereira, and K. Q. Weinberger, editors, *Advances in Neural Information Processing Systems 24*, pages 2546–2554. Curran Associates, Inc.

Rajarshi Bhowmik and Gerard de Melo. 2018. Generating fine-grained open vocabulary entity type descriptions. In *Proceedings of the 56th Annual Meeting of the Association for Computational Linguistics (Volume 1: Long Papers)*, pages 877–888, Melbourne, Australia. Association for Computational Linguistics.

Deng Cai and Wai Lam. 2020. Graph transformer for graph-to-sequence learning. *AAAI Conference on Artificial Intelligence*.

Thiago Castro Ferreira, Chris van der Lee, Emiel van Miltenburg, and Emiel Krahmer. 2019. Neural data-to-text generation: A comparison between pipeline and end-to-end architectures. In *Proceedings of the 2019 Conference on Empirical Methods in Natural Language Processing and the 9th International Joint Conference on Natural Language Processing (EMNLP-IJCNLP)*, pages 552–562, Hong Kong, China. Association for Computational Linguistics.

Mia Xu Chen, Orhan Firat, Ankur Bapna, Melvin Johnson, Wolfgang Macherey, George Foster, Llion Jones, Mike Schuster, Noam Shazeer, Niki Parmar, Ashish Vaswani, Jakob Uszkoreit, Lukasz Kaiser, Zhifeng Chen, Yonghui Wu, and Macduff Hughes. 2018. The best of both worlds: Combining recent advances in neural machine translation. In *Proceedings of the 56th Annual Meeting of the Association for Computational Linguistics (Volume 1: Long Papers)*, pages 76–86, Melbourne, Australia. Association for Computational Linguistics.

Claire Gardent, Anastasia Shimorina, Shashi Narayan, and Laura Perez-Beltrachini. 2017. The WebNLG challenge: Generating text from RDF data. In *Proceedings of the 10th International Conference on Natural Language Generation*, pages 124–133, Santiago de Compostela, Spain. Association for Computational Linguistics.

Zhijiang Guo, Yan Zhang, Zhiyang Teng, and Wei Lu. 2019. Densely connected graph convolutional networks for graph-to-sequence learning. *Transactions of the Association for Computational Linguistics*, 7:297–312.

Dan Hendrycks and Kevin Gimpel. 2016. Gaussian error linear units (gelus). *Computing Research Repository*, arXiv:1606.08415.

Sepp Hochreiter and Jürgen Schmidhuber. 1997. Long short-term memory. *Neural computation*, 9:1735–80.

Thomas N. Kipf and Max Welling. 2017. Semi-supervised classification with graph convolutional networks. In *International Conference on Learning Representations (ICLR)*.

Rik Koncel-Kedziorski, Dhanush Bekal, Yi Luan, Mirella Lapata, and Hannaneh Hajishirzi. 2019. Text Generation from Knowledge Graphs with Graph Transformers. In *Proceedings of the 2019 Conference of the North American Chapter of the Association for Computational Linguistics: Human Language Technologies, Volume 1 (Long and Short Papers)*, pages 2284–2293, Minneapolis, Minnesota. Association for Computational Linguistics.

Ranjay Krishna, Yuke Zhu, Oliver Groth, Justin Johnson, Kenji Hata, Joshua Kravitz, Stephanie Chen, Yannis Kalantidis, Li-Jia Li, David A. Shamma, Michael S. Bernstein, and Fei-Fei Li. 2017. Visual genome: Connecting language and vision using crowdsourced dense image annotations. *International Journal of Computer Vision*, 123:32–73.

Taku Kudo and John Richardson. 2018. SentencePiece: A simple and language independent subword tokenizer and detokenizer for neural text processing. In *Proceedings of the 2018 Conference on Empirical Methods in Natural Language Processing: System Demonstrations*, pages 66–71, Brussels, Belgium. Association for Computational Linguistics.

Qimai Li, Zhichao Han, and Xiao ming Wu. 2018. Deeper insights into graph convolutional networks for semi-supervised learning. *AAAI Conference on Artificial Intelligence*.

Yi Luan, Luheng He, Mari Ostendorf, and Hannaneh Hajishirzi. 2018. Multi-task identification of entities, relations, and coreference for scientific knowledge graph construction. In *Proceedings of the 2018 Conference on Empirical Methods in Natural Language Processing*, pages 3219–3232, Brussels, Belgium. Association for Computational Linguistics.

Diego Marcheggiani and Laura Perez-Beltrachini. 2018. Deep graph convolutional encoders for structured data to text generation. In *Proceedings of the 11th International Conference on Natural Language Generation*, pages 1–9, Tilburg University, The Netherlands. Association for Computational Linguistics.

Amit Moryossef, Yoav Goldberg, and Ido Dagan. 2019. Step-by-step: Separating planning from realization in neural data-to-text generation. In *Proceedings of the 2019 Conference of the North American Chapter of the Association for Computational Linguistics: Human Language Technologies, Volume 1 (Long and Short Papers)*, pages 2267–2277, Minneapolis, Minnesota. Association for Computational Linguistics.

Kishore Papineni, Salim Roukos, Todd Ward, and Wei-Jing Zhu. 2002. Bleu: a method for automatic evaluation of machine translation. In *Proceedings of the 40th Annual Meeting of the Association for Computational Linguistics*, pages 311–318, Philadelphia, Pennsylvania, USA. Association for Computational Linguistics.

Hongbin Pei, Bingzhe Wei, Kevin Chen-Chuan Chang, Yu Lei, and Bo Yang. 2020. Geom-gcn: Geometric graph convolutional networks. In *International Conference on Learning Representations (ICLR)*.

Emmanouil Antonios Platanios, Otilia Stretcu, Graham Neubig, Barnabas Poczos, and Tom Mitchell. 2019. Competence-based curriculum learning for neural machine translation. In *Proceedings of the 2019 Conference of the North American Chapter of the Association for Computational Linguistics: Human Language Technologies, Volume 1 (Long and Short Papers)*, pages 1162–1172, Minneapolis, Minnesota. Association for Computational Linguistics.

Maja Popović. 2017. chrF++: words helping character n-grams. In *Proceedings of the Second Conference on Machine Translation*, pages 612–618, Copenhagen, Denmark. Association for Computational Linguistics.

Colin Raffel, Noam Shazeer, Adam Roberts, Katherine Lee, Sharan Narang, Michael Matena, Yanqi Zhou, Wei Li, and Peter J. Liu. 2019. Exploring the limits of transfer learning with a unified text-to-text transformer. *Computing Research Repository*, arXiv:1910.10683.

Leonardo F. R. Ribeiro, Claire Gardent, and Iryna Gurevych. 2019. Enhancing AMR-to-text generation with dual graph representations. In *Proceedings of the 2019 Conference on Empirical Methods in Natural Language Processing and the 9th International Joint Conference on Natural Language Processing (EMNLP-IJCNLP)*, pages 3183–3194, Hong Kong, China. Association for Computational Linguistics.

Leonardo F. R. Ribeiro, Yue Zhang, Claire Gardent, and Iryna Gurevych. 2020. Modeling global and local node contexts for text generation from knowledge graphs. *Transactions of the Association for Computational Linguistics*, 8(0):589–604.

Martin Schmitt, Sahand Sharifzadeh, Volker Tresp, and Hinrich Schütze. 2020. An unsupervised joint system for text generation from knowledge graphs and semantic parsing. In *Proceedings of the 2020 Conference on Empirical Methods in Natural Language Processing (EMNLP)*, pages 7117–7130, Online. Association for Computational Linguistics.

Peter Shaw, Jakob Uszkoreit, and Ashish Vaswani. 2018. Self-attention with relative position representations. In *Proceedings of the 2018 Conference of the North American Chapter of the Association for Computational Linguistics: Human Language Technologies, Volume 2 (Short Papers)*, pages 464–468, New Orleans, Louisiana. Association for Computational Linguistics.

Noam Shazeer and Mitchell Stern. 2018. Adafactor: Adaptive learning rates with sublinear memory cost. In *Proceedings of the 35th International Conference on Machine Learning*, volume 80 of *Proceedings of Machine Learning Research*, pages 4596–4604. PMLR.

Bayu Distiawan Trisedya, Jianzhong Qi, Rui Zhang, and Wei Wang. 2018. GTR-LSTM: A triple encoder for sentence generation from RDF data. In *Proceedings of the 56th Annual Meeting of the Association for Computational Linguistics (Volume 1: Long Papers)*, pages 1627–1637, Melbourne, Australia. Association for Computational Linguistics.

Ashish Vaswani, Noam Shazeer, Niki Parmar, Jakob Uszkoreit, Llion Jones, Aidan N Gomez, Łukasz Kaiser, and Illia Polosukhin. 2017. Attention is all you need. In I. Guyon, U. V. Luxburg, S. Bengio, H. Wallach, R. Fergus, S. Vishwanathan, and R. Garnett, editors, *Advances in Neural Information Processing Systems 30*, page 5998–6008. Curran Associates, Inc.

Petar Veličković, Guillem Cucurull, Arantxa Casanova, Adriana Romero, Pietro Liò, and Yoshua Bengio. 2018. Graph Attention Networks. In *International Conference on Learning Representations (ICLR)*.

David S Wishart, Yannick D Feunang, An C Guo, Elvis J Lo, Ana Marcu, Jason R Grant, Tanvir Sajed, Daniel Johnson, Carin Li, Zinat Sayeeda, Nazanin Assempour, Ithayavani Iynkkaran, Yifeng Liu, Adam Maciejewski, Nicola Gale, Alex Wilson, Lucy Chin, Ryan Cummings, Diana Le, Allison Pon, Craig Knox, and Michael Wilson. 2018. DrugBank 5.0: a major update to the DrugBank database for 2018. *Nucleic Acids Research*, 46(D1):D1074–D1082.

Yonghui Wu, Mike Schuster, Zhifeng Chen, Quoc V. Le, Mohammad Norouzi, Wolfgang Macherey, Maxim Krikun, Yuan Cao, Qin Gao, Klaus Macherey, Jeff Klingner, Apurva Shah, Melvin Johnson, Xiaobing Liu, Łukasz Kaiser, Stephan Gouws, Yoshikiyo Kato, Taku Kudo, Hideto Kazawa, Keith Stevens, George Kurian, Nishant Patil, Wei Wang, Cliff Young, Jason Smith, Jason Riesa, Alex Rudnick, Oriol Vinyals, Greg Corrado, Macduff Hughes, and Jeffrey Dean. 2016. Google's neural machine translation system: Bridging the gap between human and machine translation. *Computing Research Repository*, arXiv:1609.08144.

Kai Zhang, Yaokang Zhu, Jun Wang, and Jie Zhang. 2020. Adaptive structural fingerprints for graph attention networks. In *International Conference on Learning Representations (ICLR)*.

Jie Zhu, Junhui Li, Muhua Zhu, Longhua Qian, Min Zhang, and Guodong Zhou. 2019. Modeling graph structure in transformer for better AMR-to-text generation. In *Proceedings of the 2019 Conference on Empirical Methods in Natural Language Processing and the 9th International Joint Conference on Natural Language Processing (EMNLP-IJCNLP)*, pages 5459–5468, Hong Kong, China. Association for Computational Linguistics.

## A Hyperparameter details

For AGENDA and WebNLG, a minimum and maximum decoding length were set according to the shortest and longest target text in the train set. Table 6 lists the hyperparameters used to obtain final results on both datasets. Input dropout is applied on the word embeddings directly after lookup for node labels and target text tokens before they are fed into encoder or decoder. Attention dropout is applied to all attention weights computed during multi-head (self-)attention.

For hyperparameter optimization, we only train for the first 10 (AGENDA) or 50 (WebNLG) epochs to save time. We use a combination of manual tuning and a limited number of randomly sampled runs. For the latter we apply Optuna with default parameters (Akiba et al., 2019; Bergstra et al., 2011) and median pruning, i.e., after each epoch we check if the best performance so far is worse than the median performance of previous runs at the same epoch and if so, abort. For hyperparameter tuning, we decode greedily and measure performance in corpus-level BLEU (Papineni et al., 2002).

| Hyperparameter | WebNLG | AGENDA |
|---|---|---|
| model dimension $d$ | 256 | 400 |
| # heads | 8 | 8 |
| # encoder layers $L_E$ | 3 | 4 |
| # decoder layers $L_D$ | 3 | 5 |
| feedforward dimension | 512 | 2000 |
| attention dropout | 0.3 | 0.1 |
| dropout | 0.1 | 0.1 |
| input dropout | 0.0 | 0.1 |
| text self-attention range $n_t$ | 25 | 50 |
| graph self-attention range $n_\delta$ | 4 | 6 |
| SAME range $n_p$ | 10 | 10 |
| gradient accumulation | 3 | 2 |
| gradient clipping | 1.0 | 1.0 |
| label smoothing | 0.25 | 0.3 |
| $L_2$ regularizer | $3 \cdot 10^{-3}$ | $3 \cdot 10^{-4}$ |
| batch size | 4 | 8 |
| # beams | 2 | 2 |
| length penalty | 5.0 | 5.0 |

Table 6: Hyperparameters used to obtain final experimental results on WebNLG and AGENDA.

## B Qualitative examples

Table 7 shows three example generations from our Graformer model and the CGE-LW system by Ribeiro et al. (2020). Often CGE-LW generations have a high surface overlap with the reference text while Graformer texts fluently express the same content.

| | |
|---|---|
| Ref. | julia morgan has designed many significant buildings , including the los angeles herald examiner building . |
| CGE-LW | julia morgan has designed many significant buildings including the los angeles herald examiner building . |
| Ours | one of the significant buildings designed by julia morgan is the los angeles herald examiner building . |
| Ref. | asam pedas is a dish of fish cooked in a sour and hot sauce that comes from indonesia . |
| CGE-LW | the main ingredients of asam pedas are fish cooked in a sour and hot sauce and comes from indonesia . |
| Ours | the main ingredients of asam pedas are fish cooked in sour and hot sauce . the dish comes from indonesia . |
| Ref. | banana is an ingredient in binignit which is a dessert . a cookie is also a dessert . |
| CGE-LW | banana is an ingredient in binignit , a cookie is also a dessert . |
| Ours | a cookie is a dessert , as is binignit , which contains banana as one of its ingredients . |

Table 7: Example references and texts generated by CGE-LW (Ribeiro et al., 2020) and Graformer (marked Ours) for samples from the WebNLG test set. In case of multiple references, only one is shown for brevity.

# Entity Prediction in Knowledge Graphs with Joint Embeddings

**Matthias Baumgartner**
University of Zurich
baumgartner@ifi.uzh.ch

**Daniele Dell'Aglio**
University of Aalborg
University of Zurich
dade@cs.aau.dk

**Abraham Bernstein**
University of Zurich
bernstein@ifi.uzh.ch

## Abstract

Knowledge Graphs (KGs) have become increasingly popular in the recent years. However, as knowledge constantly grows and changes, it is inevitable to extend existing KGs with entities that emerged or became relevant to the scope of the KG after its creation. Research on updating KGs typically relies on extracting named entities and relations from text. However, these approaches cannot infer entities or relations that were not explicitly stated. Alternatively, embedding models exploit implicit structural regularities to predict missing relations, but cannot predict missing entities. In this article, we introduce a novel method to enrich a KG with new entities given their textual description. Our method leverages joint embedding models, hence does not require entities or relations to be named explicitly. We show that our approach can identify new concepts in a document corpus and transfer them into the KG, and we find that the performance of our method improves substantially when extended with techniques from association rule mining, text mining, and active learning.

## 1 Introduction

Knowledge graphs (KGs) have gained popularity as a versatile, general-purpose, and domain-independent model to represent information and are the major backbone for many applications on the web (Noy et al., 2019). KGs express knowledge as collections of head-relation-tail statements, named *triples*, e.g. ($:Cheney$, $:vice\text{-}of$, $:Bush$) expresses that Cheney is the vice president of Bush. Since KGs are mostly built through automatic processes (Carlson et al., 2010; Dong et al., 2014) they are often incomplete, e.g. a KG may contain the fact that Cheney was the vice-president of Bush, but not that Cheney is a US citizen. In addition, KGs evolve and require maintenance: they grow and change as the knowledge they describe expands and adapts to the real world.

The problem of deriving missing portions of knowledge is known as *KG completion*. So far, the problem has been tackled by *link prediction*, i.e. finding relationships between previously known entities in the graph. In this paper, we focus on the problem of *adding and integrating new entities into the KG*—a task we call *entity prediction*. This is different from link prediction, where entities are ex-ante partially described in the KG. In entity prediction, *we discover the existence of an entity from an external source and the KG neither contains the entity nor any information about how it relates to the other entities in the KG.*

As external source, we target document corpora, which describe the entities and the relations between them. For example, a document corpus like Wikipedia contains a description of Joe Biden and his relations with Obama (vice president) and Cheney (successor). This lead to our core research question: *given a KG $\mathcal{G}$ and a document corpus $\mathcal{D}$, how can we complete $\mathcal{G}$ with entities (textually) described in $\mathcal{D}$ but not yet contained in $\mathcal{G}$?*

As a solution, we represent the KG and document corpus in a common metric space and exploit this space in conjunction with user feedback and graph features to derive statements describing the new entities. Specifically, we leverage *joint embedding models* for creating a numerical space to represent the KG and the background source. Whereas KG embedding models give good performance on the link prediction task (Cai et al., 2018a), joint embedding models combine a KG with a document corpus to draw conclusions in terms of similarity between documents and KG entities. Our experiments determine that joint embedding models are well-founded methods to propose new entities to a KG. We also discuss how the prediction performance can be improved by integrating user feedback and explicit graph features.

The next section discusses related literature and introduces relevant notations. Section 4 outlines



*Proceedings of the Fifteenth Workshop on Graph-Based Methods for Natural Language Processing (TextGraphs-15)*, pages 22–31
June 11, 2021. 

our solution based on joint embedding models, user feedback, and graph features. Section 5 describes the experimental setup and evaluates our hypotheses. Finally, Section 6 presents overall conclusions and outlines future work.

## 2 Related work

Like in our scenario, ontology population and ontology enrichment[1] extract information from documents (Petasis et al., 2011). Ontology population adds instances to an existing ontology, whereas the structure of the ontology remains unchanged. In contrast to our problem it does not need to learn relations between instances and assumes an ontology to guide the information extraction process (Buitelaar et al., 2006; Etzioni et al., 2004; Petasis et al., 2013). Ontology enrichment inserts new concepts or relations into an ontology. It differs from our setting in that it extends the schema of an ontology, using its concepts, instances, and schema constraints, while we solely rely on relationships between entities (Faure et al., 1998; Cimiano and Völker, 2005; Hahn and Marko, 2002).

KG enrichment aims at completing a given KG with new statements, or identifying erroneous ones (Paulheim, 2017), by predicting entity types (Nickel and Tresp, 2013; Socher et al., 2013) or links (Oren et al., 2007; Socher et al., 2013). In contrast, our goal is to complete a KG by adding new entities and statements related to them. (Paulheim, 2017) states that no such approach was known until 2015 and to the best of our knowledge, this has not changed meanwhile.

Automatic Knowledge Base Construction (AKBC) methods such as NELL or OpenIE approach a similar problem by means of text processing. They extract named entities and relations from a document, then arrange them as a KG (Verga and McCallum, 2016; Mitchell et al., 2018; Martínez-Rodríguez et al., 2018). Similarly, Entity Linking extracts named entities from text, then disambiguates and links them with a background database (Hoffart et al., 2014). These approaches assume that all entities and all relations are explicitly mentioned in the text under their canonical name. In contrast, we consider the scenario where entities are not stated in the text but described implicitly.

[1]In this study we do not distinguish between KG and ontology. We opt for ontology when it is used to refer to a known problem in literature, i.e. ontology population.

## 3 Background

This section presents the key concepts and notation used throughout the paper.

**Knowledge graphs.** We define a *knowledge graph* as $\mathcal{G} := (\mathcal{V}, \mathcal{R}, \mathcal{E})$, with $\mathcal{V}$ a set of vertices (entities), $\mathcal{R}$ a set of relations, and $\mathcal{E}$ a set of directed edges, also known as statements. A statement is a triple $(h, r, t) \in \mathcal{E}$, with $h, t \in \mathcal{V}$ the head/tail entities, and $r \in \mathcal{R}$ the relation. For example, the sentence "Joe Biden is the vice president of Barack Obama" is represented by the triple $(:Biden,\ :vice\text{-}of,\ :Obama)$. Let $\mathcal{U}$ be the the universe of the entities which can be described. $\mathcal{V}$ identifies the entities described in $\mathcal{G}$, and $\mathcal{V} \subset \mathcal{U}$, i.e., $\mathcal{G}$ does not include all possible entities that may be described, which is the case in real KGs.

**KG embedding.** Embedding models create a numeric, low-dimensional representation of a KG by learning a latent vector (embedding) for each KG entity and relation. Ideally, the distance between entity embeddings resembles the relatedness of the KG entities, e.g. the embeddings of $:Biden$ and $:Obama$ are close. Embedding models exploit structural regularities in the KG by defining an optimization problem in terms of a loss function that incorporates the graph's structure, as well as embeddings of a given size.

(Bordes et al., 2013) introduced the TransE embedding model, based on the idea that a relation $r$ is a translation from the source entity $h$ to the target entity $t$ in the embedding space, i.e.:

$$\mathcal{L} \sim \sum_{(h,r,t)\in\mathcal{E}} \|\mathbf{h} + \mathbf{r} - \mathbf{t}\|_2 \qquad (1)$$

We denote embeddings in bold font and elements of $\mathcal{V} \cup \mathcal{R}$ in italic, e.g. $\mathbf{h}$ and $\mathbf{r}$ are the embeddings of $h \in \mathcal{V}$ and $r \in \mathcal{R}$, respectively.

While there exists a range of embedding models (Wang et al., 2017; Cai et al., 2018b), we focus on TransE due to its popularity and conceptual clarity.

**Joint embedding models.** Not only do embedding models exist for KGs but also for text (Mikolov et al., 2013; Le and Mikolov, 2014). Joint embedding models combine two embedding models for different modalities, allowing to compare embeddings between them while maintaining the characteristics of the individual models. These models make two principal assumptions. First, each document $d$ from a corpus $\mathcal{D}$ is a textual description of a single entity $e \in \mathcal{U}$, e.g. the Wikipedia document $d_B$ (`https://en.wikipedia.org/wiki/Joe_Biden`) describes the entity $e_B$ (*:Biden*). The description may be implicit, i.e. not actually mention the entity name, and can mention other entities. Second, the two modalities are linked to each other via known correspondences. We define the correspondences as a bijective function $m : \mathcal{D} \rightarrow \mathcal{U}$, and its inverse $m' : \mathcal{U} \rightarrow \mathcal{D}$, e.g. $m[d_B] = e_B$ and $m'[e_B] = d_B$.

Two joint embedding models are *KADE* and *StarSpace*. Both take a KG $\mathcal{G}$, a document corpus $\mathcal{D}$, and known correspondences $m$ as input. They then create embeddings for each document, entity, and relation in a shared embedding space such that embeddings of a document and a corresponding entity are, i.e. $\mathbf{d} \sim \mathbf{e}$ if $m[d] = e$. *KADE* (Baumgartner et al., 2018) joins the TransE KG embedding model and the par2vec document embedding model (Le and Mikolov, 2014) by adding a regularizer term (weighted by $\lambda$) to both models, then training them in an alternating fashion. The regularization forces embeddings of corresponding documents and entities to be close to each other:

$$\mathcal{L}^{KADE}_{\text{Docs}} \sim \mathcal{L}_{\text{Docs}} + \lambda_d \sum_{d \in \mathcal{D}} \|\mathbf{d} - \mathbf{m}[d]\|$$

$$\mathcal{L}^{KADE}_{\text{KG}} \sim \mathcal{L}_{\text{KG}} + \lambda_g \sum_{e \in \mathcal{V}} \|\mathbf{e} - \mathbf{m}'[e]\|$$

*StarSpace* (Wu et al., 2018) models entities, relations, and words as atomic features, and defines objects as aggregates over these features. A document embedding thus becomes the sum of its words' embeddings. It then learns feature embeddings by minimizing the distance (inner product or cosine) between related objects:

$$\mathcal{L}^{SS} \sim \sum_{(h,r,t) \in \mathcal{E}} dst(\mathbf{h}+\mathbf{r}, \mathbf{t}) + \sum_{e \in \mathcal{V}} dst(\mathbf{e}, \sum_{w \in m'[e]} \mathbf{w})$$

## 4 Approach

As inputs, our approach receives a KG $\mathcal{G}$, a document corpus $\mathcal{D}$, and correspondences $m$ between the two modalities. While every entity has at least one corresponding document, we assume a number of *surplus documents* in $\mathcal{D}$ that are not associated with any entity in $\mathcal{G}$. A surplus document can either describe a novel entity we want to add to $\mathcal{G}$ or its association to an existing entity in $\mathcal{G}$ is unknown. The problem of entity prediction can then be divided into two subproblems:

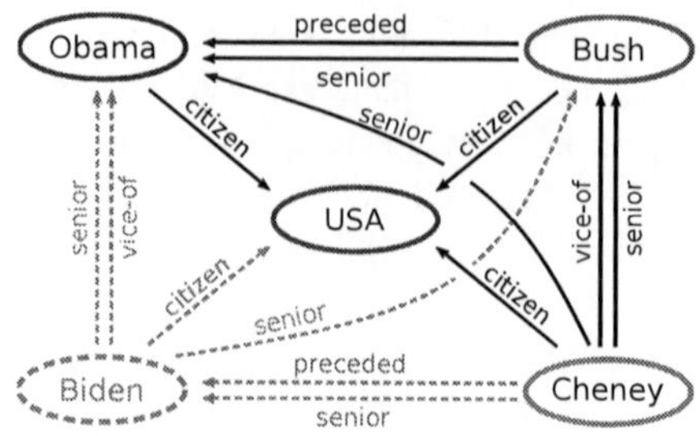


(a) The goal of entity prediction is to add the entity $:Biden$ and all red edges to the KG.

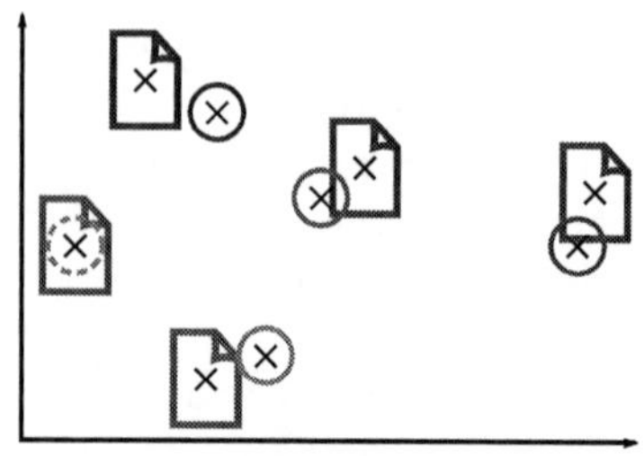

(b) The entity embedding is inferred from the document embedding in a joint embedding space.

| | $:Obama$ | $:USA$ | $:Bush$ | $:Cheney$ |
|---|---|---|---|---|
| $:citizen$ | 0.8 | 0.4 | 0.75 | 0.78 |
| $:senior$ | 0.5 | 0.9 | 0.6 | 0.7 |
| $:preceded$ | 0.6 | 0.98 | 0.7 | 0.65 |
| $:vice\text{-}of$ | 0.1 | 0.8 | 0.3 | 0.5 |

(c) Triple plausibility is estimated via the KG embedding loss on joint embeddings (lower is better).

Figure 1: An example of entity prediction via a joint embedding model.

1. Identify whether a surplus document describes a novel entity. E.g. a document that describes the entity $:Biden$ which is not part of the KG in Figure 1a.

2. Add an entity $e^*$ to $\mathcal{G}$ and propose edges between $e^*$ and the graph's current entities $\mathcal{V}$. E.g. in Figure 1a, we would ideally add $:Biden$ and all red colored edges.

We address both problems in the next sections by describing how our method adds one entity to the KG. For multiple entities, we repeat the procedure for each one independently, and leave an approach that updates the KG and its embeddings incrementally as future work to study.

### 4.1 Novelty detection

We first discuss how to distinguish surplus documents that describe novel entities from those that have an unknown association to an entity in $\mathcal{G}$. We approach this task as a binary classification problem: a surplus document is either an alternative description of an entity in $\mathcal{G}$ or a novel entity. Our intuition is that documents that describe the same entity are more similar to each other than to the remaining documents in the corpus. Since joint embeddings preserve the characteristics of the the document embedding, we measure the document similarity via the embedding distance. Hence, we train the joint embedding model, then compute the distances between surplus document's embedding to the other document embeddings. We compute the mean, variance, minimum, maximum, percentiles, span, entropy, and skew of these distances, concatenate them with the surplus document's embedding, and use the resulting feature vector as input to a binary classifier.

### 4.2 Triple reconstruction

Next, we discuss how to derive new triples that have $e^*$ as head or tail entity. This task is challenging because the number of possible triples is $2|\mathcal{V}||\mathcal{R}|$, which is orders of magnitude larger than the average number of triples an entity typically takes part in[2]. In the remainder of this section we describe the three components we use to tackle this challenge. First, we measure a potential triple's plausibility in a joint embedding space. Second, we propose a method to find likely relations with the help of user feedback. Third, we incorporate explicit features of the graph's structure into the previous methods. For the sake of brevity, we only discuss the case where $e^*$ is in the head position.

**Triple loss.** We first look into the joint embedding space to retrieve the most plausible triples. Joint embedding models strive to produce the same embedding for a corresponding document and entity. Therefore, they suggest that the entity $e^*$ is located at the same position in the embedding space as its corresponding document $d$, i.e. $\mathbf{e}^* := \mathbf{d}$. This is exemplified in Figure 1b: it shows the embeddings of all entities and documents, with corresponding items close to each other. Since $:Biden$ is missing from the graph, its embedding is proposed to be at the position of the document describing it.

KG embedding models define a triple loss $\mathcal{L}(h, r, t)$ that expresses the plausibility of a triple: *KADE* uses TransE's triple loss $\|\mathbf{h} + \mathbf{r} - \mathbf{t}\|_2$, *StarSpace* defines it as $dst(\mathbf{h} + \mathbf{r}, \mathbf{t})$. We compute the triple loss for every possible triple and collect them in a *loss matrix* $\mathbf{S}^{e^*} : \mathbb{R}^{|\mathcal{R}| \times |\mathcal{V}|}$, where each cell is defined as:

$$\mathbf{S}^{e^*}_{r,e} = \mathcal{L}(e^*, r, e) \tag{2}$$

Figure 1c presents an example triple loss matrix. For the sake of readability, we omit indices of $\mathbf{S}$ if possible, e.g. we use $\mathbf{S}^{e^*}_{r}$ to indicate the row $\mathbf{S}^{e^*}_{r,\cdot}$.

For the triple reconstruction, we are mostly interested in the ranking of losses — the triple with the lowest value in $\mathbf{S}$ is the most plausible one, irrespective of the actual value. We therefore rank triples in $\mathbf{S}$ in ascending order, i.e. assign the lowest rank to the triple that the embedding model determines to be the most plausible. Without further information, it is optimal to select the $N$ lowest ranked triples in $\mathbf{S}^{e^*}$, which we denote as the *TopN* method.

**User feedback.** We refine the triple reconstruction from joint embedding models by incorporating additional information from a user's feedback. The main challenge of the triple reconstruction is that the number of true triples to restore is much lower than the number of possible triples. To circumvent this issue, we split the triple reconstruction into two subtasks: First, we identify relations $r \in \mathcal{R}$ present at $e^*$, then we identify the tail entities given the previously found relations. We propose to involve the user in the first subtask, then to solve the second one autonomously. This is because there are typically fewer relations than vertices in a KG, thus the user has to take fewer decisions while their feedback's impact is maximized.

We formalize this idea in the *UF* procedure in Algorithm 1. We employ a logistic classifier to distinguish relations that should be present at $e^*$ from those that should not. The inputs to the classifier are the triple loss statistics of one relation $r$, i.e. the mean, median, variance, minimum, maximum, quantiles, entropy, and skew of $\mathbf{S}^{e^*}_{r}$. Its output is the likelihood of $e^*$ having any triple with relation $r$. Out of the $M$ most likely relations we then ask a user to select a correct one. For the chosen relation $r$ we add the triples with the lowest ranks in $\mathbf{S}^{e^*}_{r}$. Since $e^*$ can have multiple triples with the same relation to different entities, we pick the $N_r$ lowest ranked ones, whereas $N_r$ is the average number of $r$-triples (i.e. triples with relation $r$) at entities in $\mathcal{G}$. In addition, we discard triples that have a rank in $\mathbf{S}^{e^*}$ larger than a threshold $\theta$. The process repeats until the user judges that no relation is valid.

One issue of *UF* is that the algorithm terminates without proposing any triple if the initial set of

[2]In *FB15k-237* the average entity only occurs in about 21 out of 302'455 possible triples.

**Algorithm 1:** *UF*: Iterative triple reconstruction with user feedback. The || symbol denotes list concatenation.

**Input:** Knowledge graph $\mathcal{G}$, proposed entity $e^*$ and its loss matrix $\mathbf{S}^{e^*}$
**Result:** List of proposed triples $[(e^*, r, t)]$

/* Build relation features */
1 *features* ← [] ;
2 **for** $r \in \mathcal{R}$ **do**
3     *features*$(r)$ ← [avg($\mathbf{S}_r^{e^*}$), var($\mathbf{S}_r^{e^*}$), ...] ;
4 **end**
/* Predict initial candidate relations */
5 *candidates* ← $M$ highest scoring relations according to *clf*(*features*$(r)$) ;
6 *feedback* ← let the user select one relation from *candidates* ;
/* Select triples and iterate */
7 *triples* = [] ;
8 **while** *feedback is valid* **do**
9     $r$ ← *feedback* ;
10     $N_r$ ← mean number of $r$-triples on vertices having at least one $r$-triple ;
11     $s$ ← $\lceil N_r \rceil$ lowest ranked triples in $\mathbf{S}_r^{e^*}$ ;
12     *triples* ← *triples* || items of $s$ whose rank in $\mathbf{S}^{e^*}$ is lower than $\theta$;
13     *candidates* ← $M$ highest scoring relations according to *clf*(*features*$(r)$) ;
14     *feedback* ← let the user select one true relation from *candidates* ;
15 **end**
16 return *triples* ;

relations suggested to the user lacks a valid one. To prevent this problem, we introduce *UF-s*, which keeps generating initial candidate relations (line 5 in Algorithm 1) until the user selects one of them, then continues in the same way as *UF*.

**Graph features** We further improve the triple reconstruction performance by exploiting the graph structure. In the following, we define two features and integrate them into the *UF* method.

The first feature focuses on improving the selection of a relation in *UF*. Once a user has selected a relation, we use this new evidence to improve the estimate of other relations' likelihoods. For this, we use the *confidence* measure (*CO*) from Association Rule Learning (Agrawal et al., 1993), which expresses how certain we are about an entity having a relation $r_i$ if we know that it has $r_j$:

$$\text{conf}(r_j \Rightarrow r_i) = p(r_i|r_j) = \frac{|\{h|(h, r_j, \cdot) \in \mathcal{E}\} \cap \{h|(h, r_i, \cdot) \in \mathcal{E}\}|}{|\{h|(h, r_j, \cdot) \in \mathcal{E}\}|}$$

We integrate the confidence into *UF* by multiplying it with the respective likelihood predicted by the *clf* classifier. Note that this notion of confidence assumes that both $r_i$ and $r_j$ have the same direction, e.g. $e^*$ in the head position. To incorporate the case where their direction differs (i.e. one is inbound, the other outbound to $e^*$), we modify Algorithm 1 to alternate between reconstructing triples with $e^*$ in the head and tail position.

The second feature helps with finding the tail entities under a given relation. With no other information than the graph, it is reasonable to add an edge from $e^*$ to the entity that is most frequently used with the given relation. This measure is especially informative if the relation occurs at few entities. To express these ideas, we use the BM25 weighting scheme ($BM$), popular in information retrieval (Robertson and Zaragoza, 2009). It assigns a large weight to an edge if the entity is likely to have the relation (term frequency) and if having that relation is also informative (document frequency). We integrate this feature into the *UF* method by dividing each value in $\mathbf{S}^{e^*}$ by its BM25 score.

Both of these features can be calculated in a single pass over the graph, i.e. they have complexity $\mathcal{O}(|\mathcal{E}|)$. Training an embedding model requires multiple iterations over the graph, making their complexity $\mathcal{O}(k|\mathcal{E}|)$ with $k$ typically in the thousands. Therefore, calculating the graph statistics does not impact the scalability of the method.

## 5 Results

In this section, we first describe the experimental setup, then discuss the novelty detection, and finally show the triple reconstruction results.

### 5.1 Setup

We evaluate our methods on *FB15k-237* and *DBP50*, two popular KGs for KG embedding model benchmarking (Toutanova and Chen, 2015; Shi and Weninger, 2018). For entities from either KG, we select a random section of their respective Wikipedia article as corresponding document. To ensure that our methods do not learn from explicitly mentioned entity names, we replace all mentions of any of the entity label's words with 'entity'. For example, if the label is 'Joe Biden', we replace any occurrence of 'Joe' and 'Biden' with 'entity'. We then apply tokenization, normalization, and stopword removal on the documents. Finally, we remove entities from the graphs that cannot be associated with a unique document. Table 1 reports the resulting dataset sizes.

To test our methods, we randomly sample $k =$

|  | FB15k-237 | DBP50 |
|---|---|---|
| Entitites | 14'375 | 24'005 |
| Relations | 236 | 351 |
| Total Triples | 300'423 | 33'486 |
| Train triples | 263'907 | 31'336 |
| Unique words | 90'824 | 66'745 |

Table 1: Dataset sizes

100 entities from each KG and remove them from the respective graph, leaving $k$ surplus documents in both datasets. We then sample another $k$ of the remaining entities in both KGs and add a second document to each of them, again randomly selected from their Wikipedia article and preprocessed in the same way as before. We omit these documents from the known correspondences $m$. This produces a total of $2 \cdot k$ surplus documents: For half of them no entity exists in the KG, the other half of them have existing yet unknown entities in the graph.

We then train *StarSpace* and *KADE* on the KGs and corpora. As our goal is not to get the best performance out of the embedding models, we use common parameters for these models: for *KADE* we set $\lambda_d = \lambda_g = 0.01$, for *StarSpace* we use the inner product. In both cases, we use embedding vectors of size 100 and we train for 1000 epochs.

### 5.2 Novelty detection results

We first discuss the results of novelty detection with joint embedding models. We hypothesize that joint embedding models have a higher accuracy in distinguishing novel from unassociated documents than other unsupervised document models.

**Experiment 1: Novelty classification.** To test the novelty detection, we train a boosting decision stumps classifier on the $2 \cdot k$ surplus documents, whereas half of them describe a novel entity, half of them describe an existing one. We compare *KADE* document embeddings to a bag-of-word document representation, and evaluate the classifier in a 10-fold cross-validation setting.

Table 2 shows the two classifiers' performances in terms of accuracy (overall correct classification), type-I (mistaken as novel) and type-II errors (mistaken as unassociated), precision, and recall. The bag-of-words model achieves near-random accuracy, while *KADE* embeddings achieve a substantially higher performance. The advantage of *KADE* is mostly in its lower type-I error rate, which prevents redundancy, i.e. that existing entities are being added a second time to the KG.

|  | *FB15k-237* |  | *DBP50* |  |
|---|---|---|---|---|
|  | *KADE* | BoW | *KADE* | BoW |
| Accuracy | **0.640** | 0.505 | **0.585** | 0.515 |
| Type-I error | **0.190** | 0.285 | **0.205** | 0.275 |
| Type-II error | **0.170** | 0.210 | **0.210** | **0.210** |
| Precision | **0.626** | 0.501 | **0.578** | 0.511 |
| Recall | **0.650** | 0.590 | 0.573 | **0.581** |

Table 2: Performance of classifying documents as describing a novel or existing entity. Higher accuracy, precision, and recall are better, while lower type-I and type-II errors are better.

### 5.3 Triple reconstruction results

In the following, we compare the different triple reconstruction methods and their variations. First, we discuss the triple reconstruction considering only the embedding model's triple loss (*TopN*). Second, we investigate the impact of the separation into relation and triple prediction with user feedback (*UF*, *UF-s*). Third, we compare different combinations of graph features ($BM$, $CO$, or both) on their effect on Algorithm 1. Last, we discuss how much effort the different procedures inflict on the user.

We evaluate our methods on the binary classification metrics precision and recall. The precision indicates the portion of correct triples out of all proposed triples. The recall measures the portion of correctly proposed triples out of all correct triples. We apply our methods on the $k$ novel entities individually and report the averaged metrics.

**Experiment 2: Joint embedding model.** In this experiment, we study how joint embedding models perform in the triple reconstruction task. Specifically, we compare the two joint embedding methods *StarSpace* and *KADE* in the *TopN* setting, and investigate how well the document embedding serves as embedding of the novel entity, as proposed by these models. To test the latter, we train a TransE model on the KG (without the $k$ omitted entities) and derive the embedding of a novel entity $e^*$ according to TransE's loss function, i.e.

$$\arg\min_{\mathbf{e}^*} \sum_{(e^*,r,t)} \|\mathbf{e}^* + \mathbf{r} - \mathbf{t}\| + \sum_{(h,r,e^*)} \|\mathbf{h} + \mathbf{r} - \mathbf{e}^*\|$$

by using triples from the original KG. We denote this as *Oracle*, as it computes the optimal entity embedding from ground-truth data. As lower baseline, we use random embeddings (*Random*). For each entity embedding (from a baseline or joint embedding space), we select triples as specified by *TopN*. We set $N = 10$ which gave the best performance in our experiments. We hypothesize that the triple

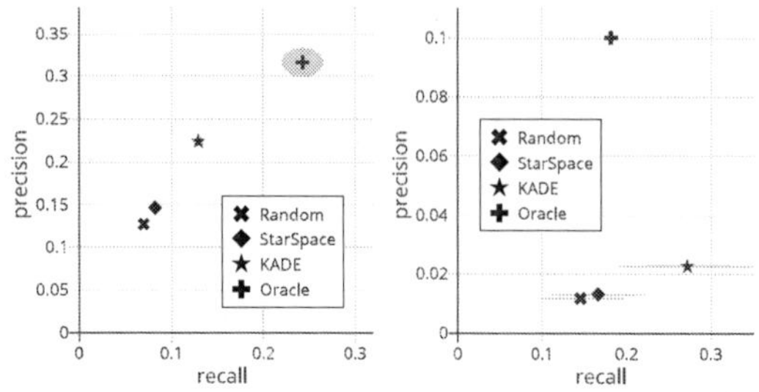


(a) Entity restoration with joint embeddings.

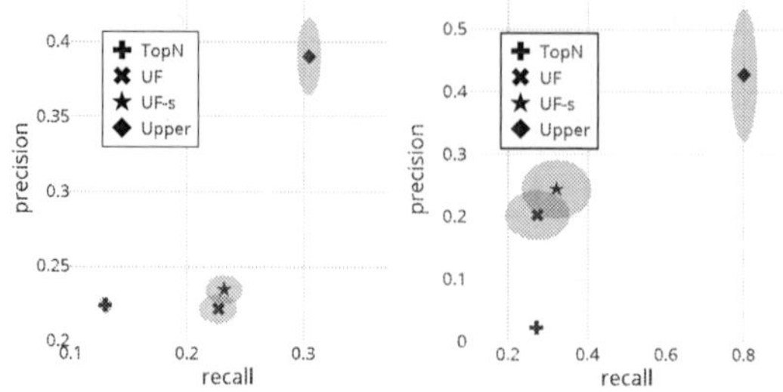


(b) Impact of user feedback.

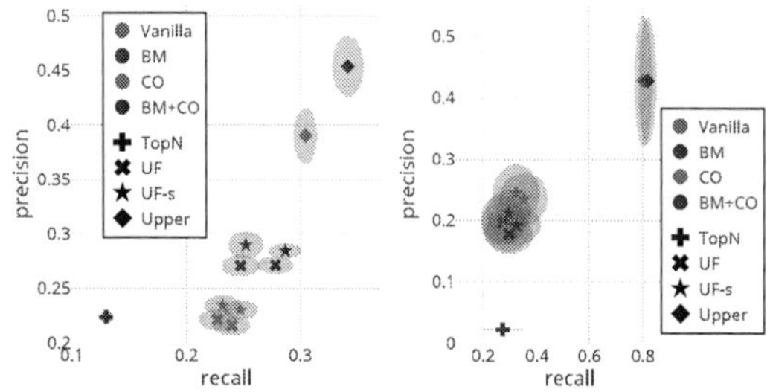


(c) Impact of user feedback and graph features combined. Marker shapes indicate the user feedback method, their color the graph features.

| | Vanilla | BM | CO | BM+CO |
|---|---|---|---|---|
| *FB15k-237* (upper baseline 103.658) | | | | |
| *UF* | 26.798 | 27.237 | 20.943 | 20.937 |
| *UF-s* | 29.002 | 29.329 | 23.799 | 23.800 |
| *DBP50* (upper baseline 80.562) | | | | |
| *UF* | 30.740 | 30.738 | 32.677 | 32.677 |
| *UF-s* | 64.037 | 64.037 | 66.429 | 66.429 |

(d) Number of user decisions per method and graph feature (lower is better).

Figure 2: Experimental results for *FB15k-237* (left plots) and *DBP50* (right plots). The red ellipses show the variance. Note that axes have different scales.

reconstruction performs substantially better with joint embeddings than the *Random* baseline.

Figure 2a shows the precision and recall of *TopN* with embeddings from the different models. It shows that *KADE* performs substantially better than *StarSpace* in both metrics and datasets, meaning that the more constrained document model used by *KADE* is advantageous in the entity prediction task. As expected, the performance of *StarSpace* and *KADE* lies between the two baselines, however compared to the *Oracle* baseline their performance is unsatisfactory, motivating further improvements.

**Experiment 3: User feedback.** Next, we hypothesise that user feedback increases precision and recall in the triple reconstruction task. For these experiments, we use *KADE* embeddings, $\theta = 500$, and $M = 10$. Since a user study would exceed the scope of this experiment, we provide user feedback by automatically selecting one random correct relation out of the suggested ones. Out of the $k$ entities omitted from the KG, one is selected as $e^*$. The other omitted entities are used to train the classifier *clf* by constructing features from their triple loss matrices as stated in Section 4.2 and using their triples from the ground-truth KG as training targets. We repeat this procedure for all $k$ entities, and report the averaged evaluation metrics.

Figure 2b contrasts the *UF* and *UF-s* methods with *TopN* and an upper bound *Upper*. The *Upper* baseline knows all true relations of $e^*$, then picks the lowest ranked $N$ triples for each of them, according to $\mathbf{S}^{e^*}$. Varying $N$ shifts the trade-off between precision and recall, whereas we use the $N$ that maximizes the F1 score (i.e. the harmonic mean of precision and recall). Note that like *Oracle*, this baseline is not practically viable as it uses ground-truth information, but rather indicates the maximum performance that could be achieved given the triple loss of the joint embeddings.

Figure 2b shows that that the user feedback has a positive impact on at least one of the two evaluation metrics, and that *UF-s* improves over *UF* with an average increase of 13.43% in precision and 9.83% in recall. The latter is expected, since *UF-s* has a guaranteed initial relation. In *FB15k-237*, the user feedback improves recall by 76.95%, implying that the classifier learns relations present at $e^*$. While more relations are considered, the ratio of correctly selected triples does not improve with *UF*, meaning that the ranking of triples within one relation is about as accurate as the rankings in the full triple loss matrix. In *DBP50*, the precision increases much more than the recall. In contrast to *FB15k-237*, this dataset is sparser (about 2.5 triples per vertex), which makes it harder to find relations. However, once a relation is known, the triple scores from the joint embedding model are reliable, i.e. the true triples have low ranks and are thus selected.

**Experiment 4: Graph statistics.** As the last part of our triple reconstruction method we evaluate the combination of user feedback and graph features. We first hypothesize that combining *UF* and *UF-s* with either $BM$ or $CO$ increases their precision and recall. Our second hypothesis is that the combination of $BM$ and $CO$ yields an improvement over having only one of them. For this experiment, we use the same setup as in the previous one and apply the BM25 parameters $b = 0.75$ and $k_1 = 2.0$. Figure 2c shows the use of the different graph features in *UF*, *UF-s*, and the *Upper* baseline, and includes *TopN* as lower baseline. Vanilla indicates no graph features were in effect. Note that the *Upper* baseline is not affected by the $CO$ feature as it does not select relations iteratively.

On *FB15k-237*, the $BM$ feature improves the precision by 23.05%, while the $CO$ feature increases the recall by 6.10% (at the cost of slightly lowering the precision). The combination of both features ($BM + CO$) amplifies these effects, with an improvement of 23.11% in recall and 22.02% in precision. These observations relate to how the features affect the different parts of Algorithm 1: $CO$ helps in finding more relations, hence increases the recall; $BM$ increases the number of retrieved true triples of a given relation, hence increases the precision. These effects are greater on *UF-s* than on *UF* because the user provides at least one relation, which in turn allows the graph features to become more effective. On *DBP50*, the graph features have no significant effect in our methods nor the *Upper* baseline; instead, the variance is larger than the difference between the methods. We attribute this to the sparsity of the dataset, since it provides too few samples to estimate frequencies accurately and small differences in the triple selection have a huge impact on the precision and recall.

**Experiment 5: User involvement.** To evaluate the user workload, we measure how many relations a user has to judge during the triple reconstruction task, assuming that the user reports the first valid relation they find in each iteration.

Figure 2d shows the number of judgements of *UF*, *UF-s*, their variations, and an upper baseline. The upper baseline expresses the case where at most one relation is valid in each iteration. The lower baseline is $2M = 20$ since the user has to review all presented relations at least once.

It is apparent that *UF-s* involves more judgements than *UF*, which comes from two factors: A higher effort to find an initial relation, and more subsequent iterations. We further observe that the number of judgements is substantially lower than the upper baseline in *FB15k-237*, meaning that it finds multiple valid relations per iteration. On the other hand, it is more difficult to find a valid relation in *DBP50*, hence the user workload is higher, especially in *UF-s*. Graph features generally show a positive impact in *FB15k-237* and a marginal negative effect in *DBP50*, in particular the $CO$ feature as it affects which relations are shown to the user.

## 6 Conclusion and Future Work

In this paper, we studied the problem of integrating new entities into a KG given their textual description. We exploited joint embeddings to identify entity candidates, and combined information from the joint embedding model with user feedback and graph features to improve the triple reconstruction. Our method solely relies on structural patterns in the data and does not need explicit mentions of entities or relations in the text. Our experiments suggest that joint embeddings are viable methods for entity prediction, and confirm that user feedback and graph features have a substantial impact on the triple reconstruction. In particular, experiments indicate that user feedback, features on relations ($CO$), and features on entities ($BM$) treat different aspects of the problem, making their combination more successful than using only one of them.

Comparing the results with the upper baselines shows that there is room for improvement. A possible way to fill this gap is to integrate explicit information into the process, e.g. considering the schema or the semantics of the relations or entities. Another approach is to study the incremental addition of new entities and triples: We restore entities and triples independently of each other, however, the restoration provides new information that can be exploited subsequently. Finally, our method could be extended in a straight-forward manner to other external data sources such as images, or to predict novel relations instead of entities.

***Acknowledgements.*** We thank the Swiss National Science Foundation for their partial support under contract number #407550_167177 and Ralph Bobrik from Swiss Re for his helpful insights.

## References


Rakesh Agrawal, Tomasz Imielinski, and Arun N. Swami. 1993. Mining association rules between sets of items in large databases. In *SIGMOD Conference*.

Matthias Baumgartner, Wen Zhang, Bibek Paudel, Daniele Dell'Aglio, Huajun Chen, and Abraham Bernstein. 2018. Aligning knowledge base and document embedding models using regularized multi-task learning. In *International Semantic Web Conference (1)*, volume 11136 of *Lecture Notes in Computer Science*, pages 21–37. Springer.

Antoine Bordes, Nicolas Usunier, Alberto García-Durán, Jason Weston, and Oksana Yakhnenko. 2013. Translating embeddings for modeling multi-relational data. In *NIPS*, pages 2787–2795.

Paul Buitelaar, Philipp Cimiano, Stefania Racioppa, and Melanie Siegel. 2006. Ontology-based information extraction with SOBA. In *LREC*, pages 2321–2324. European Language Resources Association (ELRA).

HongYun Cai, Vincent W. Zheng, and Kevin Chen-Chuan Chang. 2018a. A Comprehensive Survey of Graph Embedding: Problems, Techniques, and Applications. *IEEE Trans. Knowl. Data Eng.*, 30(9):1616–1637.

HongYun Cai, Vincent W. Zheng, and Kevin Chen-Chuan Chang. 2018b. A comprehensive survey of graph embedding: Problems, techniques, and applications. *IEEE Trans. Knowl. Data Eng.*, 30(9):1616–1637.

Andrew Carlson, Justin Betteridge, Bryan Kisiel, Burr Settles, Estevam R. Hruschka Jr, and Tom M. Mitchell. 2010. Toward an Architecture for Never-Ending Language Learning. In *AAAI*. AAAI Press.

Philipp Cimiano and Johanna Völker. 2005. Text2onto. In *NLDB*, volume 3513 of *Lecture Notes in Computer Science*, pages 227–238. Springer.

Xin Dong, Evgeniy Gabrilovich, Geremy Heitz, Wilko Horn, Ni Lao, Kevin Murphy, Thomas Strohmann, Shaohua Sun, and Wei Zhang. 2014. Knowledge vault: a web-scale approach to probabilistic knowledge fusion. In *KDD*, pages 601–610. ACM.

Oren Etzioni, Michael J. Cafarella, Doug Downey, Stanley Kok, Ana-Maria Popescu, Tal Shaked, Stephen Soderland, Daniel S. Weld, and Alexander Yates. 2004. Web-scale information extraction in knowitall: (preliminary results). In *WWW*, pages 100–110. ACM.

David Faure, Claire Nédellec, and Céline Rouveirol. 1998. Acquisition of semantic knowledge using machine learning methods: The system" asium". In *Universite Paris Sud*. Citeseer.

Udo Hahn and Kornl G Marko. 2002. Ontology and lexicon evolution by text understanding. In *Proceedings of the ECAI 2002 Workshop on Machine Learning and Natural Language Processing for Ontology Engineering (OLT 2002), Lyon, France*.

Johannes Hoffart, Yasemin Altun, and Gerhard Weikum. 2014. Discovering emerging entities with ambiguous names. In *WWW*, pages 385–396. ACM.

Quoc V. Le and Tomas Mikolov. 2014. Distributed representations of sentences and documents. In *ICML*, volume 32 of *JMLR Workshop and Conference Proceedings*, pages 1188–1196. JMLR.org.

José-Lázaro Martínez-Rodríguez, Ivan López-Arévalo, and Ana B. Rios-Alvarado. 2018. Openie-based approach for knowledge graph construction from text. *Expert Syst. Appl.*, 113:339–355.

Tomas Mikolov, Kai Chen, Greg Corrado, and Jeffrey Dean. 2013. Efficient estimation of word representations in vector space. In *ICLR (Workshop)*.

Tom M. Mitchell, William W. Cohen, Estevam R. Hruschka Jr., Partha P. Talukdar, Bo Yang, Justin Betteridge, Andrew Carlson, Bhavana Dalvi Mishra, Matt Gardner, Bryan Kisiel, Jayant Krishnamurthy, Ni Lao, Kathryn Mazaitis, Thahir Mohamed, Ndapandula Nakashole, Emmanouil A. Platanios, Alan Ritter, Mehdi Samadi, Burr Settles, Richard C. Wang, Derry Wijaya, Abhinav Gupta, Xinlei Chen, Abulhair Saparov, Malcolm Greaves, and Joel Welling. 2018. Never-ending learning. *Commun. ACM*, 61(5):103–115.

Maximilian Nickel and Volker Tresp. 2013. Tensor factorization for multi-relational learning. In *ECML/PKDD (3)*, volume 8190 of *Lecture Notes in Computer Science*, pages 617–621. Springer.

Natasha Noy, Yuqing Gao, Anshu Jain, Anant Narayanan, Alan Patterson, and Jamie Taylor. 2019. Industry-scale knowledge graphs: Lessons and challenges. *Commun. ACM*, 62(8):36–43.

Eyal Oren, Sebastian Gerke, and Stefan Decker. 2007. Simple algorithms for predicate suggestions using similarity and co-occurrence. In *ESWC*, volume 4519 of *Lecture Notes in Computer Science*, pages 160–174. Springer.

Heiko Paulheim. 2017. Knowledge graph refinement: A survey of approaches and evaluation methods. *Semantic web*, 8(3):489–508.

Georgios Petasis, Vangelis Karkaletsis, Georgios Paliouras, Anastasia Krithara, and Elias Zavitsanos. 2011. Ontology population and enrichment: State of the art. In *Knowledge-Driven Multimedia Information Extraction and Ontology Evolution*, volume 6050 of *Lecture Notes in Computer Science*, pages 134–166. Springer.

Georgios Petasis, Ralf Möller, and Vangelis Karkaletsis. 2013. BOEMIE: reasoning-based information extraction. In *NLPAR@LPNMR*, volume 1044 of *CEUR Workshop Proceedings*, pages 60–75. CEUR-WS.org.

Stephen E. Robertson and Hugo Zaragoza. 2009. The probabilistic relevance framework: BM25 and beyond. *Foundations and Trends in Information Retrieval*, 3(4):333–389.

Baoxu Shi and Tim Weninger. 2018. Open-world knowledge graph completion. In *AAAI*, pages 1957–1964. AAAI Press.

Richard Socher, Danqi Chen, Christopher D Manning, and Andrew Ng. 2013. Reasoning with neural tensor networks for knowledge base completion. In *Advances in neural information processing systems*, pages 926–934.

Kristina Toutanova and Danqi Chen. 2015. Observed versus latent features for knowledge base and text inference. In *Proceedings of the 3rd Workshop on Continuous Vector Space Models and their Compositionality*, pages 57–66, Beijing, China. Association for Computational Linguistics.

Patrick Verga and Andrew McCallum. 2016. Row-less universal schema. In *AKBC@NAACL-HLT*, pages 63–68. The Association for Computer Linguistics.

Quan Wang, Zhendong Mao, Bin Wang, and Li Guo. 2017. Knowledge graph embedding: A survey of approaches and applications. *IEEE Trans. Knowl. Data Eng.*, 29(12):2724–2743.

Ledell Yu Wu, Adam Fisch, Sumit Chopra, Keith Adams, Antoine Bordes, and Jason Weston. 2018. Starspace: Embed all the things! In *AAAI*, pages 5569–5577. AAAI Press.

# Hierarchical Graph Convolutional Networks for Jointly Resolving Cross-document Coreference of Entity and Event Mentions

**Duy Phung**[1], **Tuan Ngo Nguyen**[2] **and Thien Huu Nguyen**[2]
[1]VinAI Research, Vietnam
[2]Department of Computer and Information Science,
University of Oregon, Eugene, Oregon, USA
v.duypv1@vinai.io,{tnguyen,thien}@cs.uoregon.edu

## Abstract

This paper studies the problem of cross-document event coreference resolution (CDECR) that seeks to determine if event mentions across multiple documents refer to the same real-world events. Prior work has demonstrated the benefits of the predicate-argument information and document context for resolving the coreference of event mentions. However, such information has not been captured effectively in prior work for CDECR. To address these limitations, we propose a novel deep learning model for CDECR that introduces hierarchical graph convolutional neural networks (GCN) to jointly resolve entity and event mentions. As such, sentence-level GCNs enable the encoding of important context words for event mentions and their arguments while the document-level GCN leverages the interaction structures of event mentions and arguments to compute document representations to perform CDECR. Extensive experiments are conducted to demonstrate the effectiveness of the proposed model.

## 1 Introduction

Event coreference resolution (ECR) aims to cluster event-triggering expressions in text such that all event mentions in a group refer to the same unique event in real world. We are interested in cross-document ECR (CDECR) where event mentions might appear in the same or different documents. For instance, consider the following sentences (event mentions) **S1** and **S2** that involve "*leaving*" and "*left*" (respectively) as event trigger words (i.e., the predicates):

**S1**: *O'Brien was forced into the drastic step of* **leaving** *the 76ers.*

**S2**: *Jim O'Brien* **left** *the 76ers after one season as coach.*

An CDECR system in this case would need to recognize that both event mentions in **S1** and **S2** refer to the same event.

A major challenge in CDECR involves the necessity to model entity mentions (e.g., "*Jim O'Brien*") that participate into events and reveal their spatio-temporal information (Yang et al., 2015) (called event arguments). In particular, as event mentions might be presented in different sentences/documents, an important evidence for predicting the coreference of two event mentions is to realize that the two event mentions have the same participants in the real world and/or occur at the same location and time (i.e., same arguments).

Motivated by this intuition, prior work for CDECR has attempted to jointly resolve cross-document coreference for entities and events so the two tasks can mutually benefit from each other (iterative clustering) (Lee et al., 2012). In fact, this iterative and joint modeling approach has recently led to the state-of-the-art performance for CDECR (Barhom et al., 2019; Meged et al., 2020). Our model for CDECR follows this joint coreference resolution method; however, we advance it by introducing novel techniques to address two major limitations from previous work (Yang et al., 2015; Kenyon-Dean et al., 2018; Barhom et al., 2019), i.e., the inadequate mechanisms to capture the argument-related information for representing event mentions and the use of only lexical features to represent input documents.

As the first limitation with the event argument-related evidence, existing methods for CDECR have mainly captured the direct information of event arguments for event mention representations, thus failing to explicitly encode other important context words in the sentences to reveal fine-grained nature of relations between arguments and triggers for ECR (Yang et al., 2015; Barhom et al., 2019). For instance, consider the coreference prediction between the event mentions in **S1** and the following sentence **S3** (with "*leave*" as the event trigger word):

**S3:** *The baseball coach Jim O'Brien decided to leave the*



*Proceedings of the Fifteenth Workshop on Graph-Based Methods for Natural Language Processing (TextGraphs-15)*, pages 32–41
June 11, 2021. 

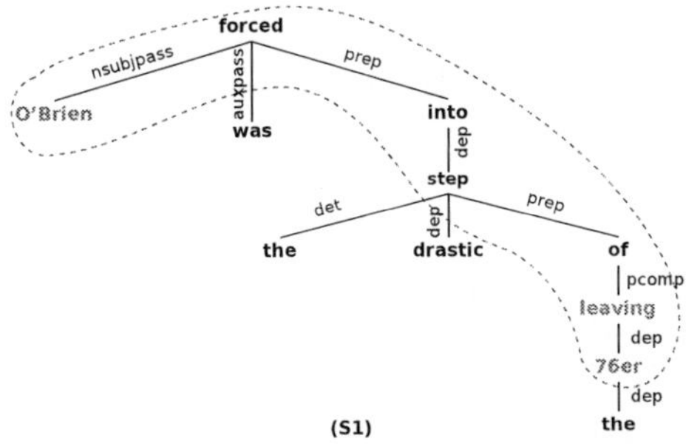


Figure 1: The pruned dependency tree for the event mention in **S1**. The trigger is red while argument heads are blue.

*club on Thursday.*

The arguments for the event mention in **S3** involves *"The baseball coach Jim O'Brien"*, *"the club"*, and *"Monday"*. If an entity coreference resolution system considers the entity mention pairs (*"O'Brien"* in **S1**, *"The baseball coach Jim O'Brien"* in **S3**) and (*"the 76ers"* in **S1** and *"the club"* in **S3**) as being coreferred, a CDECR system, which only concerns event arguments and their coreference information, would incorrectly predict the coreference between the event mentions in **S1** and **S3** in this case. However, if the CDECR system further models the important words for the relations between event triggers and arguments (i.e., the words *"was forced"* in **S1** and *"decided"* in **S3**), it can realize the unwillingness of the subject for the position ending event in **S1** and the self intent to leave the position for the event in **S3**. As such, this difference can help the system to reject the event coreference for **S1** and **S3**.

To this end, we propose to explicitly identify and capture important context words for event triggers and arguments in representation learning for CDECR. In particular, our motivation is based on the shortest dependency paths between event triggers and arguments that have been used to reveal important context words for their relations (Li et al., 2013; Sha et al., 2018; Veyseh et al., 2020a, 2021). As an example, Figure 1 shows the dependency tree of **S1** where the shortest dependency path between *"O'Brien"* and *"leaving"* can successfully include the important context word *"forced"*. As such, for each event mention, we leverage the shortest dependency paths to build a pruned and argument-customized dependency tree to simultaneously contain event triggers, arguments and the important words in a single structure. Afterward, the structure will be exploited to learn richer representation vectors for CDECR.

Second, for document representations, previous work on CDECR has proved that input documents also provide useful context information for event mentions (e.g., document topics) to enhance the clustering performance (Kenyon-Dean et al., 2018). However, the document information is only captured via lexical features in prior work, e.g., TF-IDF vectors (Kenyon-Dean et al., 2018; Barhom et al., 2019), leading to the poor generalization to unseen words/tokens and inability to encapsulate latent semantic information for CDECR. To this end, we propose to learn distributed representation vectors for input documents to enrich event mention representations and improve the generalization of the models for CDECR. In particular, as entity and event mentions are the main objects of interest for CDECR, our motivation is to focus on the context information from these objects to induce document representations for the models. To implement this idea, we propose to represent input documents via interaction graphs between their entity and event mentions, serving as the structures to generate document representation vectors.

Based on those motivations, we introduce a novel hierarchical graph convolutional neural network (GCN) that involves two levels of GCN models to learn representation vectors for the iterative and joint model for CDECR. In particular, sentence-level GCNs will consume the pruned dependency trees to obtain context-enriched representation vectors for event and entity mentions while a document-level GCN will be run over the entity-event interaction graphs, leveraging the mention representations from the sentence-level GCNs as the inputs to generate document representations for CDECR. Extensive experiments show that the proposed model achieves the state-of-the-art resolution performance for both entities and events on the ECB+ dataset. To our knowledge, this is the first work that utilizes GCNs and entity-event interaction graphs for coreference resolution.

## 2 Related Work

ECR is considered as a more challenging task than entity coreference resolution due to the more complex structures of event mentions that require argument reasoning (Yang et al., 2015). Previous work for within-document event resolution includes pairwise classifiers (Ahn, 2006; Chen et al., 2009), spectral graph clustering methods (Chen and Ji, 2009), information propagation (Liu et al., 2014), markov logic networks (Lu et al., 2016), and deep learning (Nguyen et al., 2016). For only cross-document event resolution, prior work has considered mention-pair classifiers for coreference that use granularities of event slots and lexical features of event mentions for the features (Cybulska and Vossen, 2015b,a). Within- and cross-document event coreference have also been solved simultaneously in previous work (Lee et al., 2012; Bejan and Harabagiu, 2010; Adrian Bejan and Harabagiu, 2014; Yang et al., 2015; Choubey and Huang, 2017; Kenyon-Dean et al., 2018). The most related works to us involve the joint models for entity and event coreference resolution that use contextualized word embeddings to capture the dependencies between the two tasks and lead to the state-of-the-art performance for CDECR (Lee et al., 2012; Barhom et al., 2019; Meged et al., 2020).

Finally, regarding the modeling perspective, our work is related to the models that use GCNs to learn representation vectors for different NLP tasks, e.g., event detection (Lai et al., 2020; Veyseh et al., 2019) and target opinion word extraction (Veyseh et al., 2020b), applying both sentence- and document-level graphs (Sahu et al., 2019; Tran et al., 2020; Nan et al., 2020; Tran and Nguyen, 2021; Nguyen et al., 2021). However, to our knowledge, none of the prior work has employed GCNs for ECR.

## 3 Model

Given a set of input documents $\mathcal{D}$, the goal of CDECR is to cluster event mentions in the documents of $\mathcal{D}$ according to their coreference. Our model for CDECR follows (Barhom et al., 2019) that simultaneously clusters entity mentions in $\mathcal{D}$ to benefit from the inter-dependencies between entities and events for coreference resolution. In this section, we will first describe the overall framework of our iterative method for joint entity and event coreference resolution based on (Barhom et al., 2019) (a summary of the framework is given in Algorithm 1). The novel hierarchical GCN model for inducing mention[1] representation vectors will be discussed afterward.

**Iterative Clustering for CDECR**: Following (Barhom et al., 2019), we first cluster the input document set $\mathcal{D}$ into different topics to improve the coreference performance (the set of document topics is called $T$). As we use the ECB+ dataset (Cybulska and Vossen, 2014) to evaluate the models in this work, the training phase directly utilizes the golden topics of the documents while the test phase applies the K-mean algorithm for document clustering as in (Barhom et al., 2019). Afterward, given a topic $t \in T$ with the corresponding document subset $\mathcal{D}_t \subset \mathcal{D}$, our CDECR model initializes the entity and event cluster configurations $E_t^0$ and $V_t^0$ (respectively) where: $E_t^0$ involves within-document clusters of the entity mentions in the documents in $\mathcal{D}_t$, and $V_t^0$ simply puts each event mention presented in $\mathcal{D}_t$ into its own cluster (lines 2 and 3 in Algorithm 1). In the training phase, $E_t^0$ is obtained from the golden within-document coreference information of the entity mentions (to reduce noise) while the within-document entity mention clusters returned by Stanford CoreNLP (Manning et al., 2014) are used for $E_t^0$ in the test phase, following (Barhom et al., 2019). For convenience, the sets of entity and event mentions in $\mathcal{D}_t$ are called $M_t^E$ and $M_t^V$ respectively.

**Algorithm 1** Training algorithm

1: **for** $t \in T$ **do**
2: $E_t^0 \leftarrow$ Within-doc clusters of entity mentions
3: $V_t^0 \leftarrow$ Singleton event mentions in $M_t^V$
4: $k \leftarrow 1$
5: **while** $\exists$ meaningful cluster-pair merge **do**
6: //Entities
7: Generate entity mention representations $R_E(m_{e_i}, V_t^{k-1})$ for all $m_{e_i} \in M_t^E$
8: Compute entity mention-pair coreference scores $S_E(m_{e_i}, m_{e_j})$
9: Train $R_E$ and $S_E$ using the gold entity mention clusters
10: $E_t^k \leftarrow$ Agglomeratively cluster $M_t^E$ based on $S_E(m_{e_i}, m_{e_j})$
11: //Events
12: Generate event mention representations $R_V(m_{v_i}, E_t^k)$ for all $m_{v_i} \in M_t^V$
13: Compute event mention-pair coreference scores $S_V(m_{v_i}, m_{v_j})$
14: Train $R_V$ and $S_V$ using the gold entity mention clusters
15: $V_t^k \leftarrow$ Agglomeratively cluster $M_t^V$ based on $S_V(m_{v_i}, m_{v_j})$
16: $k \leftarrow k + 1$
17: **end while**
18: **end for**

Given the initial configurations, our iterative algorithm involves a sequence of clustering iterations, generating new cluster configurations $E_t^k$ and $V_t^k$ for entities and events (respectively) after each iteration. As such, each iteration $k$ performs two independent clustering steps where entity mentions are clustered first to produce $E_t^k$, followed by event mention clustering to obtain

[1]We use mentions to refer to both event and entity mentions.

$V_t^k$ (alternating the clustering). Starting with the entity clustering at iteration $k$, each entity mention $m_{e_i}$ is first transformed into a representation vector $R_E(m_{e_i}, V_t^{k-1})$ (line 7 in Algorithm 1) that is conditioned on not only the specific context of $m_{e_i}$ but also the current event cluster configuration $V_t^{k-1}$ (i.e., to capture the event-entity inter-dependencies). Afterward, a scoring function $S_E(m_{e_i}, m_{e_j})$ is used to compute the coreference probability/score for each pair of entity mentions, leveraging their mention representations $R_E(m_{e_i}, V_t^{k-1})$ and $R_E(m_{e_j}, V_t^{k-1})$ at the current iteration ($R_E$ and $S_E$ will be discussed in the next section) (line 8). An agglomerative clustering algorithm then utilizes these coreference scores to cluster the entity mentions, leading to a new configuration $E_t^k$ for entity mention clusters (line 10). Given $E_t^k$, the same procedure is applied to cluster the event mentions for iteration $k$, including: (i) obtaining an event representation vector $R_V(m_{v_i}, E_t^k)$ for each event mention $m_{v_i}$ based on the current entity cluster configuration $E_t^k$, (ii) computing coreference scores for the event mention pairs via the scoring function $S_V(m_{v_i}, m_{v_j})$, and (iii) performing agglomerative clustering for the event mentions to produce the new configuration $V_t^k$ for event clusters (lines 12, 13, and 15).

Note that during the training process, the parameters of the representation and scoring functions for entities $R_E$ and $S_E$ (or for events with $R_V$ and $S_V$) are updated/optimized after the coreference scores are computed for all the entity (or event) mention pairs. This corresponds to lines 9 and 14 in Algorithm 1 (not used in the test phase). In particular, the loss function to optimize $R_E$ and $S_E$ in line 9 is based on the cross-entropy over every pair of entity mentions $(m_{e_i}, m_{e_j})$ in $M_t^E$: $L_t^{ent,coref} = -\sum_{m_{e_i} \neq m_{e_j}} y_{ij}^{ent} \log S_E(m_{e_i}, m_{e_j}) - (1 - y_{ij}^{ent}) \log(1 - S_E(m_{e_i}, m_{e_j})$ where $y_{ij}^{ent}$ is a golden binary variable to indicate whether $m_{e_i}$ and $m_{e_j}$ corefer or not (symmetrically for $L_t^{env,coref}$ to train $R_V$ and $S_V$ in line 14). Also, we use the predicted configurations $E_t^k$ and $V_t^{k-1}$ in the mention representation computation (instead of the golden clusters as in $y_{ij}^{ent}$ for the loss functions) during both the training and test phases to achieve a consistency (Barhom et al., 2019).

Finally, we note that the agglomerative clustering in each iteration of our model also starts with the initial clusters as in $E_t^0$ and $V_t^0$, and greedily merges multiple cluster pairs with the highest cluster-pair scores until all the scores are below a predefined threshold $\delta$. In this way, the algorithm first focuses on high-precision merging operations and postpones less precise ones until more information is available. The cluster-pair score $S_C(c_i, c_j)$ for two clusters $c_i$ and $c_j$ (mention sets) at some algorithm step is based on averaging mention linkage coreference scores: $S_C(c_i, c_j) = \frac{1}{|c_i||c_j|} \sum_{m_i \in c_i, m_j \in c_j} S_*(m_i, m_j)$ (Barhom et al., 2019) where $*$ can be $E$ or $V$ depending on whether $c_i$ and $c_j$ are entity or event clusters (respectively).

**Mention Representations**: Let $m$ be a mention (event or entity) in a sentence $W = w_1, w_2, \ldots, w_n$ of $n$ words ($w_i$ is the $i$-th word) where $w_a$ is the head word of $m$. To prepare $W$ for the mention representation computation and achieve a fair comparison with (Barhom et al., 2019), we first convert each word $w_i \in W$ into a vector $x_i$ using the ELMo embeddings (Peters et al., 2018). Here, $x_i$ is obtained by running the pre-trained ELMo model over $W$ and averaging the hidden vectors for $w_i$ at the three layers in ELMo. This transforms $W$ into a sequence of vectors $X = x_1, x_2, \ldots, x_n$ for the next steps. The mention representations in our work are based on two major elements, i.e., the modeling of important context words for event triggers and arguments, and the induction of document presentations.

**(i) Modeling Important Context Words**: A motivation for representation learning in our model is to capture event arguments and important context words (for the relations between event triggers and arguments) to enrich the event mention representations. In this work, we employ a symmetric intuition to compute a representation vector for an entity mention $m$, aiming to encode associated predicates (i.e., event triggers that accept $m$ as an argument $W$) and important context words (for the relations between the entity mention and associated event triggers). As such, following (Barhom et al., 2019), we first identify the attached arguments (if $m$ is an event mention) or predicates (if $m$ is an entity mention) in $W$ for $m$ using a semantic role labeling (SRL) system. In particular, we focus on four semantic roles of interest: `Arg0`, `Arg1`, `Location`, and `Time`. For convenience, let $A^m = \{w_{i_1}, \ldots, w_{i_o}\} \subset W$ be the set of head words of the attached event arguments or event triggers for $m$ in $W$ based on the SRL system and the four roles ($o$ is the number of head words). In particular, if $m$ is an event mention,

$A^m$ would involve the head words of the entity mentions that fill the four semantic roles for $m$ in $W$. In contrast, if $m$ is an entity mention, $A^m$ would capture the head words of the event triggers that take $m$ as an argument with one of the four roles in $W$. Afterward, to encode the important context words for the relations between $m$ and the words in $A^m$, we employ the shortest dependency paths $P_{i_j}$ between the head word $w_a$ of $m$ and the words $w_{i_j} \in A^m$. As such, starting with the dependency tree of $\mathcal{G}^m = \{\mathcal{N}^m, \mathcal{E}^m\}$ of $W$ ($\mathcal{N}^m$ involves the words in $W$), we build a pruned tree $\hat{\mathcal{G}}^m = \{\hat{\mathcal{N}}^m, \hat{\mathcal{E}}^m\}$ of $\mathcal{G}^m$ to explicitly focus on the mention $m$ and its important context words in the paths $P_{i_j}$. Concretely, the node set $\hat{\mathcal{N}}^m$ of $\hat{\mathcal{G}}^m$ contains all the words in the paths $P_{i_j}$ ($\hat{\mathcal{N}}^m = \bigcup_{j=1..o} P_{i_j}$) while the edge set $\hat{\mathcal{E}}^m$ preserves the dependency connections in $\mathcal{G}^m$ of the words in $\hat{\mathcal{N}}^m$ ($\hat{\mathcal{E}}^m = \{(a,b)|a,b \in \hat{\mathcal{N}}^m, (a,b) \in \mathcal{E}^m\}$). As such, the pruned tree $\hat{\mathcal{G}}^m$ helps to gather the relevant context words for the coreference resolution of $m$ and organize them into a single dependency graph, serving as a rich structure to learn a representation vector for $m$[2] (e.g., in Figure 1).

**(ii) Graph Convolutional Networks**: The context words and structure in $\hat{\mathcal{G}}^m$ suggest the use of Graph Convolutional Networks (GCN) (Kipf and Welling, 2017; Nguyen and Grishman, 2018) to learn the representation vector for $m$ (called the sentence-level GCN). In particular, the GCN model in this work involves several layers (i.e., $L$ layers in our case) to compute the representation vectors for the nodes in the graph $\hat{\mathcal{G}}^m$ at different abstract levels. The input vector $h_v^0$ for the node $v \in \hat{\mathcal{N}}^m$ for GCN is set to the corresponding ELMo-based vectors in $X$. After $L$ layers, we obtain the hidden vectors $h_v^L$ (in the last layer) for the nodes $v \in \hat{\mathcal{N}}^m$. We call $sent(m) = [h_{v_m}^L, max\_pool(h_v^L|v \in \hat{\mathcal{N}}^m)]$ the sentence-level GCN vector that will be used later to represent $m$ ($v_m$ is the corresponding node of the head word of $m$ in $\hat{\mathcal{N}}^m$).

**(iii) GCN Interaction**: Our discussion about the sentence-level GCN so far has been agnostic to whether $m$ is an event or entity mention and the straightforward approach is to apply the same GCN model for both entity and event mentions. However, this approach might limit the flexibility of the GCN model to focus on the necessary aspects of information that are specific to each coreference resolution task (i.e., events or entities). For example, event coreference might need to weight the information from event arguments and important context words more than those for entity coreference (Yang et al., 2015). To this end, we propose to apply two separate sentence-level GCN models for event and entity mentions, which share the architecture but differ from the parameters, to enhance representation learning (called $G^{ent}$ and $G^{evn}$ for entities and events respectively). In addition, to introduce a new source of training signals and promote the knowledge transfer between the two GCN networks, we propose to regularize the GCN models so they produce similar representation vectors for the same input sentence $W$. In particular, we apply both GCN models $G^{ent}$ and $G^{evn}$ over the full dependency tree[3] $\mathcal{G}^m$ using the ELMo-based vectors $X$ for $W$ as the input. This produces the hidden vectors $h_1^{ent}, \ldots, h_n^{ent}$ and $h_1^{env}, \ldots, h_n^{env}$ in the last layers of $G^{ent}$ and $G^{evn}$ for $W$. Afterward, we compute two versions of representation vectors for $W$ based on max-pooling: $h^{ent} = max\_pool(h_1^{ent}, \ldots, h_n^{ent})$, $h^{env} = max\_pool(h_1^{env}, \ldots, h_n^{env})$. Finally, the mean squared difference between $h^{ent}$ and $h^{env}$ is introduced into the overall loss function to regularize the models: $L_m^{reg} = ||h^{ent} - h^{env}||_2^2$. As this loss is specific to mention $m$, it will be computed independently for event and entity mentions and added into the corresponding training loss (i.e., lines 9 or 14 in Algorithm 1). In particular, the overall training loss for entity mention coreference resolution in line 9 of Algorithm 1 is: $L_t^{ent} = \alpha^{ent} L_t^{ent,coref} + (1-\alpha^{ent}) \sum_{m_e \in M_t^E} L_{m_e}^{reg}$ while those for event mention coreference resolution is: $L_t^{env} = \alpha^{env} L_t^{env,coref} + (1 - \alpha^{env}) \sum_{m_v \in M_t^V} L_{m_v}^{reg}$ (line 14). Here, $\alpha^{ent}$ and $\alpha^{env}$ are the trade-off parameters.

**(iv) Document Representation**: As motivated in the introduction, we propose to learn representation vectors for input documents to enrich mention representations and improve the generalization of the models (over the lexical features for documents). As such, our principle is to employ entity and event mentions (the main objects of interest in CDECR) and their interactions/structures to represent input documents (i.e., documents as interaction graphs of entity and event mentions). Given the mention $m$ of interest and its correspond-

[2]If $A^m$ is empty, the pruned tree $\hat{\mathcal{G}}^m$ only contains the head word of $m$.

[3]We tried the pruned dependency tree $\hat{\mathcal{G}}^m$ in this regularization, but the full dependency tree $\mathcal{G}^m$ led to better results.

ing document $d \in \mathcal{D}_t$, we start by building an interaction graph $\mathcal{G}^{doc} = \{\mathcal{N}^{doc}, \mathcal{E}^{doc}\}$ where the node set $\mathcal{N}^{doc}$ involves all the entity and event mentions in $d$. For the edge set $\mathcal{E}^{doc}$, we leverage two types of information to connect the nodes in $\mathcal{N}^{doc}$: (i) predicate-argument information: we establish a link between the nodes for an event mention $x$ and an entity mention $y$ in $\mathcal{N}^{doc}$ if $y$ is an argument of $x$ for one of the four semantic roles, i.e., Arg0, Arg1, Location, and Time (identified by the SRL system), and (ii) entity mention coreference: we connect any pairs of nodes in $\mathcal{N}^{doc}$ that correspond to two coreferring entity mentions in $d$ (using the gold within-document entity coreference in training and the predicted one in testing, as in $E_t^0$). In this way, $\mathcal{G}^{doc}$ helps to emphasize on important objects of $d$ and enables intra- and inter-sentence interactions between event mentions (via entity mentions/arguments) to produce effective document representations for CDECR.

In the next step, we feed the interaction graph $\mathcal{G}^{doc}$ into a GCN model $G^{doc}$ (called the document-level GCN) using the sentence-level GCN-based representations of the entity and event mentions in $\mathcal{N}^{doc}$ (i.e., $sent(m)$) as the initial vectors for the nodes (thus called a hierarchical GCN model). The hidden vectors produced by the last layer of $G^{doc}$ for the nodes in $\mathcal{G}^{doc}$ is called $\{h_u^d | u \in \mathcal{N}^{doc}\}$. Finally, we obtain the representation vector $doc(m)$ for $d$ based on the max-pooling: $doc(m) = max\_pool(h_u^d | u \in \mathcal{N}^{doc})$.

**(v) Final Representation**: Given the representation vectors learned so far, we form the final representation vector for $m$ ($R_E(m, V_t^{k-1})$ or $R_V(m, E_t^k)$ in lines 7 or 12 of Algorithm 1) by concatenating the following vectors:

(1) The sentence- and document-level GCN-based representation vectors for $m$ (i.e., $sent(m)$ and $doc(m)$).

(2) The cluster-based representation $cluster(m) = [\texttt{Arg0}_m, \texttt{Arg1}_m, \texttt{Location}_m, \texttt{Time}_m]$. Taking $\texttt{Arg0}_m$ as an example, it is computed by considering the mention $m'$ that is associated with $m$ via the semantic role Arg0 in $W$ using the SRL system. Here, $m'$ is an event mention if $m$ is an entity mention and vice versa (Arg0 = 0 if $m'$ does not exist). As such, let $c$ be the cluster in the current configuration (i.e., $V_t^{k-1}$ or $E_t^k$) that contain $m'$. We then obtain $\texttt{Arg0}_m$ by averaging the ELMo-based vectors (i.e., $X = x_1, \ldots, x_n$) of the head words of the mentions in $c$: $\texttt{Arg0}_m = 1/|c| \sum_{q \in c} x_{head(q)}$ ($head(q)$ is the index of the head word of mention $q$ in $W$). Note that as the current entity cluster configuration $E_t^k$ is used to generate the cluster-based representations if $m$ is an event mention (and vice verse), it serves as the main mechanism to enable the two coreference tasks to interact and benefit from each other. These vectors are inherited from (Barhom et al., 2019) for a fair comparison.

Finally, given two mentions $m_1$ and $m_2$, and their corresponding representation vectors $R(m_1)$ and $R(m_2)$ (as computed above), the coreference score functions $S_E$ and $S_V$ send the concatenated vector $[R(m_1), R(m_2), R(m_1) \odot R(m_2)]$ to two-layer feed-forward networks (separate ones for $S_E$ and $S_V$) that involve the sigmoid function in the end to produce coreference score for $m_1$ and $m_2$. Here, $\odot$ is the element-wise product. This completes the description of our CDECR model.

## 4 Experiments

**Dataset**: We use the ECB+ dataset (Cybulska and Vossen, 2014) to evaluate the CDECR models in this work. Note that ECB+ is the largest dataset with both within- and cross-document annotation for the coreference of entity and event mentions so far. We follow the setup and split for this dataset in prior work to ensure a fair comparison (Cybulska and Vossen, 2014; Kenyon-Dean et al., 2018; Barhom et al., 2019; Meged et al., 2020). In particular, this setup employs the annotation subset that has been validated for correctness by (Cybulska and Vossen, 2014) and involves a larger portion of the dataset for training. In ECB+, only a part of the mentions are annotated. This setup thus utilizes gold-standard event and entity mentions in the evaluation and does not require special treatment for unannotated mentions (Barhom et al., 2019).

Note that there is a different setup for ECB+ that is applied in (Yang et al., 2015) and (Choubey and Huang, 2017). In this setup, the full ECB+ dataset is employed, including the portions with known annotation errors. In test time, such prior work utilizes the predicted mentions from a mention extraction tool (Yang et al., 2015). To handle the partial annotation in ECB+, those prior work only evaluates the systems on the predicted mentions that are also annotated as the gold mentions. However, as shown by (Upadhyay et al., 2016), this ECB+ setup has several limitations (e.g., the ignorance of clusters with a single mention and the separate evaluation for each sub-topic). Following (Barhom et al., 2019), we thus do not evaluate the systems on this setup, i.e., not comparing our model with those models in (Yang et al., 2015) and (Choubey and Huang, 2017) due to the incompatibility.

**Hyper-Parameters**: To achieve a fair comparison, we utilize the preprocessed data and extend the implementation for the model in (Barhom et al., 2019) to include our novel hierarchical GCN model. The development dataset of ECB+ is used to tune the hyper-parameters of the proposed model (called HGCN). The suggested values and the resources for our model are reported in Appendix A.

**Comparison**: Following (Barhom et al., 2019), we compare HGCN with the following baselines:

(i) **LEMMA** (Barhom et al., 2019): This first clusters documents to topics and then groups event mentions that are in the same document clusters and share the head lemmas.

(ii) **CV** (Cybulska and Vossen, 2015b): This is a supervised learning method for CDECR that leverages discrete features to represent event mentions and documents. We compare with the best reported results for this method as in (Barhom et al., 2019).

(iii) **KCP** (Kenyon-Dean et al., 2018): This is a neural network model for CDECR. Both event mentions and document are represented via word embeddings and hand-crafted binary features.

(iv) **C-KCP** (Barhom et al., 2019): This is the KCP model that is retrained and tuned using the same document clusters in the test phase as in (Barhom et al., 2019) and our model.

(v) **BSE** (Barhom et al., 2019): This is a joint resolution model for cross-document coreference of entity and event mentions, using ELMo to compute representations for the mentions.

(v) **BSE-DJ** (Barhom et al., 2019): This is a variant of BSE that does not use the cluster-based representations $cluster(m)$ in the mention representations, thus performing event and entity coreference resolution separately.

(vii) **MCS** (Meged et al., 2020): An extension of BSE where some re-ranking features are included. Note that BSE and MCS are the current state-of-the-art (SOTA) models for CDECR on ECB+.

For cross-document entity coreference resolution, we compare our model with the LEMMA and BSE models in (Barhom et al., 2019), the only works that report the performance for event mentions on ECB+ so far. Following (Barhom et al., 2019), we use the common coreference resolution metrics to evaluate the models in this work, including MUC (Vilain et al., 1995), $B^3$, CEAF-e (Luo, 2005), and CoNLL F1 (average of three previous metrics). The official CoNLL scorer in (Pradhan et al., 2014) is employed to compute these metrics. Tables 1 and 2 show the performance (F1 scores) of the models for cross-document resolution for entity and event mentions (respectively). Note that we also report the performance of a variant (called **HGCN-DJ**) of the proposed HGCN model where the cluster-based representations $cluster(m)$ are excluded (thus separately doing event and entity resolution as BSE-DJ).

| Model | MUC | $B^3$ | CEAF-e | CoNLL |
|---|---|---|---|---|
| LEMMA (Barhom et al., 2019) | 78.1 | 77.8 | 73.6 | 76.5 |
| CV (Cybulska and Vossen, 2015b) | 73.0 | 74.0 | 64.0 | 73.0 |
| KCP (Kenyon-Dean et al. 2019) | 69.0 | 69.0 | 69.0 | 69.0 |
| CKCP (Barhom et al., 2019) | 73.4 | 75.9 | 71.5 | 73.6 |
| BSE-DJ (Barhom et al., 2019) | 79.4 | 80.4 | 75.9 | 78.5 |
| BSE (Barhom et al., 2019) | 80.9 | 80.3 | 77.3 | 79.5 |
| MCS (Meged et al., 2020) | 81.6 | 80.5 | 77.8 | 80.0 |
| HGCN-DJ | 81.3 | 80.8 | 76.1 | 79.4 |
| HGCN (proposed) | **83.1** | **82.1** | **78.8** | **81.3** |

Table 1: The cross-document event coreference resolution performance (F1) on the ECB+ test set.

| Model | MUC | $B^3$ | CEAF-e | CoNLL |
|---|---|---|---|---|
| LEMMA (Barhom et al., 2019) | 76.7 | 65.6 | 60.0 | 67.4 |
| BSE-DJ (Barhom et al., 2019) | 78.7 | 69.9 | 61.6 | 70.0 |
| BSE (Barhom et al., 2019) | 79.7 | 70.5 | 63.3 | 71.2 |
| HGCN-DJ | 80.1 | 70.7 | 62.2 | 71.0 |
| HGCN (proposed) | **82.1** | **71.7** | **63.4** | **72.4** |

Table 2: The cross-document entity coreference resolution performance (F1) on the ECB+ test set.

As can be seen, HGCN outperforms the all the baselines models on both entity and event coreference resolution (over different evaluation metrics). In particular, the CoNLL F1 score of HGCN for event coreference is 1.3% better than those for MCS (the prior SOTA model) while the CoNLL F1 improvement of HGCN over BSE (the prior SOTA model for entity coreference on ECB+) is 1.2%. These performance gaps are significant with $p < 0.001$, thus demonstrating the effectiveness of the proposed model for CDECR. Importantly, HGCN is significantly better than BSE, the most direct baseline of the proposed model, on both entity and event coreference regardless of whether the cluster-based representations $cluster(m)$ for joint entity and event resolution is used or not. This testifies to the benefits of the proposed hierarchical model for representation learning for CDECR. Finally, we evaluate the full HGCN model when ELMo embeddings are replaced with BERT embeddings (Devlin et al., 2019), leading to the CoNLL F1 scores of 79.7% and 72.3% for event and entity coreference (respectively). This performance is either worse (for events) or comparable (for entities) than those for EMLo, thus showing the advantages of ELMo for our tasks on ECB+.

**Ablation Study**: To demonstrate the benefits of the proposed components for our CDECR model, we evaluate three groups of ablated/varied models for HGCN. First, for the effectiveness of the pruned dependency tree $\hat{\mathcal{G}}^m$ and the sentence-level GCN models $G^{ent}$ and $G^{env}$, we consider the following baselines: (i) **HGCN-Sentence GCNs**: this model removes the sentence-level GCN models $G^{ent}$ and $G^{env}$ from HGCN and directly feed the ELMo-based vectors $X$ of the mention heads into the document-level GCN $G^{doc}$ (the representation vector $sent(m)$ is thus not included), and (ii) **HGCN-Pruned Tree**: this model replaces the pruned dependency tree $\hat{\mathcal{G}}^m$ with the full dependency tree $\mathcal{G}^m$ in the computation. Second, for the advantage of the GCN interaction between $G^{ent}$ and $G^{env}$, we examine two baselines: (iii) **HGCN with One Sent GCN**: this baseline only uses one sentence-level GCN model for both entity and event mentions (the regularization loss $L_m^{reg}$ for $G^{ent}$ and $G^{env}$ is thus not used as well), and (iv) **HGCN-$L_m^{reg}$**: this baseline still uses two sentence-level GCN models but excludes the regularization term $L_m^{reg}$ from the training losses. Finally, for the benefits of the document-level GCN $G^{doc}$, we study the following variants: (v) **HGCN-$G^{doc}$**: this model removes the document-level GCN model from HGCN, thus excluding the document representations $doc(m)$ from the mention representations, (vi) **HGCN-$G^{doc}$+TFIDF**: this model also excludes $G^{doc}$, but it includes the TF-IDF vectors for documents, based on uni-, bi- and tri-grams, in the mention representations (inherited from (Kenyon-Dean et al., 2018)), and (vii) **HGCN-$G^{doc}$+MP**: instead of using the GCN model $G^{doc}$, this model aggregates mention representation vectors produced by the sentence-level GCNs ($sent(m)$) to obtain the document representations $doc(m)$ using max-pooling. Table 3 presents the performance of the models for event coreference on the ECB+ test set.

| Model | MUC | $B^3$ | CEAF-e | CoNLL |
|---|---|---|---|---|
| HGCN (full) | **83.1** | **82.1** | **78.8** | **81.3** |
| HGCN-Sentence GCNs | 79.7 | 80.7 | 76.4 | 79.0 |
| HGCN-Pruned Tree | 81.8 | 81.1 | 77.1 | 80.0 |
| HGCN with One Sent GCN | 82.1 | 81.0 | 76.3 | 79.8 |
| HGCN-$L_m^{reg}$ | 81.6 | 81.6 | 77.6 | 80.3 |
| HGCN-$G^{doc}$ | 82.6 | 81.8 | 76.7 | 80.4 |
| HGCN-$G^{doc}$+TFIDF | 82.2 | 81.0 | 78.4 | 80.5 |
| HGCN-$G^{doc}$+MP | 82.0 | 81.1 | 77.0 | 80.0 |

Table 3: The CDECR F1 scores on the ECB+ test set.

It is clear from the table that all the ablated baselines are significantly worse than the full model HGCN (with $p < 0.001$), thereby confirming the necessity of the proposed GCN models (the sentence-level GCNs with pruned trees and document-level GCN) and the GCN interaction mechanism for HGCN and CDECR. In addition, the same trends for the model performance are also observed for entity coreference in this ablation study (the results are shown in Appendix B), thus further demonstrating the benefits of the proposed components in this work. Finally, we show the distribution of the error types of our HGCN model in Appendix C for future improvement.

## 5 Conclusion

We present a model to jointly resolve the cross-document coreference of entity and event mentions. Our model introduces a novel hierarchical GCN that captures both sentence and document context for the representations of entity and event mentions. In particular, we design pruned dependency trees to capture important context words for sentence-level GCNs while interaction graphs between entity and event mentions are employed for document-level GCN. In the future, we plan to explore better mechanisms to identify important context words for CDECR.

## Acknowledgments

This research has been supported by the Army Research Office (ARO) grant W911NF-21-1-0112. This research is also based upon work supported by the Office of the Director of National Intelligence (ODNI), Intelligence Advanced Research Projects Activity (IARPA), via IARPA Contract No. 2019-19051600006 under the Better Extraction from Text Towards Enhanced Retrieval (BETTER) Program. The views and conclusions contained herein are those of the authors and should not be interpreted as necessarily representing the official policies, either expressed or implied, of ARO, ODNI, IARPA, the Department of Defense, or the U.S. Government. The U.S. Government is authorized to reproduce and distribute reprints for governmental purposes notwithstanding any copyright annotation therein. This document does not contain technology or technical data controlled under either the U.S. International Traffic in Arms Regulations or the U.S. Export Administration Regulations.

## References


Cosmin Adrian Bejan and Sanda Harabagiu. 2014. Unsupervised event coreference resolution. In *Computational Linguistics*.

David Ahn. 2006. The stages of event extraction. In *Proceedings of the Workshop on Annotating and Reasoning about Time and Events*.

Shany Barhom, Vered Shwartz, Alon Eirew, Michael Bugert, Nils Reimers, and Ido Dagan. 2019. Revisiting joint modeling of cross-document entity and event coreference resolution. In *ACL*.

Cosmin Bejan and Sanda Harabagiu. 2010. Unsupervised event coreference resolution with rich linguistic features. In *ACL*.

Zheng Chen and Heng Ji. 2009. Graph-based event coreference resolution. In *Proceedings of the 2009 Workshop on Graph-based Methods for Natural Language Processing (TextGraphs-4)*.

Zheng Chen, Heng Ji, and Robert Haralick. 2009. A pairwise event coreference model, feature impact and evaluation for event coreference resolution. In *Proceedings of the Workshop on Events in Emerging Text Types*.

Prafulla Kumar Choubey and Ruihong Huang. 2017. Event coreference resolution by iteratively unfolding inter-dependencies among events. In *EMNLP*.

Agata Cybulska and Piek Vossen. 2014. Using a sledgehammer to crack a nut? lexical diversity and event coreference resolution. In *LREC*.

Agata Cybulska and Piek Vossen. 2015a. Translating granularity of event slots into features for event coreference resolution. In *Proceedings of the The 3rd Workshop on EVENTS: Definition, Detection, Coreference, and Representation*.

Agata Cybulska and Piek T. J. M. Vossen. 2015b. "bag of events" approach to event coreference resolution. supervised classification of event templates. In *Int. J. Comput. Linguistics Appl.*

Jacob Devlin, Ming-Wei Chang, Kenton Lee, and Kristina Toutanova. 2019. BERT: Pre-training of deep bidirectional transformers for language understanding. In *NAACL-HLT*.

Matthew Honnibal and Ines Montani. 2017. spaCy 2: Natural language understanding with Bloom embeddings, convolutional neural networks and incremental parsing. In *To appear*.

Kian Kenyon-Dean, Jackie Chi Kit Cheung, and Doina Precup. 2018. Resolving event coreference with supervised representation learning and clustering-oriented regularization. In *Proceedings of the Seventh Joint Conference on Lexical and Computational Semantics*.

Thomas N. Kipf and Max Welling. 2017. Semi-supervised classification with graph convolutional networks. In *ICLR*.

Viet Dac Lai, Tuan Ngo Nguyen, and Thien Huu Nguyen. 2020. Event detection: Gate diversity and syntactic importance scores for graph convolution neural networks. In *EMNLP*.

Heeyoung Lee, Marta Recasens, Angel Chang, Mihai Surdeanu, and Dan Jurafsky. 2012. Joint entity and event coreference resolution across documents. In *EMNLP*.

Qi Li, Heng Ji, and Liang Huang. 2013. Joint event extraction via structured prediction with global features. In *ACL*.

Zhengzhong Liu, Jun Araki, Eduard Hovy, and Teruko Mitamura. 2014. Supervised within-document event coreference using information propagation. In *LREC*.

Jing Lu, Deepak Venugopal, Vibhav Gogate, and Vincent Ng. 2016. Joint inference for event coreference resolution. In *COLING*.

Xiaoqiang Luo. 2005. On coreference resolution performance metrics. In *EMNLP*.

Christopher Manning, Mihai Surdeanu, John Bauer, Jenny Finkel, Steven Bethard, and David McClosky. 2014. The Stanford CoreNLP natural language processing toolkit. In *ACL System Demonstrations*.

Yehudit Meged, Avi Caciularu, Vered Shwartz, and Ido Dagan. 2020. Paraphrasing vs coreferring: Two sides of the same coin. In *ArXiv abs/2004.14979*.

Guoshun Nan, Zhijiang Guo, Ivan Sekulic, and Wei Lu. 2020. Reasoning with latent structure refinement for document-level relation extraction. In *ACL*.

Minh Van Nguyen, Viet Dac Lai, and Thien Huu Nguyen. 2021. Cross-task instance representation interactions and label dependencies for joint information extraction with graph convolutional networks. In *NAACL-HLT*.

Thien Huu Nguyen, , Adam Meyers, and Ralph Grishman. 2016. New york university 2016 system for kbp event nugget: A deep learning approach. In *TAC*.

Thien Huu Nguyen and Ralph Grishman. 2018. Graph convolutional networks with argument-aware pooling for event detection. In *AAAI*.

F. Pedregosa, G. Varoquaux, A. Gramfort, V. Michel, B. Thirion, O. Grisel, M. Blondel, P. Prettenhofer, R. Weiss, V. Dubourg, J. Vanderplas, A. Passos, D. Cournapeau, M. Brucher, M. Perrot, and E. Duchesnay. 2011. Scikit-learn: Machine learning in Python. In *Journal of Machine Learning Research*.

Matthew Peters, Mark Neumann, Mohit Iyyer, Matt Gardner, Christopher Clark, Kenton Lee, and Luke Zettlemoyer. 2018. Deep contextualized word representations. In *NAACL-HLT*.

Sameer Pradhan, Xiaoqiang Luo, Marta Recasens, Eduard Hovy, Vincent Ng, and Michael Strube. 2014. Scoring coreference partitions of predicted mentions: A reference implementation. In *ACL*.

Sunil Kumar Sahu, Fenia Christopoulou, Makoto Miwa, and Sophia Ananiadou. 2019. Inter-sentence relation extraction with document-level graph convolutional neural network. In *ACL*.

Lei Sha, Feng Qian, Baobao Chang, and Zhifang Sui. 2018. Jointly extracting event triggers and arguments by dependency-bridge rnn and tensor-based argument interaction. In *AAAI*.

M. Surdeanu, Lluís Màrquez i Villodre, X. Carreras, and P. Comas. 2007. Combination strategies for semantic role labeling. In *Journal of Artificial Intelligence Research*.

Hieu Minh Tran, Minh Trung Nguyen, and Thien Huu Nguyen. 2020. The dots have their values: Exploiting the node-edge connections in graph-based neural models for document-level relation extraction. In *EMNLP Findings*.

Minh Tran and Thien Huu Nguyen. 2021. Graph convolutional networks for event causality identification with rich document-level structures. In *NAACL-HLT*.

Shyam Upadhyay, Nitish Gupta, Christos Christodoulopoulos, and Dan Roth. 2016. Revisiting the evaluation for cross document event coreference. In *COLING*.

Amir Pouran Ben Veyseh, Franck Dernoncourt, Quan Hung Tran, Varun Manjunatha, Lidan Wang, Rajiv Jain, Doo Soon Kim, Walter Chang, and Thien Huu Nguyen. 2021. Inducing rich interaction structures between words for document-level event argument extraction. In *Proceedings of the 25th Pacific-Asia Conference on Knowledge Discovery and Data Mining (PAKDD)*.

Amir Pouran Ben Veyseh, Thien Huu Nguyen, and Dejing Dou. 2019. Graph based neural networks for event factuality prediction using syntactic and semantic structures. In *ACL*.

Amir Pouran Ben Veyseh, Tuan Ngo Nguyen, and Thien Huu Nguyen. 2020a. Graph transformer networks with syntactic and semantic structures for event argument extraction. In *EMNLP Findings*.

Amir Pouran Ben Veyseh, Nasim Nouri, Franck Dernoncourt, Dejing Dou, and Thien Huu Nguyen. 2020b. Introducing syntactic structures into target opinion word extraction with deep learning. In *EMNLP*.

Marc Vilain, John Burger, John Aberdeen, Dennis Connolly, and Lynette Hirschman. 1995. A model-theoretic coreference scoring scheme. In *Sixth Message Understanding Conference (MUC-6)*.

Bishan Yang, Claire Cardie, and Peter Frazier. 2015. A hierarchical distance-dependent Bayesian model for event coreference resolution. In *TACL*.

# GENE: Global Event Network Embedding

**Qi Zeng[1], Manling Li[1], Tuan Lai[1], Heng Ji[1], Mohit Bansal[2], Hanghang Tong[1]**
[1]University of Illinois Urbana-Champaign [2]UNC Chapel Hill
{qizeng2, manling2, tuanml2, hengji, htong}@illinois.edu
mbansal@cs.unc.edu

## Abstract

Current methods for event representation ignore related events in a corpus-level global context. For a deep and comprehensive understanding of complex events, we introduce a new task, Event Network Embedding, which aims to represent events by capturing the connections among events. We propose a novel framework, Global Event Network Embedding (GENE), that encodes the event network with a multi-view graph encoder while preserving the graph topology and node semantics. The graph encoder is trained by minimizing both structural and semantic losses. We develop a new series of structured probing tasks, and show that our approach effectively outperforms baseline models on node typing, argument role classification, and event coreference resolution. [1]

## 1 Introduction

Understanding events is a fundamental human activity. Our minds represent events at various granularity and abstraction levels, which allows us to quickly access and reason about related scenarios. A typical event mention includes an *event trigger* (the word or phrase that most clearly expresses an event occurrence) and its *arguments* (i.e., participants in events). The lexical embedding of a trigger is usually not sufficient, because the type of an event often depends on its arguments (Ritter and Rosen, 2000; Xu and Huang, 2013; Weber et al., 2018). For example, the support verb "get" may indicate a Transfer.Ownership event ("Ellison to spend $10.3 billion to **get** his company.") or a Movement.Transport event ("Airlines are **getting** flyers to destinations on time more often."). In Figure 1, the event type triggered by "execution" is Life.Die instead of project implementation. However, such kind of atomic event representation is still overly simplistic since it only captures local information and ignores related events in the global context. Real-world events are inter-connected, as illustrated in the example in Figure 1. To have a comprehensive representation of the set fire event on an embassy, we need to incorporate its causes (e.g., the preceding execution event) and recent relevant events (e.g., the protests that happened before and after it). To capture these inter-event relations in a global context, we propose the following two assumptions.

**Assumption 1. Two events can be connected through the entities involved.** On schema or type level, two event types can be connected through multiple paths and form a coherent story (Li et al., 2020). This observation is also valid on instance level. For the example in Figure 1, one of the relations between the Set Fire event and the Execution event is the blue path $\langle$*Set Fire, target, Saudi Embassy, affiliation, Saudi Arabia, agent, Execution*$\rangle$, which partially supports the fact that angry protesters revenge the death of Nimr al-Nimr against Saudi Arabia by attacking its embassy. This approximation for event-event relations lessens the problems of coarse classification granularity and low inter-annotation agreement (which may be as low as 20% as reported in (Hong et al., 2016)). Hence, we propose to construct an **Event Network**, where each event node represents a unique instance labeled with its type, arguments, and attributes. These nodes are connected through multiple instantiated meta-paths (Sun et al., 2011) consisting of their entity arguments and the entity-entity relations. These entities can be co-referential (e.g., two protests on different dates that both occur in Tehran, Iran) or involved in the same semantic relations (both protests targeted the Saudi embassy, which is affiliated with the location entity "Saudi Arabia").

**Assumption 2. The representation of one event depends on its neighboring events in the**

[1]Our code is released at https://github.com/pkuzengqi/GENE



*Proceedings of the Fifteenth Workshop on Graph-Based Methods for Natural Language Processing (TextGraphs-15)*, pages 42–53
June 11, 2021. ©2021 Association for Computational Linguistics

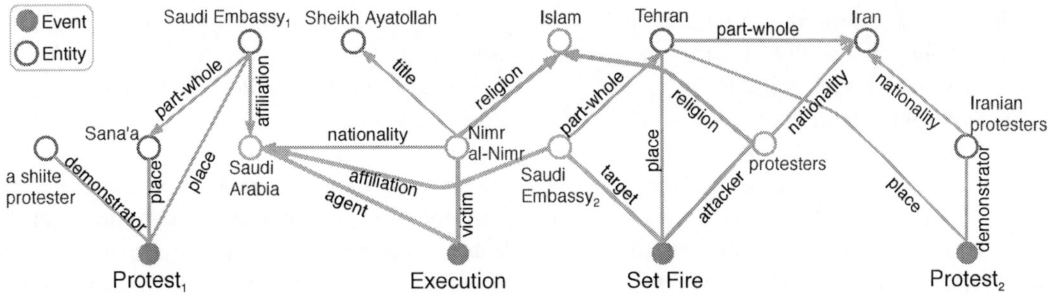


Figure 1: An example of Event Network constructed from one VOA news article, where events are connected through entities involved. Each node is an event or entity and each edge represents an argument role or entity-entity relation. In this example, *Execution* event and *Set Fire* event are connected through two paths, which tell the story of angry protesters revenge the death of Nimral-Nimr against Saudi Arabia by attacking its embassy.

**event network.** In Figure 1, a good representation of the Set Fire event should involve the Execution event because the latter clarifies the grievance motivating the former. We further enrich event representations by introducing more context from the entire event network. Compared with other methods to connect events (e.g., with event-event relations (Pustejovsky et al., 2003; Cassidy et al., 2014; Hong et al., 2016; Ikuta et al., 2014; O'Gorman et al., 2016)), our representation of each event grounded in an event network is semantically richer.

Based on these two hypotheses, we introduce a new task of **Event Network Embedding**, aiming at representing events with low-dimensional and informative embeddings by incorporating neighboring events. We also propose a novel **Global Event Network Embedding Learning (GENE)** framework for this task. To capture network topology and preserve node attributes in the event representations, GENE trains a graph encoder by minimizing both structural and semantic losses. To promote relational message passing with focus on different parts of the graph, we propose an innovative multi-view graph encoding method.

We design **Event Network Structural Probes**, an evaluation framework including a series of structural probing tasks, to check the model's capability to implicitly incorporate event network structures. In this work, the learned node embeddings are intrinsically evaluated with node typing and event argument role classification tasks, and applied to the downstream task of event coreference resolution. Experimental results on the augmented Automatic Content Extraction (ACE) dataset show that leveraging global context can significantly enrich the event representations. GENE and its variants significantly outperform the baseline methods on various tasks.

In summary, our contributions are:

- We formalize the task of event network embedding and accordingly propose a novel unsupervised learning framework, which trains the multi-view graph encoder with topology and semantics learning losses.
- We design a series of incrementally structural probing tasks, including node typing, argument role classification, and event coreference resolution, to comprehensively evaluate the event network embedding models.
- We demonstrate that our event network embedding is effective and general enough to enhance downstream applications.

## 2 Problem Formulation

**Event Network.** An event network with $n$ nodes is a heterogeneous attributed network denoted as $G = \{V, E\}$, where $V$ and $E$ are node and edge sets, respectively. Each node $v_i = \langle a_i, b_i, s_i, l_i \rangle \in V$ represents an event or entity mention, where $a_i$ and $b_i$ are the start and end word indices in sentence $s_i$, and $l_i$ is the node type label. Each edge $e_{ij} = \langle i, j, l_{ij} \rangle \in E$ represents an event-entity or entity-entity relation, where $i$ and $j$ are indices of the involved nodes and $l_{ij}$ is the edge type label.

In this work, we initialize the semantic representation of each node $v_i$ with an $m$-dimensional attribute vector $x_i$ derived from sentence context using a pretrained BERT model (Devlin et al., 2019).

**Semantic Proximity (Gao and Huang, 2018).** Given an event network $G = \{V, E\}$, the semantic proximity of node $v_i$ and node $v_j$ is determined by the similarity of node attribute vectors $x_i$ and $x_j$. If two nodes are semantically similar in the original space, they should stay similar in the new space.

**Local Neighborhood.** Given $G = \{V, E\}$, the local (one-hop) neighborhood $\mathcal{N}_i$ of node $v_i$ is defined as $\mathcal{N}_i = \{v_j \in V \mid e_{ij} \in E\}$. For example, the local neighborhood of one event is composed of its argument entities. Given event-entity node pairs, the task of argument role classification is to label the local neighborhood of events.

**Global Neighborhood.** Given $G = \{V, E\}$, node $v_j$ belongs to the global ($k$-hop with $k \geq 2$) neighborhood of node $v_i$, if node $v_i$ can walk to node $v_j$ in $k$ hops. For example, two events are 3-hop neighbors when there is a path from one event to the other through two entity nodes.

**Event Network Embedding.** Given an event network $G = \{V, E\}$ with $n$ nodes, the task of event network embedding aims to learn a mapping function $f : \{V, E\} \rightarrow Y$ or $f : \mathbb{R}^{n\times m} \times \mathbb{R}^{n\times n} \rightarrow \mathbb{R}^{n\times d}$, where $Y = [y_i] \in \mathbb{R}^{n\times d}$ is the node representation, $d$ is the embedding dimension, and $Y$ should preserve the Semantic Proximity, Local Neighborhood and Global Neighborhood.

## 3 Model

### 3.1 Approach Overview

Compared to other network embedding tasks, there are three challenges in event network embedding:

- Data Sparsity: We rely on supervised Information Extraction (IE) techniques to construct the event network, because they provide high-quality knowledge elements. However, due to the limited number of types in pre-defined ontologies, the constructed event network tends to be sparse.
- Relational Structure: The event network is heterogeneous with edges representing relations of different types. Relation types differ in semantics and will influence message passing.
- Long-Distance Dependency: Global neighborhood preservation requires node embedding to capture the distant relations between two nodes.

We first initiate the event network by event and entity extraction, event argument role labeling and entity-entity relation extraction. The nodes in the event network are events and entities. If entity coreference resolution results are available, we merge coreferential entity mentions and label the mention text with the first occurring mention. For each node $v_i$, we derive its $m$-dimensional attribute vector $x_i$ with its mention text by averaging the corresponding contextual token embeddings from a pretrained bert-base model. The edges in the event network come from the event argument roles connecting event mentions and entities, and the entity-entity relations. In addition, to alleviate the data sparsity problem we enrich the event network with external Wikipedia entity-entity relations and event narrative orders as a data preprocessing step detailed in Section 5.1.

We propose an unsupervised Global Event Network Embedding (GENE) learning framework for this task (Figure 2). We first encode the graph with a Relational Graph Convolutional Network (RGCN) (Schlichtkrull et al., 2018) based multi-view graph encoder, in which the multi-view component puts focus on various perspectives of the graph. To capture both the semantic and topological contexts, i.e. the node attributes and graph structure, in event node representation, GENE trains the graph encoder by minimizing semantic reconstruction loss and relation discrimination loss.

### 3.2 Multi-View Graph Encoder

Given an event network $G = \{V, E\}$, the graph encoder projects the nodes into a set of embeddings $Y$ while preserving the graph structure and node attributes. As shown in Figure 2, we first feed different views of $G$ to the graph encoder, then integrate encoded node embeddings into $Y$.

**RGCN.** Because of the relational structure of event network, we apply RGCN (Schlichtkrull et al., 2018), a relational variant of GCN (Kipf and Welling, 2017), as the graph encoder. RGCN induces the node embeddings based on the local neighborhood with operations on a heterogeneous graph. It differs from GCN in the type-specific weights in message propagation.

We stack two RGCN layers in the encoder. The hidden state of node $v_i$ in the first layer is initiated with node attribute $x_i$. The output of the former layer serves as the input of the next layer. Formally, in each RGCN layer the hidden state $h$ of node $v_i$ is updated through message propagation with the hidden states of neighbors (and itself) from the last layer and message aggregation with an addition

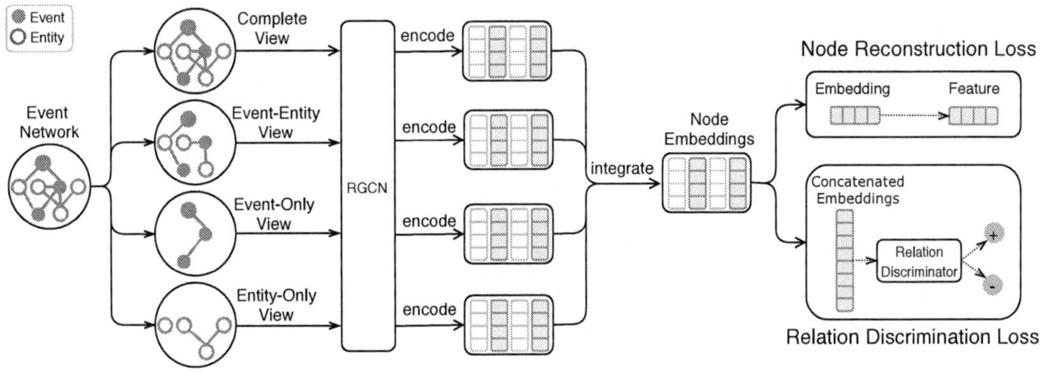


Figure 2: An overview of the proposed GENE framework. The event network is encoded by a relational graph convolutional network, which is trained with node reconstruction loss and relation discrimination loss.

operation and an element-wise activation function.

$$h_i^{(l+1)} = \sigma(W_0^{(l)} h_i^{(l)} + \sum_{r \in R} \sum_{j \in \mathcal{N}_i^r} \frac{1}{c_{i,r}} W_r^{(l)} h_j^{(l)}),$$

where $h_i^{(l)} \in \mathbb{R}^{d^{(l)}}$ is the hidden state of node $v_i$ at the $l$-th layer of RGCN, $d^{(l)}$ is the dimension of the hidden state at the $l$-th layer, $R$ is the edge relation set, $\mathcal{N}_i^r$ is the neighborhood of node $v_i$ under relation type $r \in R$, $W_r^{(l)}$ is the trainable weight matrix of relation type $r$ at the $l$-th layer, $c_{i,r} = |\mathcal{N}_i^r|$ is a normalization constant, and $\sigma$ is Leaky ReLU.

**Weight Decomposition.** In order to reduce the growing model parameter size and prevent the accompanying over-fitting problem, we follow (Schlichtkrull et al., 2018) and perform basis decomposition on relation weight matrix:

$$W_r^{(l)} = \sum_{b=1}^{B} a_{rb}^{(l)} V_b^{(l)},$$

where the edge weight $W_r^{(l)}$ is a linear combination of basis transformations $V_b^{(l)} \in \mathbb{R}^{d^{(l+1)} \times d^{(l)}}$ with coefficients $a_{rb}$. This basis decomposition method reduces model parameters by using a much smaller base set $B$ to compose relation set $R$ and can be seen as a way of weight sharing between different relation types.

**Multiple Views.** The structure of event networks can be viewed in multiple different perspectives. For example, when entity-entity relations are masked out, an event network degenerates to pieces of isolated events and only local neighborhood will be observed. The advantage of separate modeling is that it enables the graph encoder to focus on different perspectives of the graph and lessens the over-smoothing problem (the tendency of indistinguishable encoded node embeddings). Therefore, we propose to encode the network $G = \{V, E\}$ from the following views:

(1) Complete View: We keep all nodes and all edges in this view.

(2) Event-Entity View: We keep all nodes and only event-entity relations in this view. Events are isolated as single subgraphs, each of which only includes the corresponding event and its argument entities.

(3) Entity-Only View: We only keep entity nodes and entity-entity relations in this view. Information is flowed only among entity nodes and will not be influenced by events.

(4) Event-Only View: We only keep event nodes and event-event relations in this view. Similarly, events are isolated from entities.

We feed the event network in different views as separate inputs to the graph encoder, and integrate the encoded results in three ways:

**Concatenation.** Node embeddings of $\frac{d}{v}$ dimensions from $v$ views are directly concatenated with $y_{cat} = [y^0 \cdot y^1 \cdots y^{v-1}]$.

**Averaging.** Node embeddings of $d$ dimensions from $v$ views are averaged with $y_{avg} = \frac{1}{v} \sum_{j=1}^{v} y^j$.

**Weighted Averaging.** Node embeddings of $d$ dimensions from $v$ views are averaged with $y_{wavg} = \frac{1}{v} \sum_{j=1}^{v} W_v^j y^j$, where $W_v^j$ is a trainable matrix.

### 3.3 Topology Learning

To capture neighborhood information, we train the graph encoder with relation discrimination loss to learn the graph topology.

$$\mathcal{L}_T = \sum_i (\sum_{r \in R} \sum_{j \in \mathcal{N}_i^r} \mathbb{E}[\log \mathcal{D}_r(y_i, y_j)] + \sum_{r \in R} \sum_{j' \notin \mathcal{N}_i^r} \mathbb{E}[\log(1 - \mathcal{D}_r(y_i, y_{j'}))])$$

The relation-specific discriminator $\mathcal{D}_r$ determines the probability score for one node's being connected with another node in relation $r$:

$$\mathcal{D}_r(y_i, y_j) = \sigma(y_i^T W_{\mathcal{D}}^r y_j)$$

where $W_{\mathcal{D}}^r$ is a trainable bi-linear scoring matrix and $\sigma$ is Sigmoid funtion. We choose binary discriminator over multi-class classifier to capture features required for independent classification decisions.

### 3.4 Semantics Learning

To preserve the node semantics, we perform node attribute reconstruction with a two-layer feed-forward neural network:

$$\mathcal{L}_S = \sum_i \|x_i - \phi(y_i)\|_2$$

where $x_i$ represents the attributes of node $v_i$, $y_i$ represents the encoded embedding of node $v_i$, and $\phi : \mathbb{R}^{n \times d} \to \mathbb{R}^{n \times m}$ denotes the non-linear transformation function. $\mathcal{L}_S$ loss evaluates how much information required to reconstruct node attributes is preserved in the encoded node embeddings.

### 3.5 Training

To encourage the graph encoder to learn both the graph topology and node semantics, we combine the structural loss and semantics loss as the final objective function:

$$\mathcal{L} = \mathcal{L}_T + \lambda \mathcal{L}_S$$

where $\lambda$ is a weight normalization hyper-parameter.

## 4 Structural Probes for Event Network

As there is no existing work on comprehensive event representation evaluation, in this work we design an evaluation framework with a series of probing tasks to comprehensively evaluate the model's capability to capture network structures and preserve node attributes. Structural Probes are models trained to predict certain properties from inferred representations, and have been used to understand linguistic properties (Hewitt and Manning, 2019; Conneau et al., 2018).

The task of event network embedding requires the embedded distributional node representations to preserve semantic proximity, local neighborhood and global neighborhood. Accordingly, we intrinsically evaluate the semantics preservation with node typing and assess the local neighborhood preservation with event argument role classification. We also apply the node embeddings to a downstream task, event coreference resolution, to extrinsically evaluate the global neighborhood preservation.

Node Typing and Event Argument Role Classification are conducted under the same evaluation setting: given the learned node embeddings, predict the labels with a multi-layer perceptron (MLP) based classifier. If the input of the classifier is of different dimension to the event network embeddings, it will be first projected into the same dimension. The classifier is a two-layer feed-forward neural network with a linear transformation layer, a non-linear activation operation, a layer normalization, a dropout operation, and another linear transformation layer. The classifier is designed to be simple on purpose so that it will be limited in reasoning ability and thus the evidence for classification will be mainly derived from the node embeddings.

### 4.1 Node Typing

The event or entity type of each node can be inferred from the sentence context of its mentions. As the node attribute vector $x_i$ for node $v_i$ comes from the contextual word embeddings, $x_i$ naturally implies its node type. This characteristic is supposed to be preserved after the node has been further embedded and the embedding dimension has been reduced.

We evaluate the node semantics preservation by checking whether the node types can be recovered from the node embeddings. Given one event or entity node, our evaluation model predicts its type out of 45 labels, which includes 7 coarse-grained entity types, 5 value types, and 33 event types as defined in the NIST Automatic Content Extraction (ACE) task. The performance on this task is compared in terms of multi-label classification Micro F1 score.

### 4.2 Event Argument Role Classification

We detect local neighborhood preservation by evaluating whether the event-entity relation (event argument role) can be recovered from the node embeddings. Given one event node and one entity node, we predict the relation type between each pair of nodes out of 238 labels. Each label consists of an event type and an argument role type as defined in ACE. For example, the argument role label "Justice:Arrest-Jail:Agent" can only be correctly selected when the event node implies the type "Justice:Arrest-Jail" and the entity node implies its role being the "Agent". Compared to the traditional argument role labeling procedure, this setting skips the step of mention identification, which has been done in network construction process. The performance is reported with multi-label classification Micro F1 score.

### 4.3 Event Coreference Resolution

The goal of event coreference resolution is to determine which event mentions refer to the same real-world event. The features for similarity computation used in previous work are typically limited to event triggers, arguments and sentence-level contexts (Chen et al., 2009; Chen and Ji, 2009; Sammons et al., 2015; Lu and Ng, 2016; Chen and Ng, 2016; Duncan et al., 2017; Lai et al., 2021). However, event arguments are often distributed across the content of an article. Therefore a global event network can ground event mentions into a wider context with related events and help cluster coreferential mentions more accurately.

In this task we evaluate the impact of applying event network embedding as additional features on enhancing event coreference resolution. We concatenate the event embeddings learned by the event network and by a fine-tuned SpanBERT model (Joshi et al., 2020) as the input for the scoring function. The training procedure is the same as that in (Joshi et al., 2019).

We report F1 scores in terms of $B^3$ (Bagga and Baldwin, 1998), MUC (Vilain et al., 1995), $CEAF_e$ (Luo, 2005), BLANC (Recasens and Hovy, 2011) metrics, and also their averaged results (AVG).

## 5 Results and Analysis

### 5.1 Dataset

We construct corpus-level graphs for training, development, and test sets from the English subset of Automatic Content Extraction (ACE) 2005 dataset[2]. We follow the pre-processing steps in (Lin et al., 2020) and show the dataset statistics in Table 1.

[2]https://www.ldc.upenn.edu/collaborations/past-projects/ace

We perform automatic entity linking (Pan et al., 2017) to link entities to Wikipedia. Entity nodes linked to the same Wikipedia entity are merged into one node. We further retrieve entity-entity relations from Wikidata and enrich the event network with these connections, such as the part-whole relation between Tehran and Iran in Figure 1. We also add narrative event-event relations by connecting every pair of events within one document as edges in the graph.

### 5.2 Baseline

**Non-Graph Event Representation Methods.** Mention-based method represents events with contextual representations inferred by BERT (Devlin et al., 2019). Tuple-based method uses the averaged contextual representations of event mentions and its arguments.

**Graph Representation Methods.** Skip-gram (Mikolov et al., 2013) learns graph topology by increasing the predicted similarity of adjacent node embeddings and decreasing the similarity of irrelevant node embeddings with random negative sampling:

$$\mathcal{L}_G = \sum_i \Big( \sum_{j \in \mathcal{N}_i} \log \sigma(y_j^T y_i) + \sum_{j' \notin \mathcal{N}_i} \log \sigma(-y_{j'}^T y_i) \Big)$$

Deep Graph Infomax (Velickovic et al., 2019) captures graph topology by maximizing the mutual information between patch representations and higher-level subgraph summary:

$$\mathcal{L}_D = \sum_i \Big( \sum_{j \in \mathcal{N}_i} \mathbb{E}[\log \mathcal{D}(y_i, s)] + \sum_{j' \notin \mathcal{N}_i} \mathbb{E}[\log(1 - \mathcal{D}(y_{j'}, s))] \Big)$$

where the subgraph summary $s$ is read out as the average of node embeddings and $\mathcal{D}$ is the discriminator deciding the probability score for node's being contained in the summary.

For fair comparison, we train the same framework with the following graph representation learning methods.

**Event Coreference Resolution.** Besides existing methods (Bejan and Harabagiu, 2010b; Liu et al., 2014) we implement the model architecture (Lee et al., 2017) that has achieved the current state-of-the-art results in entity coreference resolution (Joshi et al., 2019) and cross-document event

| | | Article | Node | | Edge | | | | |
|---|---|---|---|---|---|---|---|---|---|
| | | | Event | Entity | Event-Entity | Entity-Entity | | Event-Event | |
| | | | | | | Original | Wiki* | Narrative* | Coref |
| ACE | train | 521 | 4,353 | 3,688 | 7,888 | 6,856 | 7,040 | 70,992 | 912 |
| | dev | 30 | 494 | 667 | 938 | 723 | 853 | 12,572 | 144 |
| | test | 40 | 424 | 750 | 897 | 796 | 1,543 | 6,154 | 121 |

Table 1: Statistics for the enhanced ACE 2005 dataset. *Wiki* and *Narrative* are enriched event-event relations.

coreference resolution (Cattan et al., 2020). We use SpanBERT (Joshi et al., 2020) for contextual embeddings. The detailed methods about the baseline event corefernece resolution framework are described in (Lai et al., 2021). In this experiment, we compare the performance with and without our event network embeddings as additional features.

### 5.3 Training Details

All models are implemented with Deep Graph Library and Pytorch framework. We train each models for 10 epochs and apply an early stopping strategy with a patience of 3 epochs (if the model does not outperform its best checkpoint for 3 epochs on validation set we will stop the training process). The batch size is 64.

The hyper-parameters are selected based on model performance on development set. The model is optimized with the Adam optimizer with a learning rate of $1e-5$ and a dropout rate of 0.1. The embedding dimension is 256 and the hidden dimension is 512. The lambda in loss function is 1.0. On average it takes approximately four hours to train a model until converge with one Tesla V100 GPU with 16GB DRAM. To improve training efficiency, neighbor pre-sampling is performed for all topology learning losses.

### 5.4 Results and Analysis

We conclude the results shown in Table 2 with the following observations:

**GENE preserves node semantics well with low-dimensional and informative embeddings.** Though with only one third of embedding dimension (typically 256, comparing to 768 in other event representation baselines), our models have higher performance on Node Typing, which shows the node semantics has been well preserved.

**Topology learning loss is crucial to event neighborhood proximity preservation.** We propose to use relation discrimination loss to learn the graph structure and exam it with argument role classification task. Methods without topology learning objectives (Event as Mention, Event as Tuple, and GENE w/ $\mathcal{L}_T$) have a significant drop of performance on this task, while our proposed model has the best performance because of the similarity and transferability between argument role classification and argument role discrimination in $\mathcal{L}_T$. Another reason is that only $\mathcal{L}_T$ is designed for heterogeneous graphs while SKG and DGI do not consider relation types.

**In general Multi-view encoder is beneficial.** Compared to the single-view variants, our multi-view encoder has overall better performance. Keeping complete view has the most closed performance, while discarding event-entity relations yields significant drop on argument role classification.

**Averaging multi-view embeddings is better than Weighted Averaging.** Intuitively weighted averaging captures the correlations among different embedding dimensions, promotes salient dimensions and/or teases out unimportant ones within the same view by performing a linear transformation within each view before averaging over views. However, results show that it is not comparable with averaging and concatenation multi-view encoders. One possible reason is that the distribution of embedding within each view is greatly restricted by the input embedding distribution.

**GENE improves the performance on event coreference resolution by connecting events through related entities.** SpanBERT model is a strong baseline with better performance compared with the former methods. We show that using our embeddings as additional features, SpanBERT can further improve all event coreference resolution scores. In the following example, SpanBERT model fails to detect the coreference link between event *sell* and event *buy* while GENE succeeds by discovering the relation between the entity arguments.

... The Times said Vivendi Universal was negotiating to **sell** its flagship theme parks to New York investment firm Blackstone Group as a the first step toward dismantlingits entertainment empire . Vivendi Universal officials in the United States were not immediately available for comment on Friday . Under the reported plans , Blackstone Group would **buy** Vivendi ' s theme park division , including ...

| Model | Node Typing | Argument Classification | Event Coreference | | | | |
|---|---|---|---|---|---|---|---|
| | | | MUC | $B^3$ | $CEAF_e$ | BLANC | AVG |
| Event Mention | 80.58 | 71.57 | 61.81 | 87.79 | 84.24 | 74.97 | 77.20 |
| Event Tuple | 68.40 | 72.13 | 63.10 | 89.06 | 85.23 | 77.6 | 78.75 |
| Skip-gram(Mikolov et al., 2013) | 75.55 | 93.42 | 59.81 | 88.09 | 83.40 | 77.30 | 77.15 |
| Deep Graph Infomax(Velickovic et al., 2019) | 74.96 | 95.32 | 59.36 | 87.05 | 82.19 | 73.41 | 75.50 |
| HDP(Bejan and Harabagiu, 2010b) | - | - | - | 83.8 | 76.7 | - | - |
| (Liu et al., 2014) | - | - | 50.98 | 89.38 | **86.47** | 70.43 | 74.32 |
| SpanBERT(Joshi et al., 2020) | - | - | 65.72 | 89.48 | 85.35 | 79.82 | 80.09 |
| **GENE** | **81.26** | **95.76** | 68.99 | 89.53 | 85.86 | 80.38 | 81.19 |
| · w/o $\mathcal{L}_T$ | 78.78 | 79.04 | **70.63** | 89.03 | 84.88 | **81.13** | 81.42 |
| · w/o $\mathcal{L}_S$ | 78.02 | 95.32 | 68.14 | 89.53 | 86.17 | 79.90 | 80.94 |
| · w/ Event-Entity view | 80.82 | 92.64 | 60.09 | 87.97 | 84.75 | 70.67 | 75.87 |
| · w/ Event-only & Entity-only views | 74.79 | 72.02 | 60.86 | 88.46 | 85.15 | 75.64 | 77.53 |
| · w/ Complete view | 79.42 | 90.52 | 63.01 | 88.11 | 84.94 | 75.50 | 77.89 |
| · w/ Concatenated integration | 78.45 | 93.87 | 70.08 | **89.81** | 85.85 | 81.08 | **81.71** |
| · w/ Weighted integration | 74.53 | 94.31 | 66.36 | 88.99 | 85.81 | 76.97 | 79.53 |

Table 2: Results on test set of ACE dataset. Node typing and argument role classification results are reported in micro F1 scores(%). Event Coreference are performed with our embeddings as additional features.

**Remaining Challenges.** One of the unsolved challenges is to capture the long distance relation in the encoder in addition to the two encoder layers. Another challenge is the limited ability in entity coreference resolution. In some failing cases, GENE model does not link two events because some of their connecting arguments are expressed as pronouns. This limitation is inherited from the upstream event extraction.

## 6 Related Work

**Event Representation.** Some previous efforts enrich event representations by introducing arguments (Levin, 1993; Goldberg, 1995; Ritter and Rosen, 2000; Huang and Ahrens, 2000; Iwata, 2005; Goldberg, 2006; Xu and Huang, 2013; Bies et al., 2016; Do et al., 2017; Kalm et al., 2019), intent and sentiment (Ding et al., 2019), and temporal information (Tong et al., 2008). (Weber et al., 2018) proposes a tensor-based event composition approach to combine a trigger and arguments to represent each event. We extend the definition of scenario to multiple inter-connected events. (Modi, 2016) captures statistical dependencies between events but limits to script data sets where the events are naturally organized in sequential temporal order. Our approach captures a rich variety of explicit semantic connections among complex events. (Hong et al., 2018) learns distributed event representations using supervised multi-task learning, while our framework is based on unsupervised learning.
**Network Embedding.** Our work falls into the scope of unsupervised learning for heterogeneous attributed network embeddings. Heterogeneous network embedding methods (Chang et al., 2015; Dong et al., 2017; Wang et al., 2019) jointly model nodes and edges. Attributed network embedding approaches (Gao and Huang, 2018; Yang et al., 2015) on the other hand put focus on preserving node attributes when encoding the networks.
**Event Coreference Resolution.** Most existing methods (Chen et al., 2009; Chen and Ji, 2009; Bejan and Harabagiu, 2010a; Zhang et al., 2015; Peng et al., 2016; Lai et al., 2021) only exploit local features including trigger, argument and sentence context matching. To prevent error propagation, some models perform joint inference between event extraction and event coreference resolution (Lee et al., 2012; Araki and Mitamura, 2015; Lu and Ng, 2017) or incorporate document topic structures (Choubey and Huang, 2018). To the best of our knowledge our method is the first to leverage the entire event networks to compute similarity features.

## 7 Conclusions and Future Work

We propose a novel continuous event representation called Event Network Embedding to capture the connections among events in a global context. This new representation provides a powerful framework for downstream applications such as event coreference resolution and event ordering.

In the future we aim to improve the ability to capture the long-distance relations in the graph encode by introducing event-event relation in the form of multiple meta-paths. The relations, or the event evolution patterns, extracted from large-scale corpora can guide event-related reasoning and act as shortcut linking event nodes. Another direction is to explore a unified automatic evaluation benchmark for event representation.

## Acknowledgement

This research is based upon work supported in part by U.S. DARPA KAIROS Program No. FA8750-19-2-1004, U.S. DARPA AIDA Program No. FA8750-18-2-0014, Air Force No. FA8650-17-C-7715. The views and conclusions contained herein are those of the authors and should not be interpreted as necessarily representing the official policies, either expressed or implied, of DARPA, or the U.S. Government. The U.S. Government is authorized to reproduce and distribute reprints for governmental purposes notwithstanding any copyright annotation therein.

## References

Jun Araki and Teruko Mitamura. 2015. Joint event trigger identification and event coreference resolution with structured perceptron. In Proceedings of the 2015 Conference on Empirical Methods in Natural Language Processing, pages 2074–2080, Lisbon, Portugal. Association for Computational Linguistics.

Amit Bagga and Breck Baldwin. 1998. Algorithms for scoring coreference chains. In The first international conference on language resources and evaluation workshop on linguistics coreference, volume 1, pages 563–566. Citeseer.

Cosmin Bejan and Sanda Harabagiu. 2010a. Unsupervised event coreference resolution with rich linguistic features. In Proceedings of the 48th Annual Meeting of the Association for Computational Linguistics, pages 1412–1422, Uppsala, Sweden. Association for Computational Linguistics.

Cosmin Adrian Bejan and Sanda M. Harabagiu. 2010b. Unsupervised event coreference resolution with rich linguistic features. In ACL 2010, Proceedings of the 48th Annual Meeting of the Association for Computational Linguistics, July 11-16, 2010, Uppsala, Sweden, pages 1412–1422. The Association for Computer Linguistics.

Ann Bies, Zhiyi Song, Jeremy Getman, Joe Ellis, Justin Mott, Stephanie Strassel, Martha Palmer, Teruko Mitamura, Marjorie Freedman, Heng Ji, and Tim O'Gorman. 2016. A comparison of event representations in DEFT. In Proceedings of the Fourth Workshop on Events, pages 27–36, San Diego, California. Association for Computational Linguistics.

Taylor Cassidy, Bill McDowell, Nathanael Chambers, and Steven Bethard. 2014. An annotation framework for dense event ordering. In Proceedings of the 52nd Annual Meeting of the Association for Computational Linguistics (Volume 2: Short Papers), pages 501–506, Baltimore, Maryland. Association for Computational Linguistics.

Arie Cattan, Alon Eirew, Gabriel Stanovsky, Mandar Joshi, and Ido Dagan. 2020. Streamlining cross-document coreference resolution: Evaluation and modeling. CoRR, abs/2009.11032.

Shiyu Chang, Wei Han, Jiliang Tang, Guo-Jun Qi, Charu C. Aggarwal, and Thomas S. Huang. 2015. Heterogeneous network embedding via deep architectures. In Proceedings of the 21th ACM SIGKDD International Conference on Knowledge Discovery and Data Mining, Sydney, NSW, Australia, August 10-13, 2015, pages 119–128.

Chen Chen and Vincent Ng. 2016. Joint inference over a lightly supervised information extraction pipeline: Towards event coreference resolution for resource-scarce languages. In Proceedings of the Thirtieth AAAI Conference on Artificial Intelligence, AAAI'16, page 2913–2920. AAAI Press.

Zheng Chen and Heng Ji. 2009. Graph-based event coreference resolution. In Proceedings of the 2009 Workshop on Graph-based Methods for Natural Language Processing (TextGraphs-4), pages 54–57, Suntec, Singapore. Association for Computational Linguistics.

Zheng Chen, Heng Ji, and Robert Haralick. 2009. A pairwise event coreference model, feature impact and evaluation for event coreference resolution. In Proceedings of the Workshop on Events in Emerging Text Types, pages 17–22, Borovets, Bulgaria. Association for Computational Linguistics.

Prafulla Kumar Choubey and Ruihong Huang. 2018. Improving event coreference resolution by modeling correlations between event coreference chains and document topic structures. In Proceedings of the 56th Annual Meeting of the Association for Computational Linguistics (Volume 1: Long Papers), pages 485–495, Melbourne, Australia. Association for Computational Linguistics.

Alexis Conneau, German Kruszewski, Guillaume Lample, Loïc Barrault, and Marco Baroni. 2018. What you can cram into a single $&!#* vector: Probing sentence embeddings for linguistic properties. In Proceedings of the 56th Annual Meeting of the Association for Computational Linguistics (Volume 1: Long Papers), pages 2126–2136, Melbourne, Australia. Association for Computational Linguistics.

Jacob Devlin, Ming-Wei Chang, Kenton Lee, and Kristina Toutanova. 2019. BERT: Pre-training of deep bidirectional transformers for language understanding. In Proceedings of the 2019 Conference of the North American Chapter of the Association for Computational Linguistics: Human Language Technologies, Volume 1 (Long and Short Papers), pages 4171–4186, Minneapolis, Minnesota. Association for Computational Linguistics.

Xiao Ding, Kuo Liao, Ting Liu, Zhongyang Li, and Junwen Duan. 2019. Event representation learning enhanced with external commonsense knowledge. In Proceedings of the 2019 Conference on Empirical Methods in Natural Language Processing and the 9th International Joint Conference on Natural Language Processing (EMNLP-IJCNLP), pages 4894–4903, Hong Kong, China. Association for Computational Linguistics.

Quynh Ngoc Thi Do, Steven Bethard, and Marie-Francine Moens. 2017. Improving implicit semantic role labeling by predicting semantic frame arguments. In Proceedings of the Eighth International Joint Conference on Natural Language Processing (Volume 1: Long Papers), pages 90–99, Taipei, Taiwan. Asian Federation of Natural Language Processing.

Yuxiao Dong, Nitesh V. Chawla, and Ananthram Swami. 2017. metapath2vec: Scalable representation learning for heterogeneous networks. In Proceedings of the 23rd ACM SIGKDD International Conference on Knowledge Discovery and Data Mining, Halifax, NS, Canada, August 13 - 17, 2017, pages 135–144.

Chase Duncan, Liang-Wei Chan, Haoruo Peng, Hao Wu, Shyam Upadhyay, Nitish Gupta, Chen-Tse Tsai, Mark Sammons, and Dan Roth. 2017. UI CCG TAC-KBP2017 submissions: Entity discovery and linking, and event nugget detection and coreference. In Proceedings of the 2017 Text Analysis Conference, TAC 2017, Gaithersburg, Maryland, USA, November 13-14, 2017. NIST.

Hongchang Gao and Heng Huang. 2018. Deep attributed network embedding. In Proceedings of the Twenty-Seventh International Joint Conference on Artificial Intelligence, IJCAI 2018, July 13-19, 2018, Stockholm, Sweden, pages 3364–3370.

Adele E. Goldberg. 1995. Constructions: A Construction Grammar Approach to Argument Structure. Chicago: University of Chicago Press.

Adele E. Goldberg. 2006. Constructions at Work: the Nature of Generalization in Language. Oxford: Oxford University Press.

John Hewitt and Christopher D. Manning. 2019. A structural probe for finding syntax in word representations. In Proceedings of the 2019 Conference of the North American Chapter of the Association for Computational Linguistics: Human Language Technologies, Volume 1 (Long and Short Papers), pages 4129–4138, Minneapolis, Minnesota. Association for Computational Linguistics.

Xudong Hong, Asad Sayeed, and Vera Demberg. 2018. Learning distributed event representations with a multi-task approach. In Proceedings of the Seventh Joint Conference on Lexical and Computational Semantics, pages 11–21, New Orleans, Louisiana. Association for Computational Linguistics.

Yu Hong, Tongtao Zhang, Tim O'Gorman, Sharone Horowit-Hendler, Heng Ji, and Martha Palmer. 2016. Building a cross-document event-event relation corpus. In Proceedings of the 10th Linguistic Annotation Workshop held in conjunction with ACL 2016 (LAW-X 2016), pages 1–6, Berlin, Germany. Association for Computational Linguistics.

Chu-Ren Huang and Kathleen Ahrens. 2000. The module-attribute representation of verbal semantics. In Proceedings of the 14th Pacific Asia Conference on Language, Information and Computation, pages 109–120, Waseda University International Conference Center, Tokyo, Japan. PACLIC 14 Organizing Committee.

Rei Ikuta, Will Styler, Mariah Hamang, Tim O'Gorman, and Martha Palmer. 2014. Challenges of adding causation to richer event descriptions. In Proceedings of the Second Workshop on EVENTS: Definition, Detection, Coreference, and Representation, pages 12–20, Baltimore, Maryland, USA. Association for Computational Linguistics.

Seizi Iwata. 2005. Locative alternation and two levels of verb meaning. Cognitive Linguistics, 16(2):355–407.

Mandar Joshi, Danqi Chen, Yinhan Liu, Daniel S. Weld, Luke Zettlemoyer, and Omer Levy. 2020. SpanBERT: Improving pre-training by representing and predicting spans. Transactions of the Association for Computational Linguistics, 8:64–77.

Mandar Joshi, Omer Levy, Luke Zettlemoyer, and Daniel Weld. 2019. BERT for coreference resolution: Baselines and analysis. In Proceedings of the 2019 Conference on Empirical Methods in Natural Language Processing and the 9th International Joint Conference on Natural Language Processing (EMNLP-IJCNLP), pages 5803–5808, Hong Kong, China. Association for Computational Linguistics.

Pavlina Kalm, Michael Regan, and William Croft. 2019. Event structure representation: Between verbs and argument structure constructions. In Proceedings of the First International Workshop on Designing Meaning Representations, pages 100–109, Florence, Italy. Association for Computational Linguistics.

Thomas N. Kipf and Max Welling. 2017. Semi-supervised classification with graph convolutional networks. In 5th International Conference on Learning Representations, ICLR 2017, Toulon, France, April 24-26, 2017, Conference Track Proceedings.

Tuan Lai, Heng Ji, Trung Bui, Quan Hung Tran, Franck Dernoncourt, and Walter Chang. 2021. A context-dependent gated module for incorporating symbolic semantics into event coreference resolution. In Proc. The 2021 Conference of the North American Chapter of the Association for Computational Linguistics - Human Language Technologies (NAACL-HLT2021).

Heeyoung Lee, Marta Recasens, Angel Chang, Mihai Surdeanu, and Dan Jurafsky. 2012. Joint entity and event coreference resolution across documents. In Proceedings of the 2012 Joint Conference on Empirical Methods in Natural Language Processing and Computational Natural Language Learning, pages 489–500, Jeju Island, Korea. Association for Computational Linguistics.

Kenton Lee, Luheng He, Mike Lewis, and Luke Zettlemoyer. 2017. End-to-end neural coreference resolution. In Proceedings of the 2017 Conference on Empirical Methods in Natural Language Processing, pages 188–197, Copenhagen, Denmark. Association for Computational Linguistics.

Beth Levin. 1993. English Verb Classes and Alternations: a Preliminary Investigation. Chicago: University of Chicago Press.

Manling Li, Qi Zeng, Ying Lin, Kyunghyun Cho, Heng Ji, Jonathan May, Nathanael Chambers, and Clare Voss. 2020. Connecting the dots: Event graph schema induction with path language modeling. In Proceedings of the 2020 Conference on Empirical Methods in Natural Language Processing. Association for Computational Linguistics.

Ying Lin, Heng Ji, Fei Huang, and Lingfei Wu. 2020. A joint neural model for information extraction with global features. In Proceedings of the 58th Annual Meeting of the Association for Computational Linguistics, pages 7999–8009, Online. Association for Computational Linguistics.

Zhengzhong Liu, Jun Araki, Eduard H. Hovy, and Teruko Mitamura. 2014. Supervised within-document event coreference using information propagation. In Proceedings of the Ninth International Conference on Language Resources and Evaluation, LREC 2014, Reykjavik, Iceland, May 26-31, 2014, pages 4539–4544. European Language Resources Association (ELRA).

Jing Lu and Vincent Ng. 2016. Event coreference resolution with multi-pass sieves. In Proceedings of the Tenth International Conference on Language Resources and Evaluation (LREC'16), pages 3996–4003, Portorož, Slovenia. European Language Resources Association (ELRA).

Jing Lu and Vincent Ng. 2017. Joint learning for event coreference resolution. In Proceedings of the 55th Annual Meeting of the Association for Computational Linguistics (Volume 1: Long Papers), pages 90–101, Vancouver, Canada. Association for Computational Linguistics.

Xiaoqiang Luo. 2005. On coreference resolution performance metrics. In Proceedings of Human Language Technology Conference and Conference on Empirical Methods in Natural Language Processing, pages 25–32.

Tomas Mikolov, Kai Chen, Greg Corrado, and Jeffrey Dean. 2013. Efficient estimation of word representations in vector space. In 1st International Conference on Learning Representations, ICLR 2013, Scottsdale, Arizona, USA, May 2-4, 2013, Workshop Track Proceedings.

Ashutosh Modi. 2016. Event embeddings for semantic script modeling. In Proceedings of The 20th SIGNLL Conference on Computational Natural Language Learning, pages 75–83, Berlin, Germany. Association for Computational Linguistics.

Tim O'Gorman, Kristin Wright-Bettner, and Martha Palmer. 2016. Richer event description: Integrating event coreference with temporal, causal and bridging annotation. In Proceedings of the 2nd Workshop on Computing News Storylines (CNS 2016), pages 47–56, Austin, Texas. Association for Computational Linguistics.

Xiaoman Pan, Boliang Zhang, Jonathan May, Joel Nothman, Kevin Knight, and Heng Ji. 2017. Cross-lingual name tagging and linking for 282 languages. In Proceedings of the 55th Annual Meeting of the Association for Computational Linguistics (Volume 1: Long Papers), pages 1946–1958, Vancouver, Canada. Association for Computational Linguistics.

Haoruo Peng, Yangqiu Song, and Dan Roth. 2016. Event detection and co-reference with minimal supervision. In Proceedings of the 2016 Conference on Empirical Methods in Natural Language Processing, pages 392–402, Austin, Texas. Association for Computational Linguistics.

James Pustejovsky, Patrick Hanks, Roser Saurí, Andrew See, Robert Gaizauskas, Andrea Setzer, Dragomir Radev, Beth Sundheim, David Day, Lisa Ferro, and Marcia Lazo. 2003. The TIMEBANK corpus. Corpus Linguistics, 2003:40.

Marta Recasens and Eduard Hovy. 2011. Blanc: Implementing the rand index for coreference evaluation. Natural Language Engineering, 17(4):485–510.

Elizabeth Ritter and Sara Thomas Rosen. 2000. Event structure and ergativity. In Events as Grammatical Objects, pages 187–238.

Mark Sammons, Haoruo Peng, Yangqiu Song, Shyam Upadhyay, Chen-Tse Tsai, Pavankumar Reddy, Subhro Roy, and Dan Roth. 2015. Illinois CCG TAC 2015 event nugget, entity discovery and linking, and slot filler validation systems. In Proceedings of the 2015 Text Analysis Conference, TAC 2015, Gaithersburg, Maryland, USA, November 16-17, 2015, 2015. NIST.

Michael Sejr Schlichtkrull, Thomas N. Kipf, Peter Bloem, Rianne van den Berg, Ivan Titov, and Max Welling. 2018. Modeling relational data with graph convolutional networks. In The Semantic Web - 15th International Conference, ESWC 2018, Heraklion, Crete, Greece, June 3-7, 2018, Proceedings, pages 593–607.

Yizhou Sun, Jiawei Han, Xifeng Yan, Philip S. Yu, and Tianyi Wu. 2011. Pathsim: Meta path-based top-k similarity search in heterogeneous information networks. Proc. VLDB Endow., 4(11):992–1003.

Hanghang Tong, Yasushi Sakurai, Tina Eliassi-Rad, and Christos Faloutsos. 2008. Fast mining of complex time-stamped events. In Proceedings of the 17th ACM Conference on Information and Knowledge Management, CIKM 2008, Napa Valley, California, USA, October 26-30, 2008, pages 759–768.

Petar Velickovic, William Fedus, William L. Hamilton, Pietro Liò, Yoshua Bengio, and R. Devon Hjelm. 2019. Deep graph infomax. In 7th International Conference on Learning Representations, ICLR 2019, New Orleans, LA, USA, May 6-9, 2019. OpenReview.net.

Marc B. Vilain, J. Burger, J. Aberdeen, D. Connolly, and L. Hirschman. 1995. A model-theoretic coreference scoring scheme. In MUC.

Xiao Wang, Houye Ji, Chuan Shi, Bai Wang, Yanfang Ye, Peng Cui, and Philip S. Yu. 2019. Heterogeneous graph attention network. In The World Wide Web Conference, WWW 2019, San Francisco, CA, USA, May 13-17, 2019, pages 2022–2032.

Noah Weber, Niranjan Balasubramanian, and Nathanael Chambers. 2018. Event representations with tensor-based compositions. In Proceedings of the Thirty-Second AAAI Conference on Artificial Intelligence, (AAAI-18), the 30th innovative Applications of Artificial Intelligence (IAAI-18), and the 8th AAAI Symposium on Educational Advances in Artificial Intelligence (EAAI-18), New Orleans, Louisiana, USA, February 2-7, 2018, pages 4946–4953.

Hongzhi Xu and Chu-Ren Huang. 2013. Primitives of events and the semantic representation. In Proceedings of the 6th International Conference on Generative Approaches to the Lexicon (GL2013), pages 54–61, Pisa, Italy. Association for Computational Linguistics.

Cheng Yang, Zhiyuan Liu, Deli Zhao, Maosong Sun, and Edward Y. Chang. 2015. Network representation learning with rich text information. In Proceedings of the Twenty-Fourth International Joint Conference on Artificial Intelligence, IJCAI 2015, Buenos Aires, Argentina, July 25-31, 2015, pages 2111–2117.

Tongtao Zhang, Hongzhi Li, Heng Ji, and Shih-Fu Chang. 2015. Cross-document event coreference resolution based on cross-media features. In Proceedings of the 2015 Conference on Empirical Methods in Natural Language Processing, pages 201–206, Lisbon, Portugal. Association for Computational Linguistics.

# Learning Clause Representation from Dependency-Anchor Graph for Connective Prediction

**Yanjun Gao** and **Ting-Hao (Kenneth) Huang** and **Rebecca J. Passonneau**
Pennsylvania State University
{yug125,txh710,rjp49}@psu.edu

## Abstract

Semantic representation that supports the choice of an appropriate connective between pairs of clauses inherently addresses discourse coherence, which is important for tasks such as narrative understanding, argumentation, and discourse parsing. We propose a novel clause embedding method that applies graph learning to a data structure we refer to as a dependency-anchor graph. The dependency anchor graph incorporates two kinds of syntactic information, constituency structure and dependency relations, to highlight the subject and verb phrase relation. This enhances coherence-related aspects of representation. We design a neural model to learn a semantic representation for clauses from graph convolution over latent representations of the subject and verb phrase. We evaluate our method on two new datasets: a subset of a large corpus where the source texts are published novels, and a new dataset collected from students' essays. The results demonstrate a significant improvement over tree-based models, confirming the importance of emphasizing the subject and verb phrase. The performance gap between the two datasets illustrates the challenges of analyzing student's written text, plus a potential evaluation task for coherence modeling and an application for suggesting revisions to students.

| | | | |
|---|---|---|---|
| $P_1$ | Bob cooked Tia a burger. | $P_1, Q_1$ | alth |
| $P_2$ | Bob cooked himself a burger. | $P_1, Q_2$ | bec |
| $Q_1$ | Bob was hungry. | $P_1, Q_3$ | none |
| $Q_2$ | Tia was hungry. | $P_1, Q_4$ | alth |
| $Q_3$ | Bob was thirsty. | $P_2, Q_1$ | bec |
| $Q_4$ | Tia was thirsty. | $P_2, Q_2$ | alth |
| alth(ough): contrast | | $P_2, Q_3$ | alth |
| bec(ause): precondition | | $P_2, Q_4$ | none |

Figure 1: For the propositions $P_m$, $Q_n$ to be joined by *although* or *because*, $P_m$ and $Q_n$. must have some semantic commonality to allow for contrast or causation. Four cases allow *although*. The two cases that allow *because* have a strong semantic relation between the predicates (*make someone a burger, be hungry*) and, there is no conflict in the *to*-object of the first clause and the subject of the second. The remaining two cases have no commonality, and neither connective can occur.

## 1 Introduction

The clause is a fundamental unit in coherent text. Much work in NLP investigates how clauses combine to form larger units, ultimately spanning a whole discourse (Wang et al., 2017; Ji and Eisenstein, 2014); how to decompose complex sentences into distinct propositions (Wang et al., 2018; Li et al., 2018; Narayan et al., 2017); how to identify explicit or implicit semantic relations between clauses (Lee and Goldwasser, 2019; Rutherford and Xue, 2015), or how to select a connective to link multiple clauses into a complex sentence (Nie et al., 2019; Malmi et al., 2018). In this paper, we focus on clause representation to support accurate connective prediction, a task which is important for coherence modeling (Pishdad et al., 2020), fine-grained opinion mining (Wiegand et al., 2015), argument mining (Kuribayashi et al., 2019; Jo et al., 2020) and argumentation (Park and Cardie, 2014). We present a case for a model that learns from a novel graph we refer to as a *dependency-anchor graph*, which retains information from dependency parses and constituency parses of input sentences that is critical for identification of the core proposition of a clause, while omitting structural information that is less relevant.

We assume that determining whether two clauses can be joined by a connective, and what connective to choose, depends primarily on the main verb in each clause, and on the arguments that occur in both clauses, particularly the grammatical subject. There are a large number of connectives and connective phrases in English; e.g., the Penn Discourse Tree Bank (Prasad et al., 2008) has 141. Here we illustrate the nature of the problem with respect to the two connectives, *although* and *because*. Figure 1 illustrates how the choice of connective to join two simple clauses $P_m$ and $Q_n$, and whether



*Proceedings of the Fifteenth Workshop on Graph-Based Methods for Natural Language Processing (TextGraphs-15)*, pages 54–66
June 11, 2021. 

a connective is appropriate at all, depends on the main verbs and their arguments. Use of *although* requires only some dimension of contrast between the joined clauses, while *because* requires that $Q_n$ be a precondition for $P_m$. The table lists two variants of $P_m$ with *cook* as the main verb, one with three distinct entities (Bob, Tia, a burger) and one with two (Bob, burger). These are considered in turn with four variants of $Q_n$ where the predicate is either closely related to *cook* (e.g.*be hungry*) or not (e.g., *be thirsty*), and the two propositions share an argument or not. In two of the eight cases, neither connective makes sense because there is no other cohesive relation (e.g., coreference, association) between the clauses. In four cases, there is some similarity and some contrast, which licenses *although*, and in two cases the more restrictive condition that licenses *because* is present. These examples illustrate that both the choice of verb, and the grammatical relations of the arguments to the verb, affect whether a connective can be used, and which one. Adding modifiers on the subject or object, or VP or sentence adverbials, would have little effect on choice of connective in these sentences.

We assume that training clause representations based on connective prediction will be useful for developing representations that capture aspects of coherence, such as those shown in Fig 1. Pishdad et al. (2020) examine a series of coherence evaluation tasks that capture different aspects of coherence. They argue that connective substitution is one of four critical tests of coherence modeling. For example, connectives that express temporal succession should not be substitutable for connectives that express simultaneity, as doing so would change the meaning. Studies of students' writing skills look at connectives with respect to quality of students' argumentative writing (Kuhn et al., 2016), and whether automated assessments differ for low-skilled versus high-skilled writers (Perin and Lauterbach, 2018). Although students can fill in correct connectives eliminated from source texts, they typically do not use connectives as precisely in their own writing (Millis et al., 1993). NLP applications aimed at supporting student revision use connectives as an indication of writing quality (Nguyen et al., 2016; Afrin and Litman, 2018), but do not help students choose correct connectives. To better evaluate model performance in connective selection, and to highlight differences between text from skillful versus developing writers, we provide two large datasets of clauses linked by connectives drawn from published fiction and from students' written text. We demonstrate the potential for a model trained on expert data to identify incorrect uses of connectives in students' writing, where students frequently misuse connectives like *and.*

Our contributions are: 1) a data structure we refer to as a *Dependency-Anchor* graph that incorporates information from both dependency and constituency trees; 2) *DAnCE* (**D**ependency-**An**chor graph representation for **C**lause **E**mbedding), a novel neural architecture that exploits bi-LSTMs at the lower layers for learning inter-word influences, and graph learning of relational structure encoded in the dependency-anchor graph; 3) two datasets for carefully edited versus student text. Our approach outperforms the state-of-the-art on connective prediction.

## 2 Motivation

The question of whether latent representations of sentence meaning can benefit from syntax has been addressed in work that compares recurrence and recursion, and finds the main benefit of recursive models to be better treatment of long-distance dependencies (Li et al., 2015). Two recent works compare tree-based models derived from dependency parses with constituency parses on semantic relatedness tasks, with no clear advantage of one grammar formalism over the other (Tai et al., 2015; Ahmed et al., 2019). As discussed in (Tai et al., 2015), dependency trees provide a more compact structure than constituency trees, through shorter paths from the root to leaf words. Further, all of a verb's arguments are its direct dependents. The recursive structure of constituency trees, on the other hand, facilitates identification of subtrees that span more of the leaf words as one moves up the tree, and that have a compositional contribution to the meaning of the sentence. Tree-based models take input from syntactic parses and compose the latent vectors through a uni-directional traversal, where the parent node representation is the sum of the child nodes. For both formalisms, many parameters are needed to encode the child-to-parent representations. For this reason, previous work strictly limits the model dimensionality (Tai et al., 2015; Ahmed et al., 2019).

To combine advantageous features from both kinds of grammar formalism, we propose dependency-anchor graphs as a compact representation that highlights the core elements of a proposition. We construct a graph with only selected components from two kinds of parse trees, thus limiting the number of parameters to learn. The subject of a clause and the main verb phrase are the two outer nodes in the graph, where we refer to the verb phrase node as the *anchor*. The subject arc from a dependency parse points from the anchor node to the subject. The anchor node is a subgraph that retains the dependency structure of words within the verb phrase. Other syntactic relations (e.g., involving words in the subject phrase or adverbial phrases), are ignored.

To encode the graph, we propose DAnCE, which applies graph convolution (GCN) (Kipf and Welling, 2017) to encode the arc between the subject and verb phrase. The input to the graph convolution comes from a bidirectional LSTM (Hochreiter and Schmidhuber, 1997) that encodes all the input tokens, including the words outside the subject and verb phrase. The interaction that DAnCE captures between subject and verb phrase has been essential in word representation but missing in tree based models (Weir et al., 2016; White et al., 2018).

We demonstrate the effectiveness of the dependency-anchor graph and DAnCE architecture through its superior performance over baselines, including tree-based models. The rest of the paper is organized as follows: we first present related work and give a detailed discussion of the Dependency-Anchor Graph and DAnCE. Then we present the datasets, experiments and discussion.

## 3 Related Work

Much research has addressed ways to learn high quality clause representations. Xu et al. (2015) propose a shortest dependency path LSTM for sentence representation in the task of relation classification. Dai and Huang (2018) propose a BiLSTM based model that combines paragraph vectors and word vectors into clause embeddings for a situation entity classification task. Connective prediction has often been addressed: Ji and Eisenstein (2015) and Rutherford et al. (2017) use recursive neural networks with parse trees as input to predict connectives and discourse relations, with solid improvements on PDTB. Malmi et al. (2018) use a decomposable attention model to predict connectives on sentences pairs extracted from Wikipedia. Our work draws on the idea of incorporating syntax into representation for connective prediction,

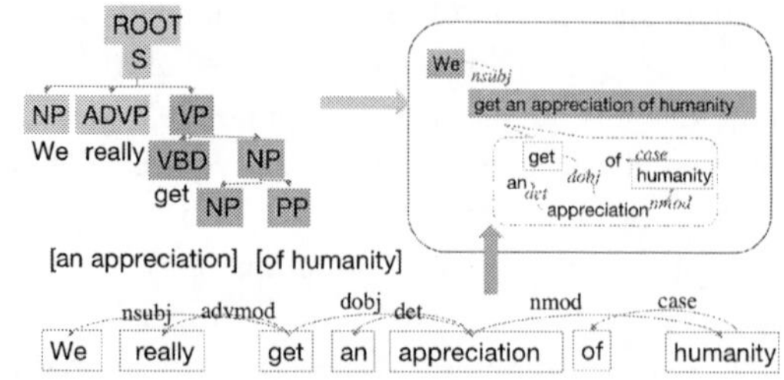


Figure 2: A dependency-anchor graph for a clause (top right) is constructed from its phrase-structure parse (top left) and dependency parse (bottom). Words spanning the VP subtree of the constituency parse (orange nodes) become a single anchor node whose internal structure preserves the dependencies among words in the VP. The nsubj dependent of the main verb is promoted to be a dependent of the entire anchor.

specifically for clauses.

Sileo et al. (2019) propose a large dataset with 170M sentence pairs with connectives for unsupervised sentence representation learning, and apply it on the SentEval task. Nie et al. (2019) develop universal sentence embeddings from a connective prediction task, and create a large corpus extracted from published fiction. They achieve state-of-the-art performance on predicting connectives, as well as on sentence embedding benchmarks from SentEval (Conneau and Kiela, 2018). Our work modifies the corpus from (Nie et al., 2019) to restrict the pairs of sentences for connective prediction to simple sentences. Our goal is to generate clause embeddings specifically for connective prediction, rather than universal sentence representation.

## 4 DAnCE Architecture

The input to DAnCE is a graph for each simple sentence that includes syntactic information from a phrase structure parse to identify the VP, and from a dependency parse to identify the grammatical subject, and dependencies within the VP.

### 4.1 Dependency-Anchor graph

The anchor VP and its subject serve as nodes in a graph, as illustrated in Figure 2. The Stanford CoreNLP dependency grammar has 58 dependency relations, eight of which are a type of subject (Van Valin, 2001; Schuster and Manning, 2016). The subject in our dependency-anchor graphs can originate as any of these eight types, and is represented as a node with a single subject edge to the anchor. The anchor node has internal graph structure, that replicates the dependency relations among the words in the VP. We align two syntax parses by the words then extract the dependencies between words inside the anchor. Each dependency-anchor graph constitutes a complete proposition. The dependency relation from the anchor to the subject, and the other dependencies for words within the VP, differentiate words by their closeness to the root verb of the dependency parse. Words outside the subject-anchor are omitted from the graph to maintain the focus of subject-VP, but they are encoded by the BiLSTM as part of the sequence and contribute to the hidden states.

### 4.2 Neural architecture

To learn a semantic representation from a dependency-anchor graph, DAnCE has the three layers illustrated in Figure 3. An initial embedding lookup layer retrieves word embeddings. A BiLSTM layer captures the hidden states over the input words at each time step. Finally, a graph convolution layer takes the subject word representation from the BiLSTM (the $\mathcal{S}$ node in Figure 3), and an *anchor embedding* that is generated from an separate module (the $\mathcal{A}$ node in Figure 3), to produce the final learned semantic representation.

The input sequence of words $x_i \in X$ is first fed into a pre-trained word embedding lookup layer, using GloVe (Pennington et al., 2014), with a bidirectional LSTM of dimension $2D$, where $D$ is the dimension of hidden states in the BiLSTM:

$$h_i = f(x_i, h_{i-1}), h_i \in \mathbb{R}^{2D} \quad (1)$$

The BiLSTM captures long-term dependencies within the clause. The resulting latent representation for the subject is fed directly to the graph convolution layer. The anchor embedding $h^A$ is computed with two alternative settings: **F**lat-**A**nchor (FA) and **G**raph-**A**nchor (GA). The main difference between the two settings is that *FA* treats the anchor as a sequence of words with their BiLSTM hidden states $h_i$, and ignores the dependency relations within the anchor. *GA* turns the dependencies into an adjacency matrix and then generates $h_i^{A_G}$ as the anchor node representation by encoding the BiLSTM hidden states within the matrix through graph attention (GAT) (Veličković et al., 2018). GAT will attend to whatever nodes are within the anchor, thus it fits well for learning the anchor representation for any length anchor. We first explain the derivation of $h_i^{A_G}$.

Following (Marcheggiani and Titov, 2017), we treat the dependency arcs within the anchor as directed. Given the latent representations of a pair of nodes within the anchor $h_i$, $h_j$, and a one-hot

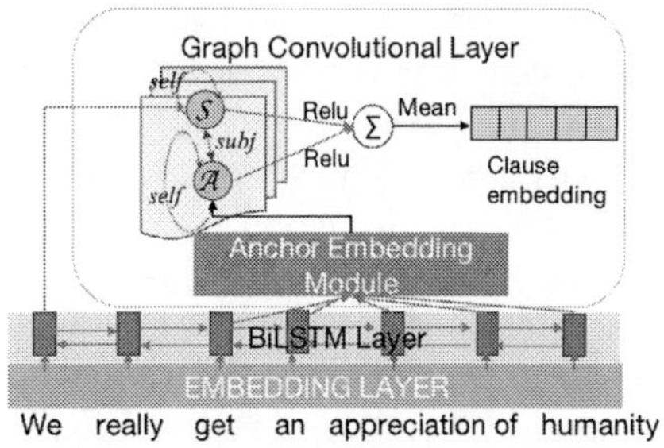


Figure 3: Overall architecture of DAnCE.

vector for each dependency arc $arc_{i,j}$, we compute an attention coefficient $e_{i,j}$:

$$e_{i,j} = a(W^h h_i, W^d[h_j||arc_{i,j}]) \quad (2)$$

where $||$ is the concatenation operation, and $a$, $W^h$, $W^d$ are learned parameters for the head and the dependent. Then we apply softmax and a Leaky ReLU activation to normalize the attention weights:

$$\alpha_{i.j} = LeakyReLU(\frac{exp(e_{i,j})}{\sum_{m \in N_A(i)} exp(e_{i,m})}) \quad (3)$$

where $N_A(i)$ represents all nodes in the anchor that are linked to $i$, including itself. Leaky Relu activation on $e_{i,j}$ enables the network to learn the importance of node $j$ and arc $i, j$ to node $i$. Therefore, $\alpha_{i,j}$ is a vector, whose length is the number of anchor words, that represents differential attention on word pairs associated with their dependency relations. We apply the attention weights on the node features from the first BiLSTM layer:

$$h_i^{A_G} = \sum_{j \in N_A(i)} \alpha_{i.j} W^{A_G} h_j \quad (4)$$

Again, there are two alternative settings to generate the anchor embedding. We use *maxpool* over all the nodes in anchor $N_A$:

$$h^A = \begin{cases} Maxpool(||_{i \in N_A} h_i) & \text{if FA} \\ Maxpool(||_{i \in N_A} h_i^{A_G}) & \text{if GA} \end{cases} \quad (5)$$

The third layer applies graph convolution (GCN) to the subject hidden states from BiLSTM and subject and anchor nodes, where the subject node is the hidden state from the BiLSTM and the anchor node is the anchor embedding $h^A$. Given a node $i$, we first compute its GCN node embedding $h_{S_i}^{k+1}$ from its neighbor $N(i)$, including a self loop, $i \in N(i)$:

$$h_{S_i}^{k+1} = ReLu(\sum_{j \in N(i)} W^{S_k} h_j^{S_k} + b^{S_k}) \quad (6)$$

where $k$ represents the $k$-order neighbor (the maximum hop between two nodes). $W^{S_k}$ and $b^{S_k}$ are the learned weights and bias. We use $k = 1$, as there is only one edge between the subject and anchor, thus $h_{S_i}^{k=0}$ is either the anchor embedding $h^A$ or the BiLSTM output for the subject word. The node representation is thus more informative by merging with its relevant neighbor through graph convolution, and enhances the final aggregation. Once the GCN node features are obtained, we compute the final embedding $h_S^K$ as the average over all node features $N_k$ at the last layer $K$,

$$h_S^K = \frac{1}{|N_K|} \sum_{v \in N_K} h_v^K, h_S^K \in \mathbb{R}^{2D} \tag{7}$$

## 5 Data Collection

This section introduces two corpora we use in our experiments. They differ in genre, size, and distribution of connectives, as well as a contrast between spontaneous student writing and carefully edited text. They also differ in the way they were annotated, and in whether they include negative examples. *DeSSE* (**De**composed **S**entences from **S**tudent **E**ssays) consists of sentences from students' opinion essays, 78% of which are complex. The annotation of DeSSE rewrites complex sentences into atomic tensed clauses, omitting any discourse connectives. Sentences are considered complex if there are at least two clauses with tensed verbs, thus a sentence consisting of a subject, verb and its clausal argument are not considered complex. The corpus also includes complex sentences with relative clauses rather than connectives, which serve as negative examples for connective prediction. We assume that a model should be able to discriminate between cases where two clauses have a cohesive relation other than one given by a connective. This is analogous to the motivation for inclusion of adversarial examples in a recent corpus for natural language arguments (Niven and Kao, 2019). In that work, it was shown that transformer models that appeared to perform well without the adversarial examples were exploiting accidental correlations, given that performance degraded significantly once adversarial examples were included. Previous work has shown similar results that neural models for summarization learn more about the position of lead sentences in news articles than about the actual meanings of sentences, due to the lead bias in news (Kedzie et al., 2018).

| Dataset | Size | Avg Length | Vocab |
|---|---|---|---|
| Book-Simpl | 644k | 7.61 | 52,957 |
| DeSSE | 70k | 10.19 | 11,186 |

Table 1: Descriptive statistics comparing Book-Simpl and DeSSE, including the number of clause pairs (Size), average clause length, and vocabulary size.

DeSSE consists of 39K source sentences, with 68 connectives of the 141 connective words and phrases identified in PDTB. Most connectives occur with very low frequency. More than 50% of pairs are connected by *and*, punctuation, or no connective. Fifty-five of the 68 connectives are rare with frequencies below 1% of the total. A detailed distribution is shown in appendix A.[1]

Our second corpus is a modification of the Book corpus, which consists of connective prediction data taken from published novels (Nie et al., 2019). The Book corpus extracts pairs of simple or complex sentences from source texts, where a connective linked the pair. The original Book corpus contains 15 connectives, and two subsets of 8 and 5 connectives. We created subsets consisting of connectives that joined simple clauses: Book-Simpl 5 with their 5 connectives (285K clause pairs), and Book-Simpl 8 with their 8 (359K clause pairs).

Table 1 shows that the average clause length for DeSSE is longer than in Book-Simpl, with one-fifth the total vocabulary. In comparison to Book-Simpl, the language in DeSSE is less formal and coherent.

### 5.1 DeSSE

DeSSE includes identification of complex sentences with tensed clauses, and excludes infinitival or gerundive clauses, as a first step towards training corpora for clause identification. It covers a wide range of intra-sentential syntactic and semantic phenomena. It includes all tensed clauses occurring in conjoined structures, including subordinating conjunctions, along with relative clauses, parentheticals, and conjoined verb phrases. It excludes clausal arguments of verbs, because the semantic relationship of the clausal argument in its sentence is given by the verb semantics. The annotation process is unique in that it involves identifying where to split the source sentence into distinct clauses, and how to rephrase the source sentence into a set of complete, independent clauses that omit any discourse connectives. It is designed for developing

[1]DeSSE is available at `https://github.com/serenayj/DeSSE`. DAnCE is available at `https://github.com/serenayj/DAnCE`.

1. (If you have not experienced *what they have experienced*), **then** you will never truly understand.
2. (I believe that *talking about race more in a civil way can only improve our society*), **but** I can see why other people may have a different opinion.

Figure 4: Original sentences from DeSSE with intra-sentential connectives, where the clause preceding the connective contains a relative clause (example 1), or a clausal argument of the main verb (example 2).

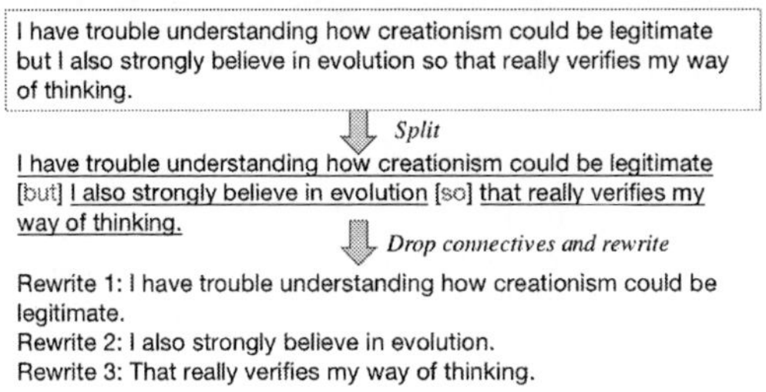


Figure 5: Example annotation from DeSSE. Annotators first split a sentence into segments (underlined text), then rewrite the segments into complete sentences, omitting connectives.

connective prediction, sentence segmentation and decomposition, and semantic representation.

Figure 4 illustrates intra-sentential connectives (*then, but*) that join two clauses. In example 1), the first clause (in parentheses) contains a free relative clause as a verb argument (in italics). In example 2), the first clause contains a clausal argument of the main verb. In both cases, however, the entire first clause is the first argument of the connective.[2]

We collected over 17,000 opinion essays written by U.S. university students in a large undergraduate social science class. Students watched video clips about race relations, and wrote essays in a blog environment to share their opinions with the class. We selected 39K sentences out of 173K for annotation, corresponding to the first 3,592 essays.

Amazon Mechanical Turk (AMT) is a popular crowdsourcing platform for NLP annotation. While it facilitates data collection, using untrained annotators requires care. In a series of pilot tasks on AMT, we iteratively designed annotation instructions and an annotation interface, while monitoring quality. Figure 5 illustrates two steps in the annotation: identification of $n$ split points between tensed clauses, and rephrasing the source into $n+1$ simple clauses, where any connectives are dropped. The final version of the instructions describes the two annotation steps, provides a list of connectives, and illustrates a positive and negative example.[3]

The ten most frequent connectives in DeSSE are *and, because, when, as, so, or, for, if, also, but*. We postprocess the corpus to identify pairs of clauses from complex sentences, and any connectives. The resulting dataset has the following distribution: a single atomic clause (22%), two clauses (45%) or more than two clauses (33%). Given sentences with exactly two atomic clauses in the source, 30% joined them with a discourse connective.

### 5.2 Book-Simpl

Nie et al. (2019) presented the Book corpus, which has 15 frequently used connectives and 4.7M pairs of sentences. Their goal was to exploit the semantic relationship given by the connective prediction task to improve sentence representation, as noted above. The Book corpus contains two versions, Book-5 with 5 connectives: *and, but, if, because, when*; and Book-8, an extended version with 3 more connectives: *before, though, so*. The sentences linked by a connective can be simple or complex.

To create a subset of the Book corpus that is more parallel to DeSSE, we selected Book corpus examples where the connective linked two simple clauses. The new Book-Simpl dataset has a distribution of connectives similar to the Book corpus (see appendix A).

## 6 Experiments

For our experiments to predict connectives, we use the same classifier used in (Nie et al., 2019). An input pair of sentence vectors representing the clauses to be joined by a connective are concatenated with vectors resulting from three pairwise vector operations: averaging, subtraction and multiplication. The concatenated vectors are fed into three fully-connected layers, then projected to a lower dimension prior to softmax over the classification categories.

Experiments on Book-Simpl predict the correct connective, given positive examples of clause pairs. Experiments on DeSSE predict the correct connective, given positive and negative examples. We compare DAnCE with four baselines on both datasets, reporting accuracy and F1. Student writing is much less coherent than much of the text that applies NLP to tasks related to discourse structure,

[2]As in (Webber and Joshi, 1998), we take connectives to be predicates whose arguments are the clauses they join.

[3]The interface checked for connectives remaining in step two to warn annotators. Details about the interface and quality control are included in appendix B.

| Group | Model | Book-Simpl 5 Acc. ($\sigma$) | F1 | Book-Simpl 8 Acc. ($\sigma$) | F1 | DeSSE 5 Acc. ($\sigma$) | F1 | DeSSE 8 Acc. ($\sigma$) | F1 |
|---|---|---|---|---|---|---|---|---|---|
| BoW | CNN | 61.89 (1.64) | 49.70 | 46.31 (1.36) | 30.62 | **53.57** (0.27) | 17.70 | **42.95** (0.22) | 9.18 |
| SeqLSTM | DisSent | 68.58 (1.55) | 58.78 | 62.92 (1.39) | 48.11 | 48.93 (0.31) | **25.27** | 39.86 (0.30) | **15.91** |
| Tree | Tree | 67.95 (1.10) | 59.67 | 59.69 (1.58) | 45.71 | 20.35 (0.74) | 9.84 | 16.63 (0.77) | 9.29 |
| LSTM | Tr-Attn | 69.08 (0.82) | 62.30 | 63.48 (1.40) | 49.06 | 18.51 (0.10) | 8.68 | 17.95 (0.72) | 12.01 |
| DAnCE | FA | **71.83** (0.45) | **63.59** | **65.60** (0.55) | **51.26** | 52.64 (0.38) | 22.29 | 41.75 (0.25) | 13.88 |
| Models | GA | 71.51 (1.45) | 59.93 | 65.38 (1.57) | 50.28 | 53.48 (0.46) | 14.73 | 12.01 (0.48) | 9.16 |

Table 2: Performance of baselines and our models on Book-Simpl 5 (N=16,538), Book-Simpl 8 (N=18,946), DeSSE 5 (N=3,466) and DeSSE (N=3,894).

such as discourse connective prediction, discourse parsing, and semantic representation of clauses. We find all models perform better on Book-Simpl than DeSSE, and DAnCE-FA yields good performance on both corpora.

### 6.1 Baselines and settings

We use three kinds of architecture as baselines: Bag-of-words feed-forward networks (*BoW*), Tree-based LSTM (*Tree-LSTM*), and sequential LSTM (*Seq-LSTM*). For BoW group, we include Glove-CNN (Kim, 2014), a widely used convolutional network for text classification that takes word vectors as input and generates sentence vectors. The Tree-LSTM group includes two models: Dependency Tree-LSTM (Tree) (Tai et al., 2015), which encodes the dependency parse, and an improved version of Tree-LSTM with attention (Tr-Attn) (Ahmed et al., 2019). The Seq-LSTM group consists of DisSent (Nie et al., 2019; Conneau et al., 2017), a BiLSTM model with max-pooling over all hidden units of sentences, and self attention. Hyperparameters are shown in Appendix D.

Our experiments ask two questions: 1) How does DAnCE, which relies on graph convolution, and whose input is a Dependency-Anchor graph, compare with tree-based models? 2) How does DAnCE compare against the two types of models that do not rely on syntax (sequence-based and BOW). The two anchor settings for DAnCE enable us also to test alternative DAnCE settings (DAnCE-FA and DAnCE-GA). Our question here is whether learning from dependency relations within verb phrases through graph attention produces better representations for connective prediction. [4]

### 6.2 Results

Table 2 reports mean accuracy and the standard deviation from 16 bootstrapped iterations on 90% of the test data, and F1 for the full test data. Bootstrapped F1 standard deviation shows the same magnitude as accuracy therefore is omitted from the table. Overall, all models report higher accuracy and F1 on Book-Simpl than DeSSE, which suggests that including "no connectives" increases the difficulty of the learning task. For Book-Simpl, increasing the number of connectives also increases the prediction difficulty, reflected in lower accuracy and F1 scores for all models on Book-Simpl 8 in comparison to Book-Simpl 5. DAnCE outperforms all baselines, DisSent falls between the two tree variants, and the BoW model has the lowest performance. On DeSSE 5 and 8, however, it is the BoW model that shows the highest accuracy. DisSent achieves the highest F1 on both versions of DeSSE. DAnCE-FA has higher accuracy but slightly lower F1 than DisSent, and both greatly outperform the two tree models and DAnCE-GA.

Recall that DeSSE includes adversarial samples, hence evaluation on DeSSE may be more revealing in comparison to Book-Simpl. Figure 6 gives a breakdown of F1 by connective on DeSSE 5 and 8 for DAnCE-FA, DisSent and Tree-Attn. It is surprising that for DeSSE 5, Tree-Attn fails completely on *and, so, as*, while it outperforms DisSent and DAnCE-FA on *because, no connective*. On DeSSE 8, Tree-Attn fails to predict *and, for, if*. DAnCE-FA and DisSent have similar F1 scores

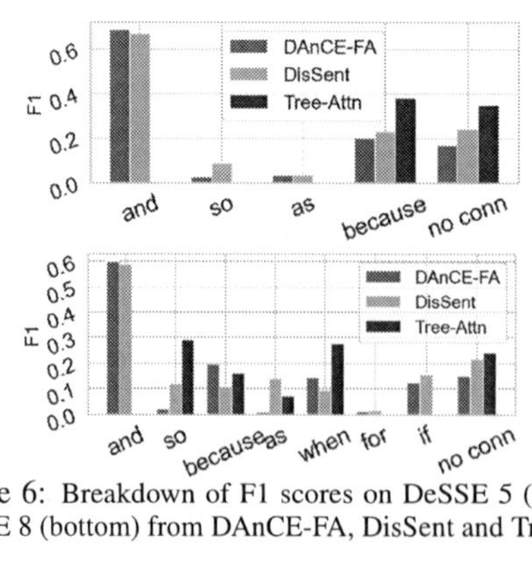


Figure 6: Breakdown of F1 scores on DeSSE 5 (top) and DeSSE 8 (bottom) from DAnCE-FA, DisSent and Tree-Attn.

[4] We attempt to train a fine-tune BERT on our dataset, however due to the size of the training set we make no success in finetuning.

| DAnCE-GA Settings | Book-Simpl (F1) 5 | 8 | DeSSE (F1) 5 | 8 |
|---|---|---|---|---|
| -GCN | 65.32 | 37.85 | 7.75 | 5.63 |
| -DIR | 58.34 | 47.85 | 17.44 | 11.75 |

Table 3: Ablation studies of DAnCE.

| DeSSE 5 *(Obs, Pred)* | Pairs | DeSSE 8 *(Obs, Pred)* | Pairs |
|---|---|---|---|
| *(and, but)* | 24.0% | *(and, but)* | 18.0% |
| *(and, and)* | 17.0% | *(and, and)* | 12.0% |
| *(because, but)* | 7.8% | *(None, but)* | 7.3% |
| *(None, but)* | 6.8% | *(because, but)* | 5.6% |
| *(so, but)* | 4.1% | *(and, when)* | 4.8% |

Table 4: For all pairs of sentences in the DeSSE test sets, we compare the observed student's usage (Obs) with the model prediction (Pred) from DAnCE-FA trained on Book Simpl, and sorted each pattern of observation and prediction by frequency. The five most frequent of these patterns are shown here for DeSSE 5 and DeSSE 8.

on *and, when, if,* but DAnCE-FA rarely or never predicts the connectives *so, for* and *as*. It may be that subtle differences in meaning based on sentence elements apart from the subject and verb phrase are predictive, given the failure of DAnCE-FA to perform at all well on these connectives. To summarize, DAnCE-FA performs comparably to DisSent and shows improvements over tree-based models. DAnCE-GA is worse than DAnCE-FA, which might be attributed to the noisy information introduced by dependency arcs within the anchor.

### 6.3 Ablation Experiment

We conducted an ablation test on DAnCE-GA to address the following questions: 1) does the performance drop if subject and verb are not highlighted? and 2) do undirected dependency arcs result in better performance within the anchor. To address the first question, we remove the GCN layer (*-GCN*). To address the second, we remove the directionality of dependency arcs inside the anchor to produce a symmetric adjacency matrix (*-DIR*). Table 3 presents F1 scores on the for sets of connectives from Book-Simpl and DeSSE. Compared to the DAnCE variants presented in Table 2, removing the emphasis on subject and verb significantly lowers the performance, especially on DeSSE. Using a symmetric adjacency matrix for graph attention results in lower performance on Book-Simpl, but surprisingly higher F1 on DeSSE. This shows that our emphasis on the subject and verb phrase enhances clause representation. However, incorporating more dependency arcs within the anchor degrades the performance.

| | | | |
|---|---|---|---|
| **Clause.1** | He said he grew up as a Christian. | | |
| **Clause.2** | He then converted to Islam. | | |
| **Student** | *and* | **DAnCE-FA** | *but* |
| **Clause.1** | He trusted his faith. | | |
| **Clause.2** | It helped him move on. | | |
| **Student** | *and* | **DAnCE-FA** | *because* |

Table 5: Example pairs of clauses from DeSSE 5, showing the connective used by the student alongside the prediction from DAnCE-FA trained on Book Simpl 5.

## 7 Discussion

Here we discuss the potential to suggest an alternative connective for students when their choice of connective differs from a connective predicted by a model that has been trained on professionally written text. The benefits of this analysis are two-fold: it explores the feasibility of an education application to help students revise their choice of connective, and it allows us to examine DAnCE's ability to model aspects of coherence that pertain to choice of connective. For all pairs of sentences in DeSSE 5 and 8, we compared the observed choice made by the student writer with the prediction from DAnCE-FA trained on Book Simpl 5 or Book Simpl 8. Table 4 shows the five most frequent pairs of student choice in DeSSE 5 or DeSSE 8 versus the prediction from the model trained on Book Simpl 5 (left columns) or trained on Book Simpl 8 (right columns). As illustrated, in many of the cases where students used *and*, the model trained on text from professional writers predicts *but*. Figure 5 shows a few examples where a student used the semantically neutral conjunction *and*, the model predicted a more specific conjunction, and the model's prediction seems more precise. Future work will investigate in detail the feasibility of suggesting alternative connectives.

## 8 Conclusion

This paper presented the dependency-anchor graph, a new data structure emphasizing the propositional structure of clauses, and DAnCE, a neural architecture with a distinct module for learning verb phrase representation, and graph convolution for semantic relation between the verb phrase and its subject.DAnCE shows good performance on two datasets for connective prediction, and introduces a potential application that could help students revise their writing through improved choice of connectives. Future work will extend DAnCE for coherence modeling within and across sentences, and for applications to support students' revisions.

## References


Tazin Afrin and Diane Litman. 2018. Annotation and classification of sentence-level revision improvement. In *Proceedings of the Thirteenth Workshop on Innovative Use of NLP for Building Educational Applications*, pages 240–246.

Mahtab Ahmed, Muhammad Rifayat Samee, and Robert E. Mercer. 2019. Improving tree-LSTM with tree attention. In *2019 IEEE 13th International Conference on Semantic Computing (ICSC)*, pages 247–254. IEEE.

Alexis Conneau and Douwe Kiela. 2018. SentEval: An evaluation toolkit for universal sentence representations. In *Proceedings of the Eleventh International Conference on Language Resources and Evaluation (LREC 2018)*.

Alexis Conneau, Douwe Kiela, Holger Schwenk, Loïc Barrault, and Antoine Bordes. 2017. Supervised learning of universal sentence representations from natural language inference data. In *Proceedings of the 2017 Conference on Empirical Methods in Natural Language Processing*, pages 670–680, Copenhagen, Denmark. Association for Computational Linguistics.

Zeyu Dai and Ruihong Huang. 2018. Building context-aware clause representations for situation entity type classification. In *Proceedings of the 2018 Conference on Empirical Methods in Natural Language Processing*, pages 3305–3315.

Chris Fournier. 2013. Evaluating text segmentation using boundary edit distance. In *Proceedings of the 51st Annual Meeting of the Association for Computational Linguistics (Volume 1: Long Papers)*, pages 1702–1712.

Sepp Hochreiter and Jürgen Schmidhuber. 1997. Long short-term memory. *Neural computation*, 9(8):1735–1780.

Yangfeng Ji and Jacob Eisenstein. 2014. Representation learning for text-level discourse parsing. In *Proceedings of the 52nd Annual Meeting of the Association for Computational Linguistics (Volume 1: Long Papers)*, pages 13–24, Baltimore, Maryland. Association for Computational Linguistics.

Yangfeng Ji and Jacob Eisenstein. 2015. One vector is not enough: Entity-augmented distributed semantics for discourse relations. *Transactions of the Association for Computational Linguistics*, 3:329–344.

Yohan Jo, Elijah Mayfield, Chris Reed, and Eduard Hovy. 2020. Machine-aided annotation for fine-grained proposition types in argumentation. In *Proceedings of The 12th Language Resources and Evaluation Conference*, pages 1008–1018.

Chris Kedzie, Kathleen McKeown, and Hal Daumé III. 2018. Content selection in deep learning models of summarization. In *Proceedings of the 2018 Conference on Empirical Methods in Natural Language Processing*, pages 1818–1828, Brussels, Belgium. Association for Computational Linguistics.

Yoon Kim. 2014. Convolutional neural networks for sentence classification. In *Proceedings of the 2014 Conference on Empirical Methods in Natural Language Processing (EMNLP)*, pages 1746–1751.

Thomas N. Kipf and Max Welling. 2017. Semi-supervised classification with graph convolutional networks. In *International Conference on Learning Representations (ICLR)*.

Deanna Kuhn, Laura Hemberger, and Valerie Khait. 2016. Tracing the development of argumentive writing in a discourse-rich context. *Written Communication*, 33(1):92–121.

Tatsuki Kuribayashi, Hiroki Ouchi, Naoya Inoue, Paul Reisert, Toshinori Miyoshi, Jun Suzuki, and Kentaro Inui. 2019. An empirical study of span representations in argumentation structure parsing. In *Proceedings of the 57th Annual Meeting of the Association for Computational Linguistics*, pages 4691–4698.

I-Ta Lee and Dan Goldwasser. 2019. Multi-relational script learning for discourse relations. In *Proceedings of the 57th Annual Meeting of the Association for Computational Linguistics*, pages 4214–4226, Florence, Italy. Association for Computational Linguistics.

Jing Li, Aixin Sun, and Shafiq Joty. 2018. SegBot: a generic neural text segmentation model with pointer network. In *Proceedings of the 27th International Joint Conference on Artificial Intelligence (IJCAI)*, pages 4166–4172.

Jiwei Li, Minh-Thang Luong, Dan Jurafsky, and Eduard Hovy. 2015. When are tree structures necessary for deep learning of representations? In *Proceedings of the 2015 Conference on Empirical Methods in Natural Language Processing*, pages 2304–2314.

Eric Malmi, Daniele Pighin, Sebastian Krause, and Mikhail Kozhevnikov. 2018. Automatic prediction of discourse connectives. In *Proceedings of the Eleventh International Conference on Language Resources and Evaluation (LREC 2018)*.

Diego Marcheggiani and Ivan Titov. 2017. Encoding sentences with graph convolutional networks for semantic role labeling. In *Proceedings of the 2017 Conference on Empirical Methods in Natural Language Processing (EMNLP)*, pages 1506–1515.

Keith K Millis, Arthur C Graesser, and Karl Haberlandt. 1993. The impact of connectives on the memory for expository texts. *Applied Cognitive Psychology*, 7(4):317–339.

Shashi Narayan, Claire Gardent, Shay Cohen, and Anastasia Shimorina. 2017. Split and rephrase. In *EMNLP 2017: Conference on Empirical Methods in Natural Language Processing*, pages 617–627.

Huy Nguyen, Wenting Xiong, and Diane Litman. 2016. Instant feedback for increasing the presence of solutions in peer reviews. In *Proceedings of the 2016 Conference of the North American Chapter of the Association for Computational Linguistics: Demonstrations*, pages 6–10.

Allen Nie, Erin Bennett, and Noah Goodman. 2019. DisSent: Learning sentence representations from explicit discourse relations. In *Proceedings of the 57th Annual Meeting of the Association for Computational Linguistics*, pages 4497–4510.

Timothy Niven and Hung-Yu Kao. 2019. Probing neural network comprehension of natural language arguments. In *Proceedings of the 57th Annual Meeting of the Association for Computational Linguistics*, pages 4658–4664.

Joonsuk Park and Claire Cardie. 2014. Identifying appropriate support for propositions in online user comments. In *Proceedings of the first workshop on argumentation mining*, pages 29–38.

Jeffrey Pennington, Richard Socher, and Christopher D Manning. 2014. Glove: Global vectors for word representation. In *Proceedings of the 2014 conference on empirical methods in natural language processing (EMNLP)*, pages 1532–1543.

Dolores Perin and Mark Lauterbach. 2018. Assessing text-based writing of low-skilled college students. *International Journal of Artificial Intelligence in Education*, 28(1):56–78.

Leila Pishdad, Federico Fancellu, Ran Zhang, and Afsaneh Fazly. 2020. How coherent are neural models of coherence? In *Proceedings of the 28th International Conference on Computational Linguistics*, pages 6126–6138.

Rashmi Prasad, Nikhil Dinesh, Alan Lee, Eleni Miltsakaki, Livio Robaldo, Aravind K Joshi, and Bonnie L Webber. 2008. The penn discourse treebank 2.0. In *LREC*. Citeseer.

Attapol Rutherford, Vera Demberg, and Nianwen Xue. 2017. A systematic study of neural discourse models for implicit discourse relation. In *Proceedings of the 15th Conference of the European Chapter of the Association for Computational Linguistics: Volume 1, Long Papers*, pages 281–291.

Attapol Rutherford and Nianwen Xue. 2015. Improving the inference of implicit discourse relations via classifying explicit discourse connectives. In *Proceedings of the 2015 Conference of the North American Chapter of the Association for Computational Linguistics: Human Language Technologies*, pages 799–808.

Sebastian Schuster and Christopher D Manning. 2016. Enhanced English universal dependencies: An improved representation for natural language understanding tasks. In *Proceedings of the Tenth International Conference on Language Resources and Evaluation (LREC'16)*, pages 2371–2378.

Damien Sileo, Tim Van De Cruys, Camille Pradel, and Philippe Muller. 2019. Mining discourse markers for unsupervised sentence representation learning. In *Proceedings of the 2019 Conference of the North American Chapter of the Association for Computational Linguistics: Human Language Technologies, Volume 1 (Long and Short Papers)*, pages 3477–3486, Minneapolis, Minnesota. Association for Computational Linguistics.

Kai Sheng Tai, Richard Socher, and Christopher D Manning. 2015. Improved semantic representations from tree-structured long short-term memory networks. In *Proceedings of the 53rd Annual Meeting of the Association for Computational Linguistics and the 7th International Joint Conference on Natural Language Processing (Volume 1: Long Papers)*, pages 1556–1566.

Robert D. Van Valin. 2001. *An introduction to syntax*. Cambridge University Press.

Petar Veličković, Guillem Cucurull, Arantxa Casanova, Adriana Romero, Pietro Lió, and Yoshua Bengio. 2018. Graph attention networks. In *Sixth International Conference on Learning Representations (ICLR)*.

Yizhong Wang, Sujian Li, and Houfeng Wang. 2017. A two-stage parsing method for text-level discourse analysis. In *Proceedings of the 55th Annual Meeting of the Association for Computational Linguistics (Volume 2: Short Papers)*, pages 184–188.

Yizhong Wang, Sujian Li, and Jingfeng Yang. 2018. Toward fast and accurate neural discourse segmentation. In *Proceedings of the 2018 Conference on Empirical Methods in Natural Language Processing*, pages 962–967.

Bonnie Webber and Aravind Joshi. 1998. Anchoring a lexicalized tree adjoining grammar for discourse. In *ACL/COLING Workshop on Discourse Relations and Discourse Markers*, pages 86–92.

David Weir, Julie Weeds, Jeremy Reffin, and Thomas Kober. 2016. Aligning packed dependency trees: a theory of composition for distributional semantics. *Computational Linguistics*, 42(4):727–761.

Aaron Steven White, Rachel Rudinger, Kyle Rawlins, and Benjamin Van Durme. 2018. Lexicosyntactic inference in neural models. In *Proceedings of the 2018 Conference on Empirical Methods in Natural Language Processing*, pages 4717–4724.

Michael Wiegand, Marc Schulder, and Josef Ruppenhofer. 2015. Opinion holder and target extraction for verb-based opinion predicates–the problem is not solved. In *Proceedings of the 6th Workshop on Computational Approaches to Subjectivity, Sentiment and Social Media Analysis*, pages 148–155.

Yan Xu, Lili Mou, Ge Li, Yunchuan Chen, Hao Peng, and Zhi Jin. 2015. Classifying relations via long short term memory networks along shortest dependency paths. In *Proceedings of the 2015 conference on empirical methods in natural language processing*, pages 1785–1794.

# A Connective distributions in Book-Simpl and DeSSE

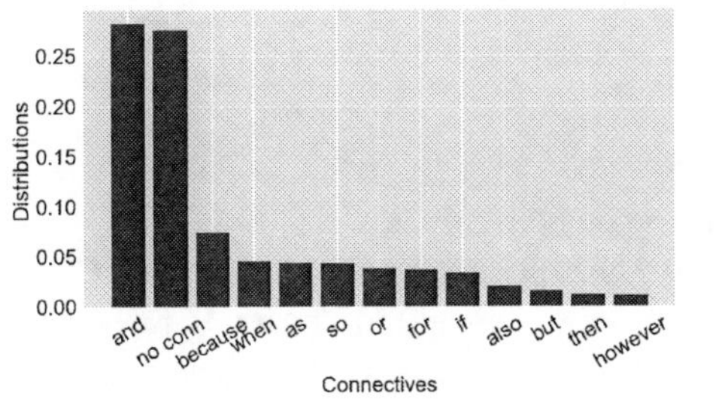


Figure 7: Connective distributions in DeSSE with threshold 1%

Here we present a detailed statistics of connective distributions on DeSSE and Book-Simpl. Figure 7 presents the connectives from DeSSE with distribution above 1%. Among 68 connectives, there are thirteen connectives above the threshold and the rest are low frequency connectives. Table 6 shows the Book-Simpl connective distribution compared to Book corpus. As illustrated, the Book-Simpl shares the same distribution as Book corpus on both Book-Simpl 5 and 8.

# B Annotation instruction in DeSSE

Here we present the instructions for annotators, as shown by Figure 8.

Complex sentences are built up from simple ones using connectives like *"and", "or", "but", "however", "because", "when", "until", "if", and relative pronouns like "which", "who", "that".*
In this HIT, you will see a complex sentence. Please:

1. Segment this sentence into several substrings, and then
2. Modify each substring to make a short, complete, new sentence, leaving out the connectives and relative pronouns.

Please convert the original long sentence into at least 1, at most 5 sub-sentences. (We usually expect 2 or 3 sub-sentences.)
Then rewrite the sub-sentences to satisfy ALL these requirements:

1. Each new simple sentence should be a complete (!), readable, grammatical sentence.
2. The content in the simple sentences should add up to the content in the complex sentences, minus all the connectives.
3. Avoid using the words that are not appeared in the original sentence for your rewriting, except the changes from singular to plural, person's name to pronouns.

NOTE: If you get an example that is a simple sentence already, not a complex sentence, just copy it and submit it as is.

Figure 8: Instruction for DeSSE annotation

The instruction illustrate the two phases of annotation. The annotator first chooses whether to add one or more split points to an input sentence, where the word after a split point represents the first word of a new segment. Once an annotator has identified the split points, which happens on the first page of the AMT interface, shown as Figure 9, a second view of the interface appears. Figure 10 shows the second view when annotators rewrite the segments. Every span of words defined by split points (or the original sentence if no split points), appears in its own text entry box for the annotator to rewrite. Annotators cannot submit if they remove all the words from a text entry box. They are instructed to rewrite each text span as a complete sentence, and to leave out the discourse connectives.

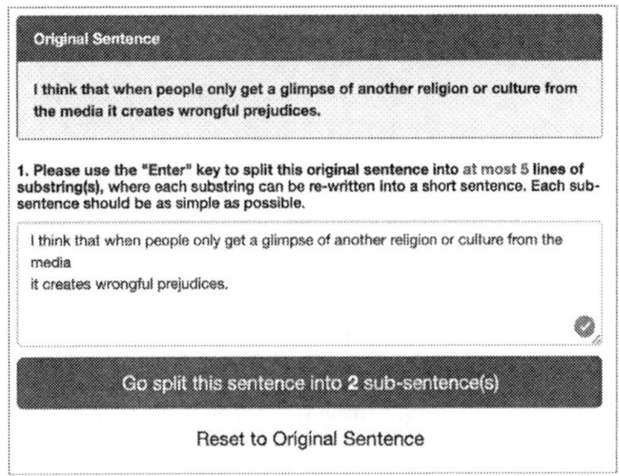


Figure 9: Interface of splitting the sentence

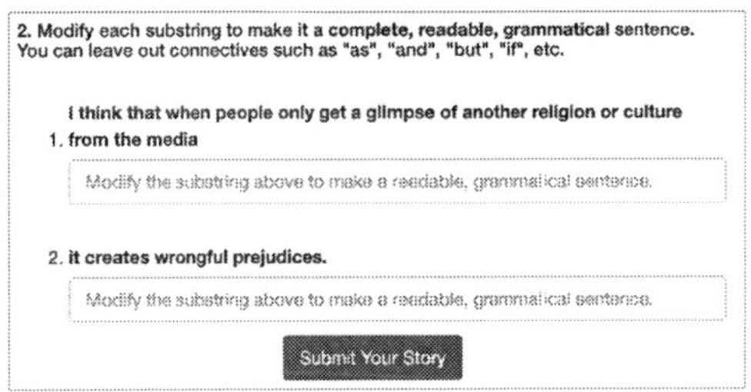


Figure 10: Interface of rewriting the segments from Figure 9 into complete sentences

Several auto-checking and warnings are applied in the interface to reassure the quality. If a rewrite contains a discourse connective, a warning box pops up asking if they should drop the discourse connective before submitting it. A warning box will show up if annotators use vocabulary outside the original sentence. To prevent annotators from failing to rewrite, we monitored the output, checking for cases where they submitted the text spans with no rewriting. Annotators are prohibited to submit if the interface detects an empty rewrite box or

| Corpus | Size | and | but | because | if | when | before | though | so |
|---|---|---|---|---|---|---|---|---|---|
| Book 5 | 3054K | 31 | 32 | 15 | 5 | 16 | *na* | *na* | *na* |
| Book-Simpl 5 | 285k | 33 | 28 | 8 | 5 | 27 | *na* | *na* | *na* |
| Book 8 | 3435K | 28 | 28 | 5 | 13 | 14 | 6 | 3 | 2 |
| Book-Simpl 8 | 359K | 29 | 24 | 4 | 7 | 23 | 8 | 3 | 1 |

Table 6: Number of sentence pairs (Size), and the distribution of connectives (as percentages) for the original Book corpus and our modified version.

the total lengths of the rewrites are too short compared to the source sentence. We warned annotators by email that if they failed to produce complete sentences in the rewrite boxes, they would be blocked. Some annotators were blocked, but most responded positively to the warnings.

## C Quality control in DeSSE

To test the clarity of instruction and interface, the initial 500 sentences were used for evaluating the task quality, each labeled by three turkers (73 turkers overall), using three measures of consistency, all in [0,1]. Average pairwise boundary similarity (Fournier, 2013), a very conservative measure of whether annotators produce the same number of segments with boundaries at nearly the same locations, was 0.55. Percent agreement on number of output substrings was 0.80. On annotations with the same number of segments, we measured the average Jaccard score (ratio of set intersection to set union) of words in segments from different annotators, which was 0.88, and words from rephrasings, which was 0.73. With all metrics close to 1, and boundary similarity above 0.5, we concluded quality was already high. During the actual data collection, quality was higher because we monitored quality on daily basis and communicated with turkers who had questions.

## D Experiment Settings

All the methods take GloVe word embeddings as input. Due to the size difference between Book-Simpl and DeSSE, we use different dimensionalities for the word embeddings ($w$) and classifier hidden layers ($h$) with the two corpora on all baseline systems: for Book-Simpl, $D_w = 300, D_h = 512$; for DeSSe $D_w = 100, D_h = 256$. We train DisSent using the original $D_h = 4096$ for Book-Simpl, and reduce it to 256 for DeSSE. Apart from this one change to DisSent, we use the published settings for all baseline systems. We train DAnCE using the same vector dimensions as for DisSent. Because DAnCE has twice the number of parameters as DisSent, we use the smaller classifier dimensionality of 256 on both corpora.

We use SGD as optimizer for DAnCE, with the learning rate at 0.01. Learning rates between [0.1,0.001] did not show obvious performance differences, and 0.01 converged faster. We use early-stopping to prevent overfitting. We did not use dropout, due to a negative impact on performance (cf. (Nie et al., 2019)).

All training is done on 4 Nvidia RTX 2080 Ti GPUs. The longest training time is 35 hours, for DAnCE on Book-Simpl 8. During testing, we perform 16 bootstrap iterations

# WikiGraphs: A Wikipedia Text - Knowledge Graph Paired Dataset

**Luyu Wang*** and **Yujia Li*** and **Ozlem Aslan** and **Oriol Vinyals**
*Equal contribution
DeepMind, London, UK
{luyuwang,yujiali,ozlema,vinyals}@google.com

## Abstract

We present a new dataset of Wikipedia articles each paired with a knowledge graph, to facilitate the research in conditional text generation, graph generation and graph representation learning. Existing graph-text paired datasets typically contain small graphs and short text (1 or few sentences), thus limiting the capabilities of the models that can be learned on the data. Our new dataset WikiGraphs is collected by pairing each Wikipedia article from the established WikiText-103 benchmark (Merity et al., 2016) with a subgraph from the Freebase knowledge graph (Bollacker et al., 2008). This makes it easy to benchmark against other state-of-the-art text generative models that are capable of generating long paragraphs of coherent text. Both the graphs and the text data are of significantly larger scale compared to prior graph-text paired datasets. We present baseline graph neural network and transformer model results on our dataset for 3 tasks: graph $\rightarrow$ text generation, graph $\rightarrow$ text retrieval and text $\rightarrow$ graph retrieval. We show that better conditioning on the graph provides gains in generation and retrieval quality but there is still large room for improvement. [1]

## 1 Introduction

Parallel datasets that pair data from different sources and modalities have enabled large amounts of research on cross modality learning. Paired image-caption datasets enable models to describe visual scenes in natural language (Lin et al., 2014; Vinyals et al., 2016), paired streams of speech and transcription data makes it possible to train speech recognition systems (Garofolo et al., 1993; Panayotov et al., 2015) or text-to-speech synthesis models (Oord et al., 2016), and parallel corpus of text in different languages enable learned machine translation models (Barrault et al., 2020).

[1]The data and the code to reproduce our baseline results are available at https://github.com/deepmind/deepmind-research/tree/master/wikigraphs

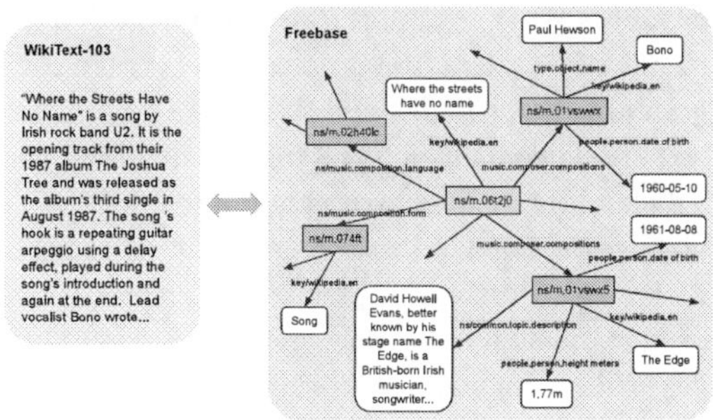


Figure 1: Illustration of a pair of Wikipedia article and the corresponding knowledge graph in our dataset.

We present a new dataset of Wikipedia text articles each paired with a relevant knowledge graph (KG), which enables building models that can generate long text conditioned on a graph structured overview of relevant topics, and also models that extract or generate graphs from a text description.

There has been many prior efforts trying to build datasets for learning graph $\rightarrow$ text generation models (Jin et al., 2020; Gardent et al., 2017; Lebret et al., 2016). However, existing graph-text paired datasets are mostly small scale, where the graphs tend to have 10-20 or even less nodes, and the text typically only contains one or a few sentences. This represents a significant contrast with the state-of-the-art text generation models (Dai et al., 2019; Brown et al., 2020), which can already generate very fluent and long text that spans thousands of tokens over multiple paragraphs.

We attempt to bridge this gap, with the goal of advancing the state-of-the-art graph $\rightarrow$ text generation models, graph representation learning models and also text-conditioned graph generative models. Each text document in our dataset is a full-length Wikipedia article, and we pair each of them with a KG that are significantly bigger than prior datasets of similar nature and includes much richer information. Hand labelling text articles with KGs is expensive and not scalable (Lebret et al., 2016),



*Proceedings of the Fifteenth Workshop on Graph-Based Methods for Natural Language Processing (TextGraphs-15)*, pages 67–82
June 11, 2021. ©2021 Association for Computational Linguistics

therefore we utilize an existing and established knowledge base, Freebase (Bollacker et al., 2008), and designed an automated process to extract a relevant subgraph from it for each Wikipedia article. To make the text generation results on our dataset directly comparable to the state-of-the-art, we chose the set of Wikipedia articles from the established language modeling benchmark WikiText-103 (Merity et al., 2016), which contains a subset of high-quality Wikipedia articles. This gives us a dataset of 23,522 graph-text pairs in total, covering 82.3% of Wikitext-103 articles. On average each graph has 38.7 nodes and 48.3 edges, and each text article contains 3,533.8 tokens. In addition to structural information, our graphs also contain rich text information with an average of 895.1 tokens in each graph. Furthermore, the automatic process we used to create this dataset can be extended to pair any Wikipedia document with Freebase, and can be scaled up to create over 3M graph-text pairs.

Out of many exciting new tasks that this dataset enables, we present 3 possibilities: graph $\rightarrow$ text generation, graph $\rightarrow$ text retrieval, and text $\rightarrow$ graph retrieval. We benchmarked a few baseline models on these tasks. The models we considered were based on the recent Transformer-XL (Dai et al., 2019) model, and we adapted it to condition the text generation on the KG in different ways. Our results show that better conditioning on the graph indeed improves the relevance of the generated text and the retrieval quality. However, there is still significant room for improvement on these tasks, which makes this an exciting dataset for research. Our data and code for baseline models will be made publicly available.

## 2 Related work

**Graph-text paired data** There has been a lot of prior work on creating graph-text paired datasets. Example applications include generating text summaries conditioned on Abstract Meaning Representation graphs (Liu et al., 2018), generating the abstract of a scientific article given a KG and title (Koncel-Kedziorski et al., 2019) and generating text from RDF triples (Gardent et al., 2017; Jin et al., 2020). In the following we will mostly review related work on KG - text paired datasets.

Annotating KG or text to create paired datasets is expensive, as a good quality annotation requires annotators that understand the content and structure of the text and the corresponding KG (Jin et al., 2020). Therefore previous KG-text paired datasets that rely on human annotation have limited scale. Among these, Gardent et al. (2017) crowdsourced human annotators to verbalize RDF triplets taken from DBpedia (Auer et al., 2007) to a few sentences (WebNLG) and this caused errors in annotation that were fixed with a few updates through years. Parikh et al. (2020) paired Wikipedia Table with one sentence text that is created by annotators that revise Wikipedia text.

| Dataset | #examples | #triples | #tokens | #vocab |
|---|---|---|---|---|
| WebNLG | 13,036 | 2.54 | 15.26 | 1,484 |
| GenWiki | **1.3M** | 1.95 | 21.46 | **476,341** |
| Ours | 23,522 | **48.3** | **3,533.8** | 238,071 |

Table 1: Our dataset contains significantly larger graphs (average #triples per graph) and longer text (average #tokens per text) than previous KG-text datasets.

Another line of research focuses on eliminating the need of human annotations by automatically matching KG-text pairs or generating KGs from text using existing tools. Lebret et al. (2016) automatically matched Wikipedia infobox of biographies with their first sentence. Koncel-Kedziorski et al. (2019) utilized an earlier information extraction system that extracts entities, co-reference and relations from given text to build KG's. The GenWiki dataset (Jin et al., 2020) is automatically constructed by querying KGs in DBpedia with the title of articles in Wikipedia followed by filtering and entity annotation.

We construct our WikiGraphs dataset by extracting a subgraph from Freebase (Bollacker et al., 2008) for each Wikipedia article following a scalable automatic process. Compared to previous work, our WikiGraphs dataset contains significantly larger graphs and longer text (Table 1).

**Models for graph-text paired data** Recent state of art language models are based on the Transformer architecture (Vaswani et al., 2017) that uses the self attention mechanism. The Transformer-XL (Dai et al., 2019) model further introduces a segment level recurrence with a novel positional encoding resulting in impressive performance in long sequences by capturing dependencies beyond a fixed length window.

Graph neural networks (GNNs) (Battaglia et al., 2018; Gilmer et al., 2017) learn representations for graph structured data through a message passing process. This class of models naturally exploit

|  | Train | Valid | Test | All |
|---|---|---|---|---|
| Num. pairs | 23,431 | 48 | 43 | 23,522 |
| % of WikiText-103 | 82.3% | 80.0% | 71.7% | 82.3% |
| Nodes per graph | 38.7 | 35.4 | 40.6 | 38.7 |
| Edges per graph | 48.3 | 42.8 | 49.5 | 48.3 |
| Avg. Node degree | 2.5 | 2.4 | 2.4 | 2.5 |
| Tokens per graph | 895.1 | 807.7 | 1,010.1 | 895.1 |
| Total graph tokens | 21.0M | 38,771 | 43,435 | 21.1M |
| Graph vocab size | - | - | - | 31,090 |
| Tokens per article | 3,531.7 | 3,644.2 | 4,564.7 | 3,533.8 |
| Total text tokens | 82.8M | 174,923 | 196,280 | 83.1M |
| Text vocab size | - | - | - | 238,071 |

Table 2: Basic statistics about our WikiGraphs dataset.

the graph structures, making them a good fit for graph data. GNNs have been used in many applications on KG's (Kipf and Welling, 2016; Wang et al., 2019; Xu et al., 2019). Fundamentally, transformers can also be understood as a special type of GNNs with a fully-connected graph structure.

The most recent prior work on graph-to-text generation follows an encoder-decoder architecture (Koncel-Kedziorski et al., 2019; Jin et al., 2020), where the graph part is encoded with a GNN model, e.g. Graph Attention Network (GAT) (Veličković et al., 2018). The text part is typically modeled using an attention based decoder with a copy mechanism (e.g. BiLSTMs as in (Jin et al., 2020)) to process input from both the KG and text.

The models we benchmarked for graph-to-text generation were based on the Transformer-XL architecture and conditioned on the graph through a GNN, making full use of the graph structure and capable of generating very long text comparable to the state-of-the-art.

## 3 Dataset

In this section we first present some properties of our dataset, and then describe the process that we used to create it.

### 3.1 Properties of the data

#### 3.1.1 Scale of the data

Basic statistics about our WikiGraphs dataset are listed in Table 2. An illustration of a graph-text pair is shown in Figure 1. A few actual examples from our dataset are included in the Appendix (Figure 7, 8). All of the articles come from the WikiText-103 dataset (Merity et al., 2016), which contains high-quality articles that fit the *Good* or *Featured* criteria specified by the Wikipedia editors when the data was collected. Merity et al. (2016) have already cleaned up and tokenized the articles, therefore they appear as plain text without any markup tags.

As will be described in Section 3.2, we try to pair each article with a subgraph from Freebase, centered at the entity node that has a Wikipedia link to the title of the article. We are not able to match every article to an entity in Freebase, but through this process we retained a significant portion of 82.3% of the WikiText-103 articles. We kept the original train/valid/test split. As we will see in Section 4.2, training models on this set gives us results that are very close to training on the full WikiText-103 dataset when evaluated on our test set. Therefore the text part of WikiGraphs appears to be sufficient to reproduce and benchmark against the state-of-the-art text generative models.

Figure 2 shows the distribution of graph sizes and article lengths across our dataset. All the distributions are skewed with a long tail. Notably, average graph size in our dataset is 38.7 nodes and 48.3 edges, considerably larger than the graphs in previous datasets (Jin et al., 2020; Gardent et al., 2017). Also the length of the text articles averages to 3,533.8 tokens and can go up to 26,994 tokens, which is orders of magnitudes longer than the text data in previous graph-text paired datasets that typically only contains a single or few sentences (Jin et al., 2020; Gardent et al., 2017; Lebret et al., 2016).

#### 3.1.2 Nodes and edges

The graphs in our dataset contains two types of nodes: entities and string literals. Each entity is labeled by a unique Freebase entity ID, e.g. `ns/m.0f9q9z`, and each string literal contains some natural language text, that could be for example a name, date, or description of an entity. Each edge in the graphs also has an associated edge label, e.g. `ns/common.topic.description`, indicating which type of edge it is. There are a total of 522 different edge types in our dataset. Figure 3 shows the frequency of all the different edge types in our dataset.

Every graph always has one entity node (we call it "center node") that has a link to the paired Wikipedia article, through a special edge `key/wikipedia.en`, and the whole graph is a 1-hop neighborhood of entities around the center node within the bigger Freebase KG, plus the string literals associated with all the entities included. Note that it is possible to have edges between the 1-hop neighbors of the center node, therefore the graphs typically are not star structured. Section 3.2

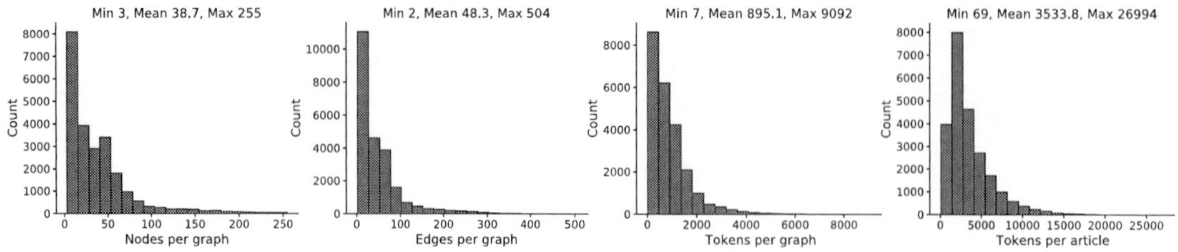


Figure 2: Distribution of graph and article sizes across our WikiGraphs dataset.

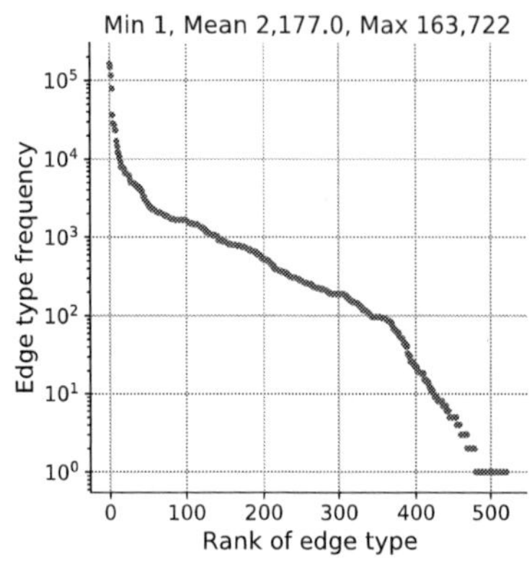


Figure 3: Edge type distribution roughly follows an inverse exponential law.

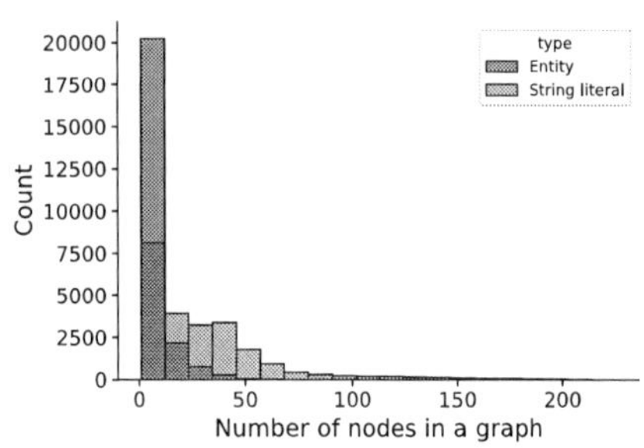


Figure 4: Distribution of the per-graph number of entity nodes and string literal nodes in our dataset.

provides more details about how these graphs are constructed and any additional filtering we did.

One special characteristic about our graph data is that the natural language text contained in the string literal nodes can sometimes be quite long (see e.g. Figure 7,8), and therefore provide much richer information not included in the graph structure itself. On average, each graph contains 895.1 tokens across all the string literal nodes in one graph (Table 2, Figure 2, "Tokens per graph").

Figure 4 shows the distribution of per-graph number of entity nodes and string literal nodes in our dataset. We can see that our graphs tend to have more string literal nodes than entity nodes, indicating that the entities are supplemented with the rich information in the string literals.

The distribution of information is not uniform across the nodes in a graph. Figure 5 shows that most entity nodes in our graph has a small degree, while few nodes have much larger degrees. Also most string literal nodes contain short text, while fewer nodes contain longer text.

The skewed distribution of nodes and edges in our dataset reflect the nature of KG's like Freebase, and presents new challenges to graph representation learning models.

### 3.2 The dataset construction process

We follow three principles when designing the dataset construction process:

1. The text part of the data should be directly comparable in complexity to the capability of state-of-the-art text generative models.
2. The graph part of the data should be constructed in an automatic and scalable way.
3. The graph part of the data should be relevant for the paired text data.

Note that our process is general, and can be applied to any set of Wikipedia articles. We have tried to pair a full dump of English Wikipedia with Freebase and managed to get over 3 million graph-text pairs. Here we restrict the process to the set of articles from the WikiText-103 dataset.

We try to map each Wikipedia article to a relevant subgraph of the existing large scale KG Freebase (Bollacker et al., 2008). We used the last public dump of Freebase[2], which contains 1.9B triples and a total of 250GB of data. We filtered the data by keeping only the entities with at least 4 string attributes (otherwise the entities are less interpretable), and keeping only the top 1024 most frequent relation types and restricting the relations to

[2]https://developers.google.com/freebase

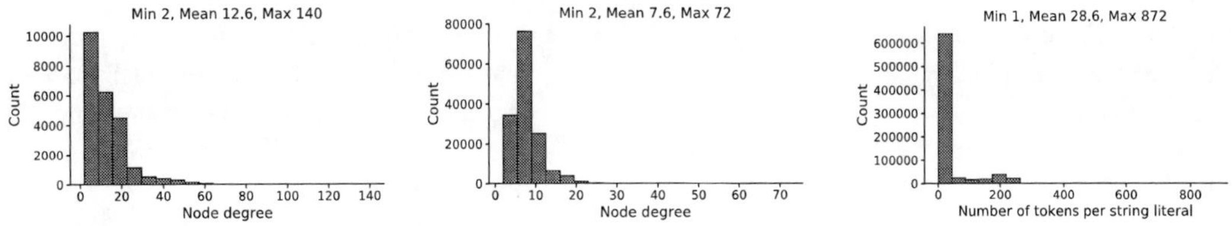


(a) Center node degree dist. (b) Non-center node degree dist. (c) String literal node length dist.

Figure 5: Node degree distribution for entity nodes and token count distribution for string literal nodes.

only those among the retained entities and between the entities and string attributes. We also simplified the entity and relation names by stripping off the irrelevant "http://rdf.freebase.com/" and further removed duplicates. This gives us a significantly cleaner and smaller backbone graph for Freebase, with about 20M nodes.

Finding the relevant subgraph for an article in such a cleaned up but still large KG remains non-trivial. Our process for this contains 3 stages: *mapping*, *expansion*, and *filtering*.

**Mapping** In the first stage of the process, we map each article into an entity in our processed Freebase KG. This is made possible through triples from Freebase like the following:

```
ns/g.11b6jbqpt4   key/wikipedia.en   "Madunnella"
```

where ns/g.11b6jbqpt4 refers to an entity in the KG, key/wikipedia.en is the type of the edge, which indicates that this entity is linked to a Wikipedia article and "Madunnella" is the title of that article. We normalize the title string (and in general any string literals) from Freebase by replacing "_" with white space and handle unicode characters properly. We extract the titles from the Wikipedia article through string matching, where titles are enclosed in a "= [title] =" pattern.

In this step we managed to map 24,345 out of 28,475 (85.5 %) article titles from WikiText-103 to an entity in our KG.

**Expansion** We treat each of the mapped entities as the center node of a subgraph, and expand 1 hop out in the entire filtered Freebase graph to include all the neighboring entities that are the most relevant to the center entity. We then expand further from this 1-hop graph out to include all the relations that connect the selected entities to string attributes as well as between these entities themselves. Note that because of these edges between the 1-hop neighbor entities the graphs are typically not star structured. This gives us a relevant but compact graph for each article. We have also investigated the possibility of a 2-hop neighborhood from the center node, and found that 2-hop neighborhoods are significantly larger than 1-hop and through some "hub" nodes like "Male" or "Female" a 2-hop neighborhood from an entity can easily include many other irrelevant entities. Based on such observations we decided to use the 1-hop neighborhood to keep the relevance of the subgraph high.

**Filtering** The last stage of the process involves more filtering and cleaning up of the data. We noticed that in Freebase it is common for one entity to have multiple relations of the same type pointing to different string attributes, like the following:

```
ns/m.07c72   key/wikipedia.en   "The SImpsons"
ns/m.07c72   key/wikipedia.en   "The Simpson"
ns/m.07c72   key/wikipedia.en   "The simsons"
ns/m.07c72   key/wikipedia.en   "Thr Simpsons"
ns/m.07c72   key/wikipedia.en   "The Simpson's"
```

It is clear that there is a lot of redundancy in this data. We reduced all such edges (from the same entity with the same edge type to string attributes) to a single edge by picking the most "canonical" one. This was done by fitting a unigram model to the characters in the collection of strings and using that model to pick the most likely string.

We also filtered the graphs based on size and created three versions of the data with maximum graph size capped at 256, 512, and 1024 nodes, respectively. All the statistics and results in the rest of the paper are based on graphs with a maximum size of 256, but all versions of the data are made available online.

## 4 Experiments

We perform a set of experiments to showcase how the text and graph information can be combined in a language model. Specifically, we consider three tasks: text generation conditioned on the graph, graph retrieval given the text, and text retrieval given the graph.

### 4.1 Graph-conditioned Transformer-XL

In order to incorporate graph information into an advanced language model, we adapt the recent Transformer-XL model (Dai et al., 2019) to also attend to the graph features. At a high-level our model embeds the graph into a set of embedding vectors, and then exposes these embeddings to the Transformer-XL model as extra "token" embeddings to condition on. The size of this set depends on the graph model we choose.

Given the features for $T$ text tokens $\mathbf{H}_t \in \mathbb{R}^{T\times d}$ and features for $T'$ graph "tokens" $\mathbf{H}_g \in \mathbb{R}^{T'\times d'}$, we illustrate the graph-conditioned attention procedure with a single head as follows:

$$\begin{aligned}\mathbf{Q}_t, \mathbf{K}_t, \mathbf{V}_t &= \mathbf{H}_t\mathbf{W}_q^t, \mathbf{H}_t\mathbf{W}_k^t, \mathbf{H}_t\mathbf{W}_v^t \\ \mathbf{K}_g, \mathbf{V}_g &= \mathbf{H}_g\mathbf{W}_k^g, \mathbf{H}_g\mathbf{W}_v^g \\ \mathbf{A}_t, \mathbf{A}_g &= \mathbf{Q}_t\mathbf{K}_t^\top, \mathbf{Q}_t\mathbf{K}_g^\top \\ \mathbf{A}, \mathbf{V} &= [\mathbf{A}_t \circ \mathbf{A}_g], [\mathbf{V}_t \circ \mathbf{V}_g] \\ \mathbf{O} &= \text{Masked-Softmax}(\mathbf{A})\mathbf{V}\end{aligned}$$

where $[a \circ b]$ stands for concatenation on the sequence dimension and thus $\mathbf{A} \in \mathbb{R}^{T\times(T+T')}$ and $\mathbf{V} \in \mathbb{R}^{(T+T')\times d_h}$, where $d_h$ is the head dimension. In other words, comparing to the original Transformer-XL, our model also computes the attention scores between the text queries $\mathbf{Q}_t$ and both the text keys $\mathbf{K}_t$ and the graph keys $\mathbf{K}_g$. As a result, the attention outputs contain information from both the graph and the text context. Note that this formulation is compatible with an additional memory (Dai et al., 2019) with minimal changes, as it simply adds in an extra set of "tokens" for the model to attend to. We don't use position encodings for the graph "tokens" as there is no sequential ordering for them.

In this work we consider three different approaches for encoding the graph structure:

- **Bag-of-words (BoW):** we construct a single bag-of-words representation of all the tokens from both the nodes and edges in the graph. Entity IDs and numeric values in the graph are replaced with special tokens <entity> and <number>. The BoW vector is further projected using a linear layer to a latent space. In this case $T' = 1$.
- **Nodes only (Nodes):** we construct separate BoW representations for each node and project each to an embedding and ignore the edges. In this case $T'$ is equal to the number of nodes in the graph.
- **Graph neural network (GNN):** we embed BoW representations for both nodes and edges and then use a graph neural network (Battaglia et al., 2018) on top of those embeddings to compute a new set of node embeddings. $T'$ is equal to the number of nodes.

The $T'$ graph embeddings from this process are shared across all the time steps for text tokens. This model can be further improved, e.g. by using word embeddings and text summarization techniques, but we leave these for future work.

#### 4.1.1 Implementation details

We reimplement the Transformer-XL model in Jax (Bradbury et al., 2018). In our experiments, we employ the base model in (Dai et al., 2019), except that we increase the tail shrinkage factor used for the adaptive softmax and input representations from 1 to 4, which saves 63% of the parameters without compromising the performance. On the full Wikitext-103 dataset, our implementation has a test perplexity of 24.2 (published result for this base model was 24.0). We train our models using the standard likelihood objective for language models with a total batch size of 64 on 8 V100 GPUs. Adam optimizer is used with an initial learning rate of $2.5 \times 10^{-4}$, which decays up to 200k steps following a cosine curve. During training, we use text segments of 150 steps and a memory of equal size. When evaluating the model, we use a sequence length of 64 and memory size 640. Unless further noted, in our experiments we use an embedding size of 256 for BoW-conditioned models. For other models, we project each node or edge represented by BoW to an embedding space of size 128. The default GNN we use has a single linear message passing layer of 256 hidden units.

### 4.2 Graph → text generation

Our first task is text generation conditioned on the graph. We evaluate model performance by (1) computing model perplexity on held-out text and (2) drawing samples from the model and comparing that to the ground truth text article. We use BLEU score (Papineni et al., 2002) to measure the similarity of our generated samples to the ground truth.

| Cond. | Test Ppl. | rBLEU | | rBLEU(w/title) | |
|---|---|---|---|---|---|
| | | Valid | Test | Valid | Test |
| None | **25.85** | 10.97 | 9.98 | 27.98 | 24.07 |
| BoW | 26.65 | 29.53 | 24.41 | 32.41 | 27.39 |
| Nodes | 27.40 | 30.51 | 25.31 | 32.60 | 27.43 |
| GNN | 26.93 | **31.39** | **26.22** | **32.65** | **28.35** |

Table 3: The perplexity and the generated text reverse-BLEU score of different types of graph-conditioned models. We show the reverse-BLEU score with or without prompting the original title at the start of the text generation.

Unlike previous use cases for BLEU score where there are many references for one generated sample, here we have only one ground truth reference but we can generate multiple samples. We therefore simply swapped the reference with the samples when computing the score, which we term as the reverse-BLEU (rBLEU). We have also tried other ways of computing the BLEU score and find that they don't change how models compare against each other.

Unless explicitly stated, we let the model sample with a memory size of 640, and condition on the graphs in the test set to generate text for up to 512 tokens per sample for a total of 20 samples per graph. The rBLEU score is computed based on these samples and corresponding ground-truth texts are truncated to the same length. We sample the texts from the distribution with a temperature of 0.8. For each case, we report the average rBLEU score of 3 sampling runs. We find the variances are insignificant which do not affect the comparison results. In Appendix A.3 we also report results for generating longer samples for up to 4096 tokens.

### 4.2.1 Main result

In Table 3, we show the perplexity and the rBLEU score of the unconditional, BoW, nodes-only, and GNN conditioned models. As a reference, a standard Transformer-XL model trained on the full Wikitext-103 training set reaches 25.08 perplexity on our test set, which contains 71.7% of the original test articles. We can see that the unconditional, i.e. text only, model trained on our dataset gets a very similar performance as trained on the full set. This is strong evidence that our dataset can be a good benchmark for state-of-the-art text generative models.

We also see that conditioned on the graphs, model perplexity didn't improve, but the relevance

| # MP layers | Test Ppl. | Test rBLEU |
|---|---|---|
| 0 | 26.65 | 25.31 |
| 1 | 27.40 | 26.22 |
| 3 | 27.20 | 26.16 |
| 5 | 26.85 | 25.91 |

Table 4: The test perplexity and the generated text reverse-BLEU score (without title prompt) of GNN-based models with different numbers of message passing layers.

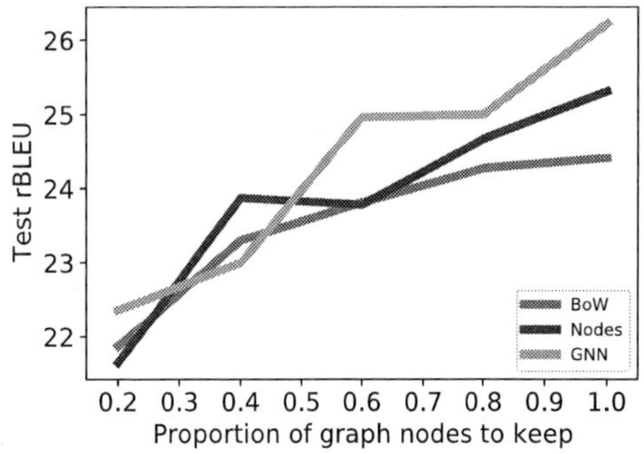


Figure 6: Performance vs size of graph to condition on. The model is trained with a smaller version of the data by subsampling the number of nodes.

of the samples measured by the BLEU scores did improve significantly. This indicates that the graph conditioned models can indeed steer the language model towards more relevant topics, but this so far cannot yet improve likelihood metrics.

To make the evaluation more fair to the text-only model, we also tried to prompt the generation with the title of the article, such that the text-only model also has some context. In this setting the graph models are still better, showing the importance of modeling the structure.

Lastly, among all the 3 graph model variants, we observe that using a set of embeddings from the nodes model is better than using a single embedding from the BoW model, and fully utilizing the graph structure through the GNN model is consistently better than ignoring the edges as in the nodes model. However the differences among the methods are relatively small. For visualizations of a few graphs in our dataset and the corresponding samples generated based on them please refer to Appendix A.

### 4.2.2 Ablation studies

We show a few ablations on the graph model and sampling parameters, to provide some insights into the models.

| Cond. | Recall@1 | Recall@5 | mAP |
|---|---|---|---|
| None | 0.02 | 0.12 | 0.10 |
| BoW | 16.28 | 30.23 | 25.98 |
| Nodes | 16.28 | **34.88** | 26.62 |
| GNN | **18.60** | **34.88** | **27.79** |

Table 5: Text retrieval given the graph.

| Cond. | Recall@1 | Recall@5 | mAP |
|---|---|---|---|
| None | 0.02 | 0.07 | 0.02 |
| BoW | 95.35 | **100.00** | 97.67 |
| Nodes | 93.02 | **100.00** | 96.51 |
| GNN | **100.00** | **100.00** | **100.00** |

Table 6: Graph Retrieval given the text.

Table 4 shows the effect of varying the number of message passing layers in the GNN. We can observe that there is a big difference between using message passing ( $\geq 1$ layers) or not (0 layers) in terms of rBLEU score, but increasing the number of message passing layers does not change the results significantly. We believe however, that these results can be improved by employing bigger and more powerful graph representation learning models, and potentially use initial node and edge representations better than bag-of-words.

In Figure 6 we show the effect of the graph size on model performance. In this experiment we subsample the nodes in each graph to control for the amount of context the model has access to. It is clear from the results that when we heavily subsample and keep only a small portion of the graphs, the GNN model performs similarly as the simpler BoW model, but GNNs benefit more as we keep more of the graph structure.

### 4.3 Graph $\rightarrow$ text retrieval

In this task, we evaluate the possibility of retrieving relevant text for a given query graph. We pair all articles with all graphs in the test set, resulting in 43×43=1849 pairs. Then the trained graph-conditioned language models are used to produce the per-token likelihood of each pair, and we use these likelihood scores to rank the text articles for each graph. We expect the learned models can rank the correct pairs higher than wrong ones. To measure the results we use standard ranking metrics including recall@K, which computes the fraction of times the correct pair is included in the top K predictions, as well as mean average precision (mAP). In Table 5, it is observed that graph-conditioned models can indeed retrieve more relevant texts from the graph than the unconditional model, among which the GNN-based model performs the best, and the unconditional model performs close to a random guess.

### 4.4 Text $\rightarrow$ graph retrieval

In this last task, we evaluate the performance of graph retrieval given a text query. We use exactly the same setting and scores as Section 4.3, but instead rank the graphs for each text article using the likelihood scores. The results are shown in Table 6. Note that this task is quite easy with our data and setup, potentially because the graphs are much more distinguishable than the text articles. All the graph-conditioned models perform almost perfectly, with the GNN model again outperforming the others.

## 5 Conclusion

In this paper, we present WikiGraphs, a new graph-text paired dataset with significantly larger graphs and longer text compared to previous datasets of similar nature. We show that the text part of this data is a good benchmark for state-of-the-art text generation models, and the paired dataset can help us benchmark models that are capable of generating long and coherent text conditioned on a graph structure.

In the first set of experiments on this dataset we showcase 3 different tasks using our dataset, and demonstrate the benefit of better models that make more use of the graph structure.

There is still significant room for improvement for these tasks on our dataset, and we hope the release of the data and baseline code can help spur more interest in developing models that can generate long text conditioned on graphs, and generate graphs given text, which is another exciting direction our dataset enables but we did not explore, and eventually bridging the graph and text modalities.

## References

Sören Auer, Christian Bizer, Georgi Kobilarov, Jens Lehmann, Richard Cyganiak, and Zachary Ives. 2007. Dbpedia: A nucleus for a web of open data. In *The Semantic Web*, pages 722–735, Berlin, Heidelberg. Springer Berlin Heidelberg.

Loïc Barrault, Magdalena Biesialska, Ondřej Bojar, Marta R Costa-jussà, Christian Federmann, Yvette Graham, Roman Grundkiewicz, Barry Haddow, Matthias Huck, Eric Joanis, et al. 2020. Findings of the 2020 conference on machine translation (wmt20). In *Proceedings of the Fifth Conference on Machine Translation*, pages 1–55.

Peter W Battaglia, Jessica B Hamrick, Victor Bapst, Alvaro Sanchez-Gonzalez, Vinicius Zambaldi, Mateusz Malinowski, Andrea Tacchetti, David Raposo, Adam Santoro, Ryan Faulkner, et al. 2018. Relational inductive biases, deep learning, and graph networks. *arXiv preprint arXiv:1806.01261*.

Kurt Bollacker, Colin Evans, Praveen Paritosh, Tim Sturge, and Jamie Taylor. 2008. Freebase: a collaboratively created graph database for structuring human knowledge. In *Proceedings of the 2008 ACM SIGMOD international conference on Management of data*, pages 1247–1250.

James Bradbury, Roy Frostig, Peter Hawkins, Matthew James Johnson, Chris Leary, Dougal Maclaurin, George Necula, Adam Paszke, Jake VanderPlas, Skye Wanderman-Milne, and Qiao Zhang. 2018. JAX: composable transformations of Python+NumPy programs.

Tom B Brown, Benjamin Mann, Nick Ryder, Melanie Subbiah, Jared Kaplan, Prafulla Dhariwal, Arvind Neelakantan, Pranav Shyam, Girish Sastry, Amanda Askell, et al. 2020. Language models are few-shot learners. *arXiv preprint arXiv:2005.14165*.

Zihang Dai, Zhilin Yang, Yiming Yang, Jaime Carbonell, Quoc V Le, and Ruslan Salakhutdinov. 2019. Transformer-xl: Attentive language models beyond a fixed-length context. *arXiv preprint arXiv:1901.02860*.

Claire Gardent, Anastasia Shimorina, Shashi Narayan, and Laura Perez-Beltrachini. 2017. The WebNLG challenge: Generating text from RDF data. In *Proceedings of the 10th International Conference on Natural Language Generation*, pages 124–133, Santiago de Compostela, Spain. Association for Computational Linguistics.

John S Garofolo, Lori F Lamel, William M Fisher, Jonathan G Fiscus, and David S Pallett. 1993. Darpa timit acoustic-phonetic continous speech corpus cd-rom. nist speech disc 1-1.1. *NASA STI/Recon technical report n*, 93:27403.

Justin Gilmer, Samuel S Schoenholz, Patrick F Riley, Oriol Vinyals, and George E Dahl. 2017. Neural message passing for quantum chemistry. In *International Conference on Machine Learning*, pages 1263–1272. PMLR.

Zhijing Jin, Qipeng Guo, Xipeng Qiu, and Zheng Zhang. 2020. GenWiki: A dataset of 1.3 million content-sharing text and graphs for unsupervised graph-to-text generation. In *Proceedings of the 28th International Conference on Computational Linguistics*, pages 2398–2409, Barcelona, Spain (Online). International Committee on Computational Linguistics.

Thomas N Kipf and Max Welling. 2016. Semi-supervised classification with graph convolutional networks. *arXiv preprint arXiv:1609.02907*.

Rik Koncel-Kedziorski, Dhanush Bekal, Yi Luan, Mirella Lapata, and Hannaneh Hajishirzi. 2019. Text Generation from Knowledge Graphs with Graph Transformers. In *Proceedings of the 2019 Conference of the North American Chapter of the Association for Computational Linguistics: Human Language Technologies, Volume 1 (Long and Short Papers)*, pages 2284–2293, Minneapolis, Minnesota. Association for Computational Linguistics.

Rémi Lebret, David Grangier, and Michael Auli. 2016. Neural text generation from structured data with application to the biography domain. In *Proceedings of the 2016 Conference on Empirical Methods in Natural Language Processing*, pages 1203–1213, Austin, Texas. Association for Computational Linguistics.

Tsung-Yi Lin, Michael Maire, Serge Belongie, James Hays, Pietro Perona, Deva Ramanan, Piotr Dollár, and C Lawrence Zitnick. 2014. Microsoft coco: Common objects in context. In *European conference on computer vision*, pages 740–755. Springer.

Fei Liu, Jeffrey Flanigan, Sam Thomson, Norman Sadeh, and Noah A Smith. 2018. Toward abstractive summarization using semantic representations. *arXiv preprint arXiv:1805.10399*.

Stephen Merity, Caiming Xiong, James Bradbury, and Richard Socher. 2016. Pointer sentinel mixture models. *arXiv preprint arXiv:1609.07843*.

Aaron van den Oord, Sander Dieleman, Heiga Zen, Karen Simonyan, Oriol Vinyals, Alex Graves, Nal Kalchbrenner, Andrew Senior, and Koray Kavukcuoglu. 2016. Wavenet: A generative model for raw audio. *arXiv preprint arXiv:1609.03499*.

Vassil Panayotov, Guoguo Chen, Daniel Povey, and Sanjeev Khudanpur. 2015. Librispeech: an asr corpus based on public domain audio books. In *2015 IEEE international conference on acoustics, speech and signal processing (ICASSP)*, pages 5206–5210. IEEE.

Kishore Papineni, Salim Roukos, Todd Ward, and Wei-Jing Zhu. 2002. Bleu: a method for automatic evaluation of machine translation. In *Proceedings of the 40th annual meeting of the Association for Computational Linguistics*, pages 311–318.

Ankur P. Parikh, Xuezhi Wang, Sebastian Gehrmann, Manaal Faruqui, Bhuwan Dhingra, Diyi Yang, and Dipanjan Das. 2020. Totto: A controlled table-to-text generation dataset.

Ashish Vaswani, Noam Shazeer, Niki Parmar, Jakob Uszkoreit, Llion Jones, Aidan N Gomez, Ł ukasz Kaiser, and Illia Polosukhin. 2017. Attention is all you need. In *Advances in Neural Information Processing Systems*, volume 30. Curran Associates, Inc.

Petar Veličković, Guillem Cucurull, Arantxa Casanova, Adriana Romero, Pietro Liò, and Yoshua Bengio. 2018. Graph attention networks. In *International Conference on Learning Representations*.

Oriol Vinyals, Alexander Toshev, Samy Bengio, and Dumitru Erhan. 2016. Show and tell: Lessons learned from the 2015 mscoco image captioning challenge. *IEEE transactions on pattern analysis and machine intelligence*, 39(4):652–663.

Hongwei Wang, Fuzheng Zhang, Mengdi Zhang, Jure Leskovec, Miao Zhao, Wenjie Li, and Zhongyuan Wang. 2019. Knowledge-aware graph neural networks with label smoothness regularization for recommender systems. In *Proceedings of the 25th ACM SIGKDD International Conference on Knowledge Discovery & Data Mining*, pages 968–977.

Kun Xu, Liwei Wang, Mo Yu, Yansong Feng, Yan Song, Zhiguo Wang, and Dong Yu. 2019. Cross-lingual knowledge graph alignment via graph matching neural network. *arXiv preprint arXiv:1905.11605*.

# A Appendix

## A.1 Graph visualization

Some example visualizations of the KG structures are shown in Figure 7 and Figure 8. The corresponding graph truth texts are shown in Table 7.

## A.2 Generated examples

The generated texts based on the graph shown in Figure 7 and Figure 8 are listed in Table 8 and Table 9, respectively.

## A.3 Ablations on sampling configurations

We show additional ablation results on the sample length (Table 10) and the temperature (Table 11) for greedy sampling. Note that for each case we show the rBLEU score based on the validation set computed with a single sampling run (20 samples per graph).

Note that the GNN model has overall the best performance. However as the sample length increases the advantage of the GNN model also decreases. This indicates that it is still very challenging to generate long text that stays on-topic, and potentially the noise overwhelms the signal when number of tokens increases to 4096.

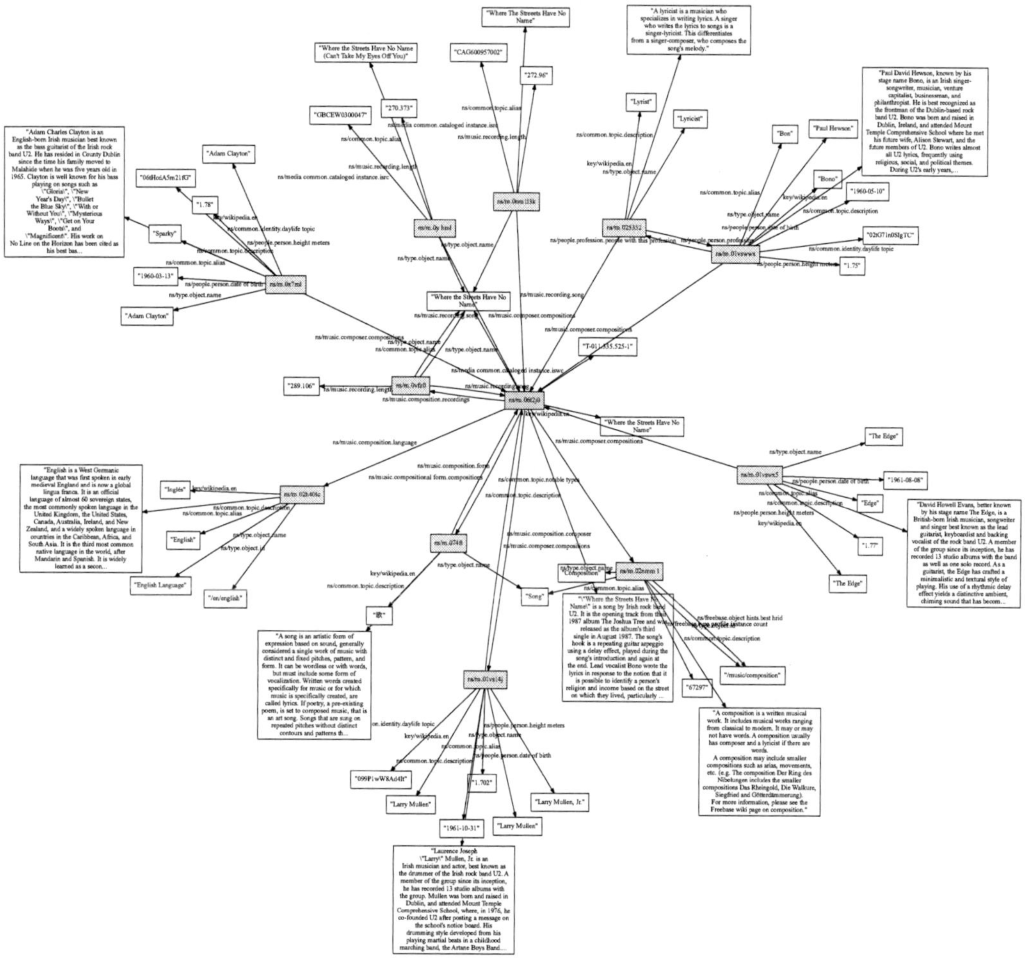

Figure 7: Visualization of the "Where the Streets Have No Name" KG in our dataset.

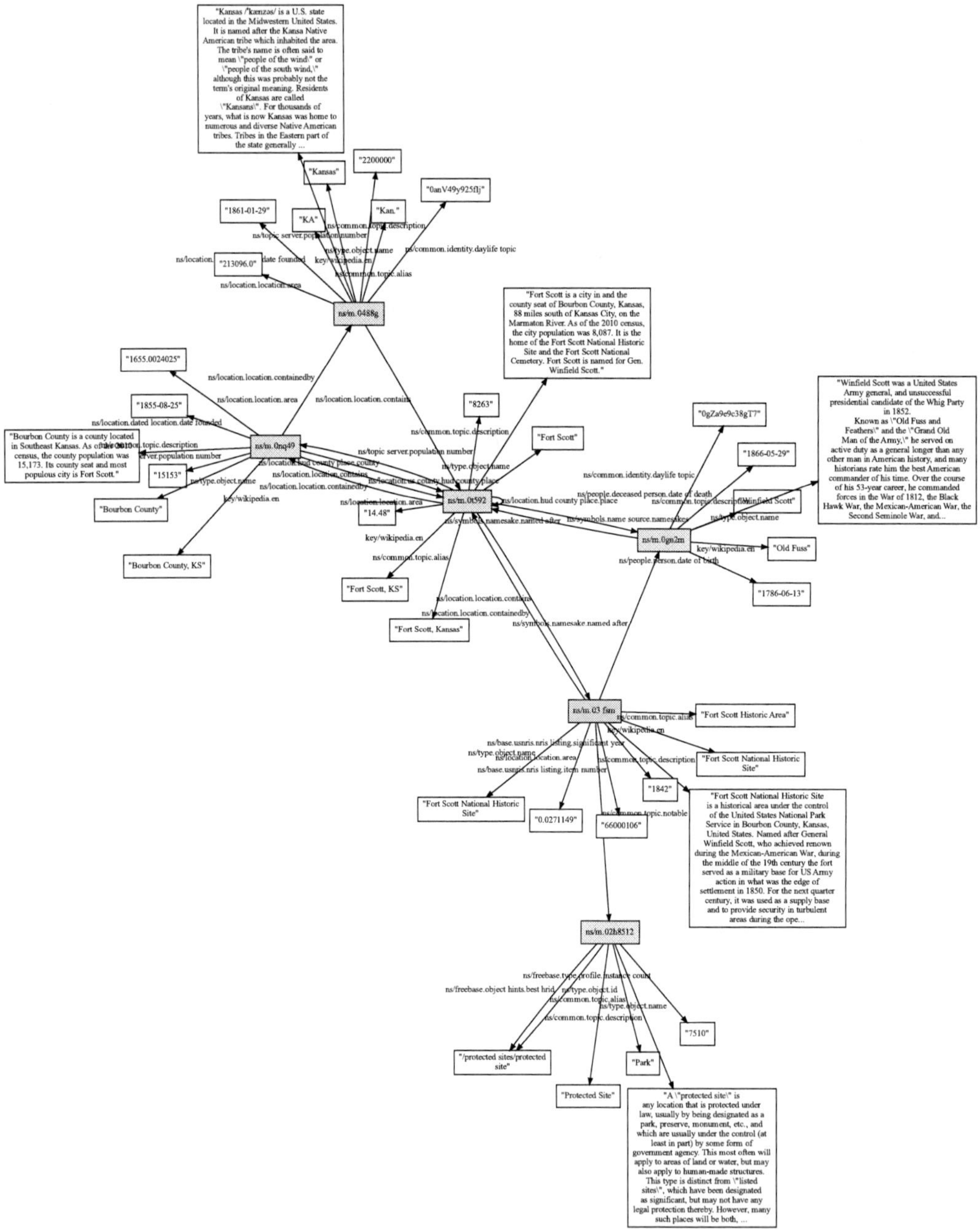

Figure 8: Visualization of the “Fort Scott National Historic Site” KG in our dataset.

| Visualization | Ground Truth Text |
|---|---|
| Figure 7 | = Where the Streets Have No Name =<br>" Where the Streets Have No Name " is a song by Irish rock band U2 . It is the opening track from their 1987 album The Joshua Tree and was released as the album 's third single in August 1987 . The song 's hook is a repeating guitar arpeggio using a delay effect , played during the song 's introduction and again at the end . Lead vocalist Bono wrote the lyrics in response to the notion that it is possible to identify a person 's religion and income based on the street on which they lived , particularly in Belfast . During the band 's difficulties recording the song , producer Brian Eno considered erasing the song 's tapes to have them start from scratch . " Where the Streets Have No Name " was praised by critics and became a commercial success , peaking at number thirteen in the US , number fourteen in Canada , number ten in the Netherlands , and number four in the United Kingdom . The song has remained a staple of their live act since the song debuted in 1987 on The Joshua Tree Tour . The song was performed on a Los Angeles rooftop for the filming of its music video , which won a Grammy Award for Best Performance Music Video .<br>= = Writing and recording = =<br>The music for " Where the Streets Have No Name " originated from a demo that guitarist The Edge composed the night before the group resumed The Joshua Tree sessions . In an upstairs room at Melbeach House — his newly purchased home — The Edge used a four @-@ track tape machine to record an arrangement of keyboards , bass , guitar , and a drum machine . Realising that the album sessions were approaching the end and that the band were short on exceptional live songs , The Edge wanted to " conjure up the ultimate U2 live @-@ song " , so he imagined what he would like to hear at a future U2 show if he were a fan . After finishing the rough mix , he felt he had come up with " the most amazing guitar part and song of [ his ] life " . With no one in the house to share the demo with , The Edge recalls dancing around and punching the air in celebration . Although the band liked the demo , it was difficult for them to record the song . Bassist Adam Clayton said , " At the time it sounded like a foreign language , whereas now we understand how it works " . The arrangement , with two time signature shifts and frequent chord changes , was rehearsed many times , but the group struggled to get a performance they liked . According to co @-@ producer Daniel Lanois , " that was the science project song . |
| Figure 8 | = Fort Scott National Historic Site =<br>Fort Scott National Historic Site is a historical area under the control of the United States National Park Service in Bourbon County , Kansas , United States . Named after General Winfield Scott , who achieved renown during the Mexican @-@ American War , during the middle of the 19th century the fort served as a military base for US Army action in what was the edge of settlement in 1850 . For the next quarter century , it was used as a supply base and to provide security in turbulent areas during the opening of the West to settlement , a period which included Bleeding Kansas and the American Civil War . The current national historic site protects 20 historic structures , a parade ground , and five acres ( 20 @,@ 000 m $^{2}$ ) of restored <unk> prairie , inside the city of Fort Scott . It is open to visitors most days of the year .<br>= = History = =<br>In 1842 , Fort Scott was named after Winfield Scott , was established on the American frontier on the military road in eastern Kansas between Fort Leavenworth and Fort Gibson . It was established to provide protection to the rapidly increasing number of settlers , who were migrating from the Eastern United States . Fort Scott became one of a chain of forts intended to protect the new settlers from the Plains Indians , as well as to protect the Indians from the settlers ' encroachment . The United States government intention to reserve permanent Indian lands west of the Missouri River gave way to the competition of settlers continuing to encroach on the Indian settlements . Fort Scott 's most active days were between 1842 and 1853 , although it was also used during the Civil War .<br>= = = Army days = = =<br>The Cherokee of Indian Territory ( now Oklahoma ) were upset to have Fort Wayne in their proximity . After some delay , the US Army decided to abandon Fort Wayne and move its soldiers to a new fort to be built between Fort Leavenworth and the site . The Army both wanted to placate the Cherokee ( who were supervised by the Department of Defense ) and provide more defense for white settlers and other Indians against the Osage , who had been conducting frequent raids in the area . On April 1 , 1842 , some soldiers of Fort Wayne left their fort and on April 22 arrived where Fort Scott would be built , in the Osage <unk> section of modern @-@ day Kansas . After haggling with the Cherokees to acquire the land , the rest of Fort Wayne 's garrison left the fort on May 26 and arrived at the Fort Scott site on May 30 . Unlike most forts for military use , the fort did not have defensive walls or structures |

Table 7: Ground truth samples.

| Cond. | Generated Text |
|---|---|
| - | = Final Fantasy Adventure =<br>Final Fantasy Adventure is a platform video game developed by Square ( now Square Enix ) and published by Square ( then Square Enix ) for the Super Nintendo Entertainment System , and published by Nintendo for the Nintendo 64 and the Nintendo 64 in North America and Europe . It was released in North America on August 10 , 1995 for the Nintendo 64 and in Europe in March 1995 for the Wii . It was also re @-@ released for the Wii in Japan on March 25 , 2015 for the Wii U 's Virtual Console service . Final Fantasy Adventure is set in the fantasy world of the fictional land of Ooo , between 1000 and 1000 years before the events of the story of the kingdom of Ooo . The story follows the protagonists , Cid , a boy who is sent to Ooo by the legendary Jörmungandr to find the Wizard of Ooo . Throughout the game , players train for a series of random battles , which are played out over a single screen . In the end , players control a " Scarlet Witch " who is summoned to the realm of Ooo . The game was well @-@ received , with praise particularly directed at its graphics and its gameplay , despite criticism for its repetitive gameplay . Critics generally praised its graphics , plot , and simplistic gameplay . The game was commercially successful , selling over 20 @,@ 000 copies , and in 2004 it was re @-@ released in Japan as part of the Final Fantasy Collections series .<br>= = Gameplay = =<br>The game is a third @-@ person shooter , with gameplay elements related to worlds , time travel , and exploration . Characters are made up of two polygons ; the main character , Aya , is a sprite @-@ based character and inhabits a world of trees and caves , where she is able to perform offensive actions along the way . The protagonist , Aya , is a heavily armored , humanoid creature with red eyes and black eyes . In contrast to other Final Fantasy games , her prominent appearances in this game are not as straightforward as in previous Final Fantasy installments . The game 's world is divided into two sections : the world of Ooo and the world of the dinosaurs . The player 's adventure begins with Aya , a girl who initially leads the plot of Twilight Town , but later returns to Ooo to save her sister . Aya explores the area and is able to save her family . After interacting with the player , Aya is able to resume the story in the future . The game 's main family member , Aya , is a woman named Alice . She is a member of the religious order , the Jehovah 's Witnesses , who is a member of |
| BoW | = Zoo Station ( song ) =<br>" Zoo Station " is a song by Australian rock band U2 from their second studio album , PopMart , released in 1992 as the album 's lead single . Rise to popularity after its release prompted U2 to record two songs with bassist Adam Clayton and guitarist Joe Bono , as they felt that it was their breakthrough album . The song comprises lyrics set in an acoustic , with lyrics that have always focused on a woman being stuck in an abusive relationship . It was developed due to the band 's involvement in the construction of Zoo Station and its accompanying soundtrack , and it was inspired by U2 's admiration of the groups they both represented . The song was inspired by a series of incidents that occurred in El Salvador when a man repeatedly attacked an apartment building . The song received positive reviews from music critics , and it was labelled a " masterpiece " by several publications . Thirty @-@ five tracks were released as singles , and the song has been covered by numerous artists , including such figures as Sam & Max , The <unk> , and Mickey Rourke . The band released their version of " Zoo Station " on non @-@ consecutive studio albums , with " Where the Streets Have No Name " and " Numb " released in 1999 and 2000 respectively . " Zoo Station " is on the band 's greatest hits album , 10 Mile Wild , and on their greatest hits album Across the Universe . It was performed live at the Vertigo Tour in 2007 . The song was included on the band 's fifth studio album , New Order ( 2008 ) , and was included on the film The Last Years ( 2012 ) .<br>= = Background = =<br>" Zoo Station " was written by U2 frontman Bono and produced by U2 and was the first song on the album . Clayton still had a strong fan base and was a regular singer . The two met while performing in the amphitheaters of Los Angeles , and in a live performance he was the lead singer on the last leg of the Vertigo Tour . The Edge and Clayton were both fans of the band , and the pair decided to collaborate on the album . Both performed on their 2004 tour , and made a solo appearance on the 2004 The Zoo TV Tour . Clayton and Clayton had been close friends , and the pair became friends again in 2008 . In late April 2004 , U2 announced that the song had been released as the first single for the album , and would be released on 31 May , five weeks after the album 's release . " Zoo Station " was released as the fourth single from PopMart and premiered on 13 June 2005 . The song is a |
| Nodes | = You Can 't Take This Away ( U2 song ) =<br>" You Can 't Take This Away ( U2 song ) " is a song by the Irish rock band U2 . It was written by vocalist Bono and produced by The Smiths for their third solo album , The Joshua Tree . Inspired by Romania roots rock and roll , " You Can 't Take This Away " is a song about a man who suffers from severe nightmares . The song was first released on the album and premiered on radio on 19 August 1996 , where it reached number 40 on the Billboard Hot 100 . " You Can 't Take This Away ( U2 song ) " received mixed reviews from critics ; some tracks , such as the opening chorus and bridge , were praised as highlights by some reviewers . The song was well received by critics , as the record company 's highest @-@ selling single at that time , where " The Edge of Forever " peaked at number 64 . It was later re @-@ released on the band 's 2006 compilation album No Line on the Horizon , but has since been re @-@ released on live performances in 2006 and 2009 . " You Can 't Take This Away ( U2 song ) " was performed on the Late Show with David Letterman on 31 December 2005 . " You Can 't Take This Away ( U2 song ) " has since been covered by many groups and has achieved enormous commercial success . A video for the song was filmed by then @-@ frontman Bono , for which it was nominated for a Grammy Award .<br>= = Background and writing = =<br>" You Can 't Take This Away ( Kingdom of Ireland song ) " is a track that features Bono and The Smiths discussing their relationship and how they changed their lives . His father , Jack Clayton , was assassinated in 1981 at the age of 23 . Bono was born in Philadelphia and worked for a business , first working as a secretary in Los Angeles , then as a photographer for a commercial for Primus . He later worked for the Coca @-@ Cola Company as a drummer in the music industry . The musician picked up the song again after Nikolai <unk> , an engineer who worked with The Smiths , heard it and decided to play it for him after U2 agreed to record it for a solo album . The band originally intended to release " You Can 't Take This Away " as a single ; however , with a critical failure , the song eventually became a single . In 2004 , " You Can 't Take This Away ( U2 song ) " is one of two songs on the album that U2 released as a single with approval of the record label . The [ ] |
| GNN | = The Edge of Glory =<br>" The Edge of Glory " is a song by Irish rock band U2 , released as a single . It was written by guitarist Larry Mullen , Jr . , who plays lead guitar on the song , and was produced by Alex <unk> , who described the song as " a track with a lot of meaning , but no connection . " The song contains several pop rock elements and is set in that time period , and is among the most prominent in the album . In addition to its lyrics , the song 's lyrics detail hypocrisy , and also deals with the effects of adultery . The song 's lyrics have been described by music critics as being autobiographical . The lyrics have been described as " a bold exploration of the figure of a New York City man " , and " an expression of the inability of freedom to live in a world that is also a place in the world of space . " The song 's lyrics describe a " Manhattan @-@ like place " , with Bono calling the arrival a " pleasant little optimism from before it came to life . " " The Edge of Glory " was a success in the United Kingdom , reaching number two in the charts in the United States , and topping the charts in Australia and New Zealand . The song has been certified platinum by the Recording Industry Association of America , and has sold over four million copies worldwide . The song has been covered by several artists , including German band U2 . The music video for " The Edge of Glory " won Best Video at the 2004 MTV Video Music Awards . The video also served as an inspiration for the film U2 360 ° ( 1998 ) .<br>= = Background = =<br>The song has been described as a " relaxed representation " of globalization , with Bono proclaiming himself the " lost king of rock ' n ' roll " , and Chris McGuinness as " the only one who has ever achieved the sound of a rock ' n ' roll . " Bono 's lyrics have been described as a parody of Lord Byron 's " My Own Time " , and as an " attack on social and political issues " .<br>= = Recording and production = =<br>Bono and U2 made the final stages of recording the song at the Abbey Road Studios in Dublin , Dublin . The sessions were divided into two sessions : Sessions at Damien the flautist and Context at the Cave of Christ . The results of the sessions were mixed by Brian Eno . U2 was very excited to record the result , with Eno referring to the recording as a " special event " , and they decided to change the track |

Table 8: Generated samples based on the “Where the Streets Have No Name” graph.

| Cond. | Generated Text |
|---|---|
| - | = Carbuncle =<br>Bloodlines is a 2011 action role @-@ playing video game developed by <unk> and published by Activision for the Wii . The game is part of a sequel of the 2013 game Eclipse : The Series . It was published by Activision on November 19 , 2011 , for Microsoft Windows , Apple II , Xbox 360 , iOS , and Xbox 360 . The game , set in the fictional Middle Ages , revolves around the player @-@ character centaurs battling for control of their universe . The protagonist of the game , Percy , the leader of the Knights of the Old Republic , is a member of the Knights of the Old Republic , and is appointed to lead a military coup to overthrow the Irish Republic and destroy the Home Nations ' military forces . Though the game mainly took place in a new version of the New York City , the original plan was to make it more easily accessible to players unfamiliar with the New Republic . It was also a commercial success , selling more than 900 @,@ 000 copies . The game received mostly positive reviews from most video game publications , with many praising the visual style and the gameplay , but many said that it was not as good as that of the previous game . Reviewers noted the game 's title forward addressing issues such as the difficulty level , a general danger of being too difficult to fight , and the difficulty of playing the game as the player @-@ character 's pattern of character .<br>= = Gameplay = =<br>Bloodlines is a crossover action role @-@ playing game that takes place in the fictional Middle Ages , which is composed of medieval countries and locales . Valhalla , a medieval stronghold , is the game 's main setting . The player @-@ character is a 3 @-@ D miniature character with a sword and shield , which have multiple colored attacks , and has two of the four abilities , which are progressively reduced from the first one and allow for greater size and movement . The available weapons are bolt @-@ fired weapons , advanced weapons , and weapons that can be used in battle . The player is able to summon magical powers to attack targets , and can use magical powers to enhance the character 's abilities . <unk> are also available via a <unk> system , which enables players to throw stones at enemies and attack enemy characters who have not encountered them . The player character also has an ability to revive foes by performing a touch @-@ screen action . The game can be played as a side @-@ scrolling through a View Mode , which can be used in the single @-@ player mode . The first act features a " <unk> " displayed from a first @-@ person perspective . The player character can move around |
| BoW | = Civil War Pass =<br>Civil War Pass , also known as the Battle of the Crater or the Battle of Fort Sumner , was an important battle fought on September 7 , 1864 , at Fort Coldwater , in the state of Montana . After seeing repeated attacks on the fort , Gen. James A. Douglas , the commander of the Confederate forces in the South , decided to abandon the fort and flee to the north . After Union forces struck the fort , they decided to flee south to the Ohio River . There they quickly encountered a group of horses , who were used to build a pontoon bridge . The ditches and wooden planks were removed and replaced with stone blocks to make them float ( plow ) . The obstacles that were created in the river valley , however , proved treacherous and were not bridged by mountain passes . The young general and his troops eventually reached the Ohio and the Mississippi rivers , but the new Presidential candidate , Abraham Lincoln , resigned after the war . After the defeat at Fort Sumner , General Douglas , the commander of the Union forces , planned and executed a number of attacks on Fort Sumner . When soldiers arrived , they found two now @-@ deserted locations . The attacks had been made more than a year before . When the line of retreat of the Union forces , which stretched from Fort Sumner to Fort Sumner , reached Fort Sumner on August 19 , 1864 , the cavalrymen captured it on September 30 . In November 1864 , General Douglas was defeated at the Battle of Lake Logan .<br>= = Background = =<br>In 1861 , with the Mexican @-@ American War nearing its conclusion , the American public began to think of an armistice treaty , or peace treaty between Mexico and the United States . On July 1 , 1861 , General Douglas sent three large armies from the Mexican @-@ American War , a series of forts west of the Rockies , to attack Fort Vicksburg . The forts were destroyed in a siege in June . These were built during the years it was fought by the Confederate States of America . The British and Americans were unprepared for the chance of victory , and the Americans were now planning to take control of the Gulf Coast . Like the Americans , the British were planning an attack into central Canada . The British were aware that the main invasion of Canada would occur on July 8 . The British were near the Niagara River and the Union were hopefully midway along the river , approaching Fort Sumner from the west . The British were reluctant to move toward the Carolinas , and so , in the event the Port of Boston was abandoned , the British would be forced to travel to the lower Mississippi . The |
| Nodes | = Fort Scott =<br>Fort Scott is an American military post located in Fort Lee , Kansas . It is named in honor of General William Scott , a U.S. Army general and the first commander of the Army of the Potomac . The site was designated as a National Historic Landmark in 1991 , and has been designated a National Historic Landmark under the title of Fort Scott Historical Site since 1929 . It is located in the Rocky Mountains in Kansas and is known as the " James Scott National Historic Site " .<br>= = History = =<br>The original having been settled by the Caddo on the Black River , and later moved to Fort Lee in present @-@ day Decatur County , Virginia . On July 10 , 1810 , the Hennepin reported that the Caddo had acquired the territory of Fort Lee , but it is unclear whether he was present there . He may have taken a position that had previously been occupied by other people . Around 1800 , the first Governor of Kansas , Colonel Andrew H. Sharpe , established Fort Scott in what is now a part of Fort Lee . The fort was constructed on a site that he had named Fort Scott , and was known as Fort Douglas . The fort was used for administrative purposes and for administration of the Missouri Territory . In 1808 , William Bolivar Buckner led a large movement to remove the western boundary of Texas , including Fort Scott . Congress authorized a survey of the territory in 1817 , and a survey of the Old South boundary was completed in 1818 , making Fort Scott the first governor to apply federal law . Although the West Texas Aftermath quickly became a national concern , the new governor was unable to raise sufficient funds to maintain Fort Scott . The fort 's construction and construction were completed in 1821 , but the state legislature refused to grant the commissioners the land they were granted . The new land , called Fort Dix , was consequently purchased by the U.S. Army . The fort 's name was later changed to Fort Lee . While the two states were in dispute by the 1832 treaty , Fort Dix was located in the Horn of the Midget Valley , part of the Pan @-@ American Native Reservation . Confederate forces launched a cavalry attack on Fort Dix in early 1835 , but both sides suffered defeats to the Union . Fort Dix was declared a U.S. Army national monument by President Andrew H. Sharpe in September 1836 . Fort Dix was named after General John Scott , a U.S. Army general and the first governor of Texas , who was killed in an assassination attempt on June 20 , 1855 . Military historian John P. Pickett wrote that it was the first military governor in the United States to serve in the Confederate States |
| GNN | = Fort Scott National Historical Park =<br>Fort Scott National Historical Park is an Illinois state historic park in the U.S. state of Kentucky . It is located at $53^{\circ}25'4''$ N $65^{\circ}41'16''$ W , at the edge of the Clay Creek valley , southwest of New Orleans . It is located at the intersection of Washington Boulevard and State Route 63 , and is the largest National Historic Landmark in the state . The site was purchased by Native Americans in 1803 and the site was added to the National Register of Historic Places in 1962 . Since 1998 , the site has been subject to an extensive series of historic markers and features that are important in preservation of American historic sites in Texas . The National Park Service includes the nation 's oldest extant log cabins , historic buildings , historic facilities , and historic structures . The park is home to the Mississippi River National Historical Park , a U.S. National Monument that supplies historic sites and historic sites . The original fort was built in 1818 to protect U.S. statehood . In 1899 , the state legislature constructed a small blockhouse at the site of the original fort to defend it from Native Americans . The blockhouse first appeared in 1868 , when land in the city of Lisbon was granted to the state . The fort has remained in use since then .<br>= = History = =<br>= = = Early history = = =<br>Fort Scott was established as a civil and military fortification in 1803 and named after an American Indian . The land that would become Fort Scott was originally part of the Louisiana Purchase , which was granted to the United States by the Louisiana Purchase Act of 1825 . The original fort was established in 1828 by an act of Congress . The American Revolutionary War came to an end in 1830 , but Independence was declared in 1831 and Independence was declared on June 3 , 1830 . The post @-@ war Treaty of Paris signed at Fort Scott ended military activity in the region . War by the United States reached an end in 1830 , and most of the land was put aside for use as a military park . Fort Scott was garrisoned by 90 soldiers from the 55th Louisiana Regiment during the War of 1812 . In 1837 , the Illinois General Assembly passed legislation creating Fort Scott as a federal park , and in the same year the state agreed to purchase the site in honor of the site 's new state of Louisiana . Originally , only about half of Fort Scott was owned , but the size of the park changed in the 1880s from a forest reserve to a dirt road . The park was significantly expanded during the 1910s , but the exact date is disputed . The |

Table 9: Generated samples based on the "Fort Scott National Historic Site" graph.

| Cond. | Valid rBLEU | | | | | Valid rBLEU (w/ title) | | | | |
|---|---|---|---|---|---|---|---|---|---|---|
| | Sample length | | | | | Sample length | | | | |
| | 256 | 512 | 1024 | 2048 | 4096 | 256 | 512 | 1024 | 2048 | 4096 |
| None | 9.53 | 10.47 | 12.22 | 14.57 | 14.60 | 29.03 | 27.78 | 27.02 | 27.24 | 26.94 |
| BoW | 30.63 | 29.44 | 29.56 | 29.92 | 30.00 | 35.03 | 32.48 | 31.50 | 31.72 | 31.46 |
| Nodes | 32.33 | 30.30 | 29.82 | 30.43 | 29.91 | 35.45 | 32.88 | 31.57 | 31.79 | 31.03 |
| GNN | 33.81 | 31.32 | 30.39 | 30.53 | 30.05 | 36.49 | 32.49 | 31.70 | 31.77 | 30.79 |

Table 10: Generated samples vs sample length.

| Cond. | Valid rBLEU | | | Valid rBLEU (w/ title) | | |
|---|---|---|---|---|---|---|
| | Temperature | | | Temperature | | |
| | 0.6 | 0.8 | 1.0 | 0.6 | 0.8 | 1.0 |
| None | 12.08 | 10.47 | 9.71 | 27.09 | 27.78 | 26.21 |
| BoW | 28.21 | 29.44 | 27.63 | 31.25 | 32.48 | 31.02 |
| Nodes | 29.55 | 30.30 | 28.48 | 31.52 | 32.88 | 31.23 |
| GNN | 29.59 | 31.32 | 29.01 | 31.55 | 32.49 | 31.20 |

Table 11: Generated samples vs temperature.

# Selective Attention Based Graph Convolutional Networks for Aspect-Level Sentiment Classification

**Xiaochen Hou***, **Jing Huang, Guangtao Wang, Peng Qi,**
**Xiaodong He, Bowen Zhou**
JD AI Research, Mountain View, CA
*xclmm1994@gmail.com

## Abstract

Recent work on aspect-level sentiment classification has employed Graph Convolutional Networks (GCN) over dependency trees to learn interactions between aspect terms and opinion words. In some cases, the corresponding opinion words for an aspect term cannot be reached within two hops on dependency trees, which requires more GCN layers to model. However, GCNs often achieve the best performance with two layers, and deeper GCNs do not bring any additional gain. Therefore, we design a novel selective attention based GCN model. On one hand, the proposed model enables the direct interaction between aspect terms and context words via the self-attention operation without the distance limitation on dependency trees. On the other hand, a top-$k$ selection procedure is designed to locate opinion words by selecting $k$ context words with the highest attention scores. We conduct experiments on several commonly used benchmark datasets and the results show that our proposed *SA-GCN* outperforms strong baseline models.

## 1 Introduction

Aspect-level sentiment classification is a fine-grained sentiment analysis task, which aims to identify the sentiment polarity (e.g., positive, negative or neutral) of a specific aspect term (also called target) appearing in a sentence. For example, "*Despite a slightly limited menu, everything prepared is done to perfection, ultra fresh and a work of food art.*", the sentiment polarity of aspect terms "menu" and "food" are negative and positive, respectively. The opinion words "limited" and "done to perfection" provide evidences for sentiment polarity predictions. This task has many applications, such as restaurant recommendation and purchase recommendation on e-commerce websites.

To solve this problem, recent studies have shown that the interactions between an aspect term and its context (which include opinion words) are crucial in identifying the sentiment polarity towards the given term. Most approaches consider the semantic information from the context words and utilize the attention mechanism to learn such interactions. However, it has been shown that syntactic information obtained from dependency parsing is very effective in capturing long-range syntactic relations that are obscure from the surface form (Zhang et al., 2018). A recent popular approach to learn syntax-aware representations is employing graph convolutional networks (GCN) (Kipf and Welling, 2017) model over dependency trees (Huang and Carley, 2019; Zhang et al., 2019; Sun et al., 2019; Wang et al., 2020; Tang et al., 2020), which introduces syntactic inductive biases into the message passing.

In some cases, the most important context words, i.e. opinion words, are more than two-hops away from the aspect term words on the dependency tree. As indicated by Figure 1, there are four hops between the target "Mac OS" and the opinion words "easily picked up" on the dependency tree. This type of cases requires more than two layers of GCN to learn interactions between them. However, previous works show that GCN models with two layers often achieve the best performance (Zhang et al., 2018; Xu et al., 2018), deeper GCNs do not bring additional gain due to the over-smoothing problem (Li et al., 2018b), which makes different nodes have similar representations and lose the distinction among nodes.

In order to solve the above problem, we propose a novel selective attention based GCN (*SA-GCN*) model, which combines the GCN model over dependency trees with a self-attention based sequence model over the sentence. On one hand, the self-attention sequence model enables the direct interaction between an aspect term and its context so that it can take care of the situation where the term is far away from the opinion words on the dependency tree. On the other hand, a top-$k$ attention selection module is applied after the self-attention opera-



*Proceedings of the Fifteenth Workshop on Graph-Based Methods for Natural Language Processing (TextGraphs-15)*, pages 83–93
June 11, 2021. 

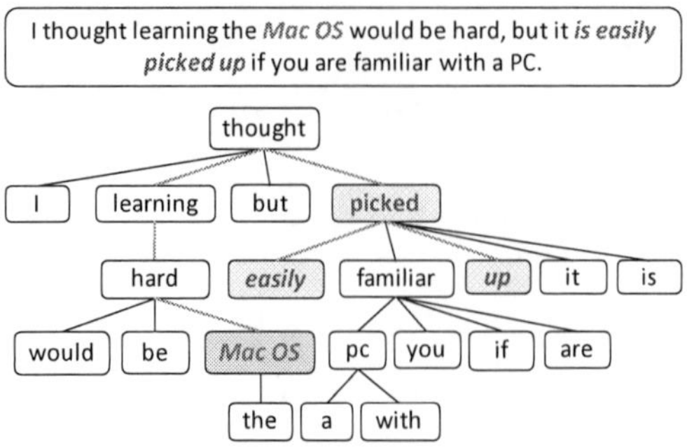


Figure 1: Example of dependency tree with multi-hop between aspect term and determined context words.

tion, which is designed to locate opinion words contained in the context for the aspect term. As shown in Figure 1, if the opinion words "easily picked up" are detected correctly through the top-$k$ selection module, it definitely could help the model to classify the sentiment as positive. To provide supervision information for the top-$k$ selection procedure, we introduce the opinion words extraction task and jointly train the task with the sentiment classification task.

Specifically, the base model is the GCN model over dependency trees. The model uses the pre-trained BERT to obtain representations of the aspect term and its context words as the initial node features on the dependency tree.

Next, the GCN outputs are fed into a multi-head top-$k$ attention selection module. For each head, the self-attention operation is applied over the sentence to get a dense attention score matrix, where $i$-th row corresponds the attention scores of all words to the $i$-th word in the sentence. Then for each word, context words with top-$k$ attention scores are selected and others are ignored, which sparsifies the attention score matrix and forms a sparse graph. We design two strategies to get the sparse graph: i) applying top-$k$ selection over the attention matrix obtained by summing attention score matrices of all heads, and thus different heads share the same sparse graph; ii) applying top-$k$ selection on individual attention score matrix of each head, and thus different heads have its own sparse graph. Finally, we apply a GCN layer again to integrate information from such sparse graph(s) for each head, and concatenate the GCN outputs w.r.t. different heads as the final word representation for sentiment analysis.

The main contributions of this work are summarized as the following:

- We propose a selective attention based GCN (*SA-GCN*) module, which takes the benefit of GCN over the dependency trees and enables the aspect term directly obtaining information from the opinion words according to most relevant context words. This helps the model handle cases when the aspect term and opinion words are located far away from each other on the dependency tree.
- We propose to jointly train the sentiment classification and opinion extraction tasks. The joint training further improves the performance of the classification task and provides explanation for sentiment prediction.

## 2 Related Work

Capturing the interaction between the aspect term and opinion words is essential for predicting the sentiment polarity towards the aspect term. In recent work, various attention mechanisms, such as co-attention, self-attention and hierarchical attention, were utilized to learn this interaction (Tang et al., 2016; Liu and Zhang, 2017; Li et al., 2018c; Wang et al., 2018; Fan et al., 2018; Chen et al., 2017; Zheng and Xia, 2018; Wang and Lu, 2018; Li et al., 2018a,c). Specifically, they first encoded the context and the aspect term by recurrent neural networks (RNNs), and then stacked several attention layers to learn the aspect term representations from important context words.

After the success of the pre-trained BERT model (Devlin et al., 2018), Song et al. (2019) utilized the pre-trained BERT as the encoder. In the study by (Xu et al., 2019), the task was considered as a review reading comprehension (RRC) problem. RRC datasets were post trained on BERT and then fine-tuned to the aspect-level sentiment classification. Rietzler et al. (2019) utilized millions of extra data based on BERT to help sentiment analysis.

The above approaches mainly considered the semantic information. Recent approaches attempted to incorporate the syntactic knowledge to learn the syntax-aware representation of the aspect term. Dong et al. (2014) proposed AdaRNN, which adaptively propagated the sentiments of words to target along the dependency tree in a bottom-up manner. Nguyen and Shirai (2015) extended RNN to obtain the representation of the target aspect by aggregating the syntactic information from the dependency and constituent tree of the sentence. He et al. (2018) proposed to use the distance between the context word and the aspect term along the dependency tree as the attention weight. Some researchers (Huang and Carley, 2019; Zhang et al., 2019; Sun et al., 2019) employed GNNs over dependency trees to aggregate information from syntactic neighbors. Most recent work in Wang et al. (2020) proposed to reconstruct the dependency tree to an aspect-oriented tree. The reshaped tree only kept the dependency structure around the aspect term and got rid of all other dependency connections, which made the learned node representations not fully syntax-aware. Tang et al. (2020) designed a mutual biaffine module between Transformer encoder and the GCN encoder to enhance the representation learning.

The downside of applying GCN over dependency trees is that it cannot elegantly handle the long distance between aspect terms and opinion words. Our proposed *SA-GCN* model effectively integrates the benefit of a GCN model over dependency trees and a self-attention sequence model to directly aggregate information from opinion words. The top-$k$ self-attention sequence model selects the most important context words, which effectively sparsifies the fully-connected graph from self-attention. Then we apply another GCN layer on top of this new sparsified graph, such that each of those important context words is directly reachable by the aspect term and the interaction between them could be learned.

# 3 Proposed Model

## 3.1 Overview of the Model

The goal of our proposed *SA-GCN* model is to predict the sentiment polarity of an aspect term in a given sentence. To improve the sentiment classification performance and provide explanations about the polarity prediction, we also introduce the opinion extraction task for joint training. The opinion extraction task aims to predict a tag sequence $\boldsymbol{y}_o = [y_1, y_2, \cdots, y_n]$ ($y_i \in \{B, I, O\}$) denotes the beginning of, inside of, and outside of opinion words. Figure 2 illustrates the overall architecture of the *SA-GCN* model. For each instance composing of a sentence-term pair, all the words in the sentence except for the aspect term are defined as context words.

## 3.2 Encoder for Aspect Term and Context

**BERT Encoder**. We use the pre-trained BERT base model as the encoder to obtain embeddings of sentence words. Suppose a sentence consists of $n$ words $\{w_1, w_2, ..., w_\tau, w_{\tau+1} ..., w_{\tau+m}, ..., w_n\}$ where $\{w_\tau, w_{\tau+1} ..., w_{\tau+m-1}\}$ stand for the aspect term containing $m$ words. First, we construct the input as "[CLS] + sentence + [SEP] + term + [SEP]" and feed it into BERT. This input format enables explicit interactions between the whole sentence and the term such that the obtained word representations are term-attended. Then, we use average pooling to summarize the information carried by sub-words from BERT and obtain final embeddings of words $\boldsymbol{X} \in \mathbb{R}^{n \times d_B}$, $d_B$ refers to the dimensionality of BERT output.

## 3.3 GCN over Dependency Trees

With words representations $\boldsymbol{X}$ as node features and dependency tree as the graph, we employ a GCN to capture syntactic relations between the term node and its neighboring nodes.

GCNs have shown to be effective for many NLP applications, such as relation extraction (Guo et al., 2019; Zhang et al., 2018), reading comprehension (Kundu et al., 2019; Tu et al., 2019), and aspect-level sentiment analysis (Huang and Carley, 2019; Zhang et al., 2019; Sun et al., 2019). In each GCN layer, a node aggregates the information from its one-hop neighbors and update its representation. In our case, the graph is represented by the dependency tree, where each word is treated as a single node and its representation is denoted as the node feature. The message passing on the graph can be formulated as follows:

$$\boldsymbol{H}^{(l)} = \sigma(\boldsymbol{A}\boldsymbol{H}^{(l-1)}\boldsymbol{W}^{(l-1)}) \tag{1}$$

where $\boldsymbol{H}^{(l)} \in \mathbb{R}^{n \times d_h}$ is the output $l$-th GCN layer, $\boldsymbol{H}^{(0)} \in \mathbb{R}^{n \times d_B}$ is the input of the first GCN layer, and $\boldsymbol{H}^{(0)} = \boldsymbol{X} \in \mathbb{R}^{n \times d_B}$. $\boldsymbol{A} \in \mathbb{R}^{n \times n}$ denotes the adjacency matrix obtained from the dependency tree, note that we add a self-loop on each node. $\boldsymbol{W}$ represents the learnable weights, where $\boldsymbol{W}^{(0)} \in \mathbb{R}^{d_B \times d_h}$ and $\boldsymbol{W}^{(l-1)} \in \mathbb{R}^{d_h \times d_h}$. $\sigma$ refers to $ReLU$ activation function.

The node features are passed through the GCN layer, the representation of each node is now further enriched by syntax information from the dependency tree.

## 3.4 SA-GCN: Selective Attention based GCN

Although performing GCNs over dependency trees brings syntax information to the representation of each word, it could still limit interactions between aspect terms and long-distance opinion words that are essential for determining the sentiment polarity. In order to alleviate the problem, we apply a

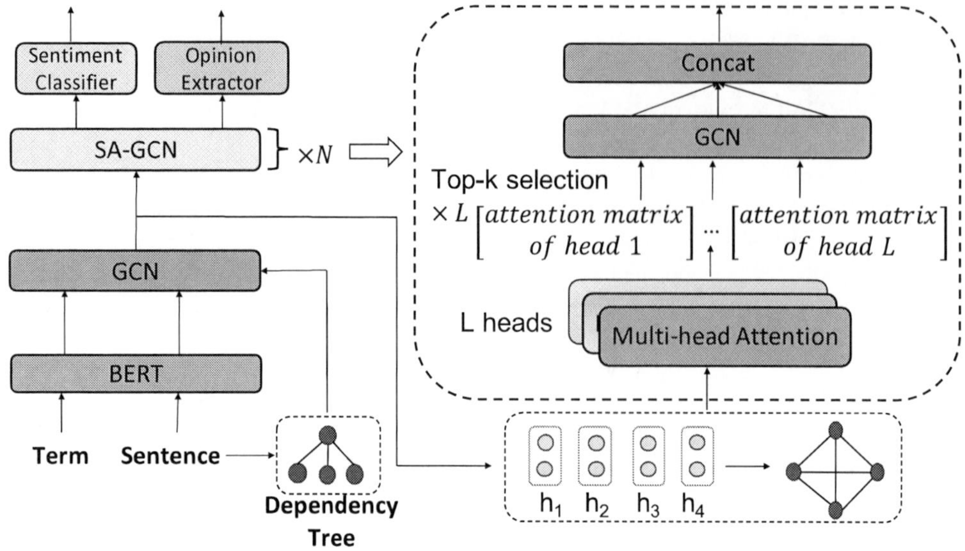


Figure 2: The *SA-GCN* model architecture: the left part is the overview of the framework, the right part shows details of a *SA-GCN* block.

Selective Attention based GCN (*SA-GCN*) block to identify the most important context words and integrate their information into the representation of the aspect term. Multiple *SA-GCN* blocks can be stacked to form a deep model. Each *SA-GCN* block is composed of three parts: a multi-head self-attention layer, top-$k$ selection and a GCN layer.

**Self-Attention.** We apply the multi-head self-attention first to get the attention score matrices $\boldsymbol{A}^i_{score} \in \mathbb{R}^{n \times n}(1 \leq i \leq L)$, $L$ is the number of heads. It can be formulated as:

$$\boldsymbol{A}^i_{score} = \frac{(\boldsymbol{H}_{k,i}\boldsymbol{W}_k)(\boldsymbol{H}_{q,i}\boldsymbol{W}_q)^T}{\sqrt{d_{head}}} \tag{2}$$

$$d_{head} = \frac{d_h}{L} \tag{3}$$

where $\boldsymbol{H}_{*,i} = \boldsymbol{H}_*[:,:,i]$, $* \in \{k\text{: key}, q\text{: query}\}$, $\boldsymbol{H}_k \in \mathbb{R}^{n \times d_{head} \times L}$ and $\boldsymbol{H}_q \in \mathbb{R}^{n \times d_{head} \times L}$ are the node representations from the previous GCN layer, $\boldsymbol{W}_k \in \mathbb{R}^{d_{head} \times d_{head}}$ and $\boldsymbol{W}_q \in \mathbb{R}^{d_{head} \times d_{head}}$ are learnable weight matrices, $d_h$ is the dimension of the input node feature, and $d_{head}$ is the dimension of each head.

The obtained attention score matrices can be considered as $L$ fully-connected (complete) graphs, where each word is connected to all the other context words with different attention weights. This kind of attention score matrix has been used in attention-guided GCNs for relation extraction (Guo et al., 2019). Although the attention weight is helpful to differentiate different words, the fully connected graph still results in the aspect node fusing all the other words information directly, and the noise is often introduced during feature aggregation in GCNs, which further hurts the sentiment prediction. Therefore, we propose a top-$k$ attention selection mechanism to sparsify the fully connected graph, and obtain a new sparse graph for feature aggregation for GCN. This is different from attention-guided GCNs (Guo et al., 2019) which performed feature aggregation over the fully-connected graph. Moreover, our experimental study (see Table 5 in Section 4) also confirms that the top-$k$ selection is quite important and definitely beneficial to the aspect-term classification task.

**Top-$k$ Selection.** For each attention score matrix $\boldsymbol{A}^i_{score}$, we find the top-$k$ important context words for each word, which effectively remove some edges in $\boldsymbol{A}^i_{score}$. The reason why we choose the top-$k$ context words is that only a few words are sufficient to determine the sentiment polarity towards an aspect term. Therefore, we discard other words with low attention scores to get rid of irrelevant noisy words.

We design two strategies for top-$k$ selection, head-independent and head-dependent. Head-independent selection determines $k$ context words by aggregating the decisions made by all heads and reaches to an agreement among heads, while head-dependent policy enables each head to keep its own selected $k$ words.

Head-independent selection is defined as following: we first sum the attention score matrix of each head element-wise, and then find top-$k$ context words using the mask generated by the function $topk$. For example, $topk([0.3, 0.2, 0.5])$ returns $[1, 0, 1]$ if $k$ is set to 2. Finally, we apply a softmax operation on the updated attention score matrix. The process could be formulated as follows:

$$\boldsymbol{A}_{sum} = \sum_{i=1}^{L} \boldsymbol{A}^i_{score} \quad (4)$$

$$\boldsymbol{A}_{m_{ind}} = topk(\boldsymbol{A}_{sum}) \quad (5)$$

$$\boldsymbol{A}^i_{h_{ind}} = softmax(\boldsymbol{A}_{m_{ind}} \circ \boldsymbol{A}^i_{score}) \quad (6)$$

where $\boldsymbol{A}^i_{score}$ is the attention score matrix of $i$-th head, $\circ$ denotes the element-wise multiplication.

Head-dependent selection finds top-$k$ context words according to the attention score matrix of each head individually. We apply the softmax operation on each top-$k$ attention matrix. This step can be formulated as:

$$\boldsymbol{A}^i_{m_{dep}} = topk(\boldsymbol{A}^i_{score}) \quad (7)$$

$$\boldsymbol{A}^i_{h_{dep}} = softmax(\boldsymbol{A}^i_{m_{dep}} \circ \boldsymbol{A}^i_{score}) \quad (8)$$

Compared to head-independent selection with exactly $k$ words selected, head-dependent usually selects a larger number (than $k$) of important context words. Because each head might choose different $k$ words thus more than $k$ words are selected in total.

From top-$k$ selection we obtain $L$ graphs based on the new attention scores and pass them to the next GCN layer. For simplicity, we will omit the $head\text{-}ind$ and $head\text{-}dep$ subscript in the later section. The obtained top-$k$ score matrix $\boldsymbol{A}$ could be treated as an adjacency matrix, where $\boldsymbol{A}(p, q)$ denotes as the weight of the edge connecting word $p$ and word $q$. Note that $\boldsymbol{A}$ does not contain self-loop, and we add a self-loop for each node.

**GCN Layer**. After top-$k$ selection on each attention score matrix $\boldsymbol{A}^i_{score}$ ($\boldsymbol{A}^i_{score}$ is not fully connected anymore), we apply a one-layer GCN and get updated node features as follows:

$$\hat{\boldsymbol{H}}^{(l,i)} = \sigma(\boldsymbol{A}^i \hat{\boldsymbol{H}}^{(l-1)} \boldsymbol{W}^i) + \hat{\boldsymbol{H}}^{(l-1)} \boldsymbol{W}^i \quad (9)$$

$$\hat{\boldsymbol{H}}^{(l)} = \|_{i=1}^{L} \hat{\boldsymbol{H}}^{(l,i)} \quad (10)$$

where $\hat{\boldsymbol{H}}^{(l)} \in \mathbb{R}^{n \times d_h}$ is the output of the $l$-th *SA-GCN* block and composed by the concatenation of $\hat{\boldsymbol{H}}^{(l,i)} \in \mathbb{R}^{n \times d_{head}}$ of $i$-th head, $\hat{\boldsymbol{H}}^{(0)} \in \mathbb{R}^{n \times d_h}$ is the input of the first *SA-GCN* block and comes from the GCN layer operating on the dependency tree, $\boldsymbol{A}^i$ is the top-$k$ score matrix of $i$-th head, $\boldsymbol{W}^i \in \mathbb{R}^{d_h \times d_{head}}$ denotes as the learnable weight matrix, and $\sigma$ refers to $ReLU$ activation function. The *SA-GCN* block can be applied multi times if needed.

### 3.5 Classifier

Based on the output $\hat{\boldsymbol{H}}_o$ of the last *SA-GCN* block, we extract the aspect term node features from $\hat{\boldsymbol{H}}_o$, and conduct average pooling to obtain the aspect term [1] representation $\hat{\boldsymbol{h}}_t \in \mathbb{R}^{1 \times d_h}$. Then we feed it into a two-layer MLP to calculate the final classification scores $\hat{\boldsymbol{y}}_s$:

$$\hat{\boldsymbol{y}}_s = softmax(\boldsymbol{W}_2 \sigma(\boldsymbol{W}_1 \hat{\boldsymbol{h}}_t^T)) \quad (11)$$

where $\boldsymbol{W}_2 \in \mathbb{R}^{C \times d_{out}}$ and $\boldsymbol{W}_1 \in \mathbb{R}^{d_{out} \times d_h}$ denote the learnable weight matrix, $C$ is the sentiment class number, and $\sigma$ refers to $ReLU$ activation function. We use cross entropy as the sentiment classification loss function:

$$L_s = -\sum_{c=1}^{C} \boldsymbol{y}_{s,c} \log \hat{\boldsymbol{y}}_{s,c} + \lambda \|\theta\|^2 \quad (12)$$

where $\lambda$ is the coefficient for L2-regularization, $\theta$ denotes the parameters that need to be regularized, $\boldsymbol{y}_s$ is the true sentiment label.

### 3.6 Opinion Extractor

The opinion extraction shares the same input encoder, i.e. the *SA-GCN* as sentiment classification. Therefore we feed the output of *SA-GCN* to a linear-chain Conditional Random Field (CRF) (Lafferty et al., 2001), which is the opinion extractor. Specifically, based on the *SA-GCN* output $\hat{\boldsymbol{H}}_o$, the output sequence $\boldsymbol{y}_o = [y_1, y_2, \cdots, y_n]$ ($y_i \in \{B, I, O\}$) is predicted as:

$$p(\boldsymbol{y}_o|\hat{\boldsymbol{H}}_o) = \frac{exp(s(\hat{\boldsymbol{H}}_o, \boldsymbol{y}_o))}{\sum_{\boldsymbol{y'}_o \in Y} exp(s(\hat{\boldsymbol{H}}_o, \boldsymbol{y'}_o))} \quad (13)$$

$$s(\hat{\boldsymbol{H}}_o, \boldsymbol{y}_o) = \sum_{i}^{n} (\boldsymbol{T}_{y_{i-1}, y_i} + \boldsymbol{P}_{i, y_i}) \quad (14)$$

$$\boldsymbol{P}_i = \boldsymbol{W}_o \hat{\boldsymbol{H}}_o[i] + \boldsymbol{b}_o \quad (15)$$

where $Y$ denotes the set of all possible tag sequences, $\boldsymbol{T}_{y_{i-1}, y_i}$ is the transition score matrix, $\boldsymbol{W}_o$ and $\boldsymbol{b}_o$ are learnable parameters. We apply Viterbi

[1]The aspect term might be composed of multiple term nodes in the graph.

| Dataset | Positive | | Neutral | | Negative | |
|---|---|---|---|---|---|---|
| | Train | Test | Train | Test | Train | Test |
| 14Lap | 991 | 341 | 462 | 169 | 867 | 128 |
| 14Rest | 2164 | 728 | 633 | 196 | 805 | 196 |
| 15Rest | 963 | 353 | 36 | 37 | 280 | 207 |
| 16Rest | 1324 | 483 | 71 | 32 | 489 | 135 |

Table 1: Statistics of Datasets.

algorithm in the decoding phase. And the loss for opinion extraction task is defined as:

$$L_o = -log(p(\boldsymbol{y}_o|\hat{\boldsymbol{H}}_o)) \tag{16}$$

Finally, the total training loss is:

$$L = L_s + \alpha L_o \tag{17}$$

where $\alpha \geq 0$ represents the weight of opinion extraction task.

## 4 Experiments

**Data Sets**. We evaluate our *SA-GCN* model on four datasets: Laptop reviews from SemEval 2014 Task 4 (14Lap), Restaurant reviews from SemEval 2014 Task 4 (Pontiki et al., 2014), SemEval 2015 Task 12 (Pontiki et al., 2015) and SemEval 2016 Task 5 (Pontiki et al., 2016) (14Rest, 15Rest and 16Rest). We remove several examples with "conflict" labels. The statistics of these datasets are listed in Table 1. The opinion words labeling for these four datasets come from (Fan et al., 2019).

**Baselines**. Since BERT(Devlin et al., 2018) model shows significant improvements over many NLP tasks, we directly implement *SA-GCN* based on BERT and compare with following BERT-based baseline models:

1. **BERT-SPC** (Song et al., 2019) feeds the sentence and term pair into the BERT model and the BERT outputs are used for prediction.
2. **AEN-BERT** (Song et al., 2019) uses BERT as the encoder and employs several attention layers.
3. **TD-GAT-BERT** (Huang and Carley, 2019) utilizes GAT on the dependency tree to propagate features from the syntactic context.
4. **DGEDT-BERT** (Tang et al., 2020) proposes a mutual biaffine module to jointly consider the flat representations learnt from Transformer and graph-based representations learnt from the corresponding dependency graph in an iterative manner.
5. **R-GAT+BERT** (Wang et al., 2020) reshapes and prunes the dependency parsing tree to an aspect-oriented tree rooted at the aspect term, and then employs relational GAT to encode the new tree for sentiment predictions.

In our experiments, we present results of the average and standard deviation numbers from seven runs of different random initialization. We use BERT-base model to compare with other published numbers. We implement our own *BERT-baseline* by directly applying a classifier on top of BERT-base encoder, *BERT+2-layer GCN* and *BERT+4-layer GCN* are models with 2-layer and 4-layer GCN respectively on dependency trees with the BERT encoder. *BERT+SA-GCN* is our proposed *SA-GCN* model with BERT encoder. *Joint SA-GCN* refers to joint training of sentiment classification and opinion extraction tasks.

**Evaluation metrics**. We train the model on training set, and evaluate the performance on test set in terms of accuracy and macro-F1 scores which are commonly-used in sentiment analysis (Sun et al., 2019; Tang et al., 2016; Wang et al., 2020).

**Parameter Setting**. During training, we set the learning rate to $10^{-5}$. The batch size is 4. We train the model up to 5 epochs with Adam optimizer. We obtain dependency trees using the Stanford Stanza (Qi et al., 2020). The dimension of BERT output $d_B$ is 768. The hidden dimensions are selected from $\{128, 256, 512\}$. We apply dropout (Srivastava et al., 2014) and the dropout rate range is $[0.1, 0.4]$. The L2 regularization is set to $10^{-6}$. We use 1 or 2 *SA-GCN* blocks in our experiments. We choose $k$ in top-$k$ selection module from $\{2, 3\}$ to achieve the best performance. For joint training, the weight range of opinion extraction loss is $[0.05, 0.15]$.[2]

### 4.1 Experimental Results

We present results of the *SA-GCN* model in two aspects: classification performance and qualitative case study.

**Classification**. Table 2 shows comparisons of *SA-GCN* with other baselines in terms of classification accuracy and Macro-F1. From this table, we observe that: *SA-GCN* achieves the best average results on 14Lap, 15Rest and 16Rest datasets, and obtains competitive results on 14Rest dataset. The joint training of sentiment classification and opin-

[2]Our code will be released at the time of publication.

| Category | Model | 14Rest | | 14Lap | | 15Rest | | 16Rest | |
|---|---|---|---|---|---|---|---|---|---|
| | | Acc | Macro-F1 | Acc | Macro-F1 | Acc | Macro-F1 | Acc | Macro-F1 |
| BERT | BERT-SPC | 84.46 | 76.98 | 78.99 | 75.03 | - | - | - | - |
| | AEN-BERT | 83.12 | 73.76 | 79.93 | 76.31 | - | - | - | - |
| BERT+DT* | TD-GAT-BERT | 83.0 | - | 80.1 | - | - | - | - | - |
| | DGEDT-BERT | 86.3 | 80.0 | 79.8 | 75.6 | 84.0 | **71.0** | **91.9** | 79.0 |
| BERT+RDT◇ | R-GAT+BERT | **86.60** | **81.35** | 78.21 | 74.07 | - | - | - | - |
| Ours | BERT-baseline | $85.56 \pm 0.30$ | $79.21 \pm 0.45$ | $79.57 \pm 0.15$ | $76.18 \pm 0.31$ | $83.45 \pm 1.13$ | $69.29 \pm 1.78$ | $91.06 \pm 0.44$ | $78.58 \pm 1.62$ |
| | BERT+2-layer GCN | $85.78 \pm 0.59$ | $80.55 \pm 0.90$ | $79.72 \pm 0.31$ | $76.31 \pm 0.35$ | $83.71 \pm 0.42$ | $69.26 \pm 1.63$ | $91.23 \pm 0.25$ | $79.29 \pm 0.51$ |
| | BERT+4-layer GCN | $85.03 \pm 0.64$ | $78.90 \pm 0.75$ | $79.57 \pm 0.15$ | $76.23 \pm 0.49$ | $83.48 \pm 0.33$ | $68.72 \pm 1.08$ | $91.02 \pm 0.26$ | $78.68 \pm 0.50$ |
| | BERT+*SA-GCN*† | $86.16 \pm 0.23$ | $80.54 \pm 0.38$ | **80.31** $\pm 0.47$ | **76.99** $\pm 0.59$ | **84.18** $\pm 0.29$ | $69.42 \pm 0.81$ | $91.41 \pm 0.39$ | **80.39** $\pm 0.93$ |
| | Joint *SA-GCN* | $86.57 \pm 0.81$ | $81.14 \pm 0.69$ | **80.61** $\pm 0.32$ | **77.12** $\pm 0.51$ | **84.63** $\pm 0.33$ | $69.1 \pm 0.78$ | $91.54 \pm 0.26$ | **80.68** $\pm 0.92$ |
| | Joint *SA-GCN* (Best◇) | **87.68** | **82.45** | **81.03** | **77.71** | **85.26** | 69.71 | **92.0** | **81.86** |

⋆ DT: Dependency Tree; ◇ RDT: Reshaped Dependency Tree.
†: Head-independent based top-$k$ Selection.
◇ The "best" denotes as the best performances of our *SA-GCN* model from the seven runs. Row "Joint-SA-GCN" reports the average and std of these seven runs.

Table 2: Comparison of *SA-GCN* with various baselines.

| Sentence | Label | GCN | *SA-GCN* |
|---|---|---|---|
| Satay is one of those favorite haunts on Washington where the service and food is always on the money. | positive | neutral | positive |
| And the fact that it comes with an i5 processor definitely speeds things up | positive | neutral | positive |
| I know real Indian food and this was n't it. | negative | neutral | negative |

Table 3: Top-$k$ visualization: the darker the shade, the larger attention weight.

ion extraction tasks further boosts the performances on all datasets.

Specifically, *BERT+2-layer GCN* outperforms *BERT-baseline*, which proves the benefit of using syntax information. *BERT+4-layer GCN* is actually worse than *BERT+2-layer GCN*, which shows that more GCN layers do not bring additional gain.

Our *BERT+SA-GCN* model further outperforms the *BERT+2-layer GCN* model. Because the *SA-GCN* block allows aspect terms to directly absorb the information from the most important context words that are not reachable within two hops in the dependency tree.

Besides, introducing the opinion extraction task provides more supervision signals for the top-$k$ selection module, which benefits the sentiment classification task.

**Qualitative Case Study**. To show the efficacy of the *SA-GCN* model on dealing long-hops between aspect term and its opinion words, we demonstrate three examples as shown in Table 3. These sentences are selected from test sets of 14Lap and 14Rest datasets and predicted correctly by the *SA-GCN* model but wrongly by *BERT+2-layer GCN*. The important thing to note here, our *SA-GCN* model could provide explanation about the prediction according to the learned attention weights, while the GCN based model (*BERT+2-layer GCN* denoted as "GCN" in Table 3) cannot. Aspect terms are colored red. Top-3 words with the largest attention weights towards the aspect term are shaded. The darker the shade, the larger attention weight.

In all three examples the aspect terms are more than three hops away from essential opinion words (Please refer to Fig. 3), thus *BERT+2-layer GCN* model cannot learn the interactions between them within two layers, while *SA-GCN* model overcomes the distance limitation and locates right opinion words.

| Model | 14Rest | 14Lap | 15Rest | 16Rest |
|---|---|---|---|---|
| | F1 | F1 | F1 | F1 |
| IOG | 80.24 | 71.39 | 73.51 | 81.84 |
| ASTE | 83.15 | 76.03 | 78.02 | 83.73 |
| Joint *SA-GCN* | **83.72** $\pm 0.51$ | **76.79** $\pm 0.33$ | **80.99** $\pm 0.43$ | **83.83** $\pm 0.50$ |

Table 4: Opinion extraction results.

**Opinion Extraction**. Table 4 shows the results of the opinion extraction task under the joint training setting. The reported numbers are obtained by averaging F1 of seven runs. In each run, the selected opinion F1 is generated from the best sentiment classification checkpoint. We compare our model with two baselines: **IOG** (Fan et al., 2019) encodes the aspect term information into context by an Inward-Outward LSTM to find the corresponding opinion words. **ASTE** (Peng et al., 2020) utilizes a GCN module to learn the mutual dependency relations between different words and to guide opinion term extraction. As shown in this table, the joint *SA-GCN* model outperforms two baseline models on all datasets, which demonstrates that the sentiment classification task is helpful for opinion extraction task as well.

### 4.2 Model Analysis

We further analyze our *SA-GCN* model from two perspectives: ablation study and sentence length analysis.

**Ablation Study**. To demonstrate effectiveness of different modules in *SA-GCN*, we conduct ablation

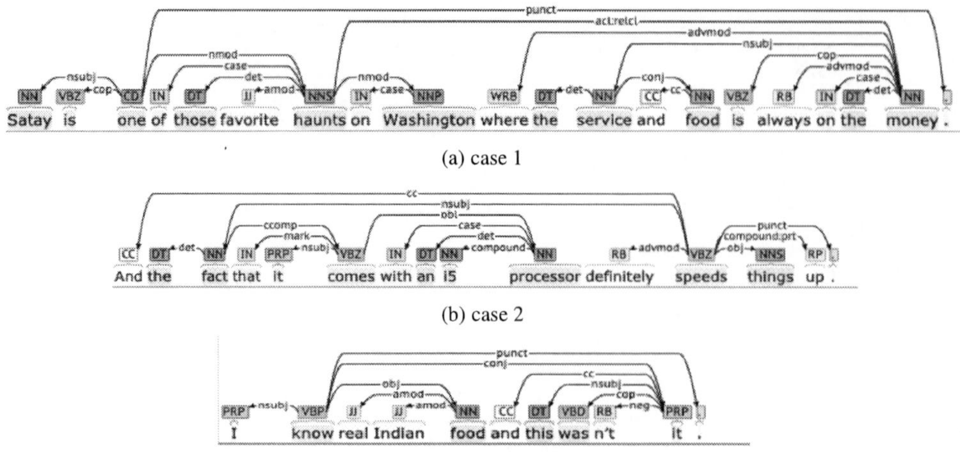


(a) case 1

(b) case 2

(c) case 3

Figure 3: Dependency trees of case study. Case 1: the aspect term "food" is four hops away from the opinion words "favorite" and "on the money". In cases 2 and 3, there are also three-hops distance between aspect terms and opinion words.

| Model | 14Rest | | 14Lap | | 15Rest | | 16Rest | |
|---|---|---|---|---|---|---|---|---|
| | Acc | Macro-F1 | Acc | Macro-F1 | Acc | Macro-F1 | Acc | Macro-F1 |
| *SA-GCN* (head-ind) | **86.16** ± 0.23 | **80.54** ± 0.38 | **80.31** ± 0.47 | **76.99** ± 0.59 | **84.18** ± 0.29 | 69.42 ± 0.81 | **91.41**± 0.39 | **80.39** ± 0.93 |
| *SA-GCN* w/o top-k | 85.06 ± 0.68 | 78.88 ± 0.83 | 79.96 ± 0.14 | 76.64 ± 0.58 | 83.15 ± 0.41 | 68.74 ± 1.48 | 90.92 ± 0.45 | 78.18 ± 0.71 |
| *SA-GCN* (head-dep)$^\diamond$ | 85.41 ± 0.21 | 79.19 ± 0.68 | 80.17 ± 0.55 | 76.83 ± 0.59 | 83.68 ± 0.54 | 68.81 ± 1.39 | 91.01 ± 0.40 | 78.88 ± 1.04 |

$^\diamond$ head-dep: head-dependent based top-$k$ selection.

Table 5: Ablation study of *SA-GCN*.

studies in Table 5. From this table, we observe that:

1. **Effect of Top-k Selection**. To examine the impact the top-k selection, we present the result of *SA-GCN w/o top-k* in Table 5. We can see that without top-k selection, both accuracy and macro-F1 decrease on all datasets. This observation proves that the top-k selection helps to reduce the noisy context and locate top important opinion words. We also conduct the effect of the hyper-parameter $k$ and the block number $N$ on *SA-GCN* under head-independent and head-dependent selection respectively (see the supplemental material).

2. **Effect of Head-independent and Head-dependent Selection**. As shown in the last row in Table 5, head-independent selection achieves better results than head-dependent selection. This is because the mechanism of head-independent selection is similar to voting. By summing up the weight scores from each head, context words with higher scores in most heads get emphasized, and words that only show importance in few heads are filtered out. Thus all heads reach to an agreement and the top-$k$ context words are decided. However for head-dependent selection, each head selects different top-$k$ context words, which is more likely to choose certain unimportant context words and introduce noise to the model prediction.

**Sentence Length Analysis**. To quantify the ability of our *SA-GCN* model dealing with long-distance problem, we conduct sentence length analysis on 14Lap and 14Rest datasets. The assumption is that the longer the sentence, the more likely the long-distance problem occurs. The results are showed in Figure 4. We measure the sentiment classification accuracy of *BERT+2-layer GCN* (denotes as GCN in Figure 4) and *BERT+SA-GCN* models under different sentence lengths. We observe that *SA-GCN* achieves better accuracy than GCN across all length ranges and is more advantageous when sentences are longer. To some extent, the results prove effectiveness of *SA-GCN* in dealing with long-distance problem.

**Hyper-parameter Analysis**. We examine the effect of the hype-parameter $k$ and the block number $N$ on our proposed model under head-independent and head-dependent selection respectively. Figure 5 shows the results on 14Rest dataset.

1. **Effect of Hyper-parameter** $k$. From Figure

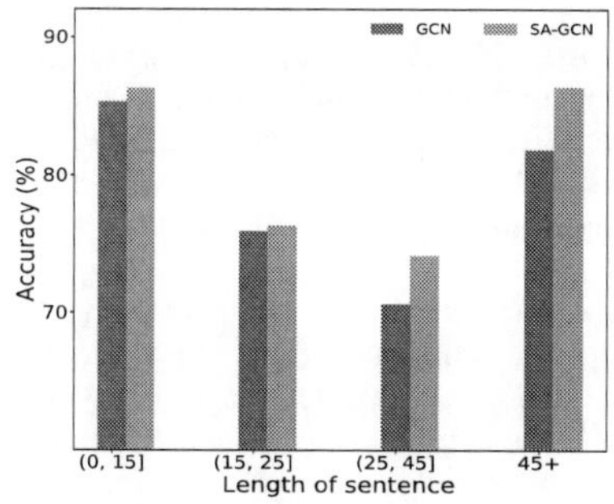


(a) Length analysis on 14Lap.

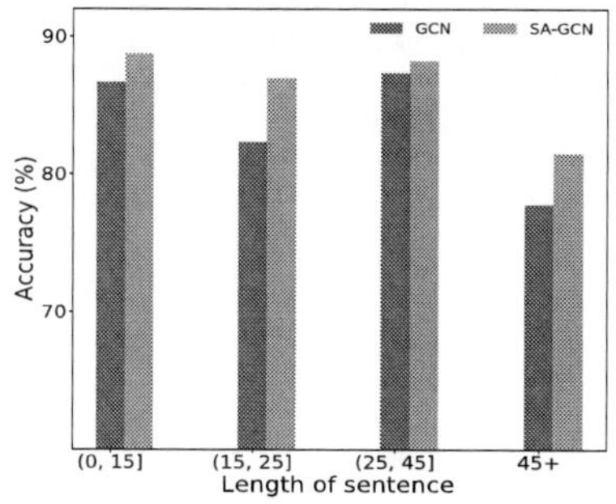


(b) Length analysis on 14Rest.

Figure 4: Sentence length analysis on 14Lap and 14Rest.

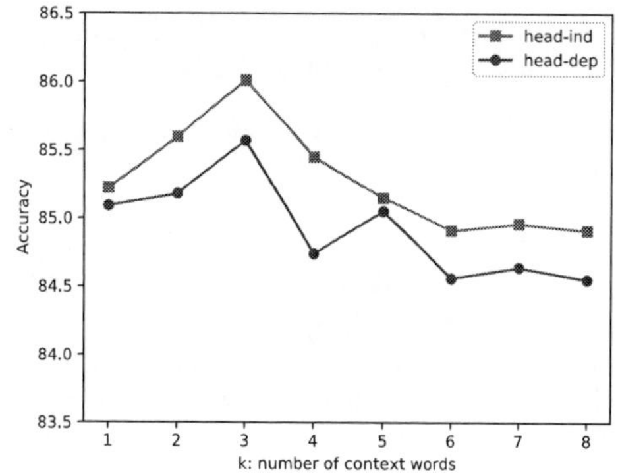


(a) Impact of $k$

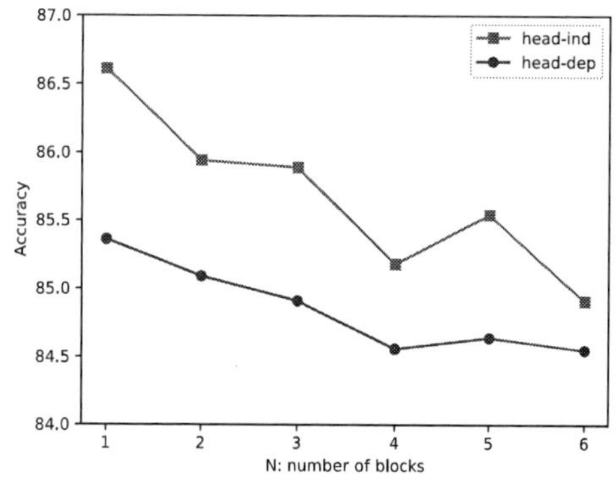


(b) Impact of block numbers

Figure 5: Impact of $k$ and block numbers on *SA-GCN* over Restaurant dataset.

5a, we observe that: 1) the highest accuracy appears when $k$ is equal to 3. As $k$ becomes bigger, the accuracy goes down. The reason is that integrating information from too many context words could introduce distractions and confuse the representation of the current word. 2) Head-independent selection performs better than head-dependent selection as $k$ increases. As mentioned before, compared with head-independent, head-dependent selection might have more than $k$ context words contribute to the aggregation and introduce some noise.

2. **Effect of Block Number**. Figure 5b shows the effect of different number of *SA-GCN* blocks. As the block number increases, the accuracy decreases for both head-independent and head-dependent selection. A single *SA-GCN* block is sufficient for selecting top-$k$ important context words. Stacking multiple blocks introduces more parameters and thus would lead to overfitting with such a small amount of training data. This might be the reason why stacking multiple blocks is not helpful. For our future work we plan to look into suitable deeper GNN models that are good for this task.

## 5 Conclusions

We propose a selective attention based GCN model for the aspect-level sentiment classification task. We first encode the aspect term and context words by pre-trained BERT to capture the interaction between them, then build a GCN on the dependency tree to incorporate syntax information. In order to handle the long distance between aspect terms and opinion words, we use the selective attention based GCN block, to select the top-$k$ important context words and employ the GCN to integrate their information for the aspect term representation learning. Further, we adopt opinion extraction problem as an auxiliary task to jointly train with sentiment classification task. We conduct experiments on several SemEval datasets. The results show that *SA-GCN* achieve better performances than previous strong baselines.

## References

Peng Chen, Zhongqian Sun, Lidong Bing, and Wei Yang. 2017. Recurrent attention network on memory for aspect sentiment analysis. In *Proceedings of the 2017 conference on empirical methods in natural language processing*, pages 452–461.

Jacob Devlin, Ming-Wei Chang, Kenton Lee, and Kristina Toutanova. 2018. Bert: Pre-training of deep bidirectional transformers for language understanding. *Proceedings of NAACL-HLT 2019*, page pages 4171–4186.

Li Dong, Furu Wei, Chuanqi Tan, Duyu Tang, Ming Zhou, and Ke Xu. 2014. Adaptive recursive neural network for target-dependent twitter sentiment classification. In *Proceedings of the 52nd annual meeting of the association for computational linguistics (volume 2: Short papers)*, pages 49–54.

Feifan Fan, Yansong Feng, and Dongyan Zhao. 2018. Multi-grained attention network for aspect-level sentiment classification. In *Proceedings of the 2018 Conference on Empirical Methods in Natural Language Processing*, pages 3433–3442.

Zhifang Fan, Zhen Wu, Xinyu Dai, Shujian Huang, and Jiajun Chen. 2019. Target-oriented opinion words extraction with target-fused neural sequence labeling. In *Proceedings of the 2019 Conference of the North American Chapter of the Association for Computational Linguistics: Human Language Technologies, Volume 1 (Long and Short Papers)*, pages 2509–2518.

Zhijiang Guo, Yan Zhang, and Wei Lu. 2019. Attention guided graph convolutional networks for relation extraction. *57th Annual Meeting of the Association for Computational Linguistics*, page 241–251.

Ruidan He, Wee Sun Lee, Hwee Tou Ng, and Daniel Dahlmeier. 2018. Effective attention modeling for aspect-level sentiment classification. In *Proceedings of the 27th International Conference on Computational Linguistics*, pages 1121–1131.

Binxuan Huang and Kathleen M Carley. 2019. Syntax-aware aspect level sentiment classification with graph attention networks. In *Proceedings of the 2019 Conference on Empirical Methods in Natural Language Processing and the 9th International Joint Conference on Natural Language Processing (EMNLP-IJCNLP)*, pages 5472–5480.

Thomas N. Kipf and Max Welling. 2017. Semi-supervised classification with graph convolutional networks. In *International Conference on Learning Representations (ICLR)*.

Souvik Kundu, Tushar Khot, Ashish Sabharwal, and Peter Clark. 2019. Exploiting explicit paths for multi-hop reading comprehension. In *Proceedings of the 57th Annual Meeting of the Association for Computational Linguistics*, pages 2737–2747. Association for Computational Linguistics.

John Lafferty, Andrew McCallum, and Fernando CN Pereira. 2001. Conditional random fields: Probabilistic models for segmenting and labeling sequence data.

Lishuang Li, Yang Liu, and AnQiao Zhou. 2018a. Hierarchical attention based position-aware network for aspect-level sentiment analysis. In *Proceedings of the 22nd Conference on Computational Natural Language Learning*, pages 181–189.

Qimai Li, Zhichao Han, and Xiao-Ming Wu. 2018b. Deeper insights into graph convolutional networks for semi-supervised learning. In *Thirty-Second AAAI Conference on Artificial Intelligence*.

Xin Li, Lidong Bing, Wai Lam, and Bei Shi. 2018c. Transformation networks for target-oriented sentiment classification. In *Proceedings of the 56th Annual Meeting of the Association for Computational Linguistics (Volume 1: Long Papers)*, pages 946–956, Melbourne, Australia. Association for Computational Linguistics.

Jiangming Liu and Yue Zhang. 2017. Attention modeling for targeted sentiment. In *Proceedings of the 15th Conference of the European Chapter of the Association for Computational Linguistics: Volume 2, Short Papers*, pages 572–577.

Thien Hai Nguyen and Kiyoaki Shirai. 2015. Phrasernn: Phrase recursive neural network for aspect-based sentiment analysis. In *Proceedings of the 2015 Conference on Empirical Methods in Natural Language Processing*, pages 2509–2514.

Haiyun Peng, Lu Xu, Lidong Bing, Fei Huang, Wei Lu, and Luo Si. 2020. Knowing what, how and why: A near complete solution for aspect-based sentiment analysis. In *AAAI*, pages 8600–8607.

Maria Pontiki, Dimitris Galanis, Haris Papageorgiou, Ion Androutsopoulos, Suresh Manandhar, Mohammad AL-Smadi, Mahmoud Al-Ayyoub, Yanyan Zhao, Bing Qin, Orphée De Clercq, Véronique Hoste, Marianna Apidianaki, Xavier Tannier, Natalia Loukachevitch, Evgeniy Kotelnikov, Nuria Bel, Salud María Jiménez-Zafra, and Gülşen Eryiğit. 2016. SemEval-2016 task 5: Aspect based sentiment analysis. In *Proceedings of the 10th International Workshop on Semantic Evaluation (SemEval-2016)*, pages 19–30, San Diego, California. Association for Computational Linguistics.

Maria Pontiki, Dimitris Galanis, Haris Papageorgiou, Suresh Manandhar, and Ion Androutsopoulos. 2015. SemEval-2015 task 12: Aspect based sentiment analysis. In *Proceedings of the 9th International Workshop on Semantic Evaluation (SemEval 2015)*, pages 486–495, Denver, Colorado. Association for Computational Linguistics.

Maria Pontiki, Dimitris Galanis, John Pavlopoulos, Harris Papageorgiou, Ion Androutsopoulos, and Suresh Manandhar. 2014. SemEval-2014 task 4: Aspect based sentiment analysis. In *Proceedings of the 8th International Workshop on Semantic Evaluation (SemEval 2014)*, pages 27–35, Dublin, Ireland. Association for Computational Linguistics.

Peng Qi, Yuhao Zhang, Yuhui Zhang, Jason Bolton, and Christopher D. Manning. 2020. Stanza: A Python natural language processing toolkit for many human languages. In *Proceedings of the 58th Annual Meeting of the Association for Computational Linguistics: System Demonstrations*.

Alexander Rietzler, Sebastian Stabinger, Paul Opitz, and Stefan Engl. 2019. Adapt or get left behind: Domain adaptation through bert language model finetuning for aspect-target sentiment classification. *arXiv preprint arXiv:1908.11860*.

Youwei Song, Jiahai Wang, Tao Jiang, Zhiyue Liu, and Yanghui Rao. 2019. Attentional encoder network for targeted sentiment classification. *arXiv preprint arXiv:1902.09314*.

Nitish Srivastava, Geoffrey Hinton, Alex Krizhevsky, Ilya Sutskever, and Ruslan Salakhutdinov. 2014. Dropout: a simple way to prevent neural networks from overfitting. *The Journal of Machine Learning Research*, 15(1):1929–1958.

Kai Sun, Richong Zhang, Samuel Mensah, Yongyi Mao, and Xudong Liu. 2019. Aspect-level sentiment analysis via convolution over dependency tree. In *Proceedings of the 2019 Conference on Empirical Methods in Natural Language Processing and the 9th International Joint Conference on Natural Language Processing (EMNLP-IJCNLP)*, pages 5683–5692.

Duyu Tang, Bing Qin, Xiaocheng Feng, and Ting Liu. 2016. Effective LSTMs for target-dependent sentiment classification. In *Proceedings of COLING 2016, the 26th International Conference on Computational Linguistics: Technical Papers*, pages 3298–3307, Osaka, Japan. The COLING 2016 Organizing Committee.

Hao Tang, Donghong Ji, Chenliang Li, and Qiji Zhou. 2020. Dependency graph enhanced dual-transformer structure for aspect-based sentiment classification. In *Proceedings of the 58th Annual Meeting of the Association for Computational Linguistics*, pages 6578–6588, Online. Association for Computational Linguistics.

Ming Tu, Guangtao Wang, Jing Huang, Yun Tang, Xiaodong He, and Bowen Zhou. 2019. Multi-hop reading comprehension across multiple documents by reasoning over heterogeneous graphs. *57th Annual Meeting of the Association for Computational Linguistics*, page pages 2704–2713.

Bailin Wang and Wei Lu. 2018. Learning latent opinions for aspect-level sentiment classification. In *Thirty-Second AAAI Conference on Artificial Intelligence*.

Kai Wang, Weizhou Shen, Yunyi Yang, Xiaojun Quan, and Rui Wang. 2020. Relational graph attention network for aspect-based sentiment analysis. In *Proceedings of the 58th Annual Meeting of the Association for Computational Linguistics*, pages 3229–3238, Online. Association for Computational Linguistics.

Shuai Wang, Sahisnu Mazumder, Bing Liu, Mianwei Zhou, and Yi Chang. 2018. Target-sensitive memory networks for aspect sentiment classification. In *Proceedings of the 56th Annual Meeting of the Association for Computational Linguistics (Volume 1: Long Papers)*, pages 957–967.

Hu Xu, Bing Liu, Lei Shu, and Philip S. Yu. 2019. Bert post-training for review reading comprehension and aspect-based sentiment analysis. In *Proceedings of the 2019 Conference of the North American Chapter of the Association for Computational Linguistics*.

Keyulu Xu, Chengtao Li, Yonglong Tian, Tomohiro Sonobe, Ken-ichi Kawarabayashi, and Stefanie Jegelka. 2018. Representation learning on graphs with jumping knowledge networks. In *Proceedings of the 35th International Conference on Machine Learning*, volume 80 of *Proceedings of Machine Learning Research*, pages 5453–5462. PMLR.

Chen Zhang, Qiuchi Li, and Dawei Song. 2019. Aspect-based sentiment classification with aspect-specific graph convolutional networks. In *Proceedings of the 2019 Conference on Empirical Methods in Natural Language Processing and the 9th International Joint Conference on Natural Language Processing (EMNLP-IJCNLP)*, pages 4560–4570.

Yuhao Zhang, Peng Qi, and Christopher D Manning. 2018. Graph convolution over pruned dependency trees improves relation extraction. *In Proceedings of the 2018 Conference on Empirical Methods in Natural Language Processing*, pages 2205–2215.

Shiliang Zheng and Rui Xia. 2018. Left-center-right separated neural network for aspect-based sentiment analysis with rotatory attention. *arXiv preprint arXiv:1802.00892*.

# Keyword Extraction Using Unsupervised Learning on the Document's Adjacency Matrix

**Eirini Papagiannopoulou** and **Grigorios Tsoumakas** and **Apostolos N. Papadopoulos**
School of Informatics, Aristotle University of Thessaloniki, 54124 Thessaloniki, Greece
{epapagia,greg,papadopo}@csd.auth.gr

## Abstract

This work revisits the information given by the graph-of-words and its typical utilization through graph-based ranking approaches in the context of keyword extraction. Recent, well-known graph-based approaches typically employ the knowledge from word vector representations during the ranking process via popular centrality measures (e.g., PageRank) without giving the primary role to vectors' distribution. We consider the adjacency matrix that corresponds to the graph-of-words of a target text document as the vector representation of its vocabulary. We propose the distribution-based modeling of this adjacency matrix using unsupervised (learning) algorithms. The efficacy of the distribution-based modeling approaches compared to state-of-the-art graph-based methods is confirmed by an extensive experimental study according to the $F_1$ score. Our code is available on GitHub[1].

## 1 Introduction

Automatic Keyword Extraction (AKE) intends to discover a limited but concise set of words that reflect the main topics discussed within a text document, avoiding the expensive and time-consuming process of manual annotation by experts (Vega-Oliveros et al., 2019). Besides, many keyphrase extraction methods form and rank the candidate phrases using the previously scored candidate unigrams by a keyword extractor, as keyphrases consist of n-grams with $n \geq 1$ (Wan and Xiao, 2008a; Hasan and Ng, 2014; Florescu and Caragea, 2017).

Both supervised and unsupervised approaches are quite famous for the AKE task (Papagiannopoulou and Tsoumakas, 2020). During the last two years, the research community pays significant attention on (supervised) deep learning methods (Chan et al., 2019; Wang et al., 2019; Zhao and Zhang, 2019; Chen et al., 2020) as the performance of the unsupervised ones shows a relative stagnation (or minimal improvements) compared to the supervised techniques. The use of standard external tools for grammatical/syntactic analysis and information sources such as (pre-trained) static word embeddings (Bennani-Smires et al., 2018; Mahata et al., 2018) that have a bias over the corpora domains used for training may also exacerbate the problem. Moreover, most methods suggest a fixed or relative with the document length number of keywords dissociating the number of returned keywords from the number of topics discussed in the document (Rousseau and Vazirgiannis, 2015). However, unsupervised methods are of timeless interest. They often are domain or language-independent and do not need any labelled data to train models compared to the supervised ones. The graph-based approaches (i.e., the most popular category of the unsupervised AKE) consider the "central" nodes of a graph-of-words as the most representative ones usually according to (variations of) the PageRank (Brin and Page, 1998) centrality, i.e., the most effective graph-based ranking method employed by the majority of the state-of-the-art (Mihalcea and Tarau, 2004; Wan and Xiao, 2008b; Florescu and Caragea, 2017; Vega-Oliveros et al., 2019). Additionally, traditional (semi-)supervised, or even deep learning approaches (Wang and Li, 2017; Gollapalli et al., 2017; Ye and Wang, 2018) utilize the unsupervised methods mentioned earlier to improve their performance.

This work takes a novel unsupervised path to keyword extraction revisiting the information provided by the graph-of-words and its conventional utilization via PageRank. Inspired by the recent approach of Papagiannopoulou et al. (2020), we investigate the effectiveness of the distribution-based modeling of the adjacency matrix, that corresponds to various versions of the (unweighted,

[1] `https://github.com/epapagia/KE_adjacency_matrix_modelling`



*Proceedings of the Fifteenth Workshop on Graph-Based Methods for Natural Language Processing (TextGraphs-15)*, pages 94–105
June 11, 2021. 

weighted or/and enhanced with positional information) graph-of-words for the target document. We also propose the use of more advanced unsupervised algorithms to model the main distribution of the adjacency matrix, determine the number of the retrieved keywords at document level, and score/rank the corresponding candidate keywords. To the best of our knowledge, this is the first work that proposes such modeling of the adjacency matrix using unsupervised machine learning approaches in the context of keyword extraction. Our empirical study confirms the efficacy of the distribution-based modeling approaches (regarding the $F_1$ score) on six datasets (full-texts of scientific publications, paper abstracts and news articles) compared to state-of-the-art graph-based methods.

The main contributions of this work are as follows: (a) We propose multiple ways for the distribution-based modeling of the adjacency matrix that corresponds to various versions of the graph-of-words for a target document. Specifically, we investigate the use of unsupervised (learning) algorithms to model the distribution of the adjacency matrix, score the candidate words, and (b) discover the appropriate number of keywords (Section 3). (c) Our empirical study provides strong evidence about the relationship between the graph-based techniques and the proposed ones emphasizing the cases that the distribution-based modeling is more promising (Section 4). Finally, Section 2 and 5 present related work on unsupervised AKE (issues/trends) as well as conclusions and future directions of our work, respectively.

## 2 Related Work

**Issues**. The comprehensive representation of the information via graphs and the efficiency of the graph-based ranking methods (e.g., PageRank (Brin and Page, 1998), HITS (Kleinberg, 1999), etc.) in many applications (including keyword extraction) led the research community to show a preference to graph-based AKE using unsupervised approaches (Papagiannopoulou and Tsoumakas, 2020). The popular TextRank (Mihalcea and Tarau, 2004) first builds an undirected, unweighted graph-of-words representation and runs the PageRank algorithm until convergence. In this vein, SingleRank (Wan and Xiao, 2008b), RAKE (Rose et al., 2010), ExpandRank (Wan and Xiao, 2008b), and CollabRank (Wan and Xiao, 2008a) are extensions of TextRank. The first two methods add weights to edges, equal to the number of co-occurrences of the two corresponding words within the predefined window, whereas, the last ones incorporate information from relevant documents. Much later, PositionRank (Florescu and Caragea, 2017) achieved significantly higher performance proposing a biased PageRank that considers both the word-word co-occurrences and the word's positions. Then, Biswas et al. (2018) and Vega-Oliveros et al. (2019) proposed graph-based keyword extraction methods that combine multiple centrality measures.

Another important issue is choosing the right number of keywords for a document. Rousseau and Vazirgiannis (2015) apply the concept of K-Core on the graph-of-words of a document retaining only the nodes from the main core as keywords. Their method is parameter-free as the K-Core principle adjusts the number of keywords concerning each graph's structure. Later, Tixier et al. (2016) show that retaining only the main core (or truss (Cohen, 2008)) is suboptimal as the complete set of a document's gold keywords cannot appear within a single subgraph and propose alternative heuristics (stopping criteria) to remove undesired words.

**Trends**. Information coming from word embeddings (Mikolov et al., 2013) proved useful for the AKE task. Numerous AKE methods use word embeddings (Mnih and Hinton, 2007; Bojanowski et al., 2017; Joulin et al., 2017) as an (external) semantic knowledge source. Representative graph-based approaches are the one of Wang et al. (2015) and Key2Vec (Mahata et al., 2018) that incorporate semantic information from pre-trained distributed word representations and word embeddings trained on a domain-specific corpus, respectively. Both methods utilize the information from word embeddings through the usual way of graph-based ranking without giving to the vector representation of terms the primary role. On the contrary, Papagiannopoulou and Tsoumakas (2018) present the Reference Vector Algorithm (RVA) that uses *local* GloVe (Pennington et al., 2014) word vectors (i.e., trained only on the target document). EmbedRank (Bennani-Smires et al., 2018) uses pre-trained sentence embeddings, Sent2Vec (Pagliardini et al., 2018), to embed both candidate terms and documents in the same high-dimensional vector space. Finally, Papagiannopoulou et al. (2020) proposed an unsupervised AKE method that uses the weighted adjacency matrix's rows as word vectors to model their distribution. The authors show that the centre of the distribution is closer to the non-keywords, as the main bulk of words are neutral or slightly relevant to the documents' topics.

## 3 Our Approach

### 3.1 Document Pre-processing

First, we eliminate from the target document punctuation marks and words that (a) are stopwords , (b) consist only of numbers, (c) have length less than two characters to avoid trivial or insignificant terms. Before we get the final set of candidate words as keywords, we use stemming.

### 3.2 Creation of the Adjacency Matrix

The majority of the graph-based approaches measure the importance of the graph-of-words' nodes using PageRank (see Section 2) that adds more value to a node connected with high-scoring nodes rather than low-scoring ones through an iterative process. However, our approach follows a different direction by identifying the most central (i.e., significant) words of the graph-of-words via the distribution-based modeling of the corresponding adjacency matrix.

We investigate our approach's effectiveness on three distinct versions of the adjacency matrix that correspond to three variants of the graph-of-words (i.e., unweighted, weighted with/without enhanced with positional information) for a target document. Specifically, given a set of unique, valid words of the text, $d \in D$, we could have one of the following types of word vectors (each row of the adjacency matrix constitutes a vector representation of a specific word):

a. *Unweighted adjacency matrix*, $A_{N \times N}$ where $N = |D|$. The $A_{N \times N}$ matrix represents the undirected[2] unweighted graph-of-words $G = (U, E)$, $U$ is the set of vertices (that correspond to the set of words $d \in D$) and $E$ is the set of edges; Each element $A_{i,j}$ is 1 when there is an edge from vertex $u_i$ to vertex $u_j$ ($u_i \neq u_j$) of $G$, i.e., the corresponding words $d_i$ and $d_j$ co-occur within a window of $T$ words, and 0 when there is no edge, $i, j \in [1..N]$.

b. *Weighted adjacency matrix*, $A'_{N \times N}$ with $N = |D|$. The $A'_{N \times N}$ matrix represents the undirected weighted graph-of-words $G' = (U, E')$, $U$ is the set of vertices and $E'$ is the set of edges; Each element $A'_{i,j}$ contains the weight of the edge from vertex $u_i$ to vertex $u_j$ ($u_i \neq u_j$), i.e., the number of co-occurrences of the corresponding words $d_i$ and $d_j$ within a window of $T$ words, $i, j \in [1..N]$. In case that there is no edge connecting the two nodes, $A'_{i,j} = 0$.

c. *Weighted adjacency matrix with positional information*, $Q_{N \times N}$ where $N = |D|$. The $Q_{N \times N}$ matrix represents the undirected weighted graph-of-words $A' = (U, E')$ but also incorporates positional information, i.e.,

$$Q = A' \odot P$$

where $\odot$ is the element-wise multiplication symbol, $A'$ is the weighted adjacency matrix, $A'_{N \times N}$, detailed in (b) and $P_{N \times N}$ is a positional matrix such that each element is defined as:

$$P_{i,j} = \frac{1}{s(d_i) + s(d_j)}$$

where $s(d)$ gives the first sentence where the word $d$ occurs in the document.

### 3.3 Distribution-based Modeling and Candidates Scoring

The next step of our approach is the distribution-based modeling of the adjacency matrix that corresponds to one of the various versions of the target document's graph-of-words described above (Section 3.2) and the candidate words' scoring. In this section, we detail three distribution-based modeling alternatives describing the intuition behind each one approach and the scoring functions used to give the final ranking of the words as keywords.

#### 3.3.1 The Mean Vector Approach

Papagiannopoulou et al. (2020) proposed *Local Vectors* (LV), an unsupervised AKE method that uses the weighted adjacency matrix of the graph-of-words as word vectors to model the distribution of the target document's words by averaging the corresponding vectors (i.e., rows of the matrix). The authors show that the centre of the distribution is closer to the non-keywords, as the main bulk of words are neutral or slightly relevant to the documents' topics. Moreover, in the same work, they show through an empirical study that the *local* word vectors coming from the weighted adjacency

[2] i.e., the adjacency matrix is symmetric.

matrix mentioned above encode statistical information equivalent to the one encoded by the local run of GloVe on a single document proposed in Papagiannopoulou and Tsoumakas (2018).

Particularly, in this work, we consider the sample's estimated mean $\boldsymbol{\mu}$ of the corresponding vector matrix, i.e., the $A_{N\times N}$ or $A'_{N\times N}$ or $Q_{N\times N}$, as the distribution's center (each word participates once in the computation). Then, we score each word with a value $S$, according to the following formula: $S(\boldsymbol{x}) = d(\boldsymbol{\mu}, \boldsymbol{x})$, where $d(\boldsymbol{\mu}, \boldsymbol{x})$ is the Euclidean distance between the mean vector $\boldsymbol{\mu}$ and the vector representation $\boldsymbol{x}$ of the word, as distance metrics that incorporate the vectors' magnitude capture the similar behaviour of the non-keywords' vectors over the keywords' ones (Papagiannopoulou et al., 2020), i.e., $d(\boldsymbol{\mu}, \boldsymbol{x}) = \sqrt{\sum_{i=1}^{N}(x_i - \mu_i)^2}$, where $N$ is the number of dimensions. The higher the score $S$, the more important the word for the document, i.e., we are interested in words with high distance values, as most of the words, which determine the distribution's center, are non-keywords. The main difference with the approach proposed by Papagiannopoulou et al. (2020) is that we score the words based only on their distance from the mean vector without involving any external heuristics such as the word's position. This way, we consider in advance any positional information via the $Q$ adjacency matrix (i.e., incorporated in the vector representation).

#### 3.3.2 Unsupervised Learning Approaches

**One-Class SVM**. Instead of calculating the distribution's center of the adjacency matrix by averaging its rows, we could use geometric concepts such as hyperspheres or hyperplanes to delimit the area of space that includes most of the word vectors (i.e., the main bulk of unimportant words) and, then, score the candidates using functions that express the vectors' deviation from the main distribution. According to this approach, the most important words are the most outlying ones (i.e., outliers) as most words are neutral or slightly relevant to the documents' topics (i.e., inliers). Tax and Duin (1999a,b) proposed a method based on SVM (Cortes and Vapnik, 1995), called One-Class SVM, that seeks the smallest hypersphere consisting of all the dataset points. Thus, training this model may reject a fraction of the positively-labelled training objects when this adequately minimizes the hypersphere volume.

There are also other approaches, such as the one of Schölkopf et al. (1999), which is similar, but instead of using a small hypersphere, it uses a hyperplane which is far from the origin (this is the version implemented by scikit-learn[3] and used in our study). This algorithm employs a function $f$ that takes the value +1 in a "small" region, covering most of the data points, and -1 elsewhere. Formally, suppose the dataset consists of the word vectors (samples) $\boldsymbol{x}$ coming from the corresponding adjacency matrix $X_{N\times N}$ (i.e., $X_{N\times N}$ can be one of the $A_{N\times N}$, $A'_{N\times N}$, $Q_{N\times N}$). Let $\Phi$ be a feature map $X \to F^4$, i.e., a specific dot product space. Then, we can separate the dataset's word vectors from the origin by solving the following quadratic optimization problem:

$$\min_{\boldsymbol{w},\xi,\rho} \frac{1}{2}||\boldsymbol{w}||^2 + \frac{1}{\nu l}\sum_i \xi_i - \rho$$

subject to $(\boldsymbol{w} \cdot \Phi(\boldsymbol{x_i})) \geq \rho - \xi_i$, $\xi_i \geq 0$
where $i$ represents the $i^{th}$ sample, $l = N$, $\nu$ is the percentage of samples considered as outliers (the expected keywords' ratio), $\xi_i$ are the slack variables that relax the constraints, $\rho$ refers to the distance of the hyperplane from the origin[5] and $\boldsymbol{w}$ represent the parameters of the SVM that define the hyperplane (we need to learn them using the dataset's samples)[6]. Then, the decision function $f(\boldsymbol{x}) = sgn((\boldsymbol{w} \cdot \Phi(\boldsymbol{x})) - \rho)$ will be positive for the most samples $\boldsymbol{x_i}$ in the dataset. In our case, an ideal scoring function that ranks the corresponding document's words is the signed distance to the separating hyperplane that will be positive for the main bulk of words and negative for the different ones. We consider only the words with a negative score as candidate keywords (the lower the value, the higher the word's importance).

We have experimented with various kernel functions, e.g., polynomial, sigmoid, etc. but the most suitable in our case is the Radial Base Function (RBF). Formally, The RBF kernel on two samples $\boldsymbol{x}$ and $\boldsymbol{x'}$ is defined as:

$$K(\boldsymbol{x}, \boldsymbol{x'}) = exp\left(-\frac{||\boldsymbol{x} - \boldsymbol{x'}||^2}{2\sigma^2}\right)$$

[3] `https://scikit-learn.org/stable/index.html`

[4] F is a dot product space such that the dot product in the image of $\Phi$ can be computed by evaluating some kernel.

[5] This distance is equal to $\frac{\rho}{||\boldsymbol{w}||}$.

[6] i.e., $\rho$ and $\boldsymbol{w}$ solve the problem.

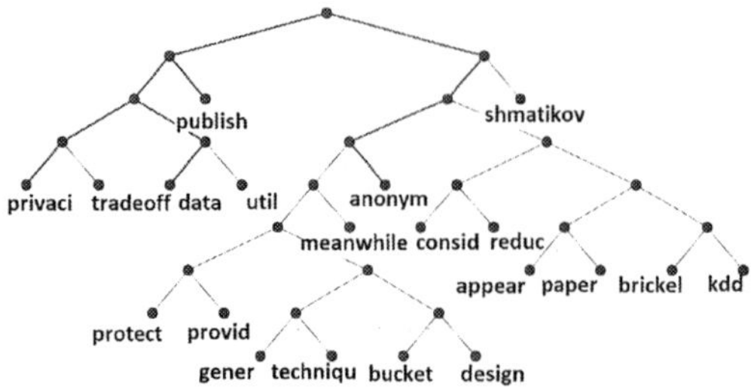


Figure 1: An isolation tree built based on the adjacency matrix's word vector representations for the article entitled "On the Tradeoff between Privacy and Utility in Data Publishing" with golden keywords: *anonymity, data, publishing, privacy*. The isolation tree recursively divides the 20 samples (i.e., words used to train the tree) by randomly selecting an attribute (matrix dimension) $b$ and a split value $m$ until either the node has only one instance or all node's data have the same values. Keywords tend to have shorter path lengths than the non-keywords that constitute the main bulk of (unimportant) words.

where $\sigma \in \mathbb{R}$ is a kernel parameter and $||x - x'||^2$ can be considered as the squared Euclidean distance between the two word vectors. These distances between the pairs of the word feature vectors incorporated by the RBF kernel make it the best choice. Moreover, distance metrics that consider the vectors' magnitude (e.g., the Euclidean distance) can capture the non-keywords' vectors' similar behavior over the keywords' ones as mentioned earlier in Section 3.3.1.

**Isolation Forest**. Instead of modeling the vectors' distribution and then estimating the distance from a reference point (e.g., the mean vector or the hyperplane), we propose to detect and rank the few different (important) word vectors via the mechanism of isolation Liu et al. (2008, 2012) utilizing the binary tree structure, called isolation tree. Because of the susceptibility to isolation, the few outlying word vectors (i.e., expected to be the important ones) are more prone to be isolated closer to the root of an isolation tree than the common ones. An isolation forest builds an ensemble of isolation trees for the given set of word vectors. The forest of random trees collectively produces shorter path lengths[7] for the outlier samples, i.e., the ones we search.

In other words, isolation forest is a tree-based algorithm built around the theory of decision trees and random forests. It also creates many isolation (decision) trees, but it calculates the *path length* necessary to isolate an observation in the tree. The idea is that keywords as a minority in a document can be treated as anomalies and thus are easier to be isolated because there are fewer conditions required to separate them from the "normal" non-keywords. Therefore, outliers (i.e., keywords) will have shorter paths than the "normal" non-keywords and reside closer to the tree's root. When many isolation trees are created, the forest is necessary to average the corresponding scores (path length calculations), providing a sense about the words that are indeed outliers.

Figure 1 shows an isolation tree built based on the Q adjacency matrix's word vector representations for a computer science abstract from the KDD collection (Caragea et al., 2014). The article entitled "On the Tradeoff between Privacy and Utility in Data Publishing" is accompanied by the following golden keywords: *anonymity, data, publishing, privacy*. The number of samples to draw from X to train each base estimator is equal to 20. We also applied PCA on X and use the two first principal components to facilitate visualization. The isolation tree recursively divides the 20 samples by randomly selecting an attribute $b$ and a split value $m$, until either the node has only one instance or all data at the node have the same values. We notice that keywords tend to have shorter path lengths than the non-keywords. Similar isolation trees, supportive of our crucial intuition, are obtained from other documents, too.

A more in-depth view of the Isolation Forest scoring function reveals that itself defines a "natural" threshold that determines whether a sample belongs to inliers or not by borrowing the analysis of Binary Search Trees (BSTs) as isolation trees have an equivalent structure (Preiss, 2000). This property is remarkable as the number of topics a document discusses should determine the corresponding number of keywords instead of suggesting a fixed or proportional to the text size number of keywords as most methods do. According to the theory, the average path length $c(\psi)$ of unsuccessful searches in a BST (i.e., the equivalent of external node terminations in an isolation tree) given a sample set of $\psi$ instances is:

$$c(\psi) = \begin{cases} 2H(\psi - 1) - 2\frac{\psi-1}{n}, & \psi > 2, \\ 1, & \psi = 2, \\ 0, & otherwise. \end{cases}$$

[7]The path length of a point x is measured by the number of edges x traverses an isolation tree from the root node until the traversal is terminated at an external node.

where $H(i)$ is the harmonic number (estimated by $ln(i)+$ the Euler's constant). Hence, the Isolation Forest scoring function is:

$$s(x, \psi) = 2^{-\frac{E(h(x))}{c(\psi)}}$$

where x is the sample, $h(x)$ is the path length of $x$ and $E(h(x))$ is the average of $h(x)$ for a collection of isolation trees. The above function ensures that samples with scores close to 1 imply diversity from the majority (i.e., $E(h(x)) \rightarrow 0$), whereas scores much lower than 0.5 indicate normal samples (i.e., $E(h(x)) \rightarrow \psi - 1$). Also, suppose all instances have a score of approximately equal to 0.5. In that case, we can consider the whole sample as a set of normal instances (i.e., $E(h(x)) \rightarrow c(\psi)$). The above findings transform the value 0.5 into an especially important threshold for determining a case as different from the whole sample or not.

## 4 Experimental Study

### 4.1 Setup

We choose six popular datasets: three collections with full-text publications, i.e., NUS (Nguyen and Kan, 2007), Semeval (SE) (Kim et al., 2010), and ACM (Krapivin et al., 2008) with 211, 244, and 2304 documents, respectively, two with scientific abstracts, i.e., KDD (Caragea et al., 2014) and WWW (Gollapalli and Caragea, 2014) with 755, and 1330 documents, respectively, and one with news texts, i.e., DUC-2001 (DUC) (Wan and Xiao, 2008b) with 308 documents. This way, we include to our study both long and short texts, either scientific or news articles. SE is already separated into training (144) and test (100) sets, and for the ACM separation, most works choose the first 400 papers from the ACM following Meng et al. (2017) as test set. However, there are no guidelines for separating the NUS, KDD, WWW, and DUC datasets. Thus, we pick the first 330 from WWW, the last 100 papers from NUS (Papagiannopoulou et al., 2020), and the last 100 from DUC, alphabetically ordered as the test data. We use the whole KDD dataset as test set as we do not use it for parameters' tuning.

In addition to the proposed approaches for AKE, i.e., the new version of LV, the Isolation Forest (IF) and the One-Class SVM (OC), four state-of-the-art unsupervised graph-based AKE methods participate in this empirical study: K-Core (K) (Seidman, 1983; Batagelj and Zaversnik, 2011), PageRank (P) (Mihalcea and Tarau, 2004; Wan and Xiao, 2008b), Betweenness (B), and Node degree (N) (the last one proposed first by Rose et al. (2010). We present the experimental results organized in three groups based on the type of information used to run (Tables 2, 3). The first two groups include the methods' runs on the unweighted and weighted graphs-of-words/adjacency matrices, i.e., with an $A$ and $A'$ subscript on the right of each method according to the notation introduced in Section 3.2, respectively (e.g., $K_A$ means that K method runs on an unweighted graph-of-words, whereas $K_{A'}$ runs on the weighted one, i.e., weighted K-Core of Batagelj and Zaversnik (2011)). The third group includes the proposed methods' runs on the $Q$ adjacency matrix (weighted with words' co-occurrences and positional information) and a Personalized weighted variant of PageRank that considers both node as well as the typical edge weights ($P_{A''}$). The node weight is equal to $\frac{1}{s}$, where $s$ is the first sentence's index that the corresponding word occurs in the document. In all cases, the methods build the graph-of-words following the pre-processing steps described in Section 3.1.

After splitting the golden keyphrases into unigrams, we use exact string matching to determine the number of correctly matched words with the golden ones for a document following the paradigm of Tixier et al. (2016). We also apply stemming to the output of the methods and the article's golden unigrams as a pre-processing step before the evaluation process. We employ the authors' keywords as a gold evaluation standard for all academic documents (long/short) except for the news dataset where only the readers' keywords are available. We used the IsolationForest and OneClassSVM classes from the scikit-learn[8] library for the IF and OC, respectively. For the implementation of the competitive approaches, we employ the PKE toolkit (Boudin, 2016), the NetworkX[9] and the gowpy[10] python libraries.

We use one dataset per text category (full-texts, abstracts, news), i.e., the training sets of NUS, WWW, DUC, to determine IF and OC models' tuning parameters to optimize the $F_1$ score. The parameters chosen for the experiments on test sets are for the IF $n_{estimators}$=200, $max_{samples}$=auto, $max_{features}$=0.75 and the OC *kernel*=rbf, *gamma*=scale. The best percentages

[8]https://scikit-learn.org/stable/index.html

[9]https://networkx.org/

[10]https://github.com/GuillaumeDD/gowpy

for the IF's *contamination* and OC's *nu* parameters (related to outliers' ratio) are 0.05, 0.1, 0.2 for the full-text publications, news texts and abstracts, respectively (used in the context of $F_1$@20 scores calculation, see Table 2). Furthermore, we compute the $F_1$ scores in Table 3 based on the number of keywords returned by the $K_A$, $K_{A'}$, $IF_A$, $IF_{A'}$ and $IF_Q$ (the value of the IF's contamination parameter is equal to *auto*[11]) approaches, i.e., $F_1@|K_A|$, $F_1@|K_{A'}|$, $F_1@|IF_A|$, $F_1@|IF_{A'}|$, $F_1@|IF_Q|$, respectively. The LV approach is parameter-free.

We follow the paradigm of existing experimental studies from the related task of keyphrase extraction (Wan and Xiao, 2008a; Bougouin et al., 2013), and set a window size $T$ equal to 10 to construct the graphs-of-words used by the graph-based approaches. Earlier, Wan and Xiao (2008b) show that in the case of weighted graphs-of-words, the greater the window size, the higher the extractor's accuracy (window sizes greater than 10 achieve more or less the same accuracy level).

| $F_1$ | NUS | | WWW | | DUC | |
|---|---|---|---|---|---|---|
| | $T_5$ | $T_{10}$ | $T_5$ | $T_{10}$ | $T_5$ | $T_{10}$ |
| $LV_A$ | 0.319 | **0.324** | 0.279 | **0.282** | 0.389 | **0.410** |
| $IF_A$ | 0.313 | **0.319** | **0.294** | 0.284 | 0.372 | **0.377** |
| $OC_A$ | 0.093 | **0.126** | 0.237 | **0.243** | 0.265 | **0.284** |
| $LV_{A'}$ | 0.311 | **0.315** | 0.283 | **0.285** | 0.401 | **0.405** |
| $IF_{A'}$ | 0.319 | **0.324** | 0.313 | **0.314** | 0.376 | **0.395** |
| $OC_{A'}$ | 0.129 | **0.142** | 0.256 | **0.261** | 0.282 | **0.293** |
| $LV_Q$ | **0.339** | 0.336 | **0.280** | 0.278 | 0.408 | **0.416** |
| $IF_Q$ | 0.338 | **0.342** | 0.321 | **0.335** | 0.383 | **0.413** |
| $OC_Q$ | **0.339** | 0.338 | 0.266 | **0.271** | **0.344** | 0.343 |

Table 1: $F_1$@20 of the LV, IF and OC keyword extraction methods using different types of adjacency matrix ($A$, $A'$, $Q$) created with two different window sizes, $T = 5$ ($T_5$) and $T = 10$, on three different datasets (NUS, WWW, DUC). The highest values appear in bold font.

Moreover, Table 1 shows the $F_1$@20 scores of LV, IF, and OC on the training sets of three representative datasets NUS, WWW and DUC (one from each category of documents, long/short scientific articles and news texts, respectively) using unweighted ($A$), weighted ($A'$), and weighted with positional information ($Q$) adjacency matrix with two different window sizes, a lower widow size $T = 5$ ($T_5$) and the usual one $T = 10$ ($T_{10}$). The highest $F_1$ scores are highlighted in bold font. The experimental results confirm that smaller window sizes led to lower $F_1$ scores for most of the proposed methods. However, in few cases where the methods with $T_5$ give higher $F_1$ scores compared to those with $T_{10}$, the differences are not statistically significant according to the two-sided Wilcoxon signed-rank nonparametric test. Finally, another reason to consider the same co-occurrence window size for both the state-of-the-art graph-based approaches and the proposed ones is our interest in investigating the methods' efficacy employing the same words' context (captured in a specific window size).

### 4.2 Performance Evaluation Results

Table 2 shows the $F_1$@20 scores of various keyword extraction methods, whereas Table 3 presents the $F_1$ scores calculated based on the returned number of keywords by $K_A$, $K_{A'}$, $IF_A$, $IF_{A'}$, and $IF_Q$ on the six datasets using unweighted ($A$), weighted ($A'$), and weighted with positional information ($Q$) graph-of-words or adjacency matrix. The highest $F_1$ scores in both tables are highlighted in red bold font. Table 2 presents the best scores for each group of methods in bold, whereas the second best are underlined. We have also checked the statistical significance of the results using two-sided Wilcoxon signed-rank nonparametric test between the graph-based (the ones in the gray background) and the distribution-based modeling approaches (LV, IF, OC) at significance level 0.01. Our analysis shows that differences in values $> 2\%$ are statistically significant. In case of statistical significance between the values of two methods whose difference is $\leq 2\%$, a superscript with the name of the corresponding graph-based method is added on the distribution-based modeling approach. We compute statistical significance separately for the groups of methods that use edge weights, node and edge weights, and no weights, respectively, to facilitate the results' interpretation.

Table 2 shows that in most cases except for the news collection (DUC), the more information we consider, i.e., both words' co-occurrences and positional info, the higher $F_1$ scores we achieve (e.g., $OC_Q$'s high scores compared to the ones of $OC_A$, $OC_{A'}$). Particularly, the transition from the unweighted graph-of-words/adjacency matrix to their weighted versions slightly improves the performance in almost all methods besides the B's (in all datasets) and LV's scores (in longer documents). $IF_{A'}$ outperforms the competitive approaches that consider edge weights to score the

[11] value for the "natural" threshold of outliers for IF, see Section 3.3.2

| $F_1$ | ACM | NUS | SE | DUC | WWW | KDD |
|---|---|---|---|---|---|---|
| $P_A$ | 0.329 | **0.331** | 0.261 | 0.381 | 0.279 | 0.265 |
| $B_A$ | 0.318 | 0.325 | 0.260 | 0.354 | 0.270 | 0.256 |
| $N_A$ | **0.330** | 0.328 | 0.263 | **0.385** | **0.284** | **0.269** |
| $LV_A$ | $0.327^{B}$ | 0.321 | 0.267 | 0.384 | $0.277^{N}$ | $0.265^{B}$ |
| $IF_A$ | $0.319^{P,N}$ | 0.320 | **0.268** | $0.362^{P}$ | $\mathbf{0.284}^{B}$ | 0.260 |
| $OC_A$ | 0.154 | 0.144 | 0.133 | 0.244 | 0.232 | 0.221 |
| $P_{A'}$ | **0.331** | **0.326** | 0.269 | 0.383 | 0.284 | 0.270 |
| $B_{A'}$ | 0.314 | 0.317 | 0.257 | 0.349 | 0.257 | 0.247 |
| $N_{A'}$ | 0.324 | 0.314 | 0.268 | **0.388** | 0.288 | 0.272 |
| $LV_{A'}$ | $0.311_{P,N}$ | 0.300 | 0.263 | 0.380 | $0.279^{N}$ | 0.269 |
| $IF_{A'}$ | $0.328^{B}$ | $\mathbf{0.326}^{N}$ | $\mathbf{0.275}^{B}$ | 0.368 | **0.316** | $\mathbf{0.289}^{P,N}$ |
| $OC_{A'}$ | 0.158 | 0.153 | 0.142 | 0.289 | 0.249 | 0.242 |
| $P_{A''}$ | **0.374** | **0.358** | **0.300** | 0.383 | 0.285 | 0.269 |
| $LV_Q$ | 0.373 | $0.343^{P}$ | 0.299 | 0.328 | $0.268^{P}$ | 0.260 |
| $IF_Q$ | 0.353 | 0.348 | 0.287 | **0.384** | **0.338** | **0.305** |
| $OC_Q$ | 0.372 | $0.340^{P}$ | 0.290 | 0.311 | 0.286 | 0.275 |

Table 2: $F_1$@20 of various keyword extraction methods using different types of graph-of-words/adjacency matrix ($A$, $A'$, $Q$) on six different datasets. Superscripts on a method's score show statistical significance between the current method and the one whose name appears as superscript (see Section 4.2). The highest values appear in bold red font. The best scores for each group of methods are in bold, whereas the second best are underlined.

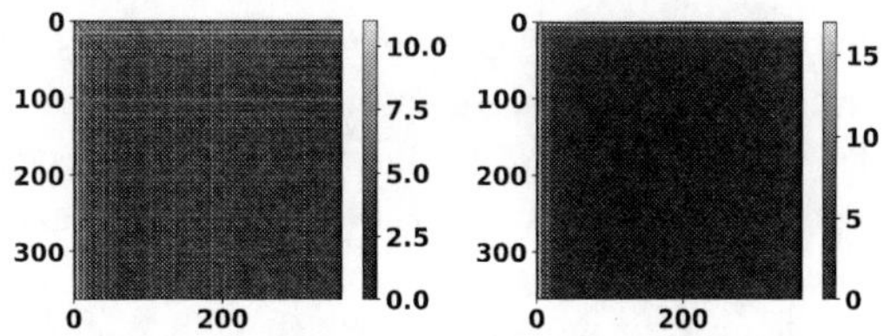


(a) (b)

Figure 2: The distances between the main bulk of word vectors from the $Q$ adjacency matrix (2b) range in low (dark) values compared to a minority of distant word vectors (yellow/green values). However, the word vectors of $A$ (2a) do not provide such clear separation between the main distribution of common words and the minority of keywords (high and low distances are just as many).

candidates ($2^{nd}$ group of methods with subscript $A'$) in four out of six datasets (NUS, SE, WWW, KDD) and achieves high scores in ACM and DUC with statistically insignificant differences compared to the competitive methods. Moreover, the addition of positional weights compared to the typical use of edge weights increases most methods' performance remarkably apart from the LV's (in shorter documents) and the P's that remains almost invariable in shorter texts. In the $3^{rd}$ group of methods, $IF_Q$ ranks first in half datasets (DUC, WWW, KDD) and performs high in NUS and SE (without statistically significant differences from $P_{A''}$). Additionally, LV achieves quite high $F_1$ scores as well.

Figure 2 shows a visual interpretation of why the additional information facilitates the distribution-based approaches to distinguish the keywords from the non-keywords via heatmaps of the Euclidean distances between the word vectors of the $A$ (2a) and $Q$ (2b), respectively, for a news text. We notice that positions combined with words' co-occurrences help the text's keyword vectors diverge from the main distribution (see the few high distances/yellow or light green values that correspond mostly to the first words of the document that include many keywords). We also see that most vectors (common words - group of inliers) are close to each other (low/dark distance values). However, the distances between word vectors of $A$ do not reveal any clear separation between the main distribution of common words and the minority of keywords making difficult the outliers' detection. Note that the words' ids (range from 0 to 363) correspond to the order of the words' presence in the text, confirming the importance of the positional information in the AKE task (keywords tend to appear at the beginning of a document). Similar plots are also obtained from multiple documents.

| $F_1$@T | ACM | NUS | SE | DUC | WWW | KDD |
|---|---|---|---|---|---|---|
| $K_A$ | 0.176 | 0.160 | 0.132 | 0.240 | 0.250 | 0.234 |
| $IF_A$ | 0.273 | 0.305 | 0.274 | 0.186 | 0.307 | 0.267 |
| $K_{A'}$ | 0.297 | 0.309 | 0.278 | **0.300** | 0.343 | **0.323** |
| $IF_{A'}$ | 0.323 | 0.372 | 0.322 | 0.183 | 0.315 | 0.283 |
| $IF_Q$ | **0.360** | **0.413** | **0.345** | 0.223 | **0.347** | 0.313 |

Table 3: $F_1$@T of $K_A$, $K_{A'}$, $IF_A$, $IF_{A'}$ and $IF_Q$ methods on the 6 datasets, where T is equal to $|K_A|$, $|K_{A'}|$, $|IF_A|$, $|IF_{A'}|$ and $|IF_Q|$, respectively. The highest values appear in red bold font.

Next, we focus on the AKE methods that determine the number of returned keywords at document level, i.e., the $K_A$, $K_{A'}$, $IF_A$, $IF_{A'}$ and $IF_Q$. We study the results of Table 3, considering Table 4

| @ | ACM | NUS | SE | DUC | WWW | KDD |
|---|---|---|---|---|---|---|
| $\|K_A\|$ | 74.1 | 70.2 | 71.5 | 53.8 | 24.5 | 25.4 |
| $\|IF_A\|$ | 10.5 | 8.7 | 10.3 | 2.6 | 5.8 | 5.4 |
| $\|K_{A'}\|$ | 8.7 | 8.4 | 7.6 | 18.1 | 12.4 | 12.4 |
| $\|IF_{A'}\|$ | 6.7 | 6.1 | 7.1 | 2.3 | 5.0 | 4.6 |
| $\|IF_Q\|$ | 7.5 | 6.6 | 7.5 | 2.3 | 4.8 | 4.4 |
| $\|V\|$ | 757.7 | 772.4 | 641.8 | 268.8 | 58.2 | 60.1 |

Table 4: Average number of keywords returned by the K and IF methods using different types of information ($A$, $A'$, $Q$). The last row shows the average number of candidate words $|V|$ per dataset.

that shows the average numbers of keywords returned by the methods mentioned earlier for each dataset. The last row in Table 4 shows the average number of candidate words $|V|$ per dataset to give an impression for the texts' vocabulary sizes. We are interested in investigating which method returns the most "accurate" keywords' sets in terms of the corresponding $F_1$ scores. However, we should keep in mind that the methods are not evaluated on the same number of keywords. Through this discussion, our goal is to discover which AKE approach is more suitable for each type of documents in a general sense. The low $F_1@|K_A|$ scores of $K_A$ compared to the $F_1$ scores of $K_{A'}$, $IF_A$, $IF_{A'}$ and $IF_Q$ are plausible due to the low precision scores of $K_A$ as the number of the words included in the K-Core of the unweighted graph-of-words is quite high (greater than 70, 53 and 24 returned keywords for the academic full-texts, news texts and scientific abstracts, respectively). In all datasets $K_{A'}$ outperforms $K_A$ giving reasonable number of keywords. Moreover, in most datasets (scientific full-texts and abstracts), $IF_Q$ outputs more accurate keyword sets (i.e., higher $F_1@|IF_Q|$ scores) than those returned by rest approaches. Exceptions are the performance on (a) the DUC (news) dataset where $IF_A$, $IF_{A'}$ and $IF_Q$ detect lower number of words as keywords compared to the golden ones and (b) the KDD collection where the $F_1@|IF_Q|$ score achieved by $IF_Q$ is slightly worse than the one of $K_{A'}$.

We also present the correlation according to the Spearman correlation coefficient between the IF's scoring function described in Section 3.3.2 and traditional weighting schemas, i.e., P, N, B, and K, for each information type used by IF and the rest graph-based methods, i.e., unweighted, weighted and weighted with positional information graphs-of-words/adjacency matrices. Table 5 shows that there is a very strong positive correlation ($\geq 0.8$) between the words' scores returned by IF and those produced by P and N for all information (input) types for almost all datasets, interpreting (partly) the comparable $F_1$ scores achieved by these methods. In this vein, there is a strong positive correlation ($\geq 0.6$) between IF and B in most cases. Moreover, the very strong positive correlation ($\geq 0.8$) on the datasets with full-texts of scientific publications goes hand-in-hand with the similar accuracy levels achieved in case there are no weights on the corresponding input. Finally, the K's output does not seem to correlate with the IF's output when no weights are used. However, if the methods use weights, the correlation between them turns into a strong/moderate positive one.

| S.C.C. | ACM | NUS | SE | DUC | WWW | KDD |
|---|---|---|---|---|---|---|
| $IF_A$-$P_A$ | **0.91** | **0.90** | **0.92** | **0.84** | **0.82** | **0.81** |
| $IF_A$-$N_A$ | **0.92** | **0.91** | **0.92** | **0.84** | **0.81** | **0.81** |
| $IF_A$-$B_A$ | **0.84** | **0.82** | **0.85** | 0.77 | 0.76 | 0.75 |
| $IF_A$-$K_A$ | 0.26 | 0.27 | 0.27 | 0.35 | 0.32 | 0.30 |
| $IF_{A'}$-$P_{A'}$ | **0.91** | **0.91** | **0.92** | **0.85** | **0.84** | **0.83** |
| $IF_{A'}$-$N_{A'}$ | **0.88** | **0.88** | **0.90** | **0.84** | **0.82** | **0.81** |
| $IF_{A'}$-$B_{A'}$ | 0.75 | 0.75 | 0.78 | 0.71 | 0.63 | 0.62 |
| $IF_{A'}$-$K_{A'}$ | 0.71 | 0.71 | 0.73 | *0.51* | *0.49* | *0.50* |
| $IF_Q$-$P_Q$ | **0.87** | **0.87** | **0.88** | 0.75 | **0.81** | **0.80** |

Table 5: Spearman's correlation coefficient (S.C.C.) between the proposed approach IF and traditional graph-based methods.

## 5 Conclusions and Future Work

In this article, we address the AKE task via the distribution-based modeling of the adjacency matrix that corresponds to various versions of the graph-of-words for a target document. More specifically, we propose capitalizing on unsupervised learning algorithms for the distribution-based modeling and scoring of the candidate words. Based on our performance evaluation, the IF approach shows the best effectiveness results in almost all datasets, concerning the $F_1$ score determining the number of keywords in document level.

There are many interesting future research directions, such as $i$) improving the scoring functions of the unsupervised learning approaches used in the context of the keyword extraction task, $ii$) adapting the proposed approach to the keyphrase extraction task , $iii$) developing novel distribution-based modeling methods that simultaneously utilize the information from one/multiple adjacency matrices , and $iv$) applying the adjacency matrix's distribution-based modeling in other tasks where only graph-based methods are used to date.

## References

Vladimir Batagelj and Matjaz Zaversnik. 2011. Fast algorithms for determining (generalized) core groups in social networks. *Adv. Data Anal. Classif.*, 5(2):129–145.

Kamil Bennani-Smires, Claudiu Musat, Andreea Hossmann, Michael Baeriswyl, and Martin Jaggi. 2018. Simple unsupervised keyphrase extraction using sentence embeddings. In *Proceedings of the 22nd Conference on Computational Natural Language Learn-*

*ing*, pages 221–229, Brussels, Belgium. Association for Computational Linguistics.

Saroj K. Biswas, Monali Bordoloi, and Jacob Shreya. 2018. A graph based keyword extraction model using collective node weight. *Expert Syst. Appl.*, 97:51–59.

Piotr Bojanowski, Edouard Grave, Armand Joulin, and Tomas Mikolov. 2017. Enriching word vectors with subword information. *Transactions of the Association for Computational Linguistics*, 5:135–146.

Florian Boudin. 2016. pke: an open source python-based keyphrase extraction toolkit. In *Proceedings of COLING 2016, the 26th International Conference on Computational Linguistics: System Demonstrations*, pages 69–73, Osaka, Japan. The COLING 2016 Organizing Committee.

Adrien Bougouin, Florian Boudin, and Béatrice Daille. 2013. TopicRank: Graph-based topic ranking for keyphrase extraction. In *Proceedings of the Sixth International Joint Conference on Natural Language Processing*, pages 543–551, Nagoya, Japan. Asian Federation of Natural Language Processing.

Sergey Brin and Lawrence Page. 1998. The anatomy of a large-scale hypertextual web search engine. *Comput. Networks*, 30(1-7):107–117.

Cornelia Caragea, Florin Adrian Bulgarov, Andreea Godea, and Sujatha Das Gollapalli. 2014. Citation-enhanced keyphrase extraction from research papers: A supervised approach. In *Proceedings of the 2014 Conference on Empirical Methods in Natural Language Processing (EMNLP)*, pages 1435–1446, Doha, Qatar. Association for Computational Linguistics.

Hou Pong Chan, Wang Chen, Lu Wang, and Irwin King. 2019. Neural keyphrase generation via reinforcement learning with adaptive rewards. In *Proceedings of the 57th Annual Meeting of the Association for Computational Linguistics*, pages 2163–2174, Florence, Italy. Association for Computational Linguistics.

Wang Chen, Hou Pong Chan, Piji Li, and Irwin King. 2020. Exclusive hierarchical decoding for deep keyphrase generation. In *Proceedings of the 58th Annual Meeting of the Association for Computational Linguistics*, pages 1095–1105, Online. Association for Computational Linguistics.

Jonathan Cohen. 2008. Trusses: Cohesive subgraphs for social network analysis. *National security agency technical report*, 16:3–29.

Corinna Cortes and Vladimir Vapnik. 1995. Support-vector networks. *Mach. Learn.*, 20(3):273–297.

Corina Florescu and Cornelia Caragea. 2017. PositionRank: An unsupervised approach to keyphrase extraction from scholarly documents. In *Proceedings of the 55th Annual Meeting of the Association for Computational Linguistics (Volume 1: Long Papers)*, pages 1105–1115, Vancouver, Canada. Association for Computational Linguistics.

Sujatha Das Gollapalli and Cornelia Caragea. 2014. Extracting keyphrases from research papers using citation networks. In *Proceedings of the Twenty-Eighth AAAI Conference on Artificial Intelligence, July 27 -31, 2014, Québec City, Québec, Canada*, pages 1629–1635. AAAI Press.

Sujatha Das Gollapalli, Xiaoli Li, and Peng Yang. 2017. Incorporating expert knowledge into keyphrase extraction. In *Proceedings of the Thirty-First AAAI Conference on Artificial Intelligence, February 4-9, 2017, San Francisco, California, USA*, pages 3180–3187. AAAI Press.

Kazi Saidul Hasan and Vincent Ng. 2014. Automatic keyphrase extraction: A survey of the state of the art. In *Proceedings of the 52nd Annual Meeting of the Association for Computational Linguistics (Volume 1: Long Papers)*, pages 1262–1273, Baltimore, Maryland. Association for Computational Linguistics.

Armand Joulin, Edouard Grave, Piotr Bojanowski, and Tomas Mikolov. 2017. Bag of tricks for efficient text classification. In *Proceedings of the 15th Conference of the European Chapter of the Association for Computational Linguistics: Volume 2, Short Papers*, pages 427–431, Valencia, Spain. Association for Computational Linguistics.

Su Nam Kim, Olena Medelyan, Min-Yen Kan, and Timothy Baldwin. 2010. SemEval-2010 task 5 : Automatic keyphrase extraction from scientific articles. In *Proceedings of the 5th International Workshop on Semantic Evaluation*, pages 21–26, Uppsala, Sweden. Association for Computational Linguistics.

Jon M. Kleinberg. 1999. Authoritative sources in a hyperlinked environment. *J. ACM*, 46(5):604–632.

Mikalai Krapivin, Aliaksandr Autayeu, and Maurizio Marchese. 2008. Large dataset for keyphrases extraction. In *Technical Report DISI-09-055*. Trento, Italy.

Fei Tony Liu, Kai Ming Ting, and Zhi-Hua Zhou. 2008. Isolation forest. In *Proceedings of the 8th IEEE International Conference on Data Mining (ICDM 2008), December 15-19, 2008, Pisa, Italy*, pages 413–422. IEEE Computer Society.

Fei Tony Liu, Kai Ming Ting, and Zhi-Hua Zhou. 2012. Isolation-based anomaly detection. *ACM Trans. Knowl. Discov. Data*, 6(1):3:1–3:39.

Debanjan Mahata, John Kuriakose, Rajiv Ratn Shah, and Roger Zimmermann. 2018. Key2Vec: Automatic ranked keyphrase extraction from scientific articles using phrase embeddings. In *Proceedings of the 2018 Conference of the North American Chapter of the Association for Computational Linguistics:*

*Human Language Technologies, Volume 2 (Short Papers)*, pages 634–639, New Orleans, Louisiana. Association for Computational Linguistics.

Rui Meng, Sanqiang Zhao, Shuguang Han, Daqing He, Peter Brusilovsky, and Yu Chi. 2017. Deep keyphrase generation. In *Proceedings of the 55th Annual Meeting of the Association for Computational Linguistics (Volume 1: Long Papers)*, pages 582–592, Vancouver, Canada. Association for Computational Linguistics.

Rada Mihalcea and Paul Tarau. 2004. TextRank: Bringing order into text. In *Proceedings of the 2004 Conference on Empirical Methods in Natural Language Processing*, pages 404–411, Barcelona, Spain. Association for Computational Linguistics.

Tomas Mikolov, Kai Chen, Greg Corrado, and Jeffrey Dean. 2013. Efficient estimation of word representations in vector space. In *1st International Conference on Learning Representations, ICLR 2013, Scottsdale, Arizona, USA, May 2-4, 2013, Workshop Track Proceedings*.

Andriy Mnih and Geoffrey E. Hinton. 2007. Three new graphical models for statistical language modelling. In *Machine Learning, Proceedings of the Twenty-Fourth International Conference (ICML 2007), Corvallis, Oregon, USA, June 20-24, 2007*, volume 227 of *ACM International Conference Proceeding Series*, pages 641–648. ACM.

Thuy Dung Nguyen and Min-Yen Kan. 2007. Keyphrase extraction in scientific publications. In *Asian Digital Libraries. Looking Back 10 Years and Forging New Frontiers, 10th International Conference on Asian Digital Libraries, ICADL 2007, Hanoi, Vietnam, December 10-13, 2007, Proceedings*, volume 4822 of *Lecture Notes in Computer Science*, pages 317–326. Springer.

Matteo Pagliardini, Prakhar Gupta, and Martin Jaggi. 2018. Unsupervised learning of sentence embeddings using compositional n-gram features. In *Proceedings of the 2018 Conference of the North American Chapter of the Association for Computational Linguistics: Human Language Technologies, Volume 1 (Long Papers)*, pages 528–540, New Orleans, Louisiana. Association for Computational Linguistics.

Eirini Papagiannopoulou and Grigorios Tsoumakas. 2018. Local word vectors guiding keyphrase extraction. *Inf. Process. Manag.*, 54(6):888–902.

Eirini Papagiannopoulou and Grigorios Tsoumakas. 2020. A review of keyphrase extraction. *Wiley Interdiscip. Rev. Data Min. Knowl. Discov.*, 10(2).

Eirini Papagiannopoulou, Grigorios Tsoumakas, and Apostolos N Papadopoulos. 2020. Keywords lie far from the mean of all words in local vector space. *arXiv preprint arXiv:2008.09513*.

Jeffrey Pennington, Richard Socher, and Christopher Manning. 2014. GloVe: Global vectors for word representation. In *Proceedings of the 2014 Conference on Empirical Methods in Natural Language Processing (EMNLP)*, pages 1532–1543, Doha, Qatar. Association for Computational Linguistics.

Bruno R. Preiss. 2000. *Data Structures and Algorithms with Object-Oriented Design Patterns in Java*. John Wiley & Sons Incorporated.

Stuart Rose, Dave Engel, Nick Cramer, and Wendy Cowley. 2010. Automatic keyword extraction from individual documents. *Text mining: applications and theory*, 1:1–20.

François Rousseau and Michalis Vazirgiannis. 2015. Main core retention on graph-of-words for single-document keyword extraction. In *Advances in Information Retrieval - 37th European Conference on IR Research, ECIR 2015, Vienna, Austria, March 29 - April 2, 2015. Proceedings*, volume 9022 of *Lecture Notes in Computer Science*, pages 382–393.

Bernhard Schölkopf, Robert C. Williamson, Alexander J. Smola, John Shawe-Taylor, and John C. Platt. 1999. Support vector method for novelty detection. In *Advances in Neural Information Processing Systems 12, [NIPS Conference, Denver, Colorado, USA, November 29 - December 4, 1999]*, pages 582–588. The MIT Press.

Stephen B Seidman. 1983. Network structure and minimum degree. *Social networks*, 5(3):269–287.

David M. J. Tax and Robert P. W. Duin. 1999a. Data domain description using support vectors. In *ESANN 1999, 7th European Symposium on Artificial Neural Networks, Bruges, Belgium, April 21-23, 1999, Proceedings*, pages 251–256.

David M. J. Tax and Robert P. W. Duin. 1999b. Support vector domain description. *Pattern Recognit. Lett.*, 20(11-13):1191–1199.

Antoine Tixier, Fragkiskos Malliaros, and Michalis Vazirgiannis. 2016. A graph degeneracy-based approach to keyword extraction. In *Proceedings of the 2016 Conference on Empirical Methods in Natural Language Processing*, pages 1860–1870, Austin, Texas. Association for Computational Linguistics.

Didier Augusto Vega-Oliveros, Pedro Spoljaric Gomes, Evangelos E. Milios, and Lilian Berton. 2019. A multi-centrality index for graph-based keyword extraction. *Inf. Process. Manag.*, 56(6).

Xiaojun Wan and Jianguo Xiao. 2008a. CollabRank: Towards a collaborative approach to single-document keyphrase extraction. In *Proceedings of the 22nd International Conference on Computational Linguistics (Coling 2008)*, pages 969–976, Manchester, UK. Coling 2008 Organizing Committee.

Xiaojun Wan and Jianguo Xiao. 2008b. Single document keyphrase extraction using neighborhood knowledge. In *Proceedings of the Twenty-Third AAAI Conference on Artificial Intelligence, AAAI 2008, Chicago, Illinois, USA, July 13-17, 2008*, pages 855–860. AAAI Press.

Liang Wang and Sujian Li. 2017. PKU_ICL at SemEval-2017 task 10: Keyphrase extraction with model ensemble and external knowledge. In *Proceedings of the 11th International Workshop on Semantic Evaluation (SemEval-2017)*, pages 934–937, Vancouver, Canada. Association for Computational Linguistics.

Rui Wang, Wei Liu, and Chris McDonald. 2015. Using word embeddings to enhance keyword identification for scientific publications. In *Databases Theory and Applications - 26th Australasian Database Conference, ADC 2015, Melbourne, VIC, Australia, June 4-7, 2015. Proceedings*, volume 9093 of *Lecture Notes in Computer Science*, pages 257–268. Springer.

Yue Wang, Jing Li, Hou Pong Chan, Irwin King, Michael R. Lyu, and Shuming Shi. 2019. Topic-aware neural keyphrase generation for social media language. In *Proceedings of the 57th Annual Meeting of the Association for Computational Linguistics*, pages 2516–2526, Florence, Italy. Association for Computational Linguistics.

Hai Ye and Lu Wang. 2018. Semi-supervised learning for neural keyphrase generation. In *Proceedings of the 2018 Conference on Empirical Methods in Natural Language Processing*, pages 4142–4153, Brussels, Belgium. Association for Computational Linguistics.

Jing Zhao and Yuxiang Zhang. 2019. Incorporating linguistic constraints into keyphrase generation. In *Proceedings of the 57th Annual Meeting of the Association for Computational Linguistics*, pages 5224–5233, Florence, Italy. Association for Computational Linguistics.

# Improving Human Text Simplification with Sentence Fusion

**Max Schwarzer**
Mila
University of Montreal
max.schwarzer@umontreal.ca

**Teerapaun Tanprasert and David Kauchak**
Computer Science Department
Pomona College
teerapaun.tanprasert@pomona.edu
david.kauchak@pomona.edu

## Abstract

The quality of fully automated text simplification systems is not good enough for use in real-world settings; instead, human simplifications are used. In this paper, we examine how to improve the cost and quality of human simplifications by leveraging crowdsourcing. We introduce a graph-based sentence fusion approach to augment human simplifications and a reranking approach to both select high quality simplifications and to allow for targeting simplifications with varying levels of simplicity. Using the Newsela dataset (Xu et al., 2015) we show consistent improvements over experts at varying simplification levels and find that the additional sentence fusion simplifications allow for simpler output than the human simplifications alone.

## 1 Introduction

Research on text simplification has largely focused on fully automated systems, including lexical systems that change words or phrases and sentence-level systems that make broader changes (Shardlow, 2014; Narayan and Gardent, 2016; Zhang and Lapata, 2017; Kriz et al., 2019). While the performance of such systems is steadily improving, for most real-world applications, the quality of these systems is still not good enough, particularly in domains where correctness is critical such as health and medical (Siddharthan, 2014; Shardlow and Nawaz, 2019). In such domains, human experts are still the main creators of simplified text (Zarcadoolas, 2010). The challenge is that these experts are costly to employ and the number of people equipped with the appropriate training and skills is limited.

In this paper, we examine a crowdsourcing approach to produce simplifications more efficiently and of higher quality using non-experts. Crowdsourcing has been suggested previously as a possible source of text simplifications (Amancio and Specia, 2014; Lasecki et al., 2015), however, no work has addressed quality control or how to deal with varying simplicity targets. The top part of Table 1 shows an example sentence to be simplified with two non-expert simplifications obtained through a crowdsourcing platform. While both of the human simplifications roughly convey the main idea in the original sentence, the quality is questionable. However, there are good portions of the simplifications, e.g., using "worried about" instead of "chief concerns". Our goal is to leverage these lower quality simplifications to generate high-quality simplifications that are as good as or better than those produced by an expert.

We make three main contributions. First, we describe a new sentence fusion technique for generating additional alternative simplifications based on the original input and the non-expert human simplifications. This allows for many additional simplifications to be generated by combining different portions of the original human simplifications. Second, we provide a supervised approach for ranking candidate simplifications, both human generated and sentence fusion generated. This allows the system to pick high quality simplifications from the candidates generated. Similar approaches have been used in translation for ranking and selecting both human and system translations (Callison-Burch, 2009; Zaidan and Callison-Burch, 2011). Third, we parameterize the ranking approach to optimize for different levels of simplicity allowing for different simplifications to be chosen depending on the simplicity target. This is particularly useful when combined with the sentence fusion technique which allows for a much broader range of possible candidates than just the human simplifications. We evaluate the proposed system against human expert simplifications and show consistently better results at varying simplicity levels for both simplicity and adequacy.



*Proceedings of the Fifteenth Workshop on Graph-Based Methods for Natural Language Processing (TextGraphs-15)*, pages 106–114
June 11, 2021. 

| Original | Bird damage is often overshadowed by weather and water as a farmer's chief concerns. |
|---|---|
| Crowdsourced 1 | Farmers problems with birds is over shadowed by weather and water. |
| Crowdsourced 2 | A farmer is mostly worried about weather and water. But a farmer might also worry about birds causing damage. |
| Generated 1 | Bird damage is often overshadowed by weather and water. |
| Generated 2 | A farmer is mostly worried about weather and water as a farmer's chief concerns. |
| Generated 3 | Farmers problems with birds is over shadowed by weather and water as a farmer's chief concerns. |

Table 1: A sentence to be simplified (*Original*) with two crowdsourced simplifications. *Generated 1-3* are example sentences produced from the fusion graph of the original and crowdsourced sentences (the fusion graph is shown in Figure 2).

## 2 Improving Human Simplification

Crowdsourcing platforms allow for data to be generated quickly with reasonable quality for a modest price (Buhrmester et al., 2011). For text simplification, given a sentence to be simplified, we can solicit human simplifications from the crowdsourcing platform. However, the quality of the resulting simplifications is often of widely varying quality (Amancio and Specia, 2014); the workers are not experts and it can be difficult to give the workers the appropriate context, e.g., the target audience, etc.

We leverage these initial human simplifications to create higher quality simplifications. Specifically, given the original sentence, $x$, and non-expert human simplifications, $s_1, s_2, ..., s_n$, the goal is to produce a high-quality simplification of $x$. Previous work in translation (Zaidan and Callison-Burch, 2011) has shown that reasonable results can be obtained by automatically selecting the highest quality non-expert translation from those solicited, however, you are limited to those options available and additional iterations of human improvements were needed to get reasonable results.

To address these limitations, we extend the candidate simplifications by generating additional alternative candidate simplifications, $s'_1, s'_2, ..., s'_m$, using a graph-based fusion of $s_1, ..., s_n$. We then rank all of the candidate simplifications, i.e., $[s_1, ..., s_n, s'_1, ..., s'_m, x]$, which includes the human simplifications, the simplifications generated by sentence fusions, and the original unsimplified sentence (to allow for no simplification), and pick the top ranked option as the final simplification. To rank the sentences, we learn a model that optimizes a scoring function that combines simplicity and adequacy, though any scoring function could be used. We give details on each of these steps below.

### 2.1 Sentence Fusion

We use a graph-based sentence fusion approach where nodes represent words and directed edges denote candidate next words. The graph is created by adding each sentence to the graph a word at a time, connecting adjacent words in the sentence with a directed edge. New nodes are created for words that do not correspond to existing nodes in the graph.

We follow a similar approach to Filippova (2010), extended in two ways to adapt it to the text simplification domain. First, we create the initial graph using the words in the original sentence. This provides an initial node ordering where the information flow is correct and avoids a bias towards any of the human simplifications. Second, we restrict which words are considered equivalent and merged into a node. The original algorithm merged words that are lexically identical. For text simplification, structural reorderings are common and can create inappropriate transitions connecting content at the end of one simplification to content at the beginning of another and vice versa. These inappropriate transitions resulted in many low quality simplifications that were not always handled well with filtering and reranking. To avoid this and reduce the burden on the reranker, we word-align each human simplification, $s_i$, with the original sentence, $x$, using the Berkeley Aligner (Liang et al., 2006) and consider words as equivalent if they are lexically identical *and* aligned in the word alignment. The result is a less dense graph with less inappropriate paths.

Figure 1 shows the fusion graph over the example in Table 1 after building the graph first with the original sentence and then adding only the first crowdsourced sentence. Each path from START to END represents one candidate simplification. The graph is initially created with just the original sentence, which can be seen as START $\rightarrow$ bird $\rightarrow$

damage → ... → END. The human simplification is then added to this graph, in this case adding an alternative way to start the sentence (START → farmers → problems) and the option to end the sentence early after "water".

Figure 2 shows the fusion graph after the second crowdsourced example is added. Several new nodes have been added representing alternative phrasings in this second sentence and many additional paths through the graph have also been added. As each additional crowdsourced sentence is added to the fusion graph, additional paths through the graph are created, resulting in more candidate sentences produced by the system. The density of the graph is dependent on the number of sentences fused, the lexical overlap between the sentences, and the diversity of phrasing. For readability, we have only shown the example with two crowdsourced sentences added. Table 1 shows three sentences generated from this graph.

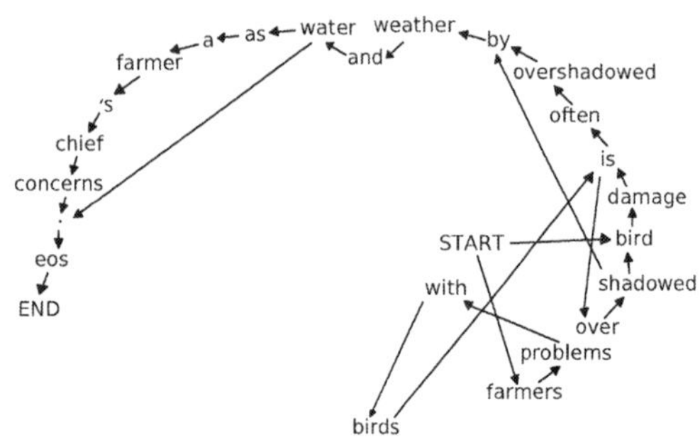


Figure 1: Fusion graph generated from only the *Original* and *Crowdsourced 1* sentences in Table 1. A directed edge $(s, t)$ indicates that word $t$ could follow word $s$ in a candidate simplification.

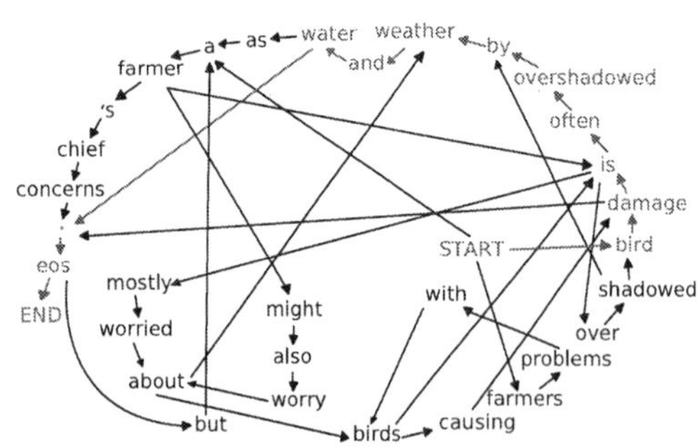


Figure 2: Fusion graph generated from the original and crowdsourced input sentences in Table 1 (the extension of Figure 1 after adding *Crowdsourced 2*). The path highlighted in red generates *Generated 1*.

## 2.2 Candidate Filtering

Any traversal of the graph from START to END represents a candidate simplification. In practice, the number of candidate simplifications encoded by the graph for actual examples can be huge and it is infeasible to generate all of the candidate options for ranking. To help identify higher quality candidate simplifications for the reranking stage we employ two techniques. First, we leverage characteristics of the words in the graph and the graph structure to impose an initial ordering of the candidate simplifications. We can then enumerate the candidate options from the graph based on this initial scoring, stopping after enough candidates have been generated. Second, we apply two additional filtering criteria to attempt to remove low quality candidates.

### 2.2.1 Graph ordering

To provide an initial ordering, we follow the heuristic from Filippova (2010) which weights edges in the graph based both on word frequency and graph path characteristics. Specifically, the weight of each edge $e_{i,j}$, representing the relationship between word $i$ and word $j$, is computed as:

$$w(e_{i,j}) = \frac{f(i) + f(j)}{\sum_{s \in S} diff(s, i, j)^{-1}}$$

where $f(k)$ is defined as the frequency of word $k$ in the sentences used to create the graph, $S$ is the set of all sentences used to create the graph, $diff(s, i, j)$ is distance from the offset position of word $i$ to word $j$ in sentence $s$.

The formula prefers edges connecting a pair of words that frequently appear close to each other as well as those with lower *word* frequencies to *edge* frequency ratio (to discourage common words that have high edge frequency with many nodes). The first condition is enforced by the denominator, which prefers nodes with many paths between them, as well as nodes with short paths between them. The second condition is enforced by the numerator; if the sum of each word's frequencies is large, $w(e_{i,j})$ is subsequently large and thus not preferred.

The quality of a path through the graph is then the sum of the edge weights along that path. Given the weighted graph, we enumerate the candidate simplifications using lowest weight path traversals since lower edge weight denotes higher quality transitions. As an example, in Figure 2, "is" is one of the nodes with several options of a successor. The edge between "is" and "often" has a weight of 1.33, while the other two outward edges, "is mostly" and "is over", both have weight 2.0. Therefore, all things being equal, the path including "is often" would be preferred over the other two.

#### 2.2.2 Filtering

We also applied two filtering criteria to try and eliminate options that were obviously bad before ranking. To avoid simplifications that were too long or short, we filtered out candidates where the compression ratio (number of words in the original sentence divided by the number in the simplification) was more than one-standard deviation from the training set. To avoid simplifications that were too dissimilar from the original sentence, we filtered out candidates where their Siamese LSTM similarity score (see Section 2.3.2) was less than the average similarity score of the human simplifications and the original sentence.

We selected the first 1,000 sentences ordered by the lowest path graph traversal that passed these two filtering criteria to move on to the ranking stage (or less if generating all possible sentences from the graph yielded less). The 1,000 candidates is generated with `shortest_simple_paths` in the NetworkX library (Python), an implementation of the shortest path algorithm without repeated nodes (Yen, 1971).

### 2.3 Ranking

To choose the final simplification we combined and ranked the original sentence (to allow for no simplification), the human simplifications, and the sentence fusion candidates. We employed a supervised, feature-based, pairwise ranking approach using a linear SVM (Lee and Lin, 2014) with the implementation from Pedregosa et al. (2012).

#### 2.3.1 Ranking Metric

Supervised ranking algorithms require training data of ranked examples. For our problem, a training example is a list of candidate simplifications, which we ranked with a quality score. Text simplification quality has been evaluated using both automated metrics, such as BLEU and SARI, and human evaluation metrics, including fluency, adequacy, and simplicity (Xu et al., 2016). Automated metrics require high-quality (i.e. expert) reference simplifications. Expert references are not available in many domains and, since our candidate outputs include crowdsourced sentences, it is unclear how a gold standard reference should be defined and obtained. Therefore, we utilize human metrics, which can be generated using non-experts.

Among the three human metrics, previous work has shown that fluency correlates with simplicity, and there is an intuitive tradeoff between simplicity and adequacy (Schwarzer and Kauchak, 2018): as sentences get simpler more content tends to be removed and the adequacy suffers. Therefore, we focus on simplicity and adequacy. The tradeoff between them can also be observed in the example shown in Table 2. For instance, the fourth sentence (*Generated 1*) is very simple, but the crucial contextual information about farmers is missing. On the other hand, the second sentence (*Crowdsourced 1*) retains most of the information in the original sentence, but also some redundant information. The tradeoff is reflected in their simplicity and adequacy scores.

To capture this tradeoff, we use a composite of simplicity and adequacy as our ranking metric during training. We define the score of a candidate simplification, $s$, as the weighted geometric mean of its normalized (0-1) adequacy, $A_s$, and simplicity, $S_s$,

$$\text{score}_\alpha(s) = \sqrt{A_s^\alpha \cdot S_s}.$$

Varying $\alpha$ biases the ranking towards simplicity (with lower $\alpha$) or adequacy (with higher $\alpha$). We only allow positive alpha. In the extremes, $\alpha = 0$ corresponds to optimizing only for simplicity and $\alpha = \infty$ only for adequacy.

#### 2.3.2 Features

We used seven features for the ranking approach including two language model features and two features that quantify the similarity between the original sentence and the candidate simplification.

**N-gram Language Model** Log-prob normalized by the number of words in the sentence of a trigram language model using Kneser-Ney smoothing trained on the billion-word language model corpus (Chelba et al., 2013) using SRILM (Stolcke, 2002).

**Neural Language Model** Log-prob normalized by the number of non-stop words in the sentence of a recurrent-convolutional character-based neural language model (Kim et al., 2016).

| Candidate Sentence | Simplicity | Adequacy | Ngram Logprob | Logprob | TF-IDF | Siamese | Comp. Ratio |
|---|---|---|---|---|---|---|---|
| Original | 0.000 | 5.000 | 6.226 | 10.986 | 0.000 | 1.000 | 1.000 |
| Crowdsourced 1 | 1.333 | 4.000 | 7.082 | 13.478 | 4.605 | 0.379 | 0.667 |
| Crowdsourced 2 | -0.667 | 3.333 | 7.151 | 10.376 | 4.493 | 0.287 | 1.556 |
| Generated 1 | 1.667 | 2.333 | 6.161 | 9.548 | 1.620 | 0.385 | 0.667 |
| Generated 2 | N/A | N/A | 6.408 | 12.322 | 2.650 | 0.497 | 0.889 |
| Generated 3 | N/A | N/A | 6.833 | 13.686 | 3.038 | 0.520 | 1.000 |

Table 2: Sentences from Table 1 (in the same order) along with the features used to rerank them. Simplicity and adequacy scores are not available for the last two candidates because they did not get picked by the decile ranker for annotation in the experiments (see **Training** in 3.1 for more details).

**TF-IDF Cosine Similarity** TF-IDF cosine similarity between the original sentence and the candidate simplification, using sentence-level IDF values calculated from the Newsela corpus.

**Siamese LSTM** Two LSTM recurrent neural networks with shared weights trained on the SemEval2014 SICK dataset (Marelli et al., 2014) using fixed, pre-trained Google News word embeddings (Mikolov et al., 2013). The similarity is calculated by comparing the hidden states of two input sentences (Mueller and Thyagarajan, 2016).

**Compression Ratio** The ratio of the number of words of the original sentence versus the candidate simplification.

**Source Label** Two binary features, one indicating if the candidate is human-generated and one indicating if it is the original sentence.

## 3 Experiments

To evaluate our approach, we collected training and testing sets consisting of an original sentence and four human simplifications. To help better train the ranker, we also collected additional training data by scoring some simplifications generated by the sentence fusion approach. To understand the effect of alpha on the output, we trained rankers over 80 values of $\alpha$, chosen to be densest near $\alpha = 1$, resulting in 80 different rankers that prioritize different levels of simplicity. We tested each of these models on the test set and compared them to four levels of expert human evaluations based on adequacy, simplicity, and fluency.

### 3.1 Data

We used the Newsela corpus (Xu et al., 2015) as the data set for evaluation. Newsela is a sentence-aligned corpus generated from articles manually simplified by experts at four simplicity levels (referred to as V1-V4, in order of increasing simplicity). We chose this dataset because it provides a strong baseline with expert simplifications and has multiple simplicity levels, which is suitable for testing our target-simplicity-specified rerankers.

**Training** We randomly selected 119 original sentences and collected 4 human simplifications and scored them for simplicity and adequacy. This data lacked examples of sentence fusion-generated simplifications that had been scored, and the initial ranker trained on it did not perform well.

To include sentence fusion examples in the data, we selected and scored some sentence fusion outputs. For each original sentence, we split the sentence fusion candidates into deciles based on the ranker (with $\alpha = 1$) and annotated the first sentence from each decile with simplicity and adequacy scores. This resulted in 10 sentence fusion simplifications per original sentence, in addition to the 4 human. We repeated this process: starting with the original sentences, annotating, and training on the freshly created dataset in each iteration. After two iterations, we observed approximate convergence in adequacy and simplicity scores on the training data and stopped iterating.

This new dataset consists of 119 original sentences, each with 4 human and 10 sentence fusion simplifications (15 candidate sentences per example, for a total of 1785 sentences) each annotated with simplicity and adequacy, and is used as the *training* data. Note that once the ranker has been trained, the only data required to apply the model to rank new sentences is the original sentence and the four crowdsourced simplifications. The generation and annotation procedure described above is only required to train the model.

**Testing** For the test set we chose an additional 200 random sentences where each original sentence was aligned with a sentence at each of the four simplicity levels (V1-V4). This allowed for a comparison of our approach against all four expert simplification levels.

**Data Collection** We used Amazon Mechanical Turk both to generate the four candidate human simplifications and to score simplifications (Callison-Burch and Dredze, 2010). The instruction for sentence simplification is to "make the sentence easier to understand" such that it "means the same thing as the original sentence". For adequacy and simplicity scores, the annotators are given the original and the simplified sentences and asked to judge to which degree the latter retains the meaning of or is simpler than the former, respectively, while fluency is annotated independently of the original sentence. We averaged judgments from three workers for each sentence. For simplicity, we asked the annotators to compare the simplification to the original on a five-point scale ranging from $-2$ (much less simple) to 2 (much simpler). Adequacy and fluency were assessed using on a five-point Likert scale with higher numbers representing better values.

Workers were required to be in the United States and have a historical 97% acceptance rate, but we placed no other restrictions on education, English proficiency, or previous simplification experience: the workers generating the simplifications were *not* experts. The full dataset (training and testing) with human evaluation scores is available online[1].

### 3.2 Results

**Simplicity and Adequacy** Figure 3 shows mean adequacy (1 to 5) and simplicity (-2 to 2) on the test set for Newsela V1-V4 and our approach (Reranked Joint) for a range of $\alpha$. Higher is better denoting simpler output for simplicity and better content retention for adequacy. One of the main benefits of our approach is that different levels of simplicity can be targeted by varying $\alpha$: the simplicity varies in the output ranging from points in the bottom right where no simplification occurs to points in the top center where significant simplification has happened. In general, the system output is both simpler and retains more information than the human expert baseline of Newsela. In particular, for all levels of Newsela (V1-V4) there is a setting of $\alpha$ where the system produces simplifications that have significantly better simplicity *and* adequacy. Table 3 gives examples along with statistical comparison based on a paired $t$-test.

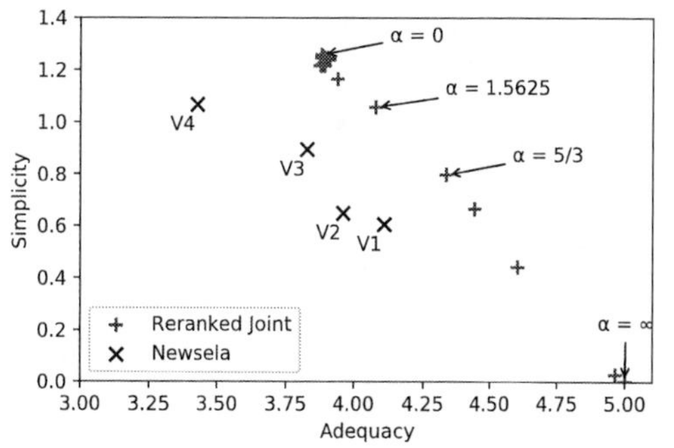


Figure 3: Average simplicity and adequacy scores for the system trained over a range of $\alpha$ compared to V1-V4 of Newsela on the test set.

| Source | Simp. | Adequacy | Fluency |
|---|---|---|---|
| System ($\alpha = 5/3$) | **0.81** | **4.33** | 4.15 |
| Newsela V1 | $0.61^{**}$ | $4.11^{***}$ | $4.26^{*}$ |
| Newsela V2 | $0.65^{*}$ | $3.96^{***}$ | **$4.26^{*}$** |
| System ($\alpha = 1.5625$) | **1.06** | **4.08** | 4.11 |
| Newsela V3 | $0.90^{**}$ | $3.83^{***}$ | **$4.24^{*}$** |
| System ($\alpha = 0$) | **1.26** | 3.88 | 4.00 |
| Human-Only ($\alpha = 0$) | $1.19^{*}$ | **3.94** | 4.05 |
| Newsela V4 | $1.06^{**}$ | $3.43^{**}$ | **$4.26^{***}$** |

Table 3: Results for three $\alpha$ with statistical significance for comparable Newsela versions *, **, *** denoting $p < 0.05$, $p < 0.01$, and $p < 0.001$, respectively.

**Fluency** Table 3 also shows the fluency scores for three different $\alpha$ settings. These alphas were selected from the range explored in the experiments to highlight how different settings of alpha produced models with significantly better performance than human experts. For all approaches, the fluency is high with values ranging from 4.00 to 4.26. The system output is less fluent than the human experts, particularly at lower levels of $\alpha$. To understand the cause of this difference, we compared the system fluency to the fluency of the *non-expert* (crowdsourced) humans that the system sentences were created from. For all three settings of $\alpha$ there is no statistically significant difference between the system output and the non-expert humans: the drop in fluency is a result of using non-expert humans.

**Qualitative** Table 4 shows an original sentence from the test dataset and the four crowdsourced simplifications. There is a fair amount of variabil-

[1] https://cs.pomona.edu/~dkauchak/simplification/

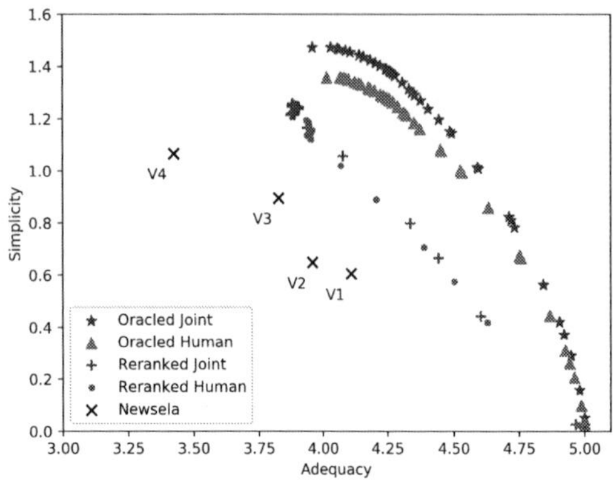


Figure 4: Simplicity and adequacy scores for reranking only the human simplifications as well as oracle output for both the full system (joint) and human only.

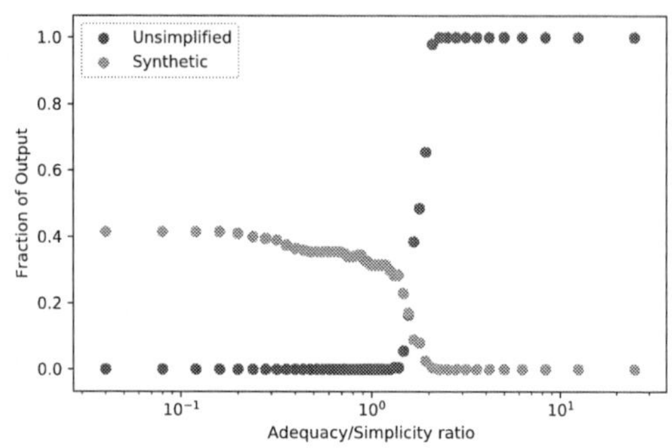


Figure 5: The fractions of output sentences coming from the sentence fusion system (synthetic) and unsimplified output sentences (the rest of the outputs are the crowdsourced simplifications), shown against the relative weightings of adequacy and simplicity.

ity in both the way that the text was simplified as well as the level of simplification. Crowdsourced 1 has only minor simplifications while the fourth is fairly aggressive. Crowdsourced 2 and 3 both split the sentence to try and make it simpler. The bottom part of the table shows the ranked output of our approach with $\alpha = 1$ (even balance between simplicity and adequacy). The top ranked choice (and therefore the one chosen) is a system fusion generated sentence; while simple, the sentence maintains the critical information in the original information. Table 4 also shows next three highest ranked options. The original sentence was ranked second (representing no simplification) followed by another system generated sentence and the first crowdsourced sentence.

### 3.3 Fusion and Ranking

We conducted additional experiments to understand the contributions of sentence fusion and ranking. To understand the contribution of the sentence fusion approach, we compared the general approach (Reranked Joint) to a version where only the four human simplifications were ranked (Reranked Human), i.e. without sentence fusion candidates (Figure 4). When adequacy is prioritized, the results are similar, however, as simplicity get prioritized more, the human simplifications are limited by the simplifications available. Adding sentence fusion allows for more varied simplifications, some of which are simpler. Table 3 gives a concrete example at $\alpha = 0$; the system is significantly simpler than the human only output, but there is no significant difference in adequacy or fluency.

Overall, the approach tends to select a combination of human and sentence fusion simplifications. Figure 5 shows the proportion of unsimplified and synthetic (fusion generated) sentences chosen as the best simplification by the ranker on the test data set for varying levels of $\alpha$. For higher $\alpha$, biasing towards adequacy, the system simply chooses not to simplify and selects the original unsimplified sentence. For the other values of $\alpha$, however, the approach utilizes a combination of the human simplifications and the fusion generated (synthetic) simplifications, using the fusion generated sentence for 30-40% of the simplifications.

We also conducted an oracle study, where we picked the best simplification candidate based on the the simplicity/adequacy annotations ("Oracled" variations in Figure 4). This is similar to the approach of Zaidan and Callison-Burch (2011), and is an option when such annotations are available. We tested this for human simplifications only (Oracled Human) and the full system with human simplifications and the top sentence fusion candidate (Oracled Joint). Again, we see that the sentence fusion approach enables more simplification, providing candidates that are significantly simpler than those generated by humans when simplicity is prioritized. The performance gap between the reranked results and the oracled result suggests that there could still be room for improving the quality of the ranking.

| **Input Sentences** | | |
|---|---|---|
| Original | | Ferguson has done dozens of studies on the subject and has consistently found that violent video games do not contribute to societal aggression. |
| Crowdsourced 1 | | Through dozens of studies on the subject, Ferguson has consistently found that violent video games do not contribute to societal aggression. |
| Crowdsourced 2 | | Ferguson found that violent video games do not contribute to societal aggression. He has done dozens of studies on the subject and has consistently come to the same conclusion. |
| Crowdsourced 3 | | Ferguson has completed many studies on the subject of violent video games. Ferguson concluded that these games do not contribute to societal aggression. |
| Crowdsourced 4 | | Ferguson did over 12 studies on it and saw that violent video games don't make people violent. |
| **Ranked Output Sentences** ($\alpha = 1.0$) | | |
| 1 | System 1 | Ferguson found that violent video games do not contribute to societal aggression. |
| 2 | Original | Ferguson has done dozens of studies on the subject and has consistently found that violent video games do not contribute to societal aggression. |
| 3 | System 2 | Ferguson has completed many studies on the subject of violent video games do not contribute to societal aggression. |
| 4 | Crowdsourced 1 | Through dozens of studies on the subject, Ferguson has consistently found that violent video games do not contribute to societal aggression. |

Table 4: An example of real input from the test data set, consisting of the original sentence and four human simplifications, and top output sentences generated and ranked by an $\alpha = 1$ reranker.

## 4 Discussion

We introduced a new approach for leveraging crowdsourced human simplification that generates additional candidate simplifications using a sentence fusion technique and a reranking approach to pick high-quality simplifications. Our proposed approach is capable of producing simplifications that outperform expert human simplifications and the sentence fusion technique is particularly good at generating simpler variants.

We also introduced the new task of generating a high-quality text simplification based on crowdsourced simplifications. Our sentence fusion algorithm followed by reranking provides one possible approach, but there are a number of areas where it could be improved. We used a graph-based fusion approach, but recent neural approaches that have been applied in abstractive summarization may be adapted (Chopra et al., 2016; Nallapati et al., 2016). Many aspects of the reranker still need to be further explored. While the reranker did a reasonable job of selecting good candidates across different simplicity levels the oracle study (Figure 4) suggests that there is still room for improvement and additional features and alternative reranking algorithms should be investigated. The question of how well our trained reranker ports to different domains is also yet to be investigated. Future research on the relationships between $\alpha$ and simplicity is needed to establish a standard for choosing appropriate values of $\alpha$ as well. We hope this paper and the associated data provides a good starting point for future research in this area.

## References

Marcelo Amancio and Lucia Specia. 2014. An analysis of crowdsourced text simplifications. In *Proceedings of the 3rd Workshop on Predicting and Improving Text Readability for Target Reader Populations (PITR)*.

Michael Buhrmester, Tracy Kwang, and Samuel D Gosling. 2011. Amazon's mechanical turk: A new source of inexpensive, yet high-quality, data? *Perspectives on Psychological Science*, 6(1):3–5.

Chris Callison-Burch. 2009. Fast, cheap, and creative: evaluating translation quality using amazon's mechanical turk. In *Proceedings of EMNLP*.

Chris Callison-Burch and Mark Dredze. 2010. Creating speech and language data with amazon's mechanical turk. In *Proceedings of NAACL-HLT Workshop on Creating Speech and Language Data with Amazon's Mechanical Turk*.

Ciprian Chelba, Tomas Mikolov, Mike Schuster, Qi Ge, Thorsten Brants, and Phillipp Koehn. 2013. One billion word benchmark for measuring progress in statistical language modeling. *arXiv:1312.3005*.

Sumit Chopra, Michael Auli, and Alexander M Rush. 2016. Abstractive sentence summarization with attentive recurrent neural networks. In *Proceedings of the 2016 Conference of the North American Chapter of the Association for Computational Linguistics: Human Language Technologies*, pages 93–98.

Katja Filippova. 2010. Multi-sentence compression: Finding shortest paths in word graphs. In *Proceedings of COLING*.

Yoon Kim, Yacine Jernite, David Sontag, and Alexander M Rush. 2016. Character-aware neural language models. In *Proceedings of AAAI*.

Reno Kriz, João Sedoc, Marianna Apidianaki, Carolina Zheng, Gaurav Kumar, Eleni Miltsakaki, and Chris Callison-Burch. 2019. Complexity-weighted loss and diverse reranking for sentence simplification. In *Proceedings of the 2019 Conference of the North American Chapter of the Association for Computational Linguistics: Human Language Technologies, Volume 1 (Long and Short Papers)*, pages 3137–3147.

Walter S Lasecki, Luz Rello, and Jeffrey P Bigham. 2015. Measuring text simplification with the crowd. In *Proceedings of Web for All Conference*.

Ching-Pei Lee and Chih-Jen Lin. 2014. Large-scale linear ranksvm. *Neural computation*.

Percy Liang, Ben Taskar, and Dan Klein. 2006. Alignment by agreement. In *Proceedings of NAACL-HLT*.

Marco Marelli, Luisa Bentivogli, Marco Baroni, Raffaella Bernardi, Stefano Menini, and Roberto Zamparelli. 2014. Semeval-2014 task 1: Evaluation of compositional distributional semantic models on full sentences through semantic relatedness and textual entailment. In *Proceedings of the International Workshop on Semantic Evaluation (SemEval)*.

Tomas Mikolov, Ilya Sutskever, Kai Chen, Greg S Corrado, and Jeff Dean. 2013. Distributed representations of words and phrases and their compositionality. In *Proceedings of NIPS*.

Jonas Mueller and Aditya Thyagarajan. 2016. Siamese recurrent architectures for learning sentence similarity. In *Proceedings of AAAI*.

Ramesh Nallapati, Bowen Zhou, Caglar Gulcehre, Bing Xiang, et al. 2016. Abstractive text summarization using sequence-to-sequence rnns and beyond. *arXiv preprint arXiv:1602.06023*.

Shashi Narayan and Claire Gardent. 2016. Unsupervised sentence simplification using deep semantics. In *The 9th International Natural Language Generation conference*, pages 111–120.

Fabian Pedregosa, Elodie Cauvet, Gaël Varoquaux, Christophe Pallier, Bertrand Thirion, and Alexandre Gramfort. 2012. Learning to rank from medical imaging data. In *Proceedings of International Workshop on Machine Learning in Medical Imaging*.

Max Schwarzer and David Kauchak. 2018. Human evaluation for text simplification: The simplicity-adequacy tradeoff. In *Proceedings of SoCal NLP Symposium*.

Matthew Shardlow. 2014. A survey of automated text simplification. *International Journal of Advanced Computer Science and Applications*.

Matthew Shardlow and Raheel Nawaz. 2019. Neural text simplification of clinical letters with a domain specific phrase table. In *Proceedings of ACL*.

Advaith Siddharthan. 2014. A survey of research on text simplification. *International Journal of Applied Linguistics*.

Andreas Stolcke. 2002. Srilm-an extensible language modeling toolkit. In *Proceedings of International Conference on Spoken Language Processing*.

Wei Xu, Chris Callison-Burch, and Courtney Napoles. 2015. Problems in current text simplification research: New data can help. *Transactions of the Association of Computational Linguistics*.

Wei Xu, Courtney Napoles, Ellie Pavlick, Quanze Chen, and Chris Callison-Burch. 2016. Optimizing statistical machine translation for text simplification. *Transactions of the Association for Computational Linguistics*.

Jin Y Yen. 1971. Finding the k shortest loopless paths in a network. *management Science*, 17(11):712–716.

Omar F Zaidan and Chris Callison-Burch. 2011. Crowdsourcing translation: Professional quality from non-professionals. In *Proceedings of NAACL-HLT*.

Christina Zarcadoolas. 2010. The simplicity complex: exploring simplified health messages in a complex world. *Health Promotion International*.

Xingxing Zhang and Mirella Lapata. 2017. Sentence simplification with deep reinforcement learning. *arXiv preprint arXiv:1703.10931*.

# Structural Realization with GGNNs

**Jinman Zhao Gerald Penn Huan Ling**
Department of Computer Science
University of Toronto
{jzhao,gpenn,linghuan}@cs.toronto.edu

## Abstract

In this paper, we define an abstract task called structural realization that generates words given a prefix of words and a partial representation of a parse tree. We also present a method for solving instances of this task using a Gated Graph Neural Network (GGNN). We evaluate it with standard accuracy measures, as well as with respect to perplexity, in which its comparison to previous work on language modelling serves to quantify the information added to a lexical selection task by the presence of syntactic knowledge. That the addition of parse-tree-internal nodes to this neural model should improve the model, with respect both to accuracy and to more conventional measures such as perplexity, may seem unsurprising, but previous attempts have not met with nearly as much success. We have also learned that transverse links through the parse tree compromise the model's accuracy at generating adjectival and nominal parts of speech.

## 1 Introduction

We conjecture that this may be an opportune time to reassess the extent to which syntax is capable of contributing to a word prediction task. *Structured realization* is a generalization of language modelling in which we receive $n - j$ words as input, together with a syntactic structure that has a yield of $n$ word positions and spans the input, plus an "overhang" of $j$ unrealized word positions. Our task is to fill in the most likely missing $j$ words. Language modelling generally possesses only the trivial annotation that consists of the words themselves and has historically assumed that $j = 1$, constituting an $n$-gram. Notable exceptions date back to the work of Chelba (2000) on *structured language modelling*, in which the syntactic annotation is partial, in that there is no overhang ($j = 0$), but structurally non-trivial, although often sparing relative to corpora that parsers are trained upon.[1] The most thorough exploration of this direction is probably that of Köhn and Baumann (2016), who equip a variety of language models with a pretrained dependency parser, which they use to predict the part of speech (POS) of the next word and some overarching syntactic structure, and then predict the next word from its POS plus an $n$-gram word history. They report a roughly 6% perplexity reduction across the different models.

In the specific case where a complete, spanning, syntactic representation is provided, but the model is evaluated solely from a zero-prefix initialization (i.e., $n = j$), this generalization can be viewed as a simple purely syntactic surface-realization problem, as one would find in a generation task.

With no fanfare whatsoever in CL circles, the machine learning community proposed an evaluation task seven years ago called "MadLibs" Kiros et al. (2014). In our terminology, the syntactic annotation provided is merely $n - j$ words followed by a string of $j$ POS tags. While it may be difficult to imagine that someone would be in possession of this POS information without also knowing how the POS tags connected together, the authors were interested in testing a new multiplicative neural language model, in which attributes (such as POS tags) can be attached to input words.

In a neural setting, parse trees can be encoded with a generalization of recurrent neural networks (RNNs) called Graph Neural Networks (GNNs). GNNs have been used as encoders to deal with a variety of different NLP problems (see related work section later). Gated GNNs (GGNNs) are an improvement over GNNs that is analogous to that of GRUs over RNNs. They train faster, and they address problems with vanishing gradients.

[1]Chelba (2000) proposes that, in order to iteratively predict one word at a time, a structured language model should predict syntactic structure over every word that it has predicted, but in his evaluation, it is very clear that he is more concerned with the first stage of word prediction.



*Proceedings of the Fifteenth Workshop on Graph-Based Methods for Natural Language Processing (TextGraphs-15)*, pages 115–124
June 11, 2021. 

We shall compare two modes of our model here using GGNN-encoded parse trees: one with parse trees from OntoNotes 5.0 (Hovy et al., 2006; Pradhan et al., 2013; Weischedel et al., 2013), and one with vestigial transitions between pre-terminal categories in sequence, which resembles the syntactic annotation selected by Kiros et al. (2014), although here the word prefix is also POS-annotated. We also test the combination of the two: a syntactic tree augmented by a linear pipeline of transitions between pre-terminals. We compute sentence-level accuracy by measuring how many words in the generated strings legitimately belong to their assigned POS categories, and compute word-level accuracy scores in three ways: accuracy at choosing a word of the appropriate part of speech (this time with the prefix of words corrected to what the corpus says, as necessary), rank of the corpus sentences by data likelihood, and word-guessing accuracy, relative to what appears in the corpus.

## 2 Method

In this paper, we exploit a Gated Graph Neural Network (GGNN) (Li et al., 2016) as a parse tree encoder. GNN encoders have been shown to be efficient for neural machine translation (Beck et al., 2018; Bastings et al., 2017) whereas in our case, we focus on structured realization. GGNNs define a propagation model that extends RNNs to arbitrary graphs and learn propagation rules between nodes. We aim to encode syntactic trees by propagating category labels throughout the tree's structure.

### 2.1 Gated Graph Neural Networks

For completeness, we briefly summarize the GGNN model (Li et al., 2016). A GGNN uses a directed graph $\{V, E\}$ where V and E are the sets of nodes and edges. We represent the initial state of a node $v$ as $s_v$ and the hidden state of node v at propagation time step t as $h_v^t$. The adjacency matrix $A \in \mathbb{R}^{|V| \times N|V|}$ determines how the nodes in the graph propagate information to each other, where $N$ represents the number of different edge types. Figure 1 is the visual representation of a GGNN; it starts with $h_v^0 = s_v$, then follows a propagation model which unrolls T steps and generates $h_v^T$ at the end. Each unroll step follows the same rule to compute $h_v^t$ from $h_v^{(t-1)}$ and A:

$$\begin{aligned} a_v^t &= A_v^\top \, [h_1^{t-1\top}, ..., h_{|V|}^{t-1\top}]^\top + b \\ r_v^t &= \sigma(W^r a_v^t + U^r h_v^{(t-1)}) \\ z_v^t &= \sigma(W^z a_v^t + U^z h_v^{(t-1)}) \\ \widetilde{h_v^t} &= tanh(W a_v^t + U(r_v^t \odot h_v^{(t-1)})) \\ h_v^t &= (1 - z_v^t) \odot h_v^{(t-1)} + z_v^t \odot \widetilde{h_v^t}. \end{aligned} \tag{1}$$

$b, W, W^r, W^z, U, U^r, U^z$ above are trainable parameters.

After information is propagated for $T$ time steps, each node's hidden state collectively represents a message about itself and its neighbourhood, which is then passed to its neighbours. Finally there is the output model. For example, Acuna et al. (2018) implemented their output model by:

$$\begin{aligned} h_v &= tanh(FC_1(h_v^T)) \\ \text{out}_v &= FC_2(h_v) \end{aligned} \tag{2}$$

where $FC_1$ and $FC_2$ are two fully connected layers.

### 2.2 Gated Graph Neural Network Models

In this part, we will describe how we use GGNNs and parse trees to build our three experimental models. Figure 2 depicts example trees for these models.

#### 2.2.1 Input Tree Construction

Since we are using GGNNs, we first need to construct the graph by giving the parse tree. We build three different models:

**Model 1:** For a given parse tree, let N be the number of nodes in the parse tree. Then the adjacency matrix of the tree, denoted as **A**, is an N × 2N matrix, concatenating two N × N matrices. **A**[:N,:] is the forward adjacency matrix of the tree and **A**[N:,:] is the backward adjacency matrix.

**Model 2:** The input does not consider interior parse tree nodes, but instead works more like a conventional language model. For each parse tree, and given a sequence of words $(w_1, w_2, ..., w_{n-1})$, we retain all and only the pre-terminal parse tree nodes, and then attempt to predict the next word $w_n$. This is the model of Kiros et al. (2014). Note that, while it is essentially a language model, the nodes of this Model are a subset of the nodes of Model 1, although the edges are completely different, encoding only transitions between the pre-terminals

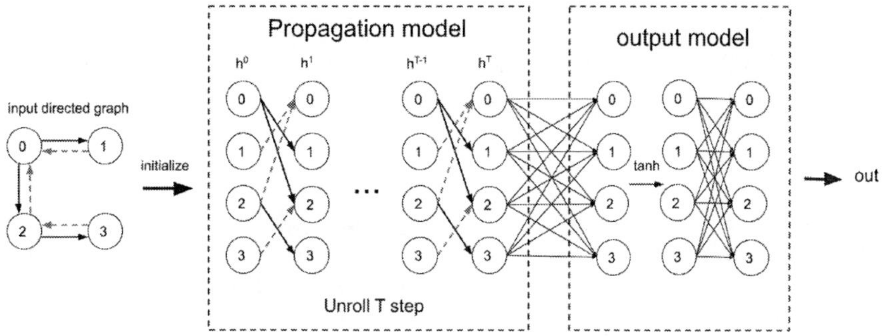


Figure 1: An example GGNN. The GGNN generates output from a directed graph. It consists of a propagation model and an output model. During the propagation step, there are two different edge types in this graph. Black arrows are the OUT edges while red arrows are the IN edges.

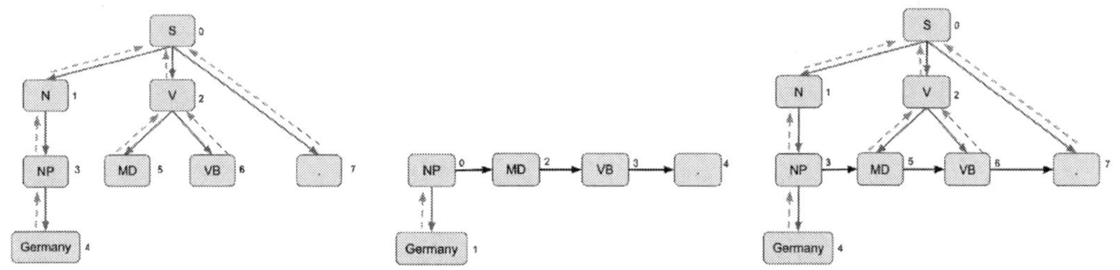


(1) (2) (3)

Figure 2: Example of an input parse tree with a given input word prefix ($w_1$ = *Germany*) and a completion consisting of POS/pre-terminal categories. The number near each node represents its index within the adjacency matrix of the tree (Figure 3). Red arrows are forward edges, green dashed arrows are backward edges and black arrows represent a transverse edge between pre-terminals. The partial trees each contain 1 terminal("Germany"), 4 pre-terminals ("NP","MD","VB",".") and, in Models (1) and (3), 3 other interior categories ("S","N","V"). We want to predict the word after *Germany*, which will be the child of pre-terminal "MD". The input of Model 1 considers tree nodes and forward/backward edges, but not transverse pre-terminal edges. The input of Model 2 does not include other parts of the tree except pre-terminals and the given terminals, yet it contains all three kinds of edges. The input of Model 3 which contains all tree nodes and all edges.

in sequence. This time, the adjacency matrix A is N × 3N which is a concatenation of three N × N matrices: $A^{forward}$, $A^{backward}$ and $A^{pre-terminal}$.

**Model 3:** This one is the combination of the above two. The number of nodes is the same as for Model 1. The adjacency matrix is the addition of each respective pair of $A^{forward}$, $A^{backward}$ and $A^{pre-terminal}$, concatenated together.

Figure 2 depicts an example for each model. By comparing the results for different models later, we will understand how essential inner nodes and edges between pre-terminals are for word prediction. Also note that Model 1 and Model 3 have the same number of nodes, but the number of nodes in Model 2 is smaller. Nevertheless, in all three models, the input may contain a prefix of $n - j$ words. As mentioned above, when this prefix is zero-length, we have three classical surface realization models. But we can also view all three models as generalizations of language models, in which:

$$P(W) = P(w_1 w_2 ... w_n) = \prod_{i=1}^{n} P(w_i | tree_{i-1}) \tag{3}$$

and $tree_{i-1}$ is the parse tree with the $1^{th}, 2^{th} ... (i-1)^{th}$ word tokens in place.

### 2.2.2 Terminal, Pre-terminal and Interior Tags

Once we have constructed the graph, we need to construct input for the model. Let $D = 100$ be the dimension of a set of word-embedding vectors over a fixed lexicon. The input to each model is an N × D matrix. All three types of nodes need

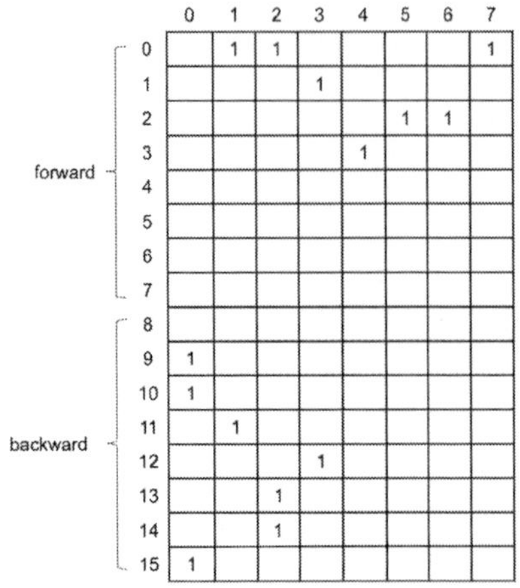


Figure 3: The adjacency matrix of the above input example (1) in Figure 2. Blank slots represent 0, meaning no edge between two nodes. A = $[A^{forward}, A^{backward}]$.

to be represented in same-dimensional vectors: 1) terminals, i.e. words, 2) pre-terminals (nodes that only appear as a parent of a leaf), and 3) interior node tags (nodes that are neither leaves nor pre-terminals). We then need to normalize all vectors.

We associate each terminal (word) with its GloVe (Pennington et al., 2014) pre-trained word vector (trained from Wikipedia 2014 + Gigaword 5, containing a 400K-word vocabulary).

For pre-terminals, we gather sequences (e.g., "NP MD VB ." in Figure 1) for each input sentence, prepare a corpus consisting only of these tags, and train embedding vectors directly on the POS tags by using the GloVe algorithms (Pennington et al., 2014). We then associate each pre-terminal with its corresponding vector.

The number of interior tags is larger than D, however, so one-hot is not appropriate in this case. For each interior node, we randomly generate a D-dimensional vector, sampling each entry of the vector from a standard Gaussian distribution.

#### 2.2.3 Predict Words

After the input presentation, the propagation step and a fully connected layer, the model will generate an N × D output matrix. In other words, all N nodes in the parse tree will have D-dimensional output. In language modelling mode, we would not care about any output except the one generated by the pre-terminal dominating the position of $w_{n-j+1}$. Let $\hat{v}$ denote this normalized D-dimensional output. The probability of $w_{n-j+1}$ given the tree, $P(w_{n-j+1} = i | tree_{n-j}) =:$

$$\frac{exp(c^2 \times (\hat{v}^T \cdot v_i))}{\sum_{j=0}^{V} exp(c^2 \times (\hat{v}^T \cdot v_j)))} \tag{4}$$

where V is the size of the pre-trained lexicon, $v_i$ and $v_j$ are vector representations for the $i$th and $j$th word types. We choose $i$ with maximum conditional probability. This is equivalent to choosing the $i$ for which $v_i$ is the closest word vector $\hat{v}$.

When $c = 1$ and $tree_{n-j}$ consists only of the sequence of input words $(w_1, w_2, ..., w_{n-j})$, Eq 4 would correspond to a standard language model. The interval $[e^{-1}, e^1]$ is too small as the range of the numerator to distinguish between good predictions and bad predictions. So instead of only normalizing them, we also multiply by a constant $c$. Thus the range of the numerator becomes $[e^{-c^2}, e^{c^2}]$. We tuned $c$ manually from 1 to 15 based on model 1. Figure 4 shows that $c = 6$ is the best, as it has the lowest cross entropy compared with other values. We will assume $c = 6$ in Section 3.

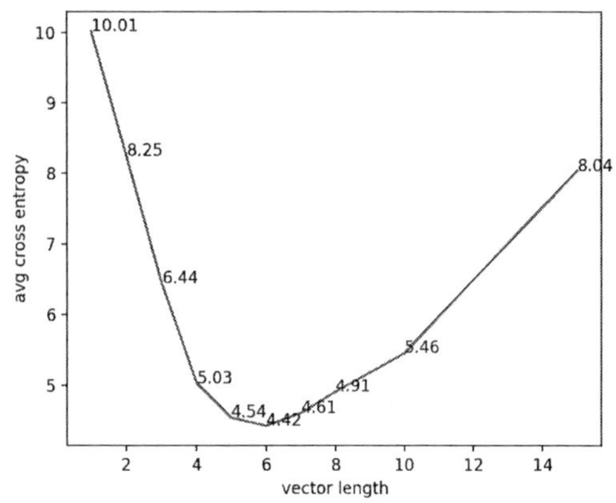


Figure 4: Average cross entropy loss of validation set using Model 1 with different magnitude of vectors.

## 3 Results

### 3.1 Datasets

We train and test all models on OntoNotes 5.0, which contains 110,000+ English sentences from print publications. We also train and evaluate the perplexity of all models on the Penn Treebank (Marcus et al., 1993), as this has become a standard among syntax-driven language models. PTB $2-21 are used as training data, $24 is for validation, and $23 is used for testing.

We excluded those trees/sentences with words that are not in GloVe's (Pennington et al., 2014) pre-trained vocabulary from both the training and validation data. The test set and validation set were excluded from our development cycle. Dataset statistics are provided in Table 1.

### 3.2 Training Details

We used 100-dimensional pre-trained GloVe vectors to represent different kinds of leaves in the tree. As the loss function, we use cross entropy loss which is calculated based on Equation 4. For each complete parse tree in the training set, let $n$ be the number of leaves/terminals in this tree. So this tree has $n$ different possible prefixes of known words($w_1 ... w_i$, $0 \leq i \leq n-1$), each with a parse tree as training input. In addition, since the number of nodes in different graphs is distinct, we use stochastic gradient descent with a learning rate of 0.01 to train the model (i.e. batch size = 1).

Perplexity relates to cross-entropy loss:

$$PPL = e^{-\frac{1}{N}\sum_i p(x) \log y(x)} \tag{5}$$

This is corpus-level perplexity, where $x$ is an arbitrary word and $p(x)$ is the function we discussed in Eq 4 and N is the number of predictions. The magnitude $c = 6$ also has lowest perplexity.

### 3.3 Realization Accuracy

A simple way to evaluate the accuracy of the models as implementations of the structured realization task is to consider their sentence output in terms of POS accuracy. If we simply remove the yields of corpus trees and attempt to regenerate them from the trees, the resulting strings will often differ from the original yields, but they may still be grammatical in the sense of the first $j$ tokens having the appropriate POS tag sequence. Table 2 shows the sentence-level word and POS accuracies on the OntoNotes test set. Both OntoNotes and PTB provide gold-standard (human labeled) syntactic constituency parse trees. We trained our model on these trees. These trees are expensive, however, so we also evaluated on trees obtained from the Berkeley neural parser (Kitaev and Klein, 2018) a state-of-the-art constituency parser with an $F_1 = 95$ score on the PTB.

### 3.4 Continuity of Latent Spaces

Some trees have the same unlabelled tree structure, although they may have different nodes. We can randomly pick two such isomorphic constituency trees $T_1$ and $T_2$, delete their leaves then linearly interpolate between their corresponding nodes and generate. For an arbitrary node of the $i^{th}$ intermediate tree, the vector representation would be:

$$\begin{aligned} node = (1-\lambda) \times T_1(node) \\ + \lambda \times T_2(node), \end{aligned} \tag{6}$$

for some value of $\lambda \in [0, 1]$. Table 3 demonstrates sentences generated from trees for various values of $\lambda$. This kind of "semantic continuity" has been demonstrated before on vector encodings, but, to our knowledge, not on structured spaces such as parallel trees of vectors.

### 3.5 Perplexity

Perplexity is perhaps the most common evaluation measure in the language modelling literature. The formula of perplexity was shown in Eq 5.

We trained and evaluated our Models on the different datasets listed in Table 1. The perplexities of the test data sets are listed in Table 4. RNNG (Dyer et al., 2016) is a state-of-the-art syntax-aware model. LSTM-256 LM is our self implemented language model using 2-layer LSTM cell with sequence length 20 and hidden state size 256. Our three models have lower perplexities across the board compared with RNNG on both OntoNotes and PTB. Model 3 on gold parse trees has the lowest perplexity overall, although it is important to remember that our models benefit from distributions from Wikipedia that are implicitly encoded in the GloVe vectors. LSTMs that use GloVe perform worse than the LSTMs with trainable word embeddings shown here.[2]

In addition, for comparion, we trained our models on PTB $2–21 excluding those trees that contain words that are not in GloVe, but tested on the entire PTB $23 with gold syntactic constituency parsing trees. For those words not in GloVe, we followed the method in RNNG (Dyer et al., 2016). First, we replace them by <UNK-XXX>(e.g. <UNK-DASH>,<UNK-NUM>). Then, for each UNK to-

[2]Kruskal-Wallis and post-hoc Mann-Whitney tests with Bonferroni correction reveal that M1–3 with benepar trees are statistically significantly different ($p < 10^{-10}$) from RNNG at the sentence level (H=56.84 PTB; 65.54 OntoNotes), and from LSTM at the word level (H=1485.94 PTB; 2561.44 OntoNotes), on both corpora, except that there was no significant difference found between M1 and RNNG with OntoNotes. All effect sizes were small (df=3, V=0.05). With OntoNotes, no significance was found between M1 and M2; with PTB, none was found between M2 and M3.

| **Dataset** | Train | Test | Valid | Vocabulary | Max_s | Ave_s | Max_t | Ave_t |
|---|---|---|---|---|---|---|---|---|
| OntoNotes | 102254 | 5430 | 5625 | 45408 | 210 | 19 | 570 | 54 |
| PTB | 31680 | 1945 | 1114 | 30924 | 116 | 23 | 308 | 68 |

Table 1: Statistics of the datasets used in this project. Max_s/Ave_s are the maximum/average lengths of sentences. Max_t/Ave_t are the maximum/average numbers of nodes in trees.

| Accuracy | M1 | M2 | M3 |
|---|---|---|---|
| word gold | 32.34 | 32.09 | **34.64** |
| word benepar | 31.47 | 31.93 | **33.96** |
| POS gold | **94.39** | 89.47 | 92.3 |
| POS benepar | **93.6** | 89.19 | 91.9 |

Table 2: Sentence-level accuracies of the models on the OntoNotes test set. "Benepar" is the Berkeley neural parser (Kitaev and Klein, 2018).

| | |
|---|---|
| $T_1$ | god was very good to me . |
| | jesus was very happy for him . |
| | god said accusatory ones while it . |
| | i made my people talking alone . |
| | he had their people talking again . |
| $T_2$ | he told their people coming again . |

Table 3: Sentences generated between two random trees that have the same unlabelled tree structure. $T_1$ = "(S (NP (NNP)) (VP (VBD) (ADJP (ADJP (RB ) (JJ )) (PP (IN ) (NP (PRP ))))) (. .))", $T_2$ = "(S (NP (PRP )) (VP (VBD ) (S (NP (PRP$ ) (NNS )) (VP (VBG ) (ADVP (RB ))))) (. .))."

| Model | | | Test ppl |
|---|---|---|---|
| KN-5-gram (Kneser and Ney, 1995) | | | 169.3 |
| LSTM-128 (Zaremba et al., 2014) | | | 113.4 |
| GRU-256 | | | 112.3 |
| RNNG (Dyer et al., 2016) | | | 102.4 |
| SO-RNNG (Kuncoro et al., 2017) | | | 101.2 |
| GA-RNNG (Kuncoro et al., 2017) | | | 100.9 |
| NVLM (Zhang and Song, 2019) | | | 91.6 |
| Model 1 (gold) | 81.05 | | |
| Model 2 (gold) | 72.09 | | |
| Model 3 (gold) | 71.07 | (benepar) | 84.44 |
| Transformer-XL | | | 54.52 |

Table 5: Perplexities of the PTB test set (entire $23). RNNG, SO-RNNG, GA-RNNG and NVLM use the same method to preprocess data, keeping only vocabulary that appear more than once in the training set. For hapaxes in the training set and words in the validation/test sets that occur once in the training set, they replace them with <UNK-POS> tokens. Their models only contain 24 000 word types, whereas ours contain 31 000. In some other language modelling settings, the vocabulary size can be as small as 10 000.

ken, we use the average of the vector representations of words labelled as XXX in the training set to obtain the vector representation of this token. The perplexity of the entire PTB $23 is listed in Table 5. RNNG, SO-RNNG, GA-RNNG and NVLM are all syntax-aware models. Our Models achieve very good perplexity. Note that while Transformer-XL does perform better, it uses roughly $2.4 \times 10^7$ parameters whereas ours uses $9 \times 10^5$. We have a larger vocabulary size because we retain words that appear in GloVe regardless of frequency. Larger vocabulary sizes generally increase perplexity.

| Model | OntoNotes | PTB | Tree type |
|---|---|---|---|
| LSTM-256 | 125.8 | 126.43 | |
| RNNG | 116.7 | 119.66 | |
| Model 1 | 92.86 | 75.14 | gold |
| Model 2 | 90.10 | 66.78 | gold |
| Model 3 | **73.65** | **65.75** | gold |
| Model 1 | 101.4 | 75.56 | benepar |
| Model 2 | 95.13 | 69.02 | benepar |
| Model 3 | **80.18** | **68.06** | benepar |

Table 4: Perplexities of the OntoNotes/PTB test trees in which all words have GloVe vectors.

### 3.6 Word-prediction Accuracy and Rank

Given a parse along with the prefix $w_1, ...w_{n-j}$, we can remove the leaves $(w_{n-j+1}, w_{n+1}, ..., w_n)$ from the parse tree, and predict $w_{n-j+1}$, where $1 \leq j \leq n$. Thus, for a tree with $n$ word positions, we can perform word prediction up to $n$ times. Unlike the structured realization accuracies above, conventional practice in language modelling evaluation is to restore the integrity of $w_{n-j}$ according to the corpus before predicting $w_{n-j+1}$ when the previous prediction step was unsuccessful. Word accuracies according to this regimen are given in Table 8, along with accuracy at predicting any word with the required part of speech.

To better evaluate the results, we also compute the rank for each predicted word. Let $\mathbf{v\prime}$ be the vector representation of the true $w_{n-j+1}$ and $\hat{\mathbf{v}}$ denote the output vector as discussed earlier. For each vector representation of a word in the pre-trained GloVe vocabulary set, compute the Euclidean distance between it and $\hat{\mathbf{v}}$. Rank r means $||\mathbf{v\prime} - \hat{\mathbf{v}}||$ is the $r^{th}$ smallest distance in comparison to the other words in the vocabulary set. If the rank is small, then the model is capable of finding a close prediction. Small rank also means the model is

| model | ≤ 10 | ≤ 100 | ≤ 1000 | ≤ 10000 | >10000 | Med | Mean |
|---|---|---|---|---|---|---|---|
| Model 1 | **55.5%** | 11.9% | 16.7% | 13.1% | 2.8% | 5 | 1057 |
| Model 2 | **55.2%** | 12.8% | 17.1% | 12.3% | 2.6% | 5 | 965 |
| Model 3 | **57.8%** | 12.2% | 15.8% | 11.9% | 2.4% | **4** | 907 |
| LSTM-256 LM | **50.7%** | 23.7% | 16.1% | 8.2% | 1.4% | 10 | **564** |

Table 6: Rank distributions for models on the OntoNotes Test Set.

| model | ≤ 10 | ≤ 100 | ≤ 1000 | ≤ 10000 | >10000 | Med | Mean |
|---|---|---|---|---|---|---|---|
| Model 1 | **55.7%** | 13.8% | 17.6% | 11.3% | 1.4% | 4 | 678 |
| Model 2 | **57.0%** | 14.5% | 16.5% | 10.7% | 1.3% | 4 | 614 |
| Model 3 | **57.2%** | 13.9% | 16.7% | 10.8% | 1.3% | 4 | 624 |
| LSTM-256 LM | **50.9%** | 22.3% | 17.1% | 8.8% | 0.9% | 10 | **470** |

Table 7: Rank distributions for models on the PTB Test Set.

able to learn the relation between the next word and the given partial parse tree.

Table 6 and Table 7 show the overall, median, and mean rank distributions of the different models, compared to LSTM-256 within the ranges $10^{\phi}$ to $10^{\phi+1}$, $0 \leq \phi \leq 4$. Most of the ranks are $\leq 10$ and the median ranks for all models are less than 5. Our GGNN based models have more predictions that rank less than or equal to 10 compared with LSTM-256. Model 1 and Model 2 have similar ranks; Model 3's are slightly better. Model 3 has the lowest median rank. Although LSTM-256 has the lowest mean rank, LSTM-256's vocabulary size is much smaller than our GGNN based models.'

### 3.7 Generating words of a specific POS

Sometimes a model has an output vector located very far from the vector representation of the true word (i.e. its rank is very large), but the predicted word can at least be assigned the correct pre-terminal POS. This means the prediction is in some sense correct, because it is more likely to be grammatically and semantically acceptable. For example, given a sequence "within three days she had," and a gold-standard next word of "worked," with parent "VBN," "turned" could be a good prediction even though it is far from "worked", because "turned" also belongs to "VBN."

Since we train terminals and pre-terminals separately, there is no prior connection defined between them. For example, given a tag "NN," we do not know which words belong to "NN" when training the vectors for the words, or when choosing the vector for "NN." So this is a learned ability. Let us denote the true $i^{th}$ word as $t$ and the predicted $i^{th}$ word as $p$. To evaluate this capability, every time the model predicts a word $p$, we count it as a correct prediction if: (1) $p$ occurs somewhere in the training data, dominated by a category $c$, and (2) $c$ also dominates this occurrence of $t$.

In Table 8, we present this accuracy rate in the second column for each of the different models. On the OntoNotes test data, Models 1 and 3 have higher rates than Model 2, while Model 2 has the highest POS accuracy on the PTB test data. Alongside this, we also compute the overall accuracy of selecting the correct word (i.e., when the true word has rank 1), as well as the macro-averaged and macro-median accuracy of selecting the correct word, broken down by the pre-terminal dominating the position to be predicted.

All three models have high POS accuracies in general (medians: 99.90, 99.93 and 99.7, respectively), but Models 2 and 3 have very bad accuracies for some POSs such as 'NN' (60.68–67.45), 'NNS' (32.32–68.31) and 'VBN' (38.5–49.1).

## 4 Related Work

**Graph Neural Networks as Graph Encoders** GNNs were first proposed by Scarselli et al. (2009). Li et al. (2016) added gating mechanisms for recurrent networks on graphs. In parallel, (Bruna et al., 2013) proposed Graph Convolutional Networks. GCNs differ from GGNNs in their graph propagation model. GGNNs exploit recurrent neural networks to learn propagation weights through time steps. Each step shares the same set of parameters. On the other hand, GCNs train unshared CNN layers through time steps. In this paper, we employed GGNNs as a design choice. Similar to our model architecture, Bastings et al. (2017); Beck et al. (2018) used graphs to incorporate syntax into neural machine translation and Marcheggiani and Titov (2017) used ERS graph convolutional networks as dependency tree encoders for semantic role labelling. Even before graph neural networks

| Model | OntoNotes | | | | PTB | | | |
|---|---|---|---|---|---|---|---|---|
| | | Word acc | | | | Word acc | | |
| | POS acc | $\mu$avg | macavg | med | POS acc | $\mu$avg | macavg | med |
| Model 1 | **94.35** | 32.4 | 26.6 | 38.6 | 94.28 | 35.47 | 41.74 | 47.46 |
| Model 2 | 89.4 | 32.0 | 37.39 | 43.52 | **97.66** | 37.12 | **43.74** | **49.22** |
| Model 3 | 92.33 | **34.7** | **37.9** | **44.3** | 95.73 | **37.27** | 41.69 | 44.37 |
| LSTM-256 LM | | 22.4 | | | | 23.57 | | |

Table 8: Percentage POS prediction accuracies and word prediction accuracies, for each model.

become popular, there were attempts akin to graph encoders. Dyer et al. (2015); Socher et al. (2013); Tai et al. (2015); Zhu et al. (2015); Le and Zuidema (2014) encoded tree structure with recursive neural networks or Tree-LSTMs.

**Surface Realization** Song et al. (2018) introduced a graph-to-sequence LSTM for AMR-to-text generation that can encode AMR structures directly. The model takes multiple recurrent transition steps in order to propagate information beyond local neighbourhoods. But this method must maintain the entire graph state at each time step. Our models also simultaneously update every node in the tree at every time step. The encoder of Trisedya et al. (2018) takes input RDF triples rendered as a graph and builds a dynamic recurrent structure that traverses the adjacency matrix of the graph one node at a time. Marcheggiani and Perez-Beltrachini (2018), again using a GCN, take only the nodes of the RDF graph as input, using the edges directly as a weight matrix. They, too, must update the entire graph at every time step.

**Language Modelling** The task of language modelling has a long and distinguished history. Although the term itself was not coined until Jelinek et al. (1975), the earliest work of Shannon (1948) on entropy presents what are effectively character-level language models as a motivating example. In both cases, given a prefix of characters/words or classes (Brown et al., 1992), the aim of the task is to predict the next such event. $n$-gram language models factor any dependency of the next event on the prefix through its dependency on the final $n-1$ events in the prefix. This long remained the dominant type of language model, but the advent of neural language models (Bengio et al., 2003), and particularly vector-space embeddings of certain lexical-semantic relations, has drastically changed that landscape. See, e.g., models using recurrent networks (Mikolov et al., 2010), year (Mikolov et al., 2011), LSTMs (Sundermeyer et al., 2012), sequence-to-sequence LSTMs models (Sutskever et al., 2014), and convolutional networks (Gehring et al., 2017) and transformers (Devlin et al., 2019).

An earlier, but ultimately unsuccessful attempt at dislodging $n$-gram language models was that of Chelba (2000), who augmented this prefix with syntactic information. Chelba (2000) did not use conventional parse trees from any of the then-common parse-annotated corpora, nor from linguistic theory, because these degraded rather than enhanced language modelling performance. Instead, he had to remain very sparing in order to realize an empirical improvement. The present model not only shares information at the dimensional level, but projects syntactic structure over the words to be predicted. While this makes structured realization a very different task from structured language modelling, this not only appears to improve perplexity, but does so without having to change the conventional representation of trees found in syntactic corpora. The present model could therefore be used to evaluate competing syntactic representations in a controlled way that quantifies their ability to assist with word prediction, as we have here.

## 5 Conclusion

GGNNs have proved to be effective as encoders of constituent parse trees from a variety of perspectives, including realization accuracy, perplexity, word-level prediction accuracy, categorical cohesion of predictions, and novel lexical selection. A limitation of this study is the comparatively modest size of its corpora, which is due to the requirement for properly curated parse-annotated data. Finding ways to scale up to larger training and test sets without the bias introduced by automated parsers remains an important issue to investigate.

## References

David Acuna, Huan Ling, Amlan Kar, and Sanja Fidler. 2018. Efficient interactive annotation of segmentation datasets with polygon-rnn++. In *CVPR*.

Joost Bastings, Ivan Titov, Wilker Aziz, Diego

Marcheggiani, and Khalil Sima'an. 2017. Graph convolutional encoders for syntax-aware neural machine translation. In *EMNLP*.

Daniel Edward Robert Beck, Gholamreza Haffari, and Trevor Cohn. 2018. Graph-to-sequence learning using gated graph neural networks. In *ACL*.

Y. Bengio, R. Ducharme, P. Vincent, and C. Jauvin. 2003. A neural probabilistic language model. *Journal of Machine Learning Research*, 3:1137–1155.

Peter F Brown, Peter V Desouza, Robert L Mercer, Vincent J Della Pietra, and Jenifer C Lai. 1992. Class-based n-gram models of natural language. *Computational linguistics*, 18(4):467–479.

Joan Bruna, Wojciech Zaremba, Arthur Szlam, and Yann LeCun. 2013. Spectral networks and locally connected networks on graphs. *CoRR*, abs/1312.6203.

C. Chelba. 2000. *Exploiting Syntactic Structure for Natural Language Modeling*. Ph.D. thesis, Johns Hopkins University.

Jacob Devlin, Ming-Wei Chang, Kenton Lee, and Kristina Toutanova. 2019. BERT: Pre-training of deep bidirectional transformers for language understanding. In *Proceedings of the 2019 Conference of the North American Chapter of the Association for Computational Linguistics: Human Language Technologies, Volume 1 (Long and Short Papers)*, pages 4171–4186, Minneapolis, Minnesota. Association for Computational Linguistics.

Chris Dyer, Miguel Ballesteros, Wang Ling, Austin Matthews, and Noah A. Smith. 2015. Transition-based dependency parsing with stack long short-term memory. In *ACL*.

Chris Dyer, Adhiguna Kuncoro, Miguel Ballesteros, and Noah A. Smith. 2016. Recurrent neural network grammars. In *Proc. of NAACL*.

Jonas Gehring, Michael Auli, David Grangier, Denis Yarats, and Yann N Dauphin. 2017. Convolutional sequence to sequence learning. In *Proceedings of the 34th International Conference on Machine Learning-Volume 70*, pages 1243–1252. JMLR. org.

Eduard Hovy, Mitchell Marcus, Martha Palmer, Lance Ramshaw, and Ralph Weischedel. 2006. Ontonotes: The 90% solution. In *Proceedings of the Human Language Technology Conference of the NAACL, Companion Volume: Short Papers*, NAACL-Short '06, pages 57–60, Stroudsburg, PA, USA. Association for Computational Linguistics.

F. Jelinek, L.R. Bahl, and R.L. Mercer. 1975. Design of a linguistic statistical decoder for the recognition of continuous speech. *IEEE Transactions on Information Theory*, IT-21(3).

Ryan Kiros, Richard Zemel, and Ruslan R Salakhutdinov. 2014. A multiplicative model for learning distributed text-based attribute representations. In Z. Ghahramani, M. Welling, C. Cortes, N. D. Lawrence, and K. Q. Weinberger, editors, *Advances in Neural Information Processing Systems 27*, pages 2348–2356. Curran Associates, Inc.

Nikita Kitaev and Dan Klein. 2018. Constituency parsing with a self-attentive encoder. *arXiv preprint arXiv:1805.01052*.

R. Kneser and H. Ney. 1995. Improved backing-off for m-gram language modeling. In *1995 International Conference on Acoustics, Speech, and Signal Processing*, volume 1, pages 181–184 vol.1.

A. Köhn and T. Baumann. 2016. Predictive incremental parsing helps language modeling. In *Proc. 26th COLING*, pages 268–277.

Adhiguna Kuncoro, Miguel Ballesteros, Lingpeng Kong, Chris Dyer, Graham Neubig, and Noah A. Smith. 2017. What do recurrent neural network grammars learn about syntax? In *Proceedings of the 15th Conference of the European Chapter of the Association for Computational Linguistics: Volume 1, Long Papers*, pages 1249–1258, Valencia, Spain. Association for Computational Linguistics.

Phong Le and Willem Zuidema. 2014. The inside-outside recursive neural network model for dependency parsing. In *Proceedings of the 2014 Conference on Empirical Methods in Natural Language Processing (EMNLP)*, pages 729–739. Association for Computational Linguistics.

Yujia Li, Daniel Tarlow, Marc Brockschmidt, and Richard S. Zemel. 2016. Gated graph sequence neural networks. *CoRR*, abs/1511.05493.

Diego Marcheggiani and Laura Perez-Beltrachini. 2018. Deep graph convolutional encoders for structured data to text generation. In *Proceedings of the 11th International Conference on Natural Language Generation*, pages 1–9, Tilburg University, The Netherlands. Association for Computational Linguistics.

Diego Marcheggiani and Ivan Titov. 2017. Encoding sentences with graph convolutional networks for semantic role labeling. In *EMNLP*.

Mitchell P. Marcus, Beatrice Santorini, and Mary Ann Marcinkiewicz. 1993. Building a large annotated corpus of English: The Penn Treebank. *Computational Linguistics*, 19(2):313–330.

Tomáš Mikolov, Martin Karafiát, Lukáš Burget, Jan Černockỳ, and Sanjeev Khudanpur. 2010. Recurrent neural network based language model. In *Eleventh annual conference of the international speech communication association*.

Tomáš Mikolov, Stefan Kombrink, Lukáš Burget, Jan Černocký, and Sanjeev Khudanpur. 2011. Extensions of recurrent neural network language model. In *2011 IEEE International Conference on Acoustics, Speech and Signal Processing (ICASSP)*, pages 5528–5531. IEEE.

Jeffrey Pennington, Richard Socher, and Christopher D. Manning. 2014. Glove: Global vectors for word representation. In *Empirical Methods in Natural Language Processing (EMNLP)*, pages 1532–1543.

Sameer Pradhan, Alessandro Moschitti, Nianwen Xue, Hwee Tou Ng, Anders Björkelund, Olga Uryupina, Yuchen Zhang, and Zhi Zhong. 2013. Towards robust linguistic analysis using OntoNotes. In *Proceedings of the Seventeenth Conference on Computational Natural Language Learning*, pages 143–152, Sofia, Bulgaria. Association for Computational Linguistics.

F. Scarselli, M. Gori, A. C. Tsoi, M. Hagenbuchner, and G. Monfardini. 2009. The graph neural network model. *IEEE Transactions on Neural Networks*, 20(1):61–80.

C.E. Shannon. 1948. A mathematical theory of communication. *Bell System Technical Journal*, 27:379–423 (July), 623–656 (October).

Richard Socher, Alex Perelygin, Jean Wu, Jason Chuang, Christopher D. Manning, Andrew Y. Ng, and Christopher Potts. 2013. Recursive deep models for semantic compositionality over a sentiment treebank. In *EMNLP*.

Linfeng Song, Yue Zhang, Zhiguo Wang, and Daniel Gildea. 2018. A graph-to-sequence model for AMR-to-text generation. In *Proceedings of the 56th Annual Meeting of the Association for Computational Linguistics (Volume 1: Long Papers)*, pages 1616–1626, Melbourne, Australia. Association for Computational Linguistics.

Martin Sundermeyer, Ralf Schlüter, and Hermann Ney. 2012. Lstm neural networks for language modeling. In *Thirteenth annual conference of the international speech communication association*.

Ilya Sutskever, Oriol Vinyals, and Quoc V Le. 2014. Sequence to sequence learning with neural networks. In *Advances in neural information processing systems*, pages 3104–3112.

Kai Sheng Tai, Richard Socher, and Christopher D. Manning. 2015. Improved semantic representations from tree-structured long short-term memory networks. In *ACL*.

Bayu Distiawan Trisedya, Jianzhong Qi, Rui Zhang, and Wei Wang. 2018. GTR-LSTM: A triple encoder for sentence generation from RDF data. In *Proceedings of the 56th Annual Meeting of the Association for Computational Linguistics (Volume 1: Long Papers)*, pages 1627–1637, Melbourne, Australia. Association for Computational Linguistics.

Ralph Weischedel, Martha Palmer, Mitchell Marcus, Eduard Hovy, Sameer Pradhan, Lance Ramshaw, Nianwen Xue, Ann Taylor, Jeff Kaufman, Michelle Franchini, et al. 2013. Ontonotes release 5.0 ldc2013t19. *Linguistic Data Consortium, Philadelphia, PA*, 23.

Wojciech Zaremba, Ilya Sutskever, and Oriol Vinyals. 2014. Recurrent neural network regularization.

Yuyu Zhang and Le Song. 2019. Language modeling with shared grammar. In *Proceedings of the 57th Annual Meeting of the Association for Computational Linguistics*, pages 4442–4453, Florence, Italy. Association for Computational Linguistics.

Xiao-Dan Zhu, Parinaz Sobhani, and Hongyu Guo. 2015. Long short-term memory over tree structures. *CoRR*, abs/1503.04881.

# MG-BERT: Multi-Graph Augmented BERT for Masked Language Modeling

**Parishad BehnamGhader** and **Hossein Zakerinia** and **Mahdieh Soleymani Baghshah**
Sharif University of Technology
Tehran, Iran
{pbehnamghader, hzakerynia}@ce.sharif.edu, soleymani@sharif.edu

## Abstract

Pre-trained models like Bidirectional Encoder Representations from Transformers (BERT), have recently made a big leap forward in Natural Language Processing (NLP) tasks. However, there are still some shortcomings in the Masked Language Modeling (MLM) task performed by these models. In this paper, we first introduce a multi-graph including different types of relations between words. Then, we propose Multi-Graph augmented BERT (MG-BERT) model that is based on BERT. MG-BERT embeds tokens while taking advantage of a static multi-graph containing global word co-occurrences in the text corpus beside global real-world facts about words in knowledge graphs. The proposed model also employs a dynamic sentence graph to capture local context effectively. Experimental results demonstrate that our model can considerably enhance the performance in the MLM task.

## 1 Introduction

In recent years, pre-trained models have led to promising results in various Natural Language Processing (NLP) tasks. Recently, Bidirectional Encoder Representations from Transformers (BERT) (Devlin et al., 2019) has received much attention as a pre-trained model that can be easily fine-tuned for a wide range of NLP tasks. BERT is pre-trained using two unsupervised tasks, Masked Language Modeling (MLM) and Next Sentence Prediction (NSP). In (Ettinger, 2019), some psycholinguistic diagnostics are introduced for assessing the linguistic capacities of pre-trained language models. These diagnostic tests consist of commonsense and pragmatic inferences, role-based event prediction, and negation. Ettinger (2019) observes some shortcomings in BERT's results and demonstrates that although BERT sometimes predicts the first candidate for the masked token almost correctly, some of its top candidates contradict each other. Besides, in the tests targeting commonsense and pragmatic inference, it is illustrated that BERT can not precisely fill the gaps based on just the input context (Ettinger, 2019).

In this paper, we incorporate co-occurrences and global information about words through graphs describing relations of words along with local contexts considered by BERT. The intention is to find more reliable and meaningful embeddings that result in better performance in MLM task. Utilizing external information about the corpus and the world in the form of graphs helps the model fill the gaps in the MLM task more easily and with more certainty. We take advantage of the rich information source accessible in knowledge graphs and also condensed information of words co-occurrence in graphs using Relational Graph Convolutional Network (R-GCN) to enrich the embedding of tokens. We also utilize the words in the current context as a dynamic complete graph using an attention mechanism. These graphs can considerably influence the performance of BERT in the MLM task as shown in the experiments.

## 2 Related Work

Knowledge graphs (KGs) are valuable sources of facts about real-world entities. Many studies have been recently introduced to utilize knowledge graphs for various purposes, such as recommender systems (Wang et al., 2019a,b; He et al., 2020) or link prediction (Feng et al., 2016; Nguyen et al., 2018; Sun et al., 2019; Zhang et al., 2020). Recently, using BERT along with knowledge graphs has also been attended for knowledge graph completion and analysis. Yao et al. (2019) employ KG-BERT in triple classification, link prediction, and relation prediction tasks. Furthermore, knowledge graphs are used in NLP tasks such as text classification (K M et al., 2018; Ostendorff et al., 2019; Zhang et al., 2019a), named entity recognition (Dekhili et al., 2019), and language



*Proceedings of the Fifteenth Workshop on Graph-Based Methods for Natural Language Processing (TextGraphs-15)*, pages 125–131
June 11, 2021. 

modeling (Ahn et al., 2016; Logan et al., 2019). ERNIE (Zhang et al., 2019b) is an enhanced language representation model incorporating knowledge graphs. In addition to BERT's pre-training objectives, it uses an additional objective that intends to select appropriate entities from the knowledge graph to complete randomly masked entity alignments. Moreover, named entity mentions in the text are recognized and aligned to their corresponding entities in KGs.

Other types of graphs have also been utilized in NLP tasks in some studies. For instance, Text GCN (Yao et al., 2018) applies Graph Convolutional Network (GCN) to the task of text classification. This paper's employed graph is a text graph created based on token co-occurrences and document-token relations in a corpus. Moreover, VGCN-BERT (Lu and Nie, 2019) enriches the word embeddings of an input sentence using the text graph inspired by Text GCN (Yao et al., 2018) and examines the obtained model in FIRE hate language detection tasks (Mandl et al., 2019).

In this paper, we aim to improve BERT's performance (in the MLM task) by incorporating a static multi-graph that includes both the knowledge graph and global co-occurrence graphs derived from the corpus as well as a dynamic graph including input sentence tokens. Static text graphs have been recently employed in VGCN-BERT (Lu and Nie, 2019) via a modified version of GCN that extends the input by a fixed number of embeddings. However, the modification of embeddings in this work is only based on input tokens. Neither other vocabularies in the static text graphs nor real-world facts (available in KGs) affect the final embeddings of tokens. On the other hand, while ENRIE (Zhang et al., 2019b) and KEPLER (Wang et al., 2019c) utilize KGs to reach an improved model, they do not employ other graphs derived from the corpus. Also, ERNIE does not learn graph-based embedding during representation learning and only adopts embeddings trained by TransE (Bordes et al., 2013). However, in our model, since we incorporate a multi-graph by extending BERT architecture and providing a graph layer of an R-GCN module and attention mechanism, a multi-graph augmented representation learning model is obtained.

## 3 Preliminaries

GCN (Kipf and Welling, 2017) is one of the most popular models for graph node embedding. R-GCN (Schlichtkrull et al., 2018) extends GCN to provide node embedding of multi-relational graphs:

$$h_i^{(l+1)} = \sigma(\sum_{r \in \mathcal{R}} \sum_{j \in \mathcal{N}_i^r} \frac{1}{c_{i,r}} W_r^{(l)} h_j^{(l)} + W_0^{(l)} h_i^{(l)}),$$

where $h_i^{(l)}$ is the $l$-th layer's hidden state of node $v_i$, $W_r^{(l)}$ is the weight matrix for relation $r$ in layer $l$, and $W_0$ is the weight matrix for self-loops. $\mathcal{N}_i^r$ is the set of $v_i$'s neighbours under relation $r$ and $c_{i,r}$ is a normalization constant.

## 4 Methodology

This section presents the overall architecture of our model, called Multi-Graph augmented BERT (MG-BERT). MG-BERT takes advantage of BERT's power in capturing context of an input text as well as a graph module including an R-GCN layer over a static multi-graph and a graph attention layer over a dynamic sentence graph. This static multi-graph includes global information about words available as facts in KGs in addition to dependencies between tokens of the input text and other words in the vocabulary which are discovered by computing co-occurrence statistics in the corpus. Two graphs are used to condense co-occurrences of words in the corpus inspired by Text GCN (Yao et al., 2018) that are also employed by VGCN-BERT (Lu and Nie, 2019). One of these graphs includes local co-occurrences of terms that is computed based on point-wise mutual information (PMI) of terms $i$ and $j$ which is calculated by:

$$p(i) = \frac{\#W(i)}{\#W}, \quad p(i,j) = \frac{\#W(i,j)}{\#W},$$
$$\text{PMI}(i,j) = log \frac{p(i,j)}{p(i)p(j)}. \quad (1)$$

In the above equations, $\#W(i)$ and $\#W(i,j)$ denote the number of fixed size windows containing term $i$ and both of the terms $i$ and $j$, respectively. $\#W$ is the whole number of windows in the corpus. The other graph includes the document level co-occurrence of tokens in the corpus computed based on term frequency-inverse document frequency (TF-IDF). The knowledge graph is also incorporated in this multi-graph. Formally, the weighted edges between token $i$ and token $j$ for three types of relations $\mathcal{R} = \{\text{KG}, \text{PMI}, \text{TF-IDF}\}$

in the multi-graph are:

$$\begin{cases} A_{ij}^{TF-IDF} = \lambda_T \sum\limits_{d \in docs} \mathrm{T}_{id}\mathrm{T}_{jd} \\ A_{ij}^{KG} = \lambda_K \sum\limits_{e \in \mathrm{KG}} \mathrm{KG}_{ie}\mathrm{KG}_{ej} & \text{if } i,j \in \mathrm{KG} \\ A_{ij}^{PMI} = \lambda_P \, \mathrm{PMI}(i,j) & \text{if } \mathrm{PMI}(i,j) > 0 \\ A_{ij}^{*} = 1 & \text{if } i = j \end{cases} \tag{2}$$

where $\mathrm{T}_{id}$ denotes the TF-IDF of token $i$ in document $d$, $\mathrm{PMI}(i,j)$ shows PMI calculated by Eq. 1, and $\mathrm{KG}_{e_1 e_2}$ is nonzero when a relation between these two entities exists in the knowledge graph. Note that we add a self-connection relation to our knowledge graph for maintaining one-hop links, while also considering two hops as in Eq. 2 to employ indirect relations through paths of length two in the knowledge graph. $\lambda_K$, $\lambda_P$, and $\lambda_T$ are also hyperparameters that can control the impact of three types of relations on tokens' embeddings. To utilize the multi-graph introduced above, we add a single-layer R-GCN described in Section 3 to the BERT model.

Furthermore, we use a graph attention mechanism to capture local information via a dynamic and complete graph in which nodes represent all tokens of the input sentence. The complete dynamic graph is used in order to obtain context-dependent new embeddings while the R-GCN layer itself provides the same new embeddings for a specific token even if the token appears in different contexts. This happens because the single R-GCN layer always performs on the same static multi-graph.

As shown in Fig. 1, the whole graph module is placed immediately after the BERT token embeddings layer since the hidden states of the whole vocabulary are available in this layer. We pass the entire multi-graph to the R-GCN module so that the global dependencies would affect embeddings of tokens properly using Eq. 3. We also use an attention mechanism as in Eq. 4 to consider the local context. The new embedding of token $i$ in sentence $s$ is computed as:

$$h_i^{'} = (1 - \lambda_{dyn}) \sum_{r \in R} \hat{A}_i^r h_i W_r \tag{3}$$

$$+ \lambda_{dyn} \left( \Big\Vert_{k=1}^{K} \sum_{j \in s} \alpha_{ij}^k h_j W_k^{Val} \right) W^O, \tag{4}$$

$$\alpha_{ij}^k = \frac{\exp((h_i W_k^{Query}).(h_j W_k^{Key}))}{\sum_{t \in s} \exp((h_i W_k^{Query}).(h_t W_k^{Key}))}, \tag{5}$$

where $\hat{A}^r$ refers to the normalized adjacency matrix of relation $r$, $W$s are trainable weight matrices (i.e. $W_r$s denote parameters of the R-GCN layer and $W_k^{Query}$, $W_k^{Key}$, and $W_k^{Val}$ denote the attention parameters), and $h_i$ is the $i^{th}$ token's embedding from the BERT token embeddings layer.

Next, we aggregate the obtained tokens' embeddings by the graph module with position embeddings and segment embeddings (similar to BERT). Afterward, we feed these representations to BERT encoders to find final embeddings. The proposed model architecture is shown in Figure 1.

In the training phase, a token from each sentence is randomly masked, and the model is trained to predict the masked token based on both the context and the incorporated static multi-graph.

## 5 Experiments

In this section, we explain the details of training MG-BERT and conduct experiments to evaluate and compare our model with the related methods recently proposed.

**Datasets.** During training, we use the WN18 knowledge graph, derived from WordNet, as an unlabeled graph (Bordes et al., 2014). We also experiment MG-BERT and other recent models on CoLA, SST-2, and Brown datasets (Warstadt et al., 2019; Socher et al., 2013; Francis and Kucera, 1979). The detailed description of these datatsets is given in Appendix A.

**Parameter Setting.** In order to capture word co-occurence statistics of the corpus, we use the BERT's tokenizer on sentences and set the sliding window size to 20 when calculating the PMI value. The whole BERT module in MG-BERT is first initialized with the pre-trained *bert-base-uncase* version of BERT in PyTorch and the model is trained on the MLM task with cross entropy loss (Wolf et al., 2019). Regarding Eq. 2, different hyper-parameter settings have been used for each dataset. $\lambda_K$, $\lambda_P$, and $\lambda_T$ are set to 0.01, 0.001, and 0.001, respectively in both CoLA and Brown datasets and 0.001, 1.0, and 0.001 in SST-2 dataset. The hyperparameter $\lambda_{dyn}$ is also set to 0.8. The graph attention mechanism is performed with 12 heads. The R-GCN and graph attention layers' output dimension are also set to 768 that equals to the dimension of the BERT token embeddings layer to substitute easily BERT's token embeddings with the embeddings

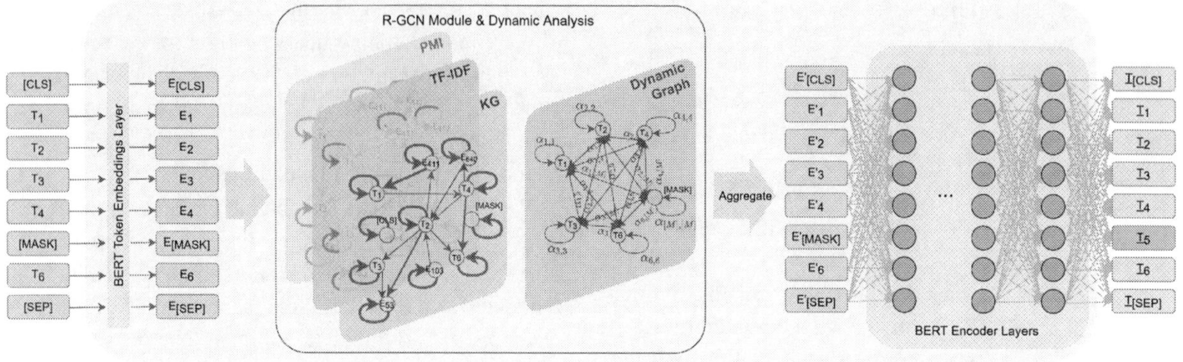


Figure 1: The architecture of MG-BERT. The "Aggregate" phase includes an aggregation of new tokens' embeddings with the position embeddings and the segment embeddings of the BERT model.

derived from the graph module. We also employ the normalization trick introduced in GCN (Kipf and Welling, 2017) to normalize each adjacency matrix in the multi-graph.

**Compared methods.** To assess our model, we compare it with BERT as the baseline. Moreover, ERNIE and VGCN-BERT are being compared as the recent methods utilizing knowledge graph and text graph, respectively (Zhang et al., 2019b; Lu and Nie, 2019). We also compare MG-BERT with MG-BERT(base) which doesn't use the dynamic graph incorporating the context according to Eq. 4. All these models are fine-tuned on the text datasets for a fair evaluation.

**Results.** We evaluate our model using Hits@1 and Hits@5 metrics. Hits@k shows the proportion of correct tokens appearing in the top $k$ results for each sample. In Table 1, we report the results of evaluations performed on the test sets of CoLA, SST-2, and Brown datasets. These results demonstrate that the proposed method outperforms other models and taking advantage of the graph module with dataset-specific hyper-parameters improves the performance.

The reason to our superiority over VGCN-BERT (Lu and Nie, 2019) is that it doesn't take advantage of real-world facts (available in KGs). Moreover, as opposed to MG-BERT, it modifies initial embeddings of tokens only based on input tokens of each sentence and other vocabularies in the text graphs don't influence the final embeddings of tokens. On the other hand, ERNIE (Zhang et al., 2019b) doesn't take full advantage of graphs since it doesn't use graphs derived from the corpus. Besides, it does not learn graph-based embeddings during representation learning. It is worth mentioning that the entity embedding model used in ERNIE has been trained on a huge subset of Wikidata[1], which is almost 120 times bigger than WN18 knowledge graph employed in our method.

The superiority of MG-BERT over MG-BERT(base) demonstrates the importance of the dynamic sentence graph and the results of MG-BERT(base) itself shows that utilizing the static multi-graph has been useful.

| Graphs | Hits@1 | Hits@5 |
|---|---|---|
| K | $70.51 \pm 1.28$ | $86.27 \pm 0.31$ |
| P | $69.63 \pm 1.78$ | $85.75 \pm 0.91$ |
| T | $69.78 \pm 1.18$ | $84.78 \pm 1.10$ |
| KP | $70.37 \pm 1.41$ | $85.66 \pm 0.92$ |
| KT | $70.50 \pm 0.99$ | $85.54 \pm 0.83$ |
| PT | $70.60 \pm 1.32$ | $85.22 \pm 0.80$ |
| KPT | $70.94 \pm 1.20$ | $85.12 \pm 1.20$ |

Table 2: Experimental results of variations of MG-BERT(base) using different graphs on CoLA dataset. The symbols K, P, and T stand for employing KG, PMI, and TF-IDF relations, respectively.

In addition, evaluation results of different variations of MG-BERT(base) on CoLA dataset, considering different graphs, are represented in Table 2, demonstrating the effect of each graph on the performance. The experimental results indicate the role of exploiting various graphs in language representation learning.

We also compare MG-BERT and MG-BERT(base) with other models using perplexity

[1]https://www.wikidata.org/

| Model | CoLA | | SST-2 | | Brown | |
|---|---|---|---|---|---|---|
| | Hits@1 | Hits@5 | Hits@1 | Hits@5 | Hits@1 | Hits@5 |
| BERT (Devlin et al., 2019) | 68.50 ±1.49 | 84.53 ±1.18 | 80.48 ±0.85 | 88.42 ±0.70 | 58.31 ±1.17 | 76.38 ±0.49 |
| ERNIE (Zhang et al., 2019b) | 69.57 ±0.89 | 84.58 ±0.72 | 81.17 ±0.77 | 88.26 ±0.57 | 57.42 ±0.73 | 75.34 ±0.65 |
| VGCN-BERT (Lu and Nie, 2019) | 69.03 ±0.78 | 84.81 ±0.62 | 80.85 ±0.48 | 88.37 ±0.58 | 57.97 ±0.97 | 76.17 ±0.67 |
| MG-BERT(base) | <u>70.95</u> ±1.20 | <u>85.12</u> ±1.20 | <u>81.28</u> ±0.51 | <u>88.56</u> ±0.79 | **58.66** ±0.11 | **76.64** ±0.61 |
| MG-BERT | **71.72** ±0.97 | **86.67** ±0.51 | **83.07** ±0.47 | **89.13** ±0.39 | <u>58.38</u> ±0.60 | <u>76.59</u> ±0.67 |

Table 1: Hits@k esults on CoLA, SST-2, and Brown datasets. The best score is highlighted in bold and the second best score is highlighted with underline.

| Model | CoLA | SST-2 | Brown |
|---|---|---|---|
| BERT (Devlin et al., 2019) | 1.33 ±0.01 | 1.43 ±0.01 | 1.66 ±0.02 |
| ERNIE (Zhang et al., 2019b) | **1.23** ±0.01 | **1.20** ±0.01 | 1.71 ±0.02 |
| VGCN-BERT (Lu and Nie, 2019) | 1.32 ±0.01 | 1.41 ±0.01 | 1.75 ±0.02 |
| MG-BERT(base) | 1.26 ±0.02 | 1.45 ±0.01 | 1.82 ±0.01 |
| MG-BERT | **1.23** ±0.01 | 1.25 ±0.01 | **1.63** ±0.01 |

Table 3: Perplexity results on CoLA, SST-2, and Brown datasets. The best score is highlighted in bold.

metric in Table 3. In this paper, the perplexity is only calculated on the masked tokens as:

$$PPL = \exp\left(\sum_{i=1}^{n} -\log \hat{y}_i^{[MASK]}\right),$$

where $\hat{y}_i^{[MASK]}$ is the predicted probability of the masked token in the $i$-th sample. A model with higher perplexity allocates lower probability to the correct masked tokens, which is not desired. The results shown in Table 3 generally demonstrate the fact that both MG-BERT and ERNIE solve the MLM task with more certainty compared to BERT and VGCN-BERT.

We also illustrate some examples of MLM task performed by MG-BERT(base) and BERT in Appendix B. These examples demonstrate that real-world information of knowledge graph and global information of co-occurrence graphs remarkably compensate BERT's shortage.

## 6 Conclusion

In this paper, we proposed a language representation learning model that enhances BERT by augmenting it with a graph module (i.e. an R-GCN layer over a static multi-graph, including global dependencies between words, and a graph attention layer over a dynamic sentence graph). The static multi-graph utilized in this work consists of a knowledge graph as a source of information about real-world facts and two other graphs built based on word co-occurrences in local windows and documents in the corpus. Therefore, the proposed model utilizes the local context, the corpus-level co-occurence statistics, and the global word dependencies (through incorporating a knowledge graph) to find the input tokens' embeddings. The results generally show the superiority of the proposed model in the Masked Language Modeling task compared to both the BERT model and the recent models employing knowledge or text graphs.

## References


Sungjin Ahn, Heeyoul Choi, Tanel Pärnamaa, and Yoshua Bengio. 2016. A neural knowledge language model. *CoRR*, abs/1608.00318.

Antoine Bordes, Xavier Glorot, Jason Weston, and Yoshua Bengio. 2014. A semantic matching energy function for learning with multi-relational data. *Machine Learning*, pages 233–259.

Antoine Bordes, Nicolas Usunier, Alberto Garcia-Duran, Jason Weston, and Oksana Yakhnenko.

2013. Translating embeddings for modeling multi-relational data. In C. J. C. Burges, L. Bottou, M. Welling, Z. Ghahramani, and K. Q. Weinberger, editors, *Advances in Neural Information Processing Systems 26*, pages 2787–2795. Curran Associates, Inc.

Gaith Dekhili, Tan Ngoc Le, and Fatiha Sadat. 2019. Augmenting named entity recognition with commonsense knowledge. In *Proceedings of the 2019 Workshop on Widening NLP*, page 142, Florence, Italy. Association for Computational Linguistics.

Jacob Devlin, Ming-Wei Chang, Kenton Lee, and Kristina Toutanova. 2019. BERT: Pre-training of deep bidirectional transformers for language understanding. In *Proceedings of the 2019 Conference of the North American Chapter of the Association for Computational Linguistics: Human Language Technologies, Volume 1 (Long and Short Papers)*, pages 4171–4186, Minneapolis, Minnesota. Association for Computational Linguistics.

Allyson Ettinger. 2019. What bert is not: Lessons from a new suite of psycholinguistic diagnostics for language models. *Transactions of the Association for Computational Linguistics*, 8:34–48.

Jun Feng, Yang Huang, Minlie andd Yang, and Xiaoyan Zhu. 2016. GAKE: Graph aware knowledge embedding. In *Proceedings of COLING 2016, the 26th International Conference on Computational Linguistics: Technical Papers*, pages 641–651, Osaka, Japan. The COLING 2016 Organizing Committee.

W. N. Francis and H. Kucera. 1979. Brown corpus manual. Technical report, Department of Linguistics, Brown University, Providence, Rhode Island, US.

Xiangnan He, K. H. Deng, Xiang Wang, Yaliang Li, Yongdong Zhang, and Meng Wang. 2020. Lightgcn: Simplifying and powering graph convolution network for recommendation. *ArXiv*, abs/2002.02126.

Annervaz K M, Somnath Basu Roy Chowdhury, and Ambedkar Dukkipati. 2018. Learning beyond datasets: Knowledge graph augmented neural networks for natural language processing. In *Proceedings of the 2018 Conference of the North American Chapter of the Association for Computational Linguistics: Human Language Technologies, Volume 1 (Long Papers)*, pages 313–322, New Orleans, Louisiana. Association for Computational Linguistics.

Thomas N. Kipf and Max Welling. 2017. Semi-Supervised Classification with Graph Convolutional Networks. In *Proceedings of the 5th International Conference on Learning Representations*, ICLR '17.

Robert Logan, Nelson F. Liu, Matthew E. Peters, Matt Gardner, and Sameer Singh. 2019. Barack's wife hillary: Using knowledge graphs for fact-aware language modeling. In *Proceedings of the 57th Annual Meeting of the Association for Computational Linguistics*, pages 5962–5971, Florence, Italy. Association for Computational Linguistics.

Zhibin Lu and Jian-Yun Nie. 2019. Raligraph at hasoc 2019: Vgcn-bert: Augmenting bert with graph embedding for offensive language detection. In *FIRE (Working Notes)*, volume 2517 of *CEUR Workshop Proceedings*, pages 221–228. CEUR-WS.org.

Thomas Mandl, Sandip Modha, Prasenjit Majumder, Daksh Patel, Mohana Dave, Chintak Mandlia, and Aditya Patel. 2019. Overview of the hasoc track at fire 2019: Hate speech and offensive content identification in indo-european languages. In *Proceedings of the 11th Forum for Information Retrieval Evaluation*, FIRE '19, page 14–17, New York, NY, USA. Association for Computing Machinery.

Dai Quoc Nguyen, Tu Dinh Nguyen, Dat Quoc Nguyen, and Dinh Phung. 2018. A novel embedding model for knowledge base completion based on convolutional neural network. In *Proceedings of the 2018 Conference of the North American Chapter of the Association for Computational Linguistics: Human Language Technologies, Volume 2 (Short Papers)*, pages 327–333, New Orleans, Louisiana. Association for Computational Linguistics.

Malte Ostendorff, Peter Bourgonje, Maria Berger, Julián Moreno Schneider, Georg Rehm, and Bela Gipp. 2019. Enriching bert with knowledge graph embeddings for document classification. *ArXiv*, abs/1909.08402.

Michael Schlichtkrull, Thomas N. Kipf, Peter Bloem, Rianne van den Berg, Ivan Titov, and Max Welling. 2018. Modeling relational data with graph convolutional networks. In *The Semantic Web - 15th International Conference, ESWC 2018, Proceedings*, Lecture Notes in Computer Science (including subseries Lecture Notes in Artificial Intelligence and Lecture Notes in Bioinformatics), pages 593–607. Springer/Verlag.

Richard Socher, Alex Perelygin, Jean Wu, Jason Chuang, Christopher D. Manning, Andrew Ng, and Christopher Potts. 2013. Recursive deep models for semantic compositionality over a sentiment treebank. In *Proceedings of the 2013 Conference on Empirical Methods in Natural Language Processing*, pages 1631–1642, Seattle, Washington, USA. Association for Computational Linguistics.

Zhiqing Sun, Zhi-Hong Deng, Jian-Yun Nie, and Jian Tang. 2019. Rotate: Knowledge graph embedding by relational rotation in complex space. *CoRR*, abs/1902.10197.

Hongwei Wang, Fuzheng Zhang, Miao Zhao, Wenjie Li, Xing Xie, and Minyi Guo. 2019a. Multi-task feature learning for knowledge graph enhanced recommendation. In *The World Wide Web Conference*, WWW '19, page 2000–2010, New York, NY, USA. Association for Computing Machinery.

Xiang Wang, Xiangnan He, Yixin Cao, Meng Liu, and Tat-Seng Chua. 2019b. Kgat: Knowledge graph attention network for recommendation. In *Proceedings of the 25th ACM SIGKDD International Conference on Knowledge Discovery & Data Mining*, KDD '19, page 950–958, New York, NY, USA. Association for Computing Machinery.

Xiaozhi Wang, Tianyu Gao, Zhaocheng Zhu, Zhiyuan Liu, Juanzi Li, and Jian Tang. 2019c. KEPLER: A unified model for knowledge embedding and pre-trained language representation. *CoRR*, abs/1911.06136.

Alex Warstadt, Amanpreet Singh, and Samuel R Bowman. 2019. Neural network acceptability judgments. *Transactions of the Association for Computational Linguistics*, 7:625–641.

Thomas Wolf, Lysandre Debut, Victor Sanh, Julien Chaumond, Clement Delangue, Anthony Moi, Pierric Cistac, Tim Rault, R'emi Louf, Morgan Funtowicz, and Jamie Brew. 2019. Huggingface's transformers: State-of-the-art natural language processing. *ArXiv*, abs/1910.03771.

Liang Yao, Chengsheng Mao, and Yuan Luo. 2018. Graph convolutional networks for text classification. *CoRR*, abs/1809.05679.

Liang Yao, Chengsheng Mao, and Yuan Luo. 2019. Kgbert: Bert for knowledge graph completion. *ArXiv*, abs/1909.03193.

Jingqing Zhang, Piyawat Lertvittayakumjorn, and Yike Guo. 2019a. Integrating semantic knowledge to tackle zero-shot text classification. In *Proceedings of the 2019 Conference of the North American Chapter of the Association for Computational Linguistics: Human Language Technologies, Volume 1 (Long and Short Papers)*, pages 1031–1040, Minneapolis, Minnesota. Association for Computational Linguistics.

Zhanqiu Zhang, Jianyu Cai, Yongdong Zhang, and Jie Wang. 2020. Learning hierarchy-aware knowledge graph embeddings for link prediction. In *The Thirty-Fourth AAAI Conference on Artificial Intelligence, AAAI 2020, The Thirty-Second Innovative Applications of Artificial Intelligence Conference, IAAI 2020, The Tenth AAAI Symposium on Educational Advances in Artificial Intelligence, EAAI 2020, New York, NY, USA, February 7-12, 2020*, pages 3065–3072. AAAI Press.

Zhengyan Zhang, Xu Han, Zhiyuan Liu, Xin Jiang, Maosong Sun, and Qun Liu. 2019b. ERNIE: Enhanced language representation with informative entities. In *Proceedings of the 57th Annual Meeting of the Association for Computational Linguistics*, pages 1441–1451, Florence, Italy. Association for Computational Linguistics.

# GTN-ED: Event Detection Using Graph Transformer Networks

**Sanghamitra Dutta**[*]
Carnegie Mellon University
sanghamd@andrew.cmu.edu

**Liang Ma**
Dataminr
lma@dataminr.com

**Tanay Kumar Saha**
Dataminr
tsaha@dataminr.com

**Di Lu**
Dataminr
dlu@dataminr.com

**Joel Tetreault**
Dataminr
jtetreault@dataminr.com

**Alejandro Jaimes**
Dataminr
ajaimes@dataminr.com

## Abstract

Recent works show that the graph structure of sentences, generated from dependency parsers, has potential for improving event detection. However, they often only leverage the edges (dependencies) between words, and discard the dependency labels (e.g., nominal-subject), treating the underlying graph edges as homogeneous. In this work, we propose a novel framework for incorporating both dependencies and their labels using a recently proposed technique called Graph Transformer Networks (GTN). We integrate GTNs to leverage dependency relations on two existing homogeneous-graph-based models, and demonstrate an improvement in the F1 score on the ACE dataset.

## 1 Introduction

Event detection is an important task in natural language processing, which encompasses predicting important incidents in texts, e.g., news, tweets, messages, and manuscripts (Yang and Mitchell, 2016; Nguyen et al., 2016; Feng et al., 2016; Zhang et al., 2020; Du and Cardie, 2020; McClosky et al., 2011; Ji and Grishman, 2008; Liao and Grishman, 2010; Li et al., 2013; Yang et al., 2019). As an example, consider the following sentence: *The plane arrived back to base safely.* Here, the word *arrived* is an event trigger that denotes an event of the type "Movement:Transport," while "*The plane*" and "*base*" are its arguments. Given a sentence, the objective of the event detection task is to predict all such event triggers and their respective types.

Recent works on event detection (Nguyen and Grishman, 2018; Liu et al., 2018; Yan et al., 2019; Balali et al., 2020) employ graph based methods (Graph Convolution Networks (Kipf and Welling, 2017)) using the dependency graph (shown in Fig. 1) generated from syntactic dependency-parsers. These methods are able to capture useful non-local dependencies between words that are relevant for event detection. However, in most of these works (with the notable exception of Cui et al. (2020)), the graph is treated as a homogeneous graph, and the dependency labels (i.e., edge-types in the graph) are ignored.

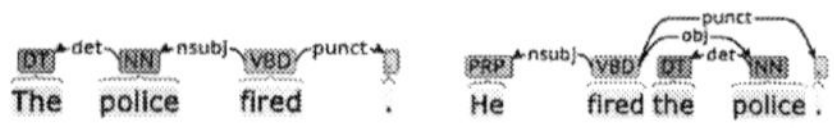


Figure 1: Examples of syntactic dependency parsing.

Dependency labels can often better inform whether a word is a trigger or not. Consider the two sentences in Fig. 1. In both the sentences, there is an edge between "*police*" and "*fired*". A model that does not take into account dependency labels will only have access to the information that they are connected. However, in the first sentence, "*fired*" is an event trigger of type "Conflict:Attack," whereas in the second sentence, it is of type "Personnel:End Position." The fact that the edge label between "*police*" and "*fired*" is a nominal-subject or an object relation serves as an indicator of the type of event trigger. Hence, leveraging the dependency labels can help improve the event detection performance.

In this work, we propose a simple method to employ the dependency labels into existing models inspired from a recently proposed technique called Graph Transformer Networks (GTN) (Yun et al., 2019). GTNs enable us to learn a soft selection of edge-types and composite relations (e.g., multi-hop connections, called *meta-paths*) among the words, thus producing heterogeneous adjacency matrices.

We integrate GTNs into two homogeneous-graph-based models (that previously ignored the dependency relations), namely, a simple gated-graph-convolution-based model inspired by Nguyen and Grishman (2018); Liu et al. (2018); Balali et al. (2020), and the near-state-of-the-art MOGANED model (Yan et al., 2019), enabling them to now leverage the dependency relations as well. Our method demonstrates a relative improvement in the

S. Dutta was a research intern at Dataminr.



*Proceedings of the Fifteenth Workshop on Graph-Based Methods for Natural Language Processing (TextGraphs-15)*, pages 132–137
June 11, 2021. 

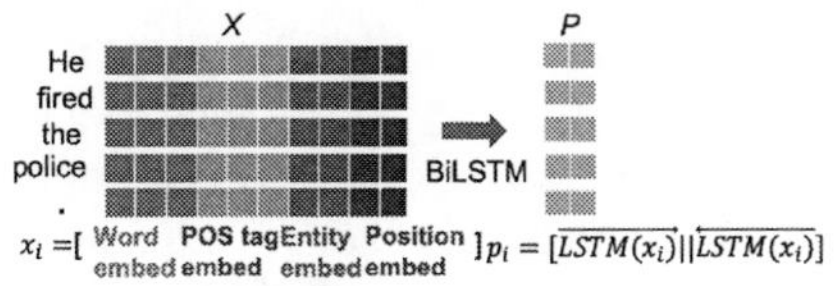


Figure 2: Embedding and BiLSTM Module.

Figure 3: Basic Gated-Graph-Convolution Network.

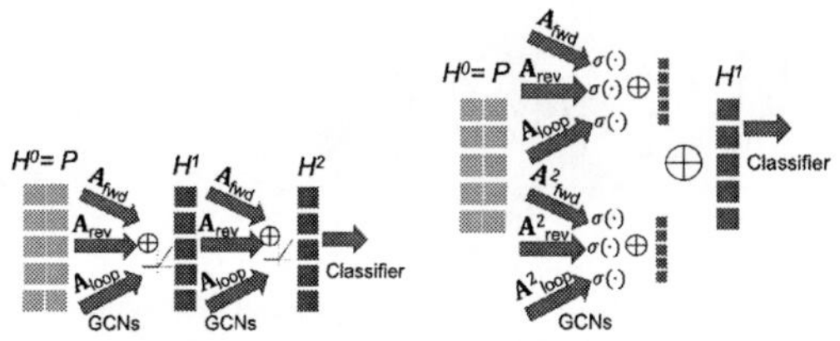


Figure 4: (Left) Model I; (Right) Model II.

F1 score on the ACE dataset (Walker et al., 2006) for both models, proving the value of leveraging dependency relations for a graph-based model. While the goal of this paper is not to establish a state-of-the-art (SOTA) method, but rather to show the merit of our approach, we do note that the improvements with our method approach the current SOTA (Cui et al., 2020) (which leverages dependency relations using embeddings instead of GTNs).

To summarize, our main contribution is *a method of enabling existing homogeneous-graph-based models to exploit dependency labels for event detection, inspired from GTNs.* Incorporating GTNs in NLP tasks has received less attention (also see recent related work Veyseh et al. (2020)).

**Notations:** We denote matrices and vectors in bold, e.g., $\boldsymbol{A}$ (matrix) or $\boldsymbol{a}$ (vector). Note that, $A(u, v)$ denotes the element at index $(u, v)$ in matrix $\boldsymbol{A}$.

## 2 Proposed Method

In this work, we incorporate GTNs onto two homogeneous-graph-based models: (i) **Model I**: a gated-graph-convolution-based model inspired by Nguyen and Grishman (2018); Liu et al. (2018); Balali et al. (2020); and (ii) **Model II**: MOGANED model (Yan et al., 2019). Both models have a similar initial embedding and BiLSTM module, followed by a graph-based module (where their differences lie), and finally a classification module.

**Embedding and BiLSTM Module:** Our initial module (shown in Fig. 2) is similar to existing works (e.g., Yan et al. (2019)). Each word of the sentence is represented by a token which consists of the word embedding, the POS tag embedding, the Named-Entity type embedding, and its positional embedding. For a sentence of $n$ words, we denote this sequence of tokens as $X = x_0, x_1, \ldots, x_{n-1}$. Next, we introduce a BiLSTM to encode $X$ into its context $P = p_0, p_1, \ldots, p_{n-1}$ where $p_i = [\overrightarrow{LSTM}(x_i)||\overleftarrow{LSTM}(x_i)]$, and $||$ denotes the concatenation operation. $P$ is then fed to the graph-based module, as discussed next.

**Graph-Based Module:** We first introduce the basic unit of both Model I and II, i.e., gated-graph-convolution network (see Fig. 3). Let $H^k = h_0^k, h_1^k, \ldots, h_{n-1}^k$ be the input and $H^{k+1} = h_0^{k+1}, h_1^{k+1}, \ldots, h_{n-1}^{k+1}$ be the output of the $k$-th layer of this module with $H^0 = P$. Given any adjacency matrix $\boldsymbol{A}$ and input $H^k$, consider the following operation at layer $k$:

$$f_u(H^k, \boldsymbol{A}) = \sum_{v=0}^{n-1} G_{\boldsymbol{A}}^k(u,v)(\boldsymbol{W}_{\boldsymbol{A}}^k h_v^k + \boldsymbol{b}_{\boldsymbol{A}}^k). \quad (1)$$

Here, $\boldsymbol{W}_{\boldsymbol{A}}^k$ and $\boldsymbol{b}_{\boldsymbol{A}}^k$ are the weight matrix and bias item for the adjacency matrix $\boldsymbol{A}$ at layer $k$, and $G_{\boldsymbol{A}}^k(u,v)$ is the gated-importance, given by $G_{\boldsymbol{A}}^k(u,v) = A(u,v)\sigma(\boldsymbol{w}_{att,\boldsymbol{A}}^k h_v^k + \epsilon_{att,\boldsymbol{A}}^k)$, where $\sigma(\cdot)$ is an activation function, and $\boldsymbol{w}_{att,\boldsymbol{A}}$ and $\epsilon_{att,\boldsymbol{A}}$ are the attention weight vector and bias item.

A dependency parser, e.g., Stanford Core NLP (Manning et al., 2014), generates a directed heterogeneous graph $\mathcal{G}$ for each sentence (recall Fig. 1). Existing works typically do not use the dependency labels (e.g., nominal-subject); they only derive three homogeneous adjacency matrices from $\mathcal{G}$ as follows: (i) $\boldsymbol{A}_{fwd}$ where $A_{fwd}(i,j) = 1$ if there is an edge from node $i$ to $j$; (ii) $\boldsymbol{A}_{rev}$ where $A_{rev}(i,j) = 1$ if there is an edge from node $j$ to $i$; and (iii) $\boldsymbol{A}_{loop}$ which is an identity matrix.

For **Model I** (see Fig. 4 (Left)), the output of the $k$-th layer (input to $k+1$-th layer) is given by $h_u^{k+1}=\text{ReLu}(\sum_{\boldsymbol{A}\in\{\boldsymbol{A}_{fwd},\boldsymbol{A}_{rev},\boldsymbol{A}_{loop}\}} f_u(H^k, \boldsymbol{A}))$. The first layer of gated-graph-convolution network captures dependencies between immediate neighbors (1-hop). To capture $K$-hop dependencies, Model I has $K$ consecutive layers of such gated-

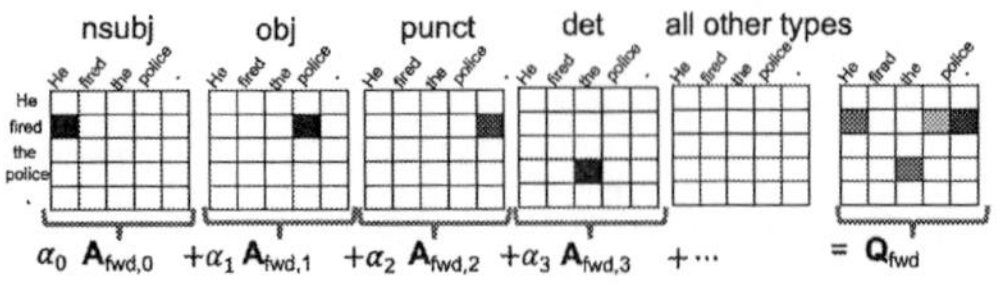


Figure 5: GTN to obtain heterogeneous adjacency matrix of meta-path length 1 (Recall Fig. 1 for the graph).

graph-convolution networks. The output of this graph-based module is then fed to a multi-layer perceptron (MLP) with attention weights for classifying each word into its event-type (or "not an event").

In **Model II**, instead of passing the BiLSTM output $P$ through a *series* of $K$ consecutive gated-graph-convolution layers (to capture $K$-hop connections), this model separately aggregates the outputs of $T$ *parallel* graph-convolution layers with separate adjacency matrices representing hops of length $1, 2, \ldots, T$ (see Fig. 4 (Right)). Let $H^0 (= P)$ be the input and $H^1$ be the output of the graph-based module of Model II (which effectively has only one layer, i.e., $k$=0). In Yan et al. (2019), the homogeneous adjacency matrices $\boldsymbol{A}_{fwd}$, $\boldsymbol{A}_{rev}$, and $\boldsymbol{A}_{loop}$ are considered with their corresponding $t$-hop adjacency matrices $\boldsymbol{A}^t_{fwd}$, $\boldsymbol{A}^t_{rev}$, and $\boldsymbol{A}^t_{loop}$ (multiplied $t$ times) respectively. The output of the graph-based module is given by: $h^1_u = \sum_{t=0}^{T-1} \boldsymbol{w}_{att,t} \boldsymbol{v}_t$ where $\boldsymbol{v}_t = \sum_{\boldsymbol{A} \in \{\boldsymbol{A}_{fwd}, \boldsymbol{A}_{rev}, \boldsymbol{A}_{loop}\}} \sigma(f_u(H^0, \boldsymbol{A}^t))$. Here, $\boldsymbol{w}_{att,t}$ is an attention-weight (further details in (Yan et al., 2019)) and $\sigma(\cdot)$ is the exponential linear unit[1]. Finally, these outputs are passed through an MLP with attention weights for classification.

**Remark.** The reason for using only three matrices instead of a separate adjacency matrix for each edge-type is that it results in an explosion of parameters for the gated-graph-convolution network, as individual weight matrices have to be learnt for each type of edge (see also Nguyen and Grishman (2018)). In this work, we replace the homogeneous matrices $\boldsymbol{A}_{fwd}$ and $\boldsymbol{A}_{rev}$ with heterogeneous adjacency matrices without a significant overhead in the number of parameters, as discussed next.

**Obtaining Heterogeneous Adjacency Matrices With GTN:** Consider a directed heterogeneous graph $\mathcal{G}$ with each edge belonging to one of $L$ types. This graph can be represented using a set of $L$ adjacency matrices $\{\boldsymbol{A}_{fwd,0}, \boldsymbol{A}_{fwd,1}, \ldots, \boldsymbol{A}_{fwd,L-1}\}$, each corresponding to a different edge-type (dependency label). $A_{fwd,l}(i, j) = 1$ if there is a directed edge from node $i$ to $j$ of type $l$. A GTN obtains a heterogeneous adjacency matrix by learning a convex combination $\boldsymbol{Q}_{fwd} = \sum_{l=0}^{L-1} \alpha_l \boldsymbol{A}_{fwd,l}$ (see Fig. 5) where $\boldsymbol{\alpha} = \text{softmax}(\boldsymbol{w})$ and $\boldsymbol{w}$ is a weight vector that the model learns. The matrix $\boldsymbol{Q}_{fwd}$ is a heterogeneous adjacency matrix with an "appropriately weighted" edge between any two nodes that have an edge in any of the $L$ original matrices.

For **Model I**, we first generate a set of $L$ adjacency matrices (for $L$ edge-types) corresponding to the directed forward edges, and another set of $L$ adjacency matrices corresponding to the reverse edges. Next, we learn heterogeneous adjacency matrices, i.e., $\boldsymbol{A}_{fwd} = \boldsymbol{Q}_{fwd}$ and $\boldsymbol{A}_{rev} = \boldsymbol{Q}_{rev}$. Our technique enables baseline Model I to leverage dependency relations by learning only $2L$ more scalar parameters which is significantly less than learning individual weight matrices for $L$ edge-types.

For **Model II**, we not only aim to learn heterogeneous adjacency matrices to replace the homogeneous $\boldsymbol{A}_{fwd}$ and $\boldsymbol{A}_{rev}$, but also learn heterogeneous adjacency matrices that have an "appropriately weighted" edge between every two nodes that are $t$-hops apart in the original graph $\mathcal{G}$ (called a meta-path of length $t$) so as to replace $\boldsymbol{A}^t_{fwd}$ and $\boldsymbol{A}^t_{rev}$. Specifically, for the case of $t = 2$, GTN first learns two convex combinations $\boldsymbol{Q}_{fwd,0}$ and $\boldsymbol{Q}_{fwd,1}$ (each corresponds to meta-paths of length 1), and then computes the product $\boldsymbol{Q}_{fwd,0}\boldsymbol{Q}_{fwd,1}$. Similarly, one can compute a product of $t$ such adjacency matrices to learn meta-paths of length $t$.

We replace all $t$-hop adjacency matrices with heterogeneous adjacency matrices of meta-path length $t$, learnt through GTNs, e.g., $\boldsymbol{A}^t_{fwd}$ is replaced by $\boldsymbol{Q}_{fwd,0}\boldsymbol{Q}_{fwd,1} \ldots \boldsymbol{Q}_{fwd,t-1}$, where each $\boldsymbol{Q}_{fwd,i}$ is a convex combination of $L$-adjacency matrices corresponding to the directed forward edges. Similar heterogeneous adjacency matrices of meta-path length $t$ are learnt for the reverse edges as well to replace $\boldsymbol{A}^t_{rev}$. This modification enables the baseline Model II to leverage the dependency relations, by only learning $2Lt$ more scalar parameters for each $t$, which is practicable.

## 3 Results

**Dataset and Evaluation Metrics:** We use the benchmark ACE2005 English dataset (Walker et al., 2006) with the same data split as in prior works (where the sentences from 529, 30, and 40 docu-

[1] The gated-importance $G^k_{\boldsymbol{A}}(u, v)$ has subtle differences between Model I and II.

| $K$ | P | R | F1 | $K$ | P | R | F1 |
|---|---|---|---|---|---|---|---|
| 1 | 72.0 | 75.5 | 73.7 | 1 | 72.9 | **76.4** | **74.6** |
| 2 | 70.7 | 75.7 | 73.1 | 2 | 72.1 | 75.9 | 74.0 |
| 3 | 72.8 | 70.7 | 71.7 | 3 | **73.8** | 73.6 | 73.7 |

Table 1: Performance of gated-graph-convolution-based models (**Model I**) for varying number of consecutive convolution layers ($K$): (Left) Baseline models with no GTNs; (Right) Proposed models with GTNs.

| Method | P | R | F1 |
|---|---|---|---|
| Baseline (no GTNs) | 79.5 | 72.3 | 75.7 |
| Proposed (with GTNs) | **80.9** | **73.2** | **76.8** |

Table 2: Performance of MOGANED (**Model II**).

ments are used as the training, validation, and test set). We use the Stanford CoreNLP toolkit (Manning et al., 2014) for sentence splitting, tokenizing, POS-tagging and dependency parsing. We use word embeddings trained over the New York Times corpus with Skip-gram algorithm following existing works (Yan et al., 2019). We evaluate the Precision (P), Recall (R) and F1 score.

**Model Settings:** For Model I, the number of consecutive layers of gated-graph-convolution networks ($K$) is varied from 1 to 3. For Model II, we use the code[2] with same hyper parameter settings.

**Performance:** For both Models I and II, GTNs demonstrate an improvement of about 1 point F1 score (see Tables 1 and 2). The 76.8 F1 score for Model II with GTNs is also quite close to the SOTA performance of 77.6 for this task (Cui et al., 2020).

**Examining Specific Predictions For Insights:** To explain the role of GTNs, we examined all the predictions on the validation set using the baseline Model II (no GTNs) and the proposed Model II (with GTNs). We include some specific instances here that we found interesting and insightful.

We observe that using GTNs makes the predictions more "precise," by reducing the number of false-positive event trigger detections. For instance, *He's now national director of Win Without War, and* ***former*** *Congressman Bob Dornan, Republican of California.* Here, "*former*" is the only event trigger (type Personnel:End-Position), as is correctly identified by our model. However, the baseline model also falsely identifies "*War*," as an event trigger of type Conflict:Attack. Another example is: *In a monstrous conflict of interest, [...].* Here, the baseline falsely identifies "*conflict*," as a trigger of type Conflict:Attack. Our model is able to identify "*War*," and "*conflict*" as non-triggers based on their context in the sentence, while the baseline seems to be over-emphasizing on their literal meaning.

In some cases, the baseline model also leads to misclassification. For instance, *The Apache troop* ***opened*** *its tank guns,[...].* Here, "*opened*," is an event trigger of type Conflict:Attack, as is correctly identified by our model; however, the baseline misclassifies it as type Movement:Transport.

Another interesting example is: *[...] Beatriz* ***walked*** *into the USCF Offices in New Windsor and immediately* ***fired*** *17 staff members.* Here, "*walked*" is an event trigger of type Movement:Transport, and "*fired*" is of type Personnel:End-Position. The baseline model misclassifies "*fired*" as Conflict:Attack, while using GTNs help classify it correctly. However, using GTNs can sometimes miss certain event triggers while attempting to be more precise, e.g., "*walked*" is missed when using GTNs while the baseline model identifies it correctly.

Lastly, there are examples where both the baseline and proposed models make the same errors. E.g., ***I visited*** *all their families.* or, *I would have* ***shot*** *the insurgent too.* Here, both models misclassify "*visited*," (type Contact:Meet) as Movement:Transport, and "*shot*," (type Life:Die) as Conflict:Attack. As future work, we are examining alternate techniques that better inform the context of the event trigger in such sentences. Another interesting example is: "*It is legal, and* ***it*** *is done.*" Both models miss "*it*," (type Transaction:Transfer-Money). For this example (and some other similar examples of anaphora resolution), we believe that it might be quite non-intuitive to classify the event trigger from the sentence alone, and dependencies among sentences from the same article might need to be leveraged to better inform the context, as we will examine in future work.

## 4 Conclusion

We developed a novel method of enabling existing event extraction models to leverage dependency relations without a significant rise in the number of parameters to be learnt. Our method relies on GTN, and demonstrates an improvement in F1 score over two strong baseline models that do not leverage dependency relations. The benefits of using GTN in an NLP task suggests that other NLP tasks could be improved in the future.

[2] https://github.com/ll0iecas/MOGANED

## References


Ali Balali, Masoud Asadpour, Ricardo Campos, and Adam Jatowt. 2020. Joint event extraction along shortest dependency paths using graph convolutional networks. *arXiv preprint arXiv:2003.08615*.

Shiyao Cui, Bowen Yu, Tingwen Liu, Zhenyu Zhang, Xuebin Wang, and Jinqiao Shi. 2020. Event detection with relation-aware graph convolutional neural networks. *arXiv preprint arXiv:2002.10757*.

Xinya Du and Claire Cardie. 2020. Event extraction by answering (almost) natural questions. *arXiv preprint arXiv:2004.13625*.

Xiaocheng Feng, Lifu Huang, Duyu Tang, Heng Ji, Bing Qin, and Ting Liu. 2016. A language-independent neural network for event detection. In *Proceedings of the 54th Annual Meeting of the Association for Computational Linguistics (Volume 2: Short Papers)*, pages 66–71.

Heng Ji and Ralph Grishman. 2008. Refining event extraction through cross-document inference. In *Proceedings of ACL-08: Hlt*, pages 254–262.

Thomas N. Kipf and Max Welling. 2017. Semi-supervised classification with graph convolutional networks. In *5th International Conference on Learning Representations, ICLR*.

Qi Li, Heng Ji, and Liang Huang. 2013. Joint event extraction via structured prediction with global features. In *Proceedings of the 51st Annual Meeting of the Association for Computational Linguistics (Volume 1: Long Papers)*, pages 73–82.

Shasha Liao and Ralph Grishman. 2010. Using document level cross-event inference to improve event extraction. In *Proceedings of the 48th Annual Meeting of the Association for Computational Linguistics*, pages 789–797.

Xiao Liu, Zhunchen Luo, and Heyan Huang. 2018. Jointly multiple events extraction via attention-based graph information aggregation. In *Proceedings of the 2018 Conference on Empirical Methods in Natural Language Processing*, pages 1247–1256, Brussels, Belgium. Association for Computational Linguistics.

Christopher D Manning, Mihai Surdeanu, John Bauer, Jenny Rose Finkel, Steven Bethard, and David McClosky. 2014. The stanford corenlp natural language processing toolkit. In *Proceedings of 52nd annual meeting of the association for computational linguistics: system demonstrations*, pages 55–60.

David McClosky, Mihai Surdeanu, and Christopher D Manning. 2011. Event extraction as dependency parsing. In *Proceedings of the 49th Annual Meeting of the Association for Computational Linguistics: Human Language Technologies*, pages 1626–1635.

Thien Huu Nguyen, Kyunghyun Cho, and Ralph Grishman. 2016. Joint event extraction via recurrent neural networks. In *Proceedings of the 2016 Conference of the North American Chapter of the Association for Computational Linguistics: Human Language Technologies*, pages 300–309.

Thien Huu Nguyen and Ralph Grishman. 2018. Graph convolutional networks with argument-aware pooling for event detection. In *Proceedings of the 32nd AAAI Conference on Artificial Intelligence*, pages 5900–5907.

Amir Pouran Ben Veyseh, Tuan Ngo Nguyen, and Thien Huu Nguyen. 2020. Graph transformer networks with syntactic and semantic structures for event argument extraction. *arXiv preprint arXiv:2010.13391*.

Christopher Walker, Stephanie Strassel, Julie Medero, and Kazuaki Maeda. 2006. Ace 2005 multilingual training corpus. *Linguistic Data Consortium, Philadelphia*, 57:45.

Haoran Yan, Xiaolong Jin, Xiangbin Meng, Jiafeng Guo, and Xueqi Cheng. 2019. Event detection with multi-order graph convolution and aggregated attention. In *Proceedings of the 2019 Conference on Empirical Methods in Natural Language Processing and the 9th International Joint Conference on Natural Language Processing (EMNLP-IJCNLP)*, pages 5770–5774.

Bishan Yang and Tom Mitchell. 2016. Joint extraction of events and entities within a document context. *arXiv preprint arXiv:1609.03632*.

Sen Yang, Dawei Feng, Linbo Qiao, Zhigang Kan, and Dongsheng Li. 2019. Exploring pre-trained language models for event extraction and generation. In *Proceedings of the 57th Annual Meeting of the Association for Computational Linguistics*, pages 5284–5294.

Seongjun Yun, Minbyul Jeong, Raehyun Kim, Jaewoo Kang, and Hyunwoo J Kim. 2019. Graph transformer networks. In *Advances in Neural Information Processing Systems*, pages 11983–11993.

Yunyan Zhang, Guangluan Xu, Yang Wang, Daoyu Lin, Feng Li, Chenglong Wu, Jingyuan Zhang, and Tinglei Huang. 2020. A question answering-based framework for one-step event argument extraction. *IEEE Access*, 8:65420–65431.

## A More Details on the MOGANED model

There are some subtle differences in the graph-attention mechanisms of Model I and II. In particular, for Model II, the gated-importance $G^0_{\boldsymbol{A}}(u, v)$ in equation (1) is redefined as follows: $G^0_{\boldsymbol{A}}(u, v)$=softmax$(E(u, v))$, where $E(u, v)=A(u, v)\gamma(\boldsymbol{W}_{c,\boldsymbol{A}}[\boldsymbol{W}_{att,\boldsymbol{A}}h^0_u||\boldsymbol{W}_{att,\boldsymbol{A}}h^0_v])$, $\gamma$ is LeakyReLU (with negative input slope $\alpha$), and $\boldsymbol{W}_{c,\boldsymbol{A}}$ and $\boldsymbol{W}_{att,\boldsymbol{A}}$ are weight matrices. Further details are provided in Yan et al. (2019).

## B Data Preprocessing

We use the same data split as several existing works (Nguyen et al., 2016; Nguyen and Grishman, 2018; Liu et al., 2018; Balali et al., 2020; Yan et al., 2019; Cui et al., 2020; Ji and Grishman, 2008; Liao and Grishman, 2010; Li et al., 2013), where the sentences from 529, 30, and 40 documents are used as the training, validation, and test set. For preprocessing, we directly used the following code[3] which uses the Stanford Core NLP toolkit (Manning et al., 2014).

## C Hyper Parameter Setting

For both the models, we select 100 as the dimension of the word embeddings, and 50 as the dimension of all the other embeddings, i.e., POS-tag embedding, Named-Entity-type embedding, and positional embedding. Following prior work, we restrict the length of each sentence to be 50 (truncating long sentences if necessary). We select the hidden units of the BiLSTM network as 100. We choose a batch size of 10, and Adam with initial learning rate of 0.0002. We select the dimension of the graph representation to be 150. When using GTNs, the number of edge-types ($L$) is 35, which is determined by the number of unique types of dependency relations, e.g., `nsubj`, `case`, etc., as obtained from the dependency parser.

[3] `https://github.com/nlpcl-lab/ace2005-preprocessing`

# Fine-grained General Entity Typing in German using GermaNet

**Sabine Weber**
University of Edinburgh
s.weber@sms.ed.ac.uk

**Mark Steedman**
University of Edinburgh
steedman@inf.ed.ac.uk

## Abstract

Fine-grained entity typing is important to tasks like relation extraction and knowledge base construction. We find however, that fine-grained entity typing systems perform poorly on general entities (e.g. "ex-president") as compared to named entities (e.g. "Barack Obama"). This is due to a lack of general entities in existing training data sets. We show that this problem can be mitigated by automatically generating training data from WordNets. We use a German WordNet equivalent, GermaNet, to automatically generate training data for German general entity typing. We use this data to supplement named entity data to train a neural fine-grained entity typing system. This leads to a 10% improvement in accuracy of the prediction of level 1 FIGER types for German general entities, while decreasing named entity type prediction accuracy by only 1%.

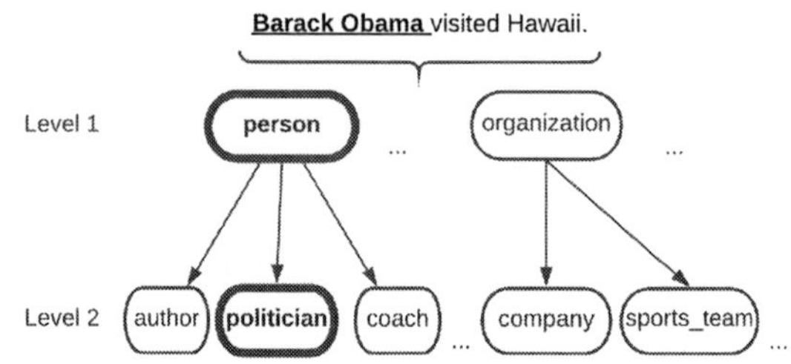


Figure 1: Fine-grained entity typing with the FIGER ontology in English. Correct types are highlighted.

## 1 Introduction

The task of fine-grained entity typing is to assign a semantic label (e.g. '/person/politician' or '/location/city') to an entity in a natural language sentence. In contrast to coarse grained entity typing it uses a larger set of types (e.g. 112 types in the FIGER ontology (Ling and Weld, 2012)), and a multilevel type hierarchy. An example of fine grained entity typing can be seen in Figure 1. Fine-grained entity typing is an important initial step in context sensitive tasks such as relation extraction (Kuang et al., 2020), question answering(Yavuz et al., 2016) and knowledge base construction (Hosseini et al., 2019).

Entities can appear in text in many forms. In the sentences 'Barack Obama visited Hawaii. The ex-president enjoyed the fine weather.' both 'Barack Obama' and 'ex-president' should be assigned the type '/person/politician' by a fine-grained entity typing system. While the typing of the **named entity** (NE) 'Barack Obama' can be performed by state of the art entity typing systems, it is unclear how well these systems perform on **general entities** (GEs) like 'ex-president'. We find that accuracy and F1 score of a state-of-the-art German fine-grained entity typing system are 17% lower on general entities than on named entities (see Table 1 and section 5). This is because the training data for these systems contains only named entities, but not general entities (e.g. Weber and Steedman (2021, under submission); Ling and Weld (2012)). This is the problem we address with our approach.

Because manual annotation of training data is costly and time intensive we propose an approach that uses existing resources to create silver annotated GE typing data. For this we use German text taken from Wikipedia, GermaNet (a German WordNet equivalent, Hamp and Feldweg (1997)) and the FIGER type ontology (Ling and Weld, 2012). The resulting data can be added to existing NE typing data for the training of a neural entity typing system. In our approach we use the hierarchical typing model of Chen et al. (2020), which builds upon contextualized word embeddings. It has shown good performance on public benchmarks and is freely available.

We compare our approach against using only NE data for training and a rule-based approach and achieve 10% improvement in accuracy of the prediction of level 1 FIGER types for German general



*Proceedings of the Fifteenth Workshop on Graph-Based Methods for Natural Language Processing (TextGraphs-15)*, pages 138–143
June 11, 2021. ©2021 Association for Computational Linguistics

entities, while decreasing named entity prediction accuracy by only 1%. Our approach can be seen as a proof of concept and a blueprint for the use of existing WordNet resources to improve entity typing quality in other languages and domains.

## 2 Related work

The problem of GE typing performance has not been examined specifically before, nor has it been addressed for the case of German. Choi et al. (2018) create a fine-grained entity typing system that is capable of typing both GE and NE in English by integrating GEs into their training data. Their approach relies on large amounts of manually annotated data, and is therefore not feasible for our case. Moreover they propose a new type hierarchy, while we stick to the widely used FIGER type hierarchy, to make the output of our system consistent with that of other systems for tasks like multilingual knowledge graph construction.

Recent advances in typing NE in English have harnessed the power of contextualized word embeddings (Peters et al., 2018; Conneau et al., 2020) to encode entities and their context. These approaches use the AIDA, BNN, OntoNotes and FIGER ontologies, which come with their own human annotated data sets (Chen et al., 2020; Dai et al., 2019; López et al., 2019). By choosing to use the model of (Chen et al., 2020), we build upon their strengths to enable GE typing in German.

German NE typing suffers from a lack of manually annotated resources. Two recent approaches by by Ruppenhofer et al. (2020) and Leitner et al. (2020) use manually annotated data from biographic interviews and court proceedings. Owing to the specific domains, the authors modify existing type onthologies (OntoNotes in the case of biographic interviews) or come up with their own type ontology (in the case of court proceedings). This limits the way their models can be applied to other domains or used for multilingual tasks. Weber and Steedman (2021, under submission) use annotation projection to create a training data set of Wikipedia text annotated with FIGER types. We build upon their data set to create a German model that types both NEs and GEs.

## 3 Method

**GermaNet** (Hamp and Feldweg, 1997) is a broad-coverage lexical-semantic net for German which contains 16.000 words and is modelled after the English WordNet (Fellbaum, 2010). The net contains links that connect nouns to their hyponyms and hypernyms. This way GermaNet implicitly contains a fine-grained ontology of nouns. Although some NE are contained in GermaNet, the vast majority of nouns are GEs.

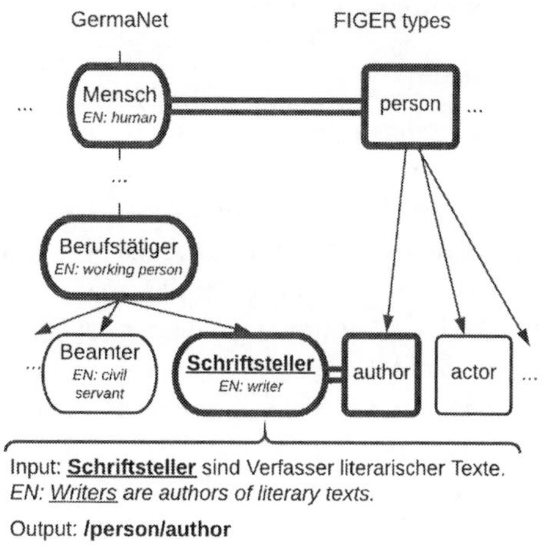


Figure 2: An example of FIGER type assignment using GermaNet. The manual mapping between GermaNet and FIGER is indicated by double lines. Whenever a word in the hypernym path of the input word is mapped to a FIGER type, the respective type gets assigned.

We manually map the 112 FIGER types to nouns in GermaNet. Starting from a German translation of the type name (e.g. the type 'person' translates to 'Mensch') we add terms that best describe the FIGER type. This mapping enables us to look up a word in GermaNet and check if any of its hypernyms are mapped to a FIGER type. If this is the case, we can assign the corresponding FIGER type to the word in question. Figure 2 illustrates this method. We use this method to generate German GE training data and as our rule-based baseline.

We use this GE training data in addition to German NE typing data to train the **hierarchical typing model** of Chen et al. (2020). In this model the entity and its context are encoded using XLM-RoBERTa (Conneau et al., 2020). For each type in the FIGER ontology the model learns a type embedding. We pass the concatenated entity and context vector trough a 2-layer feed-forward network that maps into the same space as the type embedding. The score is an inner product between the transformed entity and context vector and the type embedding. For further model details refer to Chen et al. (2020).

## 4 Experimental setup

### 4.1 Data sets

As a NE training set we use the German fine-grained entity typing corpus of Weber and Steedman (2021, under submission). This data set was generated from the WikiMatrix corpus by Schwenk et al. (2019) using annotation projection.

To create the GE training data, we use the German portion of the WikiMatrix corpus. By using the same genre we make sure that no additional noise is added by domain differences. Moreover, the original English FIGER data set was created from Wikipedia text, so we can assume that all FIGER types are well represented in the WikiMatrix data.

### 4.2 GE training data generation

To generate GE training data we take the following steps: First, we split off 100 K sentences from the top of the German part of the WikiMatrix corpus. We use spaCy (Honnibal et al., 2020) for part of speech tagging. Every word tagged as a noun is looked up in GermaNet. We use the method described in Section 3 to assign FIGER types to the noun.

This lookup in GermaNet is not context-aware, so polysemous words are assigned multiple contradicting types. We only include words in our training data that have less than two level 1 types and not more than one level 2 type. This filter discards about 41% of all input words. We discuss the implications of this filter in Section 6. The resulting corpus consists of 200K sentences of German FIGER typed GE data [1].

### 4.3 Training set up

In our experiments we compare six different training setups against a rule-based baseline using only GermaNet.

**Only NE data:** In this setup we train the hierarchical typing model on 200K sentences taken from the German fine-grained NE typing corpus by Weber and Steedman (2021, under submission).

**Mixing NE and GE data:** In this setup we add either 20K, 40K, 60K, 80K or 100K sentences of automatically generated GE training data to 200K sentences taken from the corpus of Weber and Steedman (2021, under submission) and train the hierarchical typing model on it. We shuffle the sentence order before training.

**Baseline:** We compare these two neural approaches against using only GermaNet. In this baseline we use the approach described in Section 3 and Figure 2 to type our test data.

### 4.4 Evaluation

**Metrics** Following previous fine-grained entity typing literature we evaluate the results of our model using strict accuracy (Acc) and micro F1 score. The strict accuracy is the ratio of instances where the predicted type set is exactly the same as the gold type set. The micro F1 score computes F1 score biased by class frequency. We also evaluate per hierarchy level accuracy (level 1 type labels being more coarse grained and level 2 labels more fine grained).

**Test sets** We use the German NE typing test set of Weber and Steedman (2021, under submission) for testing the performance of our systems on the task of NE typing. The test set consists of 500 manually annotated sentences.

We create our GE typing data sets by taking that same test set and manually replacing the named entities in it with plausible general entities (e.g. swapping 'Barack Obama' for 'ex-president'). Where this was not possible, we chose another noun from the sentence and manually added the correct type. In all other cases we removed the sentence from the data set. The resulting GE data set consists of 400 sentences, which we split into a 100 sentence development set and a 300 sentence test set.

## 5 Results

Table 1 shows the accuracy and F1 scores on the gold German test set. Additionally, development set results are presented in appendix A. We compare the performance of models trained with different amounts of GE data on the GE and NE test sets described in section 4.4.

The test set performance on NE is best when no GE data is added, but GE performance is at its lowest. After adding 20K sentences of GE training data the level 1 accuracy and F1 score on the GE test set rises by 9%. Increasing the amount of GE training data to 40K improves the GE test set performance further with best level 1 results at 40K sentences GE data and best level 2 results at 60K sentences GE data. Adding more GE data beyond these points decreases GE performance.

[1] The generation code and generated data can be found here: https://github.com/webersab/german_general_entity_typing

| Model | Acc L1 NE | Acc L1 GE | F1 L1 NE | F1 L1 GE | Acc L2 NE | Acc L2 GE | F1 L2 NE | F1 L2 GE |
|---|---|---|---|---|---|---|---|---|
| 200K (only NE) | 0.74 | 0.57 | 0.79 | 0.62 | 0.39 | 0.25 | 0.44 | 0.30 |
| 220K | 0.73 | 0.66 | 0.78 | 0.71 | 0.37 | 0.29 | 0.42 | 0.34 |
| 240K | **0.73** | **0.67** | **0.77** | **0.72** | 0.38 | 0.29 | 0.43 | 0.34 |
| 260K | 0.72 | 0.66 | 0.77 | 0.70 | **0.39** | **0.30** | **0.44** | **0.35** |
| 280K | 0.72 | 0.66 | 0.77 | 0.71 | 0.37 | 0.30 | 0.42 | 0.35 |
| 300K | 0.70 | 0.64 | 0.75 | 0.68 | 0.37 | 0.30 | 0.42 | 0.34 |
| GermaNet BL | 0.10 | 0.48 | 0.10 | 0.48 | 0.27 | 0.08 | 0.27 | 0.08 |

Table 1: Accuracy and micro F1 score based on training input, tested on 500 NE annotated sentences and 300 GE annotated sentences. GE Level 1 accuracy and Level 1 F1 rises by 9% when 20K sentences of GE training data are added, while NE accuracy and F1 declines by only 1%.

Although NE performance is worsened by adding GE training data, the decrease in level 1 performance in both accuracy and F1 is only 1% for 20K and 40K GE sentences, with a maximum decrease of 3% when 100K GE sentences are added.

Adding GE training data has a smaller effect on level 2 performance than on level 1 performance, with level 2 accuracy and F1 on the GE test set increasing by 5% when 60K sentences of GE data are added. Adding GE training data initially decreases performance on NE level 2 types, but at 60K sentences of GE data is just as good as without them.

Adding more than 60K sentences of GE data does not improve GE test set performance, but decreases both NE and GE test set performance in accuracy and F1 score. We can also see that the GermaNet baseline is outperformed by all systems, although its performance on level 2 GE types is close to our best models. We will discuss possible explanations in the next section.

## 6 Discussion

The results show that the models' performance on GE typing can be improved using a simple data augmentation method using WordNet, while only lightly impacting the performance on NE typing.

All neural models outperform the GermaNet baseline. This raises the question why the neural systems were able to perform better than GermaNet on GE, although the training data was generated from GermaNet. We speculate that the hierarchical typing model is very context sensitive because of its usage of contextualized word embeddings (XLM-RoBERTa) to encode entities and their context during training. While our GE data provides it with high confidence non-polysemous examples, it is able to learn which context goes with which type. At test time this awareness of context enables the neural systems to disambiguate polysemous cases, even though it has not observed these cases at training time. This intuition is supported by our test results: For the best performing model (240K) 40% of the general entities that occur in our test set are never seen in the training data.

A second reason why the neural models outperform GermaNet is that GermaNet does not represent every German noun. A certain word might not be part of GermaNet and therefor no type can be assigned. This is the case for 23% of words seen during training data generation. The neural models do not have this problem because our vocabulary is larger than the 16.000 words contained in GermaNet and because the neural models assign type labels to out of vocabulary words on the basis of the language model XML-RoBERTa.

Despite these factors the neural models' performance is closely matched by the GermaNet baseline on level 2 labels. Level 2 types are underrepresented in the data, because their prevalence follows their occurrence in the Wikipedia data. This leads to some low-level types being very rare: a signal that is too weak to be learned sufficiently by a neural model. On the other hand, a lookup of words in a preexisting data base like GermaNet is not affected by this issue. While the neural models offer high recall at low precision, GermaNet has higher precision at low recall.

The results also show that 20K sentences of GE data produce the highest increase of GE performance while impacting NE performance least. Adding GE data beyond 60K sentences does not only worsen NE performance by also GE performance. This is due to noise in the GE typing data. A manual error analysis of 100 GE training data sentences shows that 35% have incorrect type assignments. With more GE training data the model starts to overfit to this noise, which leads to decreasing test set performance, affecting NE performance slightly more than GE performance.

## 7 Conclusion and future work

In this paper we have shown that it is possible to improve the performance of a German fine-grained entity typing system using GermaNet. We create silver annotated general entity typing data for training a fine-grained entity typing model that builds upon contextualised word embeddings (in our case, XLM-RoBERTa). Our results can be taken as a blueprint for improving fine-grained entity typing performance in other languages and domains, as there are WordNets for over 40 different languages. Moreover, the manual mapping we introduced could be replaced by machine-translating English type labels into the language of the WordNet, which would require less resources for human annotation than a manual mapping.

Avenues for future work could be a combination between high-precison but low recall WordNets and neural models, e.g. through incorporating the models' prediction confidence to make a decision whether a WordNet look-up should be trusted over the models' own prediction.

The problem of general entity typing could also be viewed through the lens of coreference resolution: The type of a general entity could be inferred from a named entity that the general entity refers to. However, there might be cases in which no named entity referent exists, or domains and languages where coreference resolution systems are unavailable. In all of these cases combining our method with existing approaches opens new possibilities.

## References


Tongfei Chen, Yunmo Chen, and Benjamin Van Durme. 2020. Hierarchical entity typing via multi-level learning to rank. In *Proceedings of the 58th Annual Meeting of the Association for Computational Linguistics, ACL 2020, Online, July 5-10, 2020*, pages 8465–8475.

Eunsol Choi, Omer Levy, Yejin Choi, and Luke Zettlemoyer. 2018. Ultra-fine entity typing. In *Proceedings of the 56th Annual Meeting of the Association for Computational Linguistics (Volume 1: Long Papers)*, pages 87–96.

Alexis Conneau, Kartikay Khandelwal, Naman Goyal, Vishrav Chaudhary, Guillaume Wenzek, Francisco Guzmán, E. Grave, Myle Ott, Luke Zettlemoyer, and Veselin Stoyanov. 2020. Unsupervised cross-lingual representation learning at scale. In *ACL*.

Hongliang Dai, Donghong Du, Xin Li, and Yangqiu Song. 2019. Improving fine-grained entity typing with entity linking. In *Proceedings of the 2019 Conference on Empirical Methods in Natural Language Processing and the 9th International Joint Conference on Natural Language Processing (EMNLP-IJCNLP)*, pages 6211–6216.

Christiane Fellbaum. 2010. Wordnet. In *Theory and applications of ontology: computer applications*, pages 231–243. Springer.

Birgit Hamp and Helmut Feldweg. 1997. Germanet-a lexical-semantic net for german. In *Automatic information extraction and building of lexical semantic resources for NLP applications*.

Matthew Honnibal, Ines Montani, Sofie Van Landeghem, and Adriane Boyd. 2020. spaCy: Industrial-strength Natural Language Processing in Python.

Mohammad Javad Hosseini, Shay B Cohen, Mark Johnson, and Mark Steedman. 2019. Duality of link prediction and entailment graph induction. In *Proceedings of the 57th Annual Meeting of the Association for Computational Linguistics*, pages 4736–4746.

Jun Kuang, Yixin Cao, Jianbing Zheng, Xiangnan He, Ming Gao, and Aoying Zhou. 2020. Improving neural relation extraction with implicit mutual relations. In *2020 IEEE 36th International Conference on Data Engineering (ICDE)*, pages 1021–1032. IEEE.

Elena Leitner, Georg Rehm, and Julián Moreno-Schneider. 2020. A dataset of german legal documents for named entity recognition. *arXiv preprint arXiv:2003.13016*.

Xiao Ling and Daniel S Weld. 2012. Fine-grained entity recognition. In *AAAI*, volume 12, pages 94–100.

Federico López, Benjamin Heinzerling, and Michael Strube. 2019. Fine-grained entity typing in hyperbolic space. In *Proceedings of the 4th Workshop on Representation Learning for NLP (RepL4NLP-2019)*, pages 169–180, Florence, Italy. Association for Computational Linguistics.

Matthew E. Peters, Mark Neumann, Mohit Iyyer, Matt Gardner, Christopher Clark, Kenton Lee, and Luke Zettlemoyer. 2018. Deep contextualized word representations. In *Proc. of NAACL*.

Josef Ruppenhofer, Ines Rehbein, and Carolina Flinz. 2020. Fine-grained named entity annotations for german biographic interviews.

Holger Schwenk, Vishrav Chaudhary, Shuo Sun, Hongyu Gong, and Francisco Guzmán. 2019. Wikimatrix: Mining 135m parallel sentences in 1620

| | Acc L1 | | F1 L1 | | Acc L2 | | F1 L2 | |
|---|---|---|---|---|---|---|---|---|
| | dev | test | dev | test | dev | test | dev | test |
| 200K | 0.62 | 0.57 | 0.64 | 0.62 | 0.32 | 0.25 | 0.35 | 0.30 |
| 220K | 0.62 | 0.66 | 0.73 | 0.71 | 0.34 | 0.29 | 0.36 | 0.34 |
| 240K | **0.73** | **0.67** | **0.75** | **0.72** | **0.36** | 0.29 | **0.38** | 0.34 |
| 260K | 0.71 | 0.66 | 0.73 | 0.70 | 0.35 | **0.30** | 0.37 | **0.35** |
| 280K | 0.73 | 0.66 | 0.73 | 0.71 | 0.36 | 0.30 | 0.38 | 0.35 |
| 300K | 0.69 | 0.64 | 0.71 | 0.68 | 0.35 | 0.30 | 0.37 | 0.34 |

Table 2: We report development set and test set performance of the fine-grained entity typing model trained with different amounts of general entity training data. Best development set performance aligns with best test set performance on Level 1 metrics, and is only off by 1% for Level 2 metrics.

language pairs from wikipedia. *arXiv preprint arXiv:1907.05791*.

Sabine Weber and Mark Steedman. 2021, under submission. Fine-grained named entity typing beyond english using annotation projection.

Semih Yavuz, Izzeddin Gur, Yu Su, Mudhakar Srivatsa, and Xifeng Yan. 2016. Improving semantic parsing via answer type inference. In *Proceedings of the 2016 Conference on Empirical Methods in Natural Language Processing*, pages 149–159.

## A Development set results

Development set results can be seen in Table 2. We use the development set to determine which amount of of added GEs achieves the best result. The exact amount of GEs necessary for an ideal result might vary depending on the fine-grained entity typing model and the NE data used. The development set enables the user to determine this amount for their individual application. Best development set performance aligns with best test set performance on Level 1 metrics, and is only off by 1% for Level 2 metrics.

## B Reproducibility

In keeping with the NAACL reproducibility guildines we report the following implementation details of our model: We trained all models using a single GeForce RTX 2080 Ti GPU. Training each of the models took under an hour. The number of model parameters is 50484362. All hyperparameters of the model were taken from the implementation of Chen et al. (2020). All additional code used and all of our data sets are available on github.com/webersab/german_general_entity_typing.

# On Geodesic Distances and Contextual Embedding Compression for Text Classification

**Rishi Jha*** and **Kai Mihata***
Paul G. Allen School of Computer Science & Engineering,
University of Washington, Seattle, WA, USA
{rjha01, kaim2}@cs.washington.edu

## Abstract

In some memory-constrained settings like IoT devices and over-the-network data pipelines, it can be advantageous to have smaller contextual embeddings. We investigate the efficacy of projecting contextual embedding data (BERT) onto a manifold, and using nonlinear dimensionality reduction techniques to compress these embeddings. In particular, we propose a novel post-processing approach, applying a combination of Isomap and PCA. We find that the geodesic distance estimations, estimates of the shortest path on a Riemannian manifold, from Isomap's k-Nearest Neighbors graph bolstered the performance of the compressed embeddings to be comparable to the original BERT embeddings. On one dataset, we find that despite a 12-fold dimensionality reduction, the compressed embeddings performed within 0.1% of the original BERT embeddings on a downstream classification task. In addition, we find that this approach works particularly well on tasks reliant on syntactic data, when compared with linear dimensionality reduction. These results show promise for a novel geometric approach to achieve lower dimensional text embeddings from existing transformers and pave the way for data-specific and application-specific embedding compressions.

## 1 Introduction

Contextual embeddings, like those BERT (Devlin et al., 2019) generates, improve on non-contextual word embeddings by providing contextual semantics to the real-valued representation of a text. Although these models have been shown to achieve state-of-the-art performance on most NLP tasks, they are notably expensive to train. To help combat this, as mentioned by May et al. (2019), model compression techniques like data quantization (Gong et al., 2014), model pruning (Han et al., 2016), and knowledge distillation (Sanh et al., 2019, Hinton et al., 2015) have been developed. However, at 768 dimensions, the embeddings themselves can be prohibitively large for some tasks and settings.

Smaller embeddings both enable more compact data sizes in storage-constrained settings and over-the-air data pipelines, and help lower the requisite memory for using the embeddings for downstream tasks. For non-contextual word embeddings, Ling et al. (2016) note that loading matrices can take multiple gigabytes of memory, a prohibitively large amount for some phones and IoT devices. While contextual embeddings are smaller, downstream models will face similar headwind for large corpora.

Although there has been more extensive study in the efficacy of compressing non-contextual word embeddings (Raunak et al., 2019, Mu and Viswanath, 2018), to the best of our knowledge few contextual embedding compression post-processing approaches have been proposed (Li and Eisner, 2019). In their work, Li and Eisner (2019) propose the Variational Information Bottleneck, an autoencoder to create smaller, task specific embeddings for different languages. While effective, the computational expense of additional training loops is not appropriate for some memory constrained applications.

Our approach more closely mirrors the work of Raunak et al. (2019) who propose a Principal Component Analysis (PCA)-based post-processing algorithm to lower the dimensionality of non-contextual word embeddings. They find that they can replicate, or, in some cases, increase the performance of the original embeddings. One limitation to this approach is the lack of support for nonlinear data patterns. Nonlinear dimensionality reductions, like the Isomap shown in Figure 1, can pick up on latent textual features that evade linear algorithms like PCA. To achieve this nonlinearity, we extend this approach to contextual embeddings, adding in

*Equal contribution



*Proceedings of the Fifteenth Workshop on Graph-Based Methods for Natural Language Processing (TextGraphs-15)*, pages 144–149
June 11, 2021. ©2021 Association for Computational Linguistics

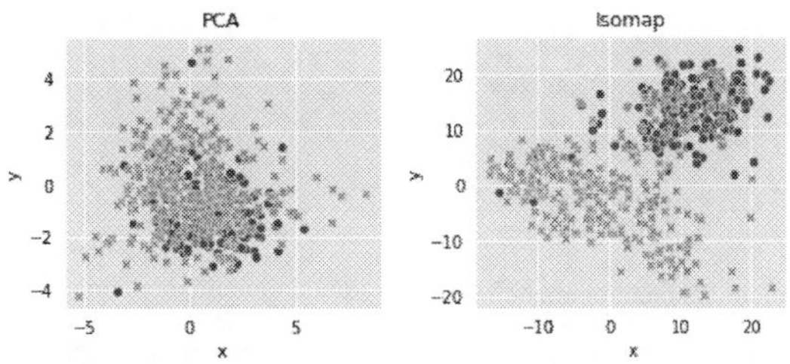


Figure 1: Visualization of two-dimensional PCA and Isomap compressions based on BERT embeddings for the SMS-SPAM dataset (Almeida et al., 2013). Spam is represented by a blue dot and ham by an orange x. We see that for this dataset in two dimensions, the Isomap compression appears more linearly separable than the PCA compression, making classification easier for the former.

additional geodesic distance information via the Isomap algorithm (Tenenbaum et al., 2000). To the best of our knowledge, the application of graph-based techniques to reduce the dimensionality of contextual embeddings is novel.

The goal of this paper is not to compete with state-of-the-art models, but, rather, (1) to show that 12-fold dimensionality reductions of contextual embeddings can, in some settings, conserve much of the original performance, (2) to illustrate the efficacy of geodesic similarity metrics in improving the downstream performance of contextual embedding compressions, and (3) propose the creation of more efficient, geodesic-distance-based transformer architectures. In particular, our main result is showing that a 64-dimensional concatenation of compressed PCA and Isomap embeddings are comparable to the original BERT embeddings and outperform our PCA baseline. We attribute this success to the locality data preserved by the k-Nearest Neighbors (k-NN) graph generated by the Isomap algorithm.

## 2 Related Work

As best we know, there is very little literature regarding the intersection of contextual embedding compression and geodesic distances. Most of the existing work in related spaces deals with non-contextual word embeddings. Despite the rapid growth in the popularity of transformers, these embeddings still retain popularity.

For non-contextual word embeddings, Mu and Viswanath (2018) propose a post-processing algorithm that projects embedded data away from the dominant principal components, in order to greater differentiate the data. Raunak et al. (2019) expand on this algorithm by combining it with PCA reductions. Both approaches are effective, but, are limited to linear dimensionality reductions.

Some nonlinear approaches include Andrews (2016) and Li and Eisner (2019) who both use autoencoder-based compressions. Notably, the former only addresses non-contextual embeddings.

Meanwhile the usage of graphs in NLP is well established, but their usage in the compression of contextual embeddings is not well documented. Wiedemann et al. (2019) use a k-NN classification to achieve state-of-the-art word sense disambiguation. Their work makes clear the effectiveness of the k-NN approach in finding distinctions in hyper-localized data.

## 3 Method

With the goal of reducing the contextual embedding dimensionality, we first processed our data using a pre-trained, uncased BERT Base model. Then, we compressed the data to a lower dimension using both PCA and Isomap as described in Section 3.2. This method aims to capture as much information as possible from the original BERT embeddings while preserving graphical locality information and nonlinearities in the final contextual embeddings.

### 3.1 Isomap and Geodesic Distances

For this paper, to blend geodesic distance information and dimensionality reduction, we use Tenenbaum's Isomap (Tenenbaum et al., 2000). Isomap relies on a weighted neighborhood graph that allows for the inclusion of complex, nonlinear patterns in the data, unlike a linear algorithm like PCA. In specific, this graph is constructed so that the edges between each vertex (datapoint) and its k-nearest neighbors have weight corresponding to the pairwise Euclidean distance on a Riemannian manifold. Dijkstra's shortest path between two points then estimates their true geodesic distance.

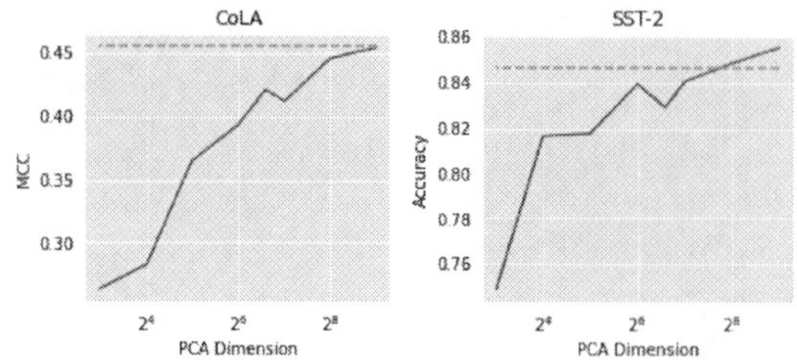


Figure 2: PCA baseline performance on CoLA (Warstadt et al., 2019) and SST-2 (Socher et al., 2013). PCA embedding performance by dimension is represented by the solid blue line. Regression at 768 dimensions is represented by an orange dashed line. On these two datasets, even at much smaller dimensionality, we see that PCA has comparable performance.

These geodesics are particularly useful for delineating points that are close in Euclidean space but not on a manifold i.e. similar BERT embeddings with different meanings.

If we assume the data follows a manifold, Isomap can exploit the Riemannian locality of these complex contextual embeddings. As Figure 1 shows, in some cases this is a good assumption to make since we are then able to dissect complex embeddings into near-linearly separable clusters. Notably, there are some limitations to this approach. If the manifold is sparse, i.e. there are few data points on certain regions of the manifold, or k is too small, the shortest path estimation of the geodesic distance can be unrepresentative of the true distance. On the contrary, if k is too large, Isomap overgeneralizes and loses its fine-grained estimation of the Riemannian surface.

Nonetheless, we hypothesize that these global geodesic distance approximations explain the empirical advantage Isomap has in our setting over other popular nonlinear dimensionality reduction techniques. Many alternatives, like Locally Linear Embeddings (Roweis and Saul, 2000) focus, instead, on preserving intra-neighborhood distance information that may not encompass inter-neighborhood relationships as Isomap does.

### 3.2 Our Approach

We applied our post-processing method to the BERT embeddings through three different dimensionality reductions. We used (1) PCA, (2) Isomap, and (3) a concatenation of embeddings from the two before training a small regression model on the embeddings. This approach aims to use linear and nonlinear dimensionality reduction techniques to best capture the data's geodesic locality information.

**PCA.** To compute linearly-reduced dimensionality embeddings, we used PCA to reduce the 768-dimensional BERT embeddings down to a number of components ranging from 16 to 256. While there are other linear dimensionality reduction techniques, PCA is a standard benchmark and empirically performed the best. These serve as a linear baseline for reduced dimension embeddings.

**Isomap.** To compute geodesic locality information, we post-processed our BERT embeddings with Isomap. The final Isomap embeddings ranged from 16 to 96 dimensions, all computed with 96 neighbors and Euclidean distance.

**Concatenated Embeddings.** To include features from both of these reductions, we combined an Isomap embedding with a PCA embedding to form concatenations of several dimensions. We experimented with ratios of PCA embedding size to Isomap embedding size from 0 to $\frac{1}{2}$ at $\frac{1}{8}$ intervals. We found that this ratio was the main determinant of relative accuracy, so for analysis we fixed the total dimension to 64.

## 4 Experiments and Results

We assess the results of these compression techniques on two text classification datasets. We provide the code for our experiments[1].

### 4.1 Data

We evaluate our method on two text classification tasks: the Corpus of Linguistic Acceptability (CoLA) (Warstadt et al., 2019), a 10657 sentence binary classification dataset on grammatical correctness and the Stanford Sentiment Treebank v2 (SST-2) (Socher et al., 2013), a 70042 sentence

[1]https://github.com/kaimihata/geo-bert

| Embedding | Isomap Dim | PCA Dim | CoLA | SST-2 |
|---|---|---|---|---|
| PCA | N/A | 64 | 0.339 | 0.842 |
| Concatenation* | 16 | 48 | 0.421 | 0.846 |
| Concatenation | 32 | 32 | 0.384 | 0.822 |
| Concatenation | 48 | 16 | 0.357 | 0.817 |
| Isomap | 64 | N/A | 0.332 | 0.814 |
| BERT | N/A | N/A | 0.455 | 0.847 |

Table 1: 64-dimensional embedding performance on CoLA (Warstadt et al., 2019) and SST-2 (Socher et al., 2013). CoLA is measured by Matthews correlation and SST-2 by accuracy. While Isomap did not perform the best outright, on these datasets we found that some inclusion of locality data proved meaningful. This shows the trade-off between locality information and performance mentioned in Section 4.4. The best 12-fold compression performance is asterisked.

binary (positive / negative) sentiment classification dataset.

For CoLA, we used the predefined, 9594 data-point train set and for SST-2, we used the first 8000 samples of their training set to construct ours due to computational limitations. For testing and evaluation, we used the corresponding datasets defined by GLUE (Wang et al., 2018). In addition, for all of our evaluations, we used the same pre-trained BERT embeddings for consistency.

### 4.2 Training and Evaluation

All of these post-processed embeddings, as well as the BERT embeddings, were trained on a downstream regression model consisting of one hidden layer (64 dim) with ReLU activation, a learning rate of $1 \times 10^{-4}$, and were optimized via ADAM (Kingma and Ba, 2015). The BERT embeddings are used as a baseline for comparison.

To evaluate our embeddings on CoLA and SST-2, we used their GLUE-defined metrics of Matthews correlation and validation accuracy, respectively. For each embedding experiment, our procedure consisted of running our post-processing method on the BERT embeddings then training the downstream model. Each reported metric is the average of three of these procedures.

### 4.3 Baseline Comparison

Agnostic of post-processing algorithm, we found reduced-dimensionality embeddings were competitive with the original embeddings. Although smaller reduction factors, understandably, performed better, we found that even when reduced by a factor as large as 12, our PCA embeddings experienced small losses in performance on both datasets (Figure 2). To demonstrate the effect of the inclusion of locality data, we picked an embedding size of 64 dimensions (a reduction factor of 12) to balance embedding size and performance for our main experiment.

In comparison to our 768-dimensional baseline, at 64 dimensions, the best reduction results were within 7.5% and 0.1% for CoLA and SST-2, respectively (Table 1). These results show that with or without the presence of locality data, compressed embeddings can perform comparably to the original embeddings.

### 4.4 Locality Information Trade-off

As shown in Table 1, on neither dataset did the fully PCA or Isomap embeddings perform the best. The best performer was, instead, a combination of these two approaches. This indicates that there must exist a trade-off on the effectiveness of locality data. While without locality data, the embedding obviously misses out on geodesic relationships, too much locality information may replace more useful features that the PCA embeddings extract. Just as the quality of the geodesic distance estimations rely on how well the data fits the underlying manifold, as discussed in Section 3, so, too, does its effectiveness. To explain this phenomenon, we hypothesize that the addition of small amounts of locality data bolsters performance by describing the geodesic relationships without drowning out important syntactic and semantic information provided by PCA.

### 4.5 Task-Specific Locality

While the best reduction consisted of a concatenation of 16-dimensional Isomap and 48-dimensional PCA embeddings, whether the other concatenations performed better than our PCA baseline was dependent on the task. For CoLA, we found that all three concatenated embeddings performed better than PCA, whereas for SST-2, only the top performing concatenated embedding beat out our baseline. To describe this disparity we look towards the nature of the datasets and tasks. Notably, CoLA requires models to identify proper grammar, a syntactic task, while SST-2 requires models to understand the sentiment of sentences, a semantic task. Syntactic data often has some intrinsic structure to it, and perhaps our manifold approach encompasses this information well. Based on this result, exploring this distinction could be an exciting avenue for further study.

## 5 Conclusions and Future Work

We present a novel approach for compressing BERT embeddings into effective lower dimension representations. Our method shows promise for the inclusion of geodesic locality information in transformers and future compression methods. We hope our results lead to more work investigating the geometric structure of transformer embeddings and developing more computationally efficient NLP training pipelines. To further this work, we plan to investigate the efficacy of (1) other graph dimensionality reduction techniques, (2) non-Euclidean distance metrics, and (3) our approach on different transformers. In addition, we would like to investigate whether datasets for other tasks can be effectively projected onto a manifold.

## Acknowledgments

We would like to thank Raunak Kumar, Rohan Jha, and our three reviewers for their thoughtful and thorough comments on improving our paper. In addition, we would like to thank our deep learning professor Joseph Redmon for inspiring this project.

## References

Tiago Almeida, Jose Gomez Hidalgo, and Tiago Silva. 2013. Towards sms spam filtering: Results under a new dataset. *International Journal of Information Security Science*, 2:1–18.

Martin Andrews. 2016. Compressing word embeddings. In *Neural Information Processing*, pages 413–422, Cham. Springer International Publishing.

Jacob Devlin, Ming-Wei Chang, Kenton Lee, and Kristina Toutanova. 2019. BERT: Pre-training of deep bidirectional transformers for language understanding. In *Proceedings of the 2019 Conference of the North American Chapter of the Association for Computational Linguistics: Human Language Technologies, Volume 1 (Long and Short Papers)*, pages 4171–4186, Minneapolis, Minnesota. Association for Computational Linguistics.

Yunchao Gong, Liu Liu, Ming Yang, and Lubomir Bourdev. 2014. Compressing Deep Convolutional Networks using Vector Quantization. *arXiv e-prints*, page arXiv:1412.6115.

Song Han, Huizi Mao, and William J Dally. 2016. Deep compression: Compressing deep neural networks with pruning, trained quantization and huffman coding. *International Conference on Learning Representations (ICLR)*.

Geoffrey Hinton, Oriol Vinyals, and Jeffrey Dean. 2015. Distilling the knowledge in a neural network. In *NIPS Deep Learning and Representation Learning Workshop*.

Diederik P. Kingma and Jimmy Ba. 2015. Adam: A method for stochastic optimization. In *3rd International Conference on Learning Representations, ICLR 2015, San Diego, CA, USA, May 7-9, 2015, Conference Track Proceedings*.

Xiang Lisa Li and Jason Eisner. 2019. Specializing word embeddings (for parsing) by information bottleneck. In *Proceedings of the 2019 Conference on Empirical Methods in Natural Language Processing and the 9th International Joint Conference on Natural Language Processing (EMNLP-IJCNLP)*, pages 2744–2754, Hong Kong, China. Association for Computational Linguistics.

Shaoshi Ling, Yangqiu Song, and Dan Roth. 2016. Word embeddings with limited memory. In *Proceedings of the 54th Annual Meeting of the Association for Computational Linguistics (Volume 2: Short Papers)*, pages 387–392, Berlin, Germany. Association for Computational Linguistics.

Avner May, Jian Zhang, Tri Dao, and Christopher Ré. 2019. On the Downstream Performance of Compressed Word Embeddings. *arXiv e-prints*, page arXiv:1909.01264.

Jiaqi Mu and Pramod Viswanath. 2018. All-but-the-top: Simple and effective postprocessing for word representations. In *International Conference on Learning Representations*.

Vikas Raunak, Vivek Gupta, and Florian Metze. 2019. Effective dimensionality reduction for word embeddings. In *Proceedings of the 4th Workshop on Representation Learning for NLP (RepL4NLP-2019)*, pages 235–243, Florence, Italy. Association for Computational Linguistics.

Sam T. Roweis and Lawrence K. Saul. 2000. Nonlinear Dimensionality Reduction by Locally Linear Embedding. *Science*, 290(5500):2323–2326.

Victor Sanh, Lysandre Debut, Julien Chaumond, and Thomas Wolf. 2019. Distilbert, a distilled version of bert: smaller, faster, cheaper and lighter. *ArXiv*, abs/1910.01108.

Richard Socher, Alex Perelygin, Jean Wu, Jason Chuang, Christopher D. Manning, Andrew Ng, and Christopher Potts. 2013. Recursive deep models for semantic compositionality over a sentiment treebank. In *Proceedings of the 2013 Conference on Empirical Methods in Natural Language Processing*, pages 1631–1642, Seattle, Washington, USA. Association for Computational Linguistics.

Joshua B. Tenenbaum, Vin de Silva, and John C. Langford. 2000. A global geometric framework for nonlinear dimensionality reduction. *Science*, 290(5500):2319–2323.

Alex Wang, Amanpreet Singh, Julian Michael, Felix Hill, Omer Levy, and Samuel Bowman. 2018. GLUE: A multi-task benchmark and analysis platform for natural language understanding. In *Proceedings of the 2018 EMNLP Workshop BlackboxNLP: Analyzing and Interpreting Neural Networks for NLP*, pages 353–355, Brussels, Belgium. Association for Computational Linguistics.

Alex Warstadt, Amanpreet Singh, and Samuel R. Bowman. 2019. Neural network acceptability judgments. *Transactions of the Association for Computational Linguistics*, 7:625–641.

Gregor Wiedemann, Steffen Remus, Avi Chawla, and Chris Biemann. 2019. Does bert make any sense? interpretable word sense disambiguation with contextualized embeddings. In *Proceedings of the 15th Conference on Natural Language Processing (KONVENS 2019): Long Papers*, pages 161–170, Erlangen, Germany. German Society for Computational Linguistics & Language Technology.

# Semi-Supervised Joint Estimation of Word and Document Readability

**Yoshinari Fujinuma**
University of Colorado Boulder
fujinumay@gmail.com

**Masato Hagiwara**
Octanove Labs
masato@octanove.com

## Abstract

Readability or difficulty estimation of words and documents has been investigated independently in the literature, often assuming the existence of extensive annotated resources for the other. Motivated by our analysis showing that there is a recursive relationship between word and document difficulty, we propose to jointly estimate word and document difficulty through a graph convolutional network (GCN) in a semi-supervised fashion. Our experimental results reveal that the GCN-based method can achieve higher accuracy than strong baselines, and stays robust even with a smaller amount of labeled data.[1]

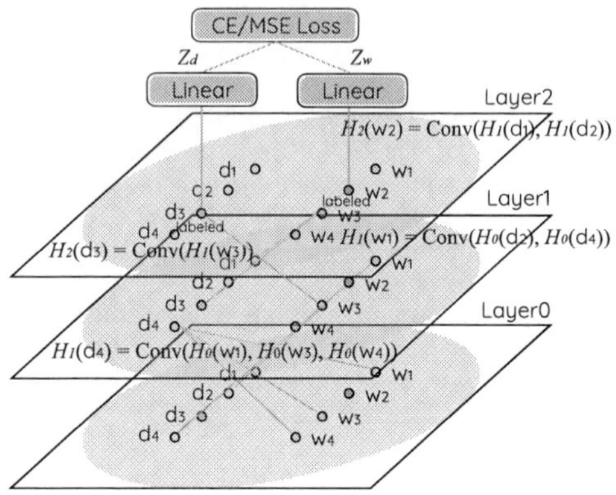


Figure 1: Overview of the proposed GCN architecture which recursively connects word $w_i$ and document $d_j$ to exploit the recursive relationship of their difficulty.

## 1 Introduction

Accurately estimating the readability or difficulty of words and text has been an important fundamental task in NLP and education, with a wide range of applications including reading resource suggestion (Heilman et al., 2008), text simplification (Yimam et al., 2018), and automated essay scoring (Vajjala and Rama, 2018).

A number of linguistic resources have been created either manually or semi-automatically for non-native learners of languages such as English (Capel, 2010, 2012), French (François et al., 2014), and Swedish (François et al., 2016; Alfter and Volodina, 2018), often referencing the Common European Framework of Reference (Council of Europe, 2001, CEFR). However, few linguistic resources exist outside these major European languages and manually constructing such resources demands linguistic expertise and efforts.

This led to the proliferation of NLP-based *readability* or *difficulty assessment* methods to automatically estimate the difficulty of words and texts (Vajjala and Meurers, 2012; Wang and Andersen, 2016; Alfter and Volodina, 2018; Vajjala and Rama, 2018; Settles et al., 2020). However, bootstrapping lexical resources with difficulty information often assumes the existence of textual datasets (e.g., digitized coursebooks) annotated with difficulty. Similarly, many text readability estimation methods (Wang and Andersen, 2016; Xia et al., 2016) assume the existence of abundant lexical or grammatical resources annotated with difficulty information. Individual research studies focus only on one side, either words or texts, although in reality they are closely intertwined—there is a *recursive relationship between word and text difficulty*, where the difficulty of a word is correlated to the *minimum* difficulty of the document where that word appears, and the difficulty of a document is correlated to the *maximum* difficulty of a word in that document (Figure 2).

We propose a method to jointly estimate word and text readability in a semi-supervised fashion from a smaller number of labeled data by leveraging the recursive relationship between words and documents. Specifically, we leverage recent developments in graph convolutional networks (Kipf and Welling, 2017, GCNs) and predict the difficulty of

[1]Our code is at https://github.com/akkikiki/diff_joint_estimate



*Proceedings of the Fifteenth Workshop on Graph-Based Methods for Natural Language Processing (TextGraphs-15)*, pages 150–155
June 11, 2021. 

words and documents simultaneously by modeling those as nodes in a graph structure and recursively inferring their embeddings using the convolutional layers (Figure 1). Our model leverages not only the supervision signals but also the recursive nature of word-document relationship. The contributions of this paper are two fold:

- We reframe the word and document readability estimation task as a semi-supervised, joint estimation problem motivated by their recursive relationship of difficulty.
- We show that GCNs are effective for solving this by exploiting unlabeled data effectively, even when less labeled data is available.

## 2 Task Definition

Given a set of words $\mathcal{W}$ and documents $\mathcal{D}$, the goal of the joint readability estimation task is to find a function $f$ that maps both words and documents to their difficulty label $f : \mathcal{W} \cup \mathcal{D} \rightarrow Y$. Documents here can be text of an arbitrary length, although we use paragraphs as the basic unit of prediction. This task can be solved as a classification problem or a regression problem where $Y \in \mathbb{R}$. We use six CEFR-labels representing six levels of difficulty, such as $Y \in \{$A1 (lowest), A2, B1, B2, C1, C2 (highest)$\}$ for classification, and a real-valued readability estimate $\beta \in \mathbb{R}$ inspired by the item response theory (Lord, 1980, IRT) for regression[2]. The $\beta$ for each six CEFR level are A1$= -1.38$, A2$= -0.67$, B1$= -0.21$, B2$= 0.21$, C1$= 0.67$, and C2$= 1.38$.

Words and documents consist of mutually exclusive unlabeled subsets $\mathcal{W}_U$ and $\mathcal{D}_U$ and labeled subsets $\mathcal{W}_L$ and $\mathcal{D}_L$. The function $f$ is inferred using the supervision signal from $\mathcal{W}_L$ and $\mathcal{D}_L$, and potentially other signals from $\mathcal{W}_U$ and $\mathcal{D}_U$ (e.g., relationship between words and documents).

## 3 Exploiting Recursive Relationship by Graph Convolutional Networks

We first show how the readability of words and documents are recursively related to each other. We then introduce a method based on graph convolutional networks (GCN) to capture such relationship.

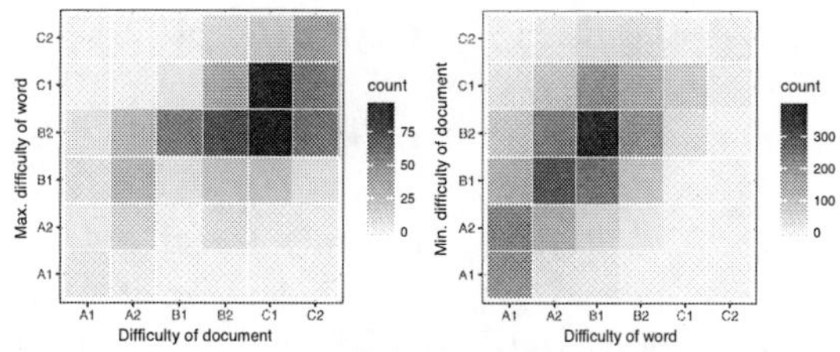


Figure 2: Recursive relationship of word/document difficulty. Word difficulty is correlated to the *minimum* difficulty of the document where that word appears, and document difficulty is correlated to the *maximum* difficulty of a word in that document.

### 3.1 Recursive Relationship of Word and Document Difficulty

The motivation of using a graph-based method for difficulty classification is the recursive relationship of word and document difficulty. Figure 2 shows such recursive relationship using the difficulty-labeled datasets explained in Section 5. One insight here is the strong correlation between the difficulty of a document and *the maximum difficulty of a word in that document*. This is intuitive and shares motivation with a method which exploits hierarchical structure of a document (Yang et al., 2016). However, the key insight here is the strong correlation between the difficulty of a word and *the minimum difficulty of a document where that word appears*, indicating that the readability of words informs that of documents, and vise versa.

### 3.2 Graph Convolutional Networks on Word-Document Graph

To capture the recursive, potentially nonlinear relationship between word and document readability while leveraging supervision signals and features, we propose to use graph convolutional networks (Kipf and Welling, 2017, GCNs) specifically built for text classification (Yao et al., 2019), which treats words and documents as nodes. Intuitively, the hidden layers in GCN, which recursively connects word and document nodes, encourage exploiting the recursive word-document relationship.

Given a heterogeneous word-document graph $G = (V, E)$ and its adjacency matrix $A \in \mathbb{R}^{|V| \times |V|}$, the hidden states for each layer $H_n \in \mathbb{R}^{|V| \times h_n}$ in a GCN with $N$ hidden layers is com-

[2]We assumed the difficulty estimate $\beta$ is normally distributed and used the mid-point of six equal portions of $N(0,1)$ when mapping CEFR levels to $\beta$.

puted using the previous layer $H_{n-1}$ as:

$$H_n = \sigma(\tilde{A}H_{n-1}W_n) \quad (1)$$

where $\sigma$ is the ReLU function[3], $\tilde{A} = D^{-\frac{1}{2}}AD^{-\frac{1}{2}}$ i.e., a symmetrically normalized matrix of $A$ with its degree matrix $D$, and $W_n \in \mathbb{R}^{h_{n-1}\times h_n}$ is the weight matrix for the $n$th layer. The input to the first layer $H_1$ is $H_0 = X$ where $X \in \mathbb{R}^{|V|\times h_0}$ is the feature matrix with $h_0$ dimensions for each node in $V$. We use three different edge weights following Yao et al. (2019): (1) $A_{ij} = \text{tfidf}_{ij}$ if $i$ is a document and $j$ is a word, (2) the normalized point-wise mutual information (PMI) i.e., $A_{ij} = \text{PMI}(i, j)$ if both $i$ and $j$ are words, and (3) self-loops, i.e., $A_{ii} = 1$ for all $i$.

We now describe the components which differs from Yao et al. (2019). We use separate final linear layers for words and documents[4]:

$$Z_w = H_N W_w + b_w \quad (2)$$

$$Z_d = H_N W_d + b_d \quad (3)$$

where $W$ and $b$ are the weight and bias of the layer, and used a linear combination of word and document losses weighted by $\alpha$ (Figure 1)

$$\mathcal{L} = \alpha\mathcal{L}(Z_w) + (1-\alpha)\mathcal{L}(Z_d) \quad (4)$$

For regression, we used $Z$ ($Z_w$ for words and $Z_d$ for documents) as the prediction of node $v$ and used the mean squared error (MSE):

$$\mathcal{L}(Z) = \frac{1}{|V_L|}\sum_{v\in V_L}(Z_v - Y_v)^2 \quad (5)$$

where $V_L = \mathcal{W}_L \cup \mathcal{D}_L$ is the set of labeled nodes. For classification, we use a softmax layer followed by a cross-entropy (CE) loss:

$$\mathcal{L}(Z) = -\sum_{v\in V_L}\log\frac{\exp(Z_{v,Y_v})}{\sum_i \exp(Z_{v,i})}. \quad (6)$$

Since GCN is transductive, node set $V$ also includes the unlabeled nodes from the evaluation sets and have predicted difficulty labels assigned when training is finished.

[3]A simplified version of GCN with linear layers (Wu et al., 2019) in preliminary experiments shows that hidden layers with ReLU performed better.

[4]A model variant with a common linear layer (i.e., original GCN) for both words and documents did not perform as well.

| Dataset | Train | Dev | Test |
|---|---|---|---|
| Words (CEFR-J + C1/C2) | 2,043 | 447 | 389 |
| Documents (Cambridge + A1) | 482 | 103 | 98 |

Table 1: Dataset size for words and documents

## 4 Experiments

**Datasets** We use publicly available English CEFR-annotated resources for second language learners, such as CEFR-J (Negishi et al., 2013) Vocabulary Profile as words and Cambridge English Readability Dataset (Xia et al., 2016) as documents (Table 1). Since these two datasets lack C1/C2-level words and A1 documents, we hired a linguistic PhD to write these missing portions[5].

**Baselines** We compare our method against methods used in previous work (Feng et al., 2010; Vajjala and Meurers, 2012; Martinc et al., 2019; Deutsch et al., 2020): (1) logistic regression for classification (LR cls), (2) linear regression for regression (LR regr), (3) Gradient Boosted Decision Tree (GBDT), and (4) Hierarchical Attention Network (Yang et al., 2016, HAN), which is reported as one of the state-of-the-art methods in readability assessment for documents (Martinc et al., 2019; Deutsch et al., 2020).

**Features** For all methods except for HAN, we use both surface or "traditional" (Vajjala and Meurers, 2012) and embedding features on words and documents which are shown to be effective for readability estimation (Culligan, 2015; Settles et al., 2020; Deutsch et al., 2020). For words, we use their length (in characters), the log frequency in Wikipedia (Ginter et al., 2017), and GloVe (Pennington et al., 2014). For documents, we use the number of NLTK (Loper and Bird, 2002)-tokenized words in a document, and the output of embeddings from BERT-base model (Devlin et al., 2019) which are averaged over all tokens in a given sentence.

**Hyperparameters** We conduct random hyperparameter search with 200 samples, separately selecting two different sets of hyperparameters, one optimized for word difficulty and the other for document. We set the number of hidden layers $N = 2$ with $h_n = 512$ for documents and $N = 1$ with $h_n = 64$ for words. See Appendix A for the details on other hyperparameters.

[5]The dataset is available at `https://github.com/openlanguageprofiles/olp-en-cefrj`.

| Method | Word | | Document | |
|---|---|---|---|---|
| | Acc | Corr | Acc | Corr |
| HAN | - | - | 0.367 | 0.498 |
| LR (regr) | 0.409 | 0.534 | 0.480 | 0.657 |
| LR (cls+m) | 0.440 | 0.514 | 0.765 | 0.723 |
| LR (cls+w) | 0.440 | 0.540 | 0.765 | 0.880 |
| GBDT | 0.432 | 0.376 | 0.765 | 0.833 |
| GCN (regr) | 0.434 | 0.579 | 0.643 | 0.849 |
| GCN (cls+m) | **0.476** | 0.536 | **0.796** | 0.878 |
| GCN (cls+w) | **0.476** | **0.592** | **0.796** | **0.891** |

Table 2: Difficulty estimation results in accuracy (Acc) and correlation (Corr) on classification outputs converted to continuous values by taking the max (cls+m) or weighted sum (cls+w) and regression (regr) variants for the logistic regression (LR) and GCN.

**Evaluation** We use accuracy and Spearman's rank correlation as the metrics. When calculating the correlation for a classification model, we convert the discrete outputs into continuous values in two ways: (1) convert the CEFR label with the maximum probability into corresponding $\beta$ in Section 2, (cls+m), or (2) take a sum of all $\beta$ in six labels weighted by their probabilities (cls+w).

### 4.1 Results

Table 2 shows the test accuracy and correlation results. GCNs show increase in both document accuracy and word accuracy compared to the baseline. We infer that this is because GCN is good at capturing the relationship between words and documents. For example, the labeled training documents include an A1 document and that contains the word "bicycle," and the difficulty label of the document is explicitly propagated to the "bicycle" word node, whereas the logistic regression baseline mistakenly predicts as A2-level, since it relies solely on the input features to capture its similarities.

### 4.2 Ablation Study on Features

Table 3 shows the ablation study on the features explained in Section 4. By comparing Table 2 and Table 3, which are experimented on the same datasets, GCN without using any traditional or embedding features ("None") shows comparative results to some baselines, especially on word-level accuracy. Therefore, the structure of the word-document graph provides effective and complementary signal for readability estimation.

Overall, the BERT embedding is a powerful feature for predicting document readability on Cambridge Readabilty Dataset. Ablating the BERT embeddings (Table 3) significantly decreases the document accuracy ($-0.112$) which is consistent with the previous work (Martinc et al., 2019; Deutsch et al., 2020) that BERT being one of the best-performing method for predicting document readability on one of the datasets they used, and HAN performing relatively low due to not using the BERT embeddings.

| Features | Word | | Document | |
|---|---|---|---|---|
| | Acc | Corr | Acc | Corr |
| All | 0.476 | 0.592 | 0.796 | 0.891 |
| −word freq. | 0.476 | 0.591 | 0.796 | 0.899 |
| −doc length | 0.481 | 0.601 | 0.796 | 0.890 |
| −GloVe | 0.463 | 0.545 | 0.714 | 0.878 |
| −BERT | 0.450 | 0.547 | 0.684 | 0.830 |
| None | 0.440 | 0.436 | 0.520 | 0.669 |

Table 3: Ablation study on the features used. "None" is when applying GCN without any features ($X = I$ i.e., one-hot encoding per node), which solely relies on the word-document structure of the graph.

### 4.3 Training on Less Labeled Data

To analyze whether GCN is robust when training dataset is small, we compare the baseline and GCN by varying the amount of labeled training data. In Figure 3, we observe consistent improvement in GCN over the baseline especially in word accuracy. This outcome suggests that the performance of GCN stays robust even with smaller training data by exploiting the signals gained from the recursive word-document relationship and their structure. Another trend observed in Figure 3 is the larger gap in word accuracy compared to document accuracy when the training data is small likely due to GCN explicitly using context given by word-document edges.

## 5 Conclusion

In this paper, we proposed a GCN-based method to jointly estimate the readability on both words and documents. We experimentally showed that GCN achieves higher accuracy by capturing the recursive difficulty relationship between words and documents, even when using a smaller amount of labeled data. GCNs are a versatile framework that allows inclusion of diverse types of nodes, such as

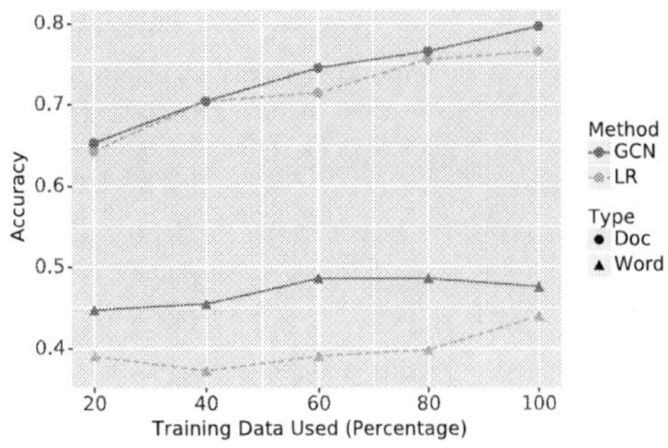


Figure 3: Word and document accuracy with different amount of training data used.

subwords, paragraphs, and even grammatical concepts. We leave this investigation as future work.

## Acknowledgements

The authors would like to thank Adam Wiemerslage, Michael J. Paul, and anonymous reviewers for their detailed and constructive feedback. We also thank Kathleen Hall for her help with annotation.

## References


David Alfter and Elena Volodina. 2018. Towards single word lexical complexity prediction. In *Proceedings of the Thirteenth Workshop on Innovative Use of NLP for Building Educational Applications*.

Annette Capel. 2010. A1–B2 vocabulary: insights and issues arising from the English Profile Wordlists project. *English Profile Journal*, 1.

Annette Capel. 2012. Completing the english vocabulary profile: C1 and C2 vocabulary. *English Profile Journal*, 3.

Council of Europe. 2001. *Common European Framework of Reference for Languages: Learning, Teaching, Assessment*. Press Syndicate of the University of Cambridge.

Brent Culligan. 2015. A comparison of three test formats to assess word difficulty. *Language Testing*, 32(4):503–520.

Tovly Deutsch, Masoud Jasbi, and Stuart Shieber. 2020. Linguistic features for readability assessment. In *Proceedings of the Fifteenth Workshop on Innovative Use of NLP for Building Educational Applications*.

Jacob Devlin, Ming-Wei Chang, Kenton Lee, and Kristina Toutanova. 2019. BERT: Pre-training of deep bidirectional transformers for language understanding. In *Proceedings of the North American Chapter of the Association for Computational Linguistics: Human Language Technologies*.

Lijun Feng, Martin Jansche, Matt Huenerfauth, and Noémie Elhadad. 2010. A comparison of features for automatic readability assessment.

Thomas François, Nùria Gala, Patrick Watrin, and Cédrick Fairon. 2014. FLELex: a graded lexical resource for French foreign learners. In *Proceedings of the Language Resources and Evaluation Conference*.

Thomas François, Elena Volodina, Ildikó Pilán, and Anaïs Tack. 2016. SVALex: a CEFR-graded lexical resource for Swedish foreign and second language learners. In *Proceedings of the Language Resources and Evaluation Conference*.

Filip Ginter, Jan Hajič, Juhani Luotolahti, Milan Straka, and Daniel Zeman. 2017. CoNLL 2017 shared task - automatically annotated raw texts and word embeddings. LINDAT/CLARIAH-CZ digital library at the Institute of Formal and Applied Linguistics (ÚFAL), Faculty of Mathematics and Physics, Charles University.

Michael Heilman, Le Zhao, Juan Pino, and Maxine Eskenazi. 2008. Retrieval of reading materials for vocabulary and reading practice. In *Proceedings of the Third Workshop on Innovative Use of NLP for Building Educational Applications*, pages 80–88.

Thomas N. Kipf and Max Welling. 2017. Semi-supervised classification with graph convolutional networks. In *Proceedings of the International Conference on Learning Representations*.

Edward Loper and Steven Bird. 2002. NLTK: The natural language toolkit. In *Proceedings of the ACL Workshop on Effective Tools and Methodologies for Teaching Natural Language Processing and Computational Linguistics*.

Frederic M. Lord. 1980. *Applications of Item Response Theory To Practical Testing Problems*. Lawrence Erlbaum Associates.

Matej Martinc, Senja Pollak, and Marko Robnik-Sikonja. 2019. Supervised and unsupervised neural approaches to text readability. *CoRR*, abs/1907.11779.

Masashi Negishi, Tomoko Takada, and Yukio Tono. 2013. A progress report on the development of the CEFR-J. In *Exploring language frameworks: Proceedings of the ALTE Kraków Conference*, pages 135–163.

Jeffrey Pennington, Richard Socher, and Christopher D. Manning. 2014. GloVe: Global vectors for word representation. In *Proceedings of Empirical Methods in Natural Language Processing*.

Burr Settles, Geoffrey T. LaFlair, and Masato Hagiwara. 2020. Machine learning–driven language assessment. *Transactions of the Association for Computational Linguistics*, 8:247–263.

Sowmya Vajjala and Detmar Meurers. 2012. On improving the accuracy of readability classification using insights from second language acquisition. In *Proceedings of the Seventh Workshop on Building Educational Applications Using NLP*.

Sowmya Vajjala and Taraka Rama. 2018. Experiments with universal CEFR classification. In *Proceedings of the Thirteenth Workshop on Innovative Use of NLP for Building Educational Applications*.

Shuhan Wang and Erik Andersen. 2016. Grammatical templates: Improving text difficulty evaluation for language learners.

Felix Wu, Tianyi Zhang, Amauri Holanda de Souza Jr., Christopher Fifty, Tao Yu, and Kilian Q. Weinberger. 2019. Simplifying graph convolutional networks. In *Proceedings of the International Conference of Machine Learning*.

Menglin Xia, Ekaterina Kochmar, and Ted Briscoe. 2016. Text readability assessment for second language learners. In *Proceedings of the 11th Workshop on Innovative Use of NLP for Building Educational Applications*.

Zichao Yang, Diyi Yang, Chris Dyer, Xiaodong He, Alex Smola, and Eduard Hovy. 2016. Hierarchical attention networks for document classification. In *Proceedings of the North American Chapter of the Association for Computational Linguistics: Human Language Technologies*.

Liang Yao, Chengsheng Mao, and Yuan Luo. 2019. Graph convolutional networks for text classification. In *Association for the Advancement of Artificial Intelligence*.

Seid Muhie Yimam, Chris Biemann, Shervin Malmasi, Gustavo Paetzold, Lucia Specia, Sanja Štajner, Anaïs Tack, and Marcos Zampieri. 2018. A report on the complex word identification shared task 2018. In *Proceedings of the Thirteenth Workshop on Innovative Use of NLP for Building Educational Applications*.

## A Hyperparameter Details

We conduct random hyperparameter search with 200 samples in the following ranges: $\alpha \in \{0.1, 0.2, ..., 0.9\}$, the learning rate from $\{1, 2, 5, 10, 20, 50, 100\} \times 10^{-4}$, dropout probability from $\{0.1, 0.2, ..., 0.5\}$, the number of epochs from $\{250, 500, 1000, 1500, 2000\}$, the number of hidden units $h_n \in \{32, 64, 128, 256, 512, 1024\}$, the number of hidden layers from $\{1, 2, 3\}$, and the PMI window width from $\{\text{disabled}, 5, 10, 15, 20\}$.

We now describe the selected best combination of hyperparameters for each setting. For GCN in the classification setting, the selected hyperparameters for document difficulty estimation are:

- $\alpha$: $0.3$
- Learning rate: $5 \cdot 10^{-4}$
- Dropout probability: $0.5$
- The number of epochs: $500$
- The number of hidden units $h_n$: $512$
- The number of hidden layers $N$: $2$
- PMI window width: $5$

and for word difficulty estimation, the selected hyperparameters are:

- $\alpha$: $0.2$
- Learning rate: $5 \cdot 10^{-3}$
- Dropout probability: $0.2$
- The number of epochs: $250$
- The number of hidden units $h_n$: $64$
- The number of hidden layers $N$: $1$
- PMI window width: disabled

For GCN in the regression setting, the selected hyperparameters for document difficulty estimation are:

- $\alpha$: $0.4$
- Learning rate: $2 \cdot 10^{-4}$
- Dropout probability: $0.3$
- The number of epochs: $1500$
- The number of hidden units $h_n$: $128$
- The number of hidden layers $N$: $2$
- PMI window width: $5$

and for word difficulty estimation, the selected hyperparameters are:

- $\alpha$: $0.2$
- Learning rate: $1 \cdot 10^{-3}$
- Dropout probability: $0.1$
- The number of epochs: $500$
- The number of hidden units $h_n$: $512$
- The number of hidden layers $N$: $2$
- PMI window width: disabled

# TextGraphs 2021 Shared Task on Multi-Hop Inference for Explanation Regeneration

**Mokanarangan Thayaparan**
Department of Computer Science
University of Manchester, UK
mokanarangan.thayaparan@manchester.ac.uk

**Marco Valentino**
Department of Computer Science
University of Manchester, UK
marco.valentino@manchester.ac.uk

**Peter Jansen**
School of Information
University of Arizona, USA
pajansen@email.arizona.edu

**Dmitry Ustalov**
Crowdsourcing Research Group
Yandex, Russia
dustalov@yandex-team.ru

## Abstract

The Shared Task on Multi-Hop Inference for Explanation Regeneration asks participants to compose large multi-hop explanations to questions by assembling large chains of facts from a supporting knowledge base. While previous editions of this shared task aimed to evaluate *explanatory completeness* – finding a set of facts that form a complete inference chain, without gaps, to arrive from question to correct answer, this 2021 instantiation concentrates on the subtask of determining relevance in large multi-hop explanations. To this end, this edition of the shared task makes use of a large set of approximately 250k manual explanatory relevancy ratings that augment the 2020 shared task data. In this summary paper, we describe the details of the explanation regeneration task, the evaluation data, and the participating systems. Additionally, we perform a detailed analysis of participating systems, evaluating various aspects involved in the multi-hop inference process. The best performing system achieved an NDCG of 0.82 on this challenging task, substantially increasing performance over baseline methods by 32%, while also leaving significant room for future improvement.

## 1 Introduction

Multi-hop inference is the task of aggregating more than one fact to perform an inference. In the context of natural language processing, multi-hop inference is typically evaluated using auxiliary tasks such as question answering, where multiple sentences from external corpora need to be retrieved and composed to form reasoning chains that support the correct answer (see Figure 1). As such, multi-hop inference represents a crucial step towards explainability in complex question answering, as the set of supporting facts can be interpreted as an explanation for the underlying inference process (Thayaparan et al., 2020).

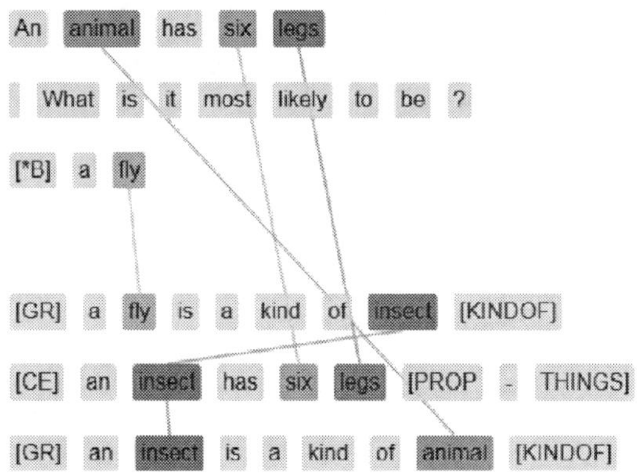


Figure 1: The motivating example provided to participants. Given a question and correct answer *(top)*, the explanation regeneration task requires participating models to find sets of facts that, taken together, provide a detailed chain-of-reasoning for the answer *(bottom)*. This 2021 instantiation of the shared task focuses on the subtask of collecting the most relevant facts for building explanations.

Constructing long inference chains can be extremely challenging for existing models, which generally exhibit a large drop in performance when composing explanations and inference chains requiring more than 2 inference steps (Fried et al., 2015; Jansen et al., 2017, 2018; Khashabi et al.,



*Proceedings of the Fifteenth Workshop on Graph-Based Methods for Natural Language Processing (TextGraphs-15)*, pages 156–165
June 11, 2021. 

2019; Yadav et al., 2020). To this end, this Shared Task on Multi-hop Inference for Explanation Regeneration (Jansen and Ustalov, 2019, 2020) has focused on expanding the capacity of models to compose long inference chains, where participants are asked to develop systems capable of reconstructing detailed explanations for science exam questions drawn from the WorldTree explanation corpus (Xie et al., 2020; Jansen et al., 2018), which range in compositional complexity from 1 to 16 facts (with the average explanation including 6 facts).

Large explanations are typically evaluated on two dimensions: *relevance* and *completeness*. *Relevance* refers to whether each fact in an explanation is relevant, topical, and required to complete the chain of inference that moves from question to correct answer. Conversely, *completeness* evaluates whether the entire set of facts in the explanation, together, composes a complete chain of inference from question to answer, without significant gaps. In practice, both of these are challenging to evaluate automatically (Buckley and Voorhees, 2004; Voorhees, 2002), given that multi-hop datasets typically include a single example of a complete explanation, in large part due to the time and expense associated with generating such annotation. Underscoring this difficulty, post-competition manual analyses on participating systems in the previous two iterations of this shared task showed that models may be performing up to 20% better at *retrieving* correct facts to build their explanation from, highlighting this significant methodological challenge.

This 2021 instantiation of the Shared Task on Explanation Regeneration focuses on the theme of determining relevance in large multi-hop explanations. To this end, participants were given access to a large pre-release dataset of approximately 250k explanatory relevancy ratings that augment the 2020 shared task data (Jansen and Ustalov, 2020), and were tasked with ranking the facts most critical to assembling large explanations for a given question highest. Similarly to the previous instances of our competition, the shared task has been organized on the CodaLab platform.[1] We released train and development datasets along with the baseline solution in advance to allow one to get to know the task specifics.[2] We ran the *practice* phase from February 15 till March 9, 2021. Then we released the test dataset without answers and ran the official *evaluation* phase from March 10 till March 24, 2021. After that we established *post-competition* phase to enable long-term evaluation of the methods beyond our shared task. Participating systems substantially increased task performance compared to a supplied baseline system by 32%, while achieving moderate overall absolute task performance – highlighting both the success of this shared task, as well as the continued challenge of determining relevancy in large multi-hop inference problems.

[1] https://competitions.codalab.org/competitions/23615

[2] https://github.com/cognitiveailab/tg2021task

## 2 Related Work

**Semantic Drift.** Multi-hop question answering systems suffer from the tendency of composing out-of-context inference chains as the number of required hops (aggregated facts) increases. This phenomenon, known as semantic drift, has been observed in a number of works (Fried et al., 2015; Jansen, 2017), which have empirically demonstrated that multi-hop inference models exhibit a substantial drop in performance when aggregating more than 2 facts or paragraphs. Semantic drift has been observed across a variety of representations and traversal methods, including word and dependency level (Pan et al., 2017; Fried et al., 2015), sentence level (Jansen et al., 2017), and paragraph level (Clark and Gardner, 2018). Khashabi et al. (2019) have demonstrated that ongoing efforts on "very long" multi-hop reasoning are unlikely to succeed without the adoption of a richer underlying representation that allows for reasoning with fewer hops.

**Many-hop multi-hop training data.** There is a recent explosion of explanation-centred datasets for multi-hop question answering (Jhamtani and Clark, 2020; Xie et al., 2020; Jansen et al., 2018; Khot et al., 2020; Yang et al., 2018; Thayaparan et al., 2020; Wiegreffe and Marasović, 2021). However, most of these datasets require the aggregation of only two sentences or paragraphs, making it hard to evaluate the robustness of the models in terms of semantic drift. On the other hand, the WorldTree corpus (Xie et al., 2020; Jansen et al., 2018) used in this shared task is explicitly designed to test multi-hop inference models on the reconstruction of long inference chains requiring the aggregation of an average of 6 facts, and as many as 16 facts.

**Question**: Which of the following best explains why the Sun appears to move across the sky every day?
**Answer**: Earth rotates on its axis.

**Explanatory Relevance Ratings**

| # | Fact (Table Row) | Relevance |
|---|---|---|
| 1 | The Earth rotating on its axis causes the Sun to appear to move across the sky during the day | 6 |
| 2 | If a human is on a rotating planet then other celestial bodies will appear to move from that human's perspective due to the rotation of that planet | 6 |
| 3 | The Earth rotates on its tilted axis | 6 |
| 4 | Diurnal motion is when objects in the sky appear to move due to Earth's rotation on its axis | 6 |
| 5 | Apparent motion is when an object appears to move relative to another object's perspective / another object 's position | 5 |
| 6 | Earth rotating on its axis occurs once per day | 4 |
| 7 | Rotation is a kind of motion | 4 |
| 8 | A rotation is a kind of movement | 4 |
| 9 | The Sun sets in the west | 2 |
| 10 | The Sun is a kind of star | 2 |
| 11 | Earth is a kind of planet | 2 |
| 12 | Earth's angle of tilt causes the length of day and night to vary | 0 |
| 13 | The Earth being tilted on its rotating axis causes seasons | 0 |
| 14 | Revolving is a kind of motion | 0 |
| 15 | The Earth revolving around the Sun causes stars to appear in different areas in the sky at different times of year | 0 |

Table 1: An example of the relevance ratings used in the 2021 shared task. *(top)* The question and correct answer. *(bottom)* Facts from the corpus, and their associated relevance rating, sorted from most-relevant to least-relevant. While the dataset provides manual relevancy ratings for the top 30 rows, only 15 are shown here for space.

**Explanation regeneration approaches on WorldTree.** A number of approaches have been proposed for the explanation regeneration task on WorldTree, including those from previous iterations of this shared task. These approaches adopt a set of diverse techniques ranging from graph-based learning (Li et al., 2020), to Transformer-based language models (Cartuyvels et al., 2020; Das et al., 2019; Pawate et al., 2020; Chia et al., 2019), Integer Linear Programming (Gupta and Srinivasaraghavan, 2020), and sparse retrieval models (Valentino et al., 2021; Chia et al., 2019). The current state-of-the-art on the explanation regeneration task is represented by a model that employs a combination of language models and Graph Neural Networks (GNN) (Li et al., 2020), with the bulk of performance contributed from the language model. Strong performance is also achieved by transformer models adapted to rank inference chains (Das et al., 2019) or operating in an iterative and recursive fashion (Cartuyvels et al., 2020). In contrast with neural-based models, recent works (Valentino et al., 2021) have shown that the explanatory patterns emerging in the WorldTree corpus can be leveraged to improve sparse retrieval models and provide a viable way to alleviate semantic drift.

## 3 Task Description

Following the previous editions of the shared task, we frame explanation generation as a ranking problem. Specifically, for a given science question, a model is supplied both the question and correct answer text, and must then selectively rank all the atomic scientific and world knowledge facts in the knowledge base such that those that were labelled as most relevant to building an explanation by a human annotator are ranked the highest. Additional details on the ranking problem are described in the 2019 shared task summary paper (Jansen and Ustalov, 2019).

## 4 Training and Evaluation Dataset

**Questions and Explanations:** The 2021 shared task adopts the same set of questions and knowledge base included in the 2020 shared task (Jansen and Ustalov, 2020), with additional relevance annotation described below. The questions and explanations are drawn from the WorldTree V2 explanation corpus (Xie et al., 2020), a set of detailed multi-fact explanations to standardized elementary and middle-school science exam questions drawn from the Aristo Reasoning Challenge (ARC) corpus(Clark et al., 2018). WorldTree V2 contains 2207 train, 496 development, and 1665 held-out test questions and explanations.

| Team | Performance (NDCG) |
|---|---|
| DeepBlueAI | 0.820 |
| RedDragonAI | 0.771 |
| Google-BERT | 0.700 |
| Huawei_noah | 0.683 |
| Baseline | 0.501 |

Table 2: Overall task performance systems participating in the 2021 Shared Task on Multi-Hop Inference for Explanation Regeneration. Performance is measured using Normalized Discounted Cumulative Gain (NDCG).

**Relevancy Ratings:** The WorldTree V2 dataset used in previous iterations of the shared task includes a single complete explanation per question, supplied as a list of binary classifications that describe which facts are included in the gold explanation for a given question. This 2021 edition of the shared task augments these original WorldTree explanations with a pre-release dataset[3] of approximately 250,000 manual relevancy ratings. Specifically, for each question in the corpus, a set of 30 facts determined to be the most likely facts relevant to building an explanation were manually assigned relevancy ratings by annotators. Ratings are on a 7-point scale (0-6), where facts rated as a 6 are the most critical to building an explanation, while facts rated as 0 are unrelated to the question. An example of these relevance ratings is shown in Table 1.

**Evaluation Metrics:** Historically, performance on the explanation regeneration task was evaluated using Mean Average Precision (MAP) , using the binary ratings (gold or not gold) associated with each fact for a given explanation. To leverage the new graded annotation schema, here we switch to evaluate system performance using Normalized Discounted Cumulative Gain (NDCG) (Järvelin and Kekäläinen, 2002; Wang et al., 2013).

## 5 System Descriptions and Performance

The 2021 shared task received 4 submissions, with 3 teams choosing to submit system description papers. The performance of the submitted systems are shown in Table 2. Overall, we observe that all participating teams substantially improved upon the NDCG score achieved by the baseline model, with increases of up to 30%. In this section, we summarize the key features of the approaches proposed by the teams.

**Baseline (tf.idf).** We adopt a term frequency-inverse document frequency *(tf.idf)* baseline (see, e.g. Manning et al., 2008, Ch. 6). Specifically, given a question and its correct answer, the baseline calculates the cosine similarity between a query vector (representing the question and correct answer) and document vectors (representing a given fact) for each fact in the knowledge base. The model then adopts the tf.idf weighting scheme to rank each fact in the knowledge base for a given question-answer pair. This baseline achieves a NDCG score of 0.501 on the test set.

**DeepBlueAI.** The model presented by Pan et al. (2021) represents the top-performing system in this edition of the shared task with a NDCG score of 0.820 – representing a substantial 32% improvement when compared to the tf.idf baseline. The model employs a two step retrieval strategy. In the first step, a pre-trained language model is fine-tuned to retrieve the top-K ($K > 100$) relevant facts for each question and answer pair. Subsequently, the same architecture is adopted to build a re-ranking model to refine the list of the top-K candidate facts. The authors propose the use of a triplet loss for the fine-tuning of the model. Specifically, the triplet loss minimizes the distance between an anchor and a positive example, while maximizing the distance between the same anchor and a negative example. The team treats question and correct answer as the anchor, while the facts annotated with high ratings are adopted as positive examples. Different experiments are conducted with three negative sampling strategies for retrieval and re-ranking. The best results are obtained when sampling negative examples from the same tables of highly relevant facts. The authors find that the best performance is obtained when averaging the results from RoBERTa (Liu et al., 2019) and ERNIE 2.0 (Sun et al., 2020) with different random seeds.

**RedDragonAI.** The system developed by Kalyan et al. (2021) combines iterative information retrieval with an ensemble of language models, achieving a NDCG score of 0.771. The first step of the proposed approach is to retrieve a limited number of facts to be subsequently re-ranked by language models. The first step is a modification of the approach proposed by Chia et al. (2020), where the model iteratively selects the closest $n$

[3]We thank the authors of this dataset for allowing it to be used anonymously for this shared task, while it is under consideration for publication.

| Table type | DeepBlueAI | RedDragonAI | Google-BERT | Baseline (tf.idf) |
|---|---|---|---|---|
| Retrieval | **0.775** | 0.736 | 0.671 | 0.477 |
| Inference-supporting | **0.716** | 0.712 | 0.683 | 0.433 |
| Complex inference | **0.738** | 0.688 | 0.664 | 0.406 |

Table 3: Performance (NDCG) of the systems when considering different types of knowledge.

| Relevance (>) | DeepBlueAI | RedDragonAI | Google-BERT | Baseline (tf.idf) |
|---|---|---|---|---|
| 0 | **0.820** | 0.771 | 0.700 | 0.501 |
| 2 | **0.818** | 0.764 | 0.686 | 0.489 |
| 4 | **0.831** | 0.692 | 0.601 | 0.416 |

Table 4: Performance (NDCG) when restricted to examining facts with a given minimum relevance rating.

facts to the question using BM25 vectors and then update the query vector via a $max$ operation. The iterative retrieval step is performed until a list of $K = 200$ facts is selected from the knowledge base. Subsequently, the top $K$ explanation facts are re-ranked using language models. The best model consists of an ensemble of BERT (Devlin et al., 2019) and SciBERT (Beltagy et al., 2019). These models are fine-tuned to predict the target explanatory relevance ratings using the following input: `Question + Answer [SEP] Explanation`. Specifically, the authors frame the problem as a regression via mean squared error loss. The ensemble is achieved by linearly combining the scores of the models. The authors reported two negative results obtained using a two-stage approach and different negative sampling techniques. In the two-stage approach, the facts were firstly categorized using binary scores to discriminate between relevant and irrelevant sentences, and then re-ranked predicting the target explanatory relevance rating. Regarding the negative sampling strategy, the authors noticed that highest percentage of errors occurring at inference time was due to irrelevant facts that are lexically close to highly relevant explanation sentences. They attempted to alleviate this problem by randomly sampling facts from the knowledge base and retrieving close negative examples during training. Neither of these two methods resulted in significant improvements.

**Google-BERT.** Xiang et al. (2021) propose a framework composed of three main steps. In the first step, the model adopts a simple tf.idf model with cosine similarity to retrieve the top-K relevant explanation sentences ($K = 50$) for each question and correct answer pair. In the second step, the authors employ an autoregressive model which selects the most relevant facts in a iterative manner. Specifically, the authors propose the adoption of a BERT-based model (Devlin et al., 2019) that selects the facts at iteration $n$ given the facts retrieved in the previous step. The model uses up to 4 iterations. Finally, the authors employ a re-ranking module to re-score the retrieved candidate explanations computing the relevance between each fact and the question-answer pairs. The re-ranking model is implemented using a BERT model for binary classification. The ablation study shows that the first two steps allow achieving a performance of 0.679 NDCG, that is improved up to 0.700 NDCG using the re-ranking model. Moreover, the experiments show that the best performance is achieved when the re-ranking model is adopted to re-score the top $K = 30$ facts.

## 6 Detailed Analysis

In order to better understand the behavior and contribution of the proposed systems, we perform a detailed analysis by grouping the explanatory facts in the supporting knowledge base in different categories. Specifically, we adopt categories that cover various aspects of the multi-hop inference process, ranging from different kinds of knowledge to different degrees of explanatory relevance and lexical overlap, to analyse the performance of each model beyond the overall explanation regeneration score.

### 6.1 Performance by Table Knowledge Types

Similarly to the previous editions of the shared task (Jansen and Ustalov, 2019, 2020), we present the results achieved by the systems considering

| Precison@$k$ | DeepBlueAI | RedDragonAI | Google-BERT | Baseline (tf.idf) |
|---|---|---|---|---|
| $k = 1$ | **0.941** | 0.918 | 0.845 | 0.715 |
| $k = 3$ | **0.878** | 0.849 | 0.791 | 0.582 |
| $k = 5$ | **0.817** | 0.784 | 0.743 | 0.501 |
| $k = 10$ | **0.686** | 0.661 | 0.647 | 0.381 |
| $k = 20$ | 0.512 | 0.507 | **0.523** | 0.272 |
| $k = 50$ | 0.296 | 0.303 | **0.315** | 0.161 |

Table 5: Precision@$k$ for each model across varying values of $k$.

| Overlaps ($\leq T$) | DeepBlueAI | RedDragonAI | Google-BERT | Baseline (tf.idf) |
|---|---|---|---|---|
| 100.0% | **0.820** | 0.771 | 0.700 | 0.501 |
| 90.0% | **0.820** | 0.771 | 0.700 | 0.501 |
| 80.0% | **0.820** | 0.771 | 0.699 | 0.501 |
| 70.0% | **0.818** | 0.769 | 0.698 | 0.497 |
| 60.0% | **0.816** | 0.766 | 0.695 | 0.493 |
| 50.0% | **0.813** | 0.763 | 0.691 | 0.487 |
| 40.0% | **0.804** | 0.754 | 0.679 | 0.471 |
| 30.0% | **0.791** | 0.738 | 0.661 | 0.443 |
| 20.0% | **0.751** | 0.704 | 0.628 | 0.382 |
| 10.0% | **0.653** | 0.603 | 0.559 | 0.261 |
| 0.0% | **0.467** | 0.358 | 0.425 | 0.134 |

Table 6: Percentage of lexical overlap and respective NDCG scores for each model. In this experiment, we measure the performance of the systems considering only those facts that have a percentage of overlap $\leq$ a given threshold $T$. The percentage of overlap is computed by dividing the number of shared terms between question-answer pair and a fact by the total number of unique terms. To evaluate the systems in the most challenging setting, we gradually decrease the value of $T$ down to 0.

different knowledge types in the knowledge base. The explanatory facts in the WorldTree corpus are stored in semi-structured tables that are broadly divided into three main categories:

- *Retrieval*: Facts that generally encode knowledge about taxonomic relations or properties.
- *Inference-Supporting*: Facts that include knowledge about actions, affordances, uses of materials or devices, sources of things, requirements, or affect relationships.
- *Complex Inference*: Facts that encode knowledge of causality, processes, changes, coupled relationships, and if/then relationships.

We break down the NDCG performance of each model across these knowledge types and report the results in Table 3.

In line with previous editions of the shared task, we observe that the performance of the models tends to be higher for the retrieval type, while decreasing for inference-supporting and complex inference facts. This can be explained by the fact that retrieval knowledge is generally specific to the concepts in the questions and therefore easier to rank, while inference-supporting and complex facts typically include more abstract scientific knowledge requiring multi-hop inference. These results are consistent across all the models except from Google-BERT, which exhibits the best performance on the inference-supporting type and more stable results in general. We attribute this outcome to the autoregressive component adopted by the system, which may facilitate the ranking of more challenging explanatory facts. With respect to the general performance of the models, we observe that DeepBlueAI consistently outperforms other approaches across all knowledge categories.

### 6.2 Performance by Relevance Ratings

As described in Section 4, the dataset for the 2021 shared task includes relevance ratings that range from 0 *(not relevant)* to 6 *(highly relevant)*. To better understand the quality of the facts retrieved by each model, we calculated the NDCG score of each model broken down by relevance ratings. The results of this analysis are reported in Table 4.

Similar to the results obtained on different knowledge types, we observe that DeepBlueAI consistently outperforms other approaches across all relevance rating bins. In contrast to other models, DeepBlueAI exhibits increasing performance for higher relevance ratings, confirming that the model is particularly suited for retrieving highly relevant facts (i.e., facts with relevance ratings $> 4$). We conjecture that these results are due to the particular training configuration adopted by the system, which employs a triplet loss to encourage the retrieval of highly relevant facts.

### 6.3 Precision@k

We compute the Precision@$k$ to complement the results obtained via the NDCG metric. In contrast to NDCG which weights facts based on relevancy ratings, here for this evaluation we consider all the facts with a rating greater than 0 as gold. The results of the analysis are reported in Table 5. The results show that DeepBlueAI substantially outperforms other models for values of $k \leq 10$. As $k$ becomes large, other models overtake it's performance, though the difference between models becomes small.

### 6.4 Performance by Lexical Overlap

One of the crucial issues regarding the evaluation of multi-hop inference models is the possibility to achieve strong overall performance without using real compositional methods (Min et al., 2019; Chen and Durrett, 2019; Trivedi et al., 2020). Therefore, in order to evaluate multi-hop inference more explicitly, we break down the performance of each model with respect to the difficulty of accessing specific facts in an explanation via direct lexical overlap. This comes from the assumption that facts sharing many terms with question or answer are relatively easier to find and rank highly.

Table 6 reports the performance of the systems by considering a difference percentage $L$ of lexical overlaps between question-answer pairs and facts computed as follows:

$$L = \frac{|t(Q||A) \cap t(F_i)|}{|t(Q||A) \cup t(F_i)|} \times 100$$

In the equation above, $t(Q||A)$ represents the set of unique terms (without stop-words) in question and correct answer, while $t(F_i)$ is the set of unique terms in a given fact $F_i$. The percentage of overlaps is then derived by dividing the number of shared terms between a question-answer pair and a fact by the number of their unique terms. Therefore, a value of $L$ equal to 50%, for example, means that 50% of the unique terms in a question-answer pair and a fact are shared.

Given a question and a value $L$ computed for each fact annotated with relevance ratings, we measure the performance of the systems considering only those facts that have a percentage of overlaps $\leq$ a given threshold $T$. To evaluate the systems in the most challenging setting, we gradually decrease the value of $T$ down to 0.

Overall, we observe that DeepBlueAI consistently outperforms all the other models across all the considered categories. Interestingly, we observe that Google-BERT performs better than RedDragonAI when considering facts that have zero lexical overlaps with question or answer, confirming the importance of performing specific analysis for the evaluation of multi-hop inference.

Despite the substantial improvement on the baseline obtained by the competing models, we still observe a significant drop in performance with low degrees of lexical overlaps. This drop indicates that the proposed models still struggle to retrieve abstract explanatory facts requiring multi-hop inference, leaving wide space for future improvements.

## 7 Conclusion

The 2021 edition of the Shared Task on Multi-Hop Inference for Explanation Regeneration was a success, with 4 participating teams each substantially improving performance over the baseline model. The best performing team, DeepBlueAI, produced a system that improves absolute performance by 32%, up to 0.820 NDCG, bringing overall state-of-the-art performance at this relevancy ranking aspect of multi-hop inference to a moderate level. We hope that future systems for many-hop multi-hop inference that aim to build large detailed explanations for question answering will be able to leverage these results to build strong relevancy retrieval subcomponents to augment their compositional inference algorithms.

## Acknowledgements

Peter Jansen's work on the shared task was supported by National Science Foundation (NSF

Award #1815948, "Explainable Natural Language Inference"). This edition of the shared task would not have been possible without the hard work of a number of relevance annotators, and their generous offer to anonymously use their data while their work is under review. A special thanks to André Freitas for the helpful discussions. Additionally, we would like to thank the Computational Shared Facility of the University of Manchester for providing the infrastructure to run our experiments.

## References

Iz Beltagy, Kyle Lo, and Arman Cohan. 2019. SciBERT: A Pretrained Language Model for Scientific Text. In *Proceedings of the 2019 Conference on Empirical Methods in Natural Language Processing and the 9th International Joint Conference on Natural Language Processing (EMNLP-IJCNLP)*, pages 3615–3620, Hong Kong. Association for Computational Linguistics.

Chris Buckley and Ellen M. Voorhees. 2004. Retrieval Evaluation with Incomplete Information. In *Proceedings of the 27th Annual International ACM SIGIR Conference on Research and Development in Information Retrieval*, SIGIR '04, pages 25–32, Sheffield, UK. Association for Computing Machinery.

Ruben Cartuyvels, Graham Spinks, and Marie-Francine Moens. 2020. Autoregressive Reasoning over Chains of Facts with Transformers. In *Proceedings of the 28th International Conference on Computational Linguistics*, COLING 2020, pages 6916–6930, Barcelona, Spain (Online). International Committee on Computational Linguistics.

Jifan Chen and Greg Durrett. 2019. Understanding Dataset Design Choices for Multi-hop Reasoning. In *Proceedings of the 2019 Conference of the North American Chapter of the Association for Computational Linguistics: Human Language Technologies, Volume 1 (Long and Short Papers)*, NAACL-HLT 2019, pages 4026–4032, Minneapolis, MN, USA. Association for Computational Linguistics.

Yew Ken Chia, Sam Witteveen, and Martin Andrews. 2019. Red Dragon AI at TextGraphs 2019 Shared Task: Language Model Assisted Explanation Generation. In *Proceedings of the Thirteenth Workshop on Graph-Based Methods for Natural Language Processing (TextGraphs-13)*, pages 85–89, Hong Kong. Association for Computational Linguistics.

Yew Ken Chia, Sam Witteveen, and Martin Andrews. 2020. Red Dragon AI at TextGraphs 2020 Shared Task : LIT : LSTM-Interleaved Transformer for Multi-Hop Explanation Ranking. In *Proceedings of the Graph-based Methods for Natural Language Processing (TextGraphs)*. Association for Computational Linguistics.

Christopher Clark and Matt Gardner. 2018. Simple and Effective Multi-Paragraph Reading Comprehension. In *Proceedings of the 56th Annual Meeting of the Association for Computational Linguistics (Volume 1: Long Papers)*, ACL 2018, pages 845–855, Melbourne, VIC, Australia. Association for Computational Linguistics.

Peter Clark, Isaac Cowhey, Oren Etzioni, Tushar Khot, Ashish Sabharwal, Carissa Schoenick, and Oyvind Tafjord. 2018. Think you have Solved Question Answering? Try ARC, the AI2 Reasoning Challenge.

Rajarshi Das, Ameya Godbole, Manzil Zaheer, Shehzaad Dhuliawala, and Andrew McCallum. 2019. Chains-of-Reasoning at TextGraphs 2019 Shared Task: Reasoning over Chains of Facts for Explainable Multi-hop Inference. In *Proceedings of the Thirteenth Workshop on Graph-Based Methods for Natural Language Processing (TextGraphs-13)*, pages 101–117, Hong Kong. Association for Computational Linguistics.

Jacob Devlin, Ming-Wei Chang, Kenton Lee, and Kristina Toutanova. 2019. BERT: Pre-training of Deep Bidirectional Transformers for Language Understanding. In *Proceedings of the 2019 Conference of the North American Chapter of the Association for Computational Linguistics: Human Language Technologies, Volume 1 (Long and Short Papers)*, NAACL-HLT 2019, pages 4171–4186, Minneapolis, MN, USA. Association for Computational Linguistics.

Daniel Fried, Peter Jansen, Gustave Hahn-Powell, Mihai Surdeanu, and Peter Clark. 2015. Higher-order Lexical Semantic Models for Non-factoid Answer Reranking. *Transactions of the Association for Computational Linguistics*, 3:197–210.

Aayushee Gupta and Gopalakrishnan Srinivasaraghavan. 2020. Explanation Regeneration via Multi-Hop ILP Inference over Knowledge Base. In *Proceedings of the Graph-based Methods for Natural Language Processing (TextGraphs)*, pages 109–114. Association for Computational Linguistics.

Peter Jansen. 2017. A Study of Automatically Acquiring Explanatory Inference Patterns from Corpora of Explanations: Lessons from Elementary Science Exams. In *6th Workshop on Automated Knowledge Base Construction (AKBC) 2017*.

Peter Jansen, Rebecca Sharp, Mihai Surdeanu, and Peter Clark. 2017. Framing QA as Building and Ranking Intersentence Answer Justifications. *Computational Linguistics*, 43(2):407–449.

Peter Jansen and Dmitry Ustalov. 2019. TextGraphs 2019 Shared Task on Multi-Hop Inference for Explanation Regeneration. In *Proceedings of the Thirteenth Workshop on Graph-Based Methods for Natural Language Processing (TextGraphs-13)*, pages 63–77, Hong Kong. Association for Computational Linguistics.

Peter Jansen and Dmitry Ustalov. 2020. TextGraphs 2020 Shared Task on Multi-Hop Inference for Explanation Regeneration. In *Proceedings of the Graph-based Methods for Natural Language Processing (TextGraphs)*, pages 85–97, Barcelona, Spain (Online). Association for Computational Linguistics.

Peter Jansen, Elizabeth Wainwright, Steven Marmorstein, and Clayton Morrison. 2018. WorldTree: A Corpus of Explanation Graphs for Elementary Science Questions supporting Multi-hop Inference. In *Proceedings of the Eleventh International Conference on Language Resources and Evaluation*, LREC 2018, pages 2732–2740, Miyazaki, Japan. European Language Resources Association (ELRA).

Kalervo Järvelin and Jaana Kekäläinen. 2002. Cumulated Gain-Based Evaluation of IR Techniques. *ACM Transactions on Information Systems*, 20(4):422–446.

Harsh Jhamtani and Peter Clark. 2020. Learning to explain: Datasets and models for identifying valid reasoning chains in multihop question-answering.

Sureshkumar Vivek Kalyan, Sam Witteveen, and Martin Andrews. 2021. TextGraphs-15 Shared Task System Description : Multi-Hop Inference Explanation Regeneration by Matching Expert Ratings. In *Proceedings of TextGraphs-15: Graph-based Methods for Natural Language Processing*. Association for Computational Linguistics.

Daniel Khashabi, Erfan Sadeqi Azer, Tushar Khot, Ashish Sabharwal, and Dan Roth. 2019. On the Possibilities and Limitations of Multi-hop Reasoning Under Linguistic Imperfections.

Tushar Khot, Peter Clark, Michal Guerquin, Peter Jansen, and Ashish Sabharwal. 2020. QASC: A Dataset for Question Answering via Sentence Composition. In *The Thirty-Fourth AAAI Conference on Artificial Intelligence (AAAI-20)*, pages 8082–8090, New York, NY, USA.

Weibin Li, Yuxiang Lu, Zhengjie Huang, Weiyue Su, Jiaxiang Liu, Shikun Feng, and Yu Sun. 2020. PGL at TextGraphs 2020 Shared Task: Explanation Regeneration using Language and Graph Learning Methods. In *Proceedings of the Graph-based Methods for Natural Language Processing (TextGraphs)*, pages 98–102. Association for Computational Linguistics.

Yinhan Liu, Myle Ott, Naman Goyal, Jingfei Du, Mandar Joshi, Danqi Chen, Omer Levy, Mike Lewis, Luke Zettlemoyer, and Veselin Stoyanov. 2019. RoBERTa: A Robustly Optimized BERT Pretraining Approach.

Christopher D. Manning, Prabhakar Raghavan, and Hinrich Schütze. 2008. *Introduction to Information Retrieval*. Cambridge University Press.

Sewon Min, Eric Wallace, Sameer Singh, Matt Gardner, Hannaneh Hajishirzi, and Luke Zettlemoyer. 2019. Compositional Questions Do Not Necessitate Multi-hop Reasoning. In *Proceedings of the 57th Annual Meeting of the Association for Computational Linguistics*, ACL 2019, pages 4249–4257, Florence, Italy. Association for Computational Linguistics.

Boyuan Pan, Hao Li, Zhou Zhao, Bin Cao, Deng Cai, and Xiaofei He. 2017. MEMEN: Multi-layer Embedding with Memory Networks for Machine Comprehension.

Chunguang Pan, Bingyan Song, and Zhipeng Luo. 2021. DeepBlueAI at TextGraphs 2021 Shared Task: Treating Multi-Hop Inference Explanation Regeneration as A Ranking Problem. In *Proceedings of TextGraphs-15: Graph-based Methods for Natural Language Processing*. Association for Computational Linguistics.

Aditya Girish Pawate, Varun Madhavan, and Devansh Chandak. 2020. ChiSquareX at TextGraphs 2020 Shared Task: Leveraging Pretrained Language Models for Explanation Regeneration. In *Proceedings of the Graph-based Methods for Natural Language Processing (TextGraphs)*, pages 103–108. Association for Computational Linguistics.

Yu Sun, Shuohuan Wang, Yu-Kun Li, Shikun Feng, Hao Tian, Hua Wu, and Haifeng Wang. 2020. ERNIE 2.0: A Continual Pre-Training Framework for Language Understanding. In *The Thirty-Fourth AAAI Conference on Artificial Intelligence (AAAI-20)*, pages 8968–8975, New York, NY, USA.

Mokanarangan Thayaparan, Marco Valentino, and André Freitas. 2020. A Survey on Explainability in Machine Reading Comprehension.

Harsh Trivedi, Niranjan Balasubramanian, Tushar Khot, and Ashish Sabharwal. 2020. Is Multihop QA in DIRE Condition? Measuring and Reducing Disconnected Reasoning. In *Proceedings of the 2020 Conference on Empirical Methods in Natural Language Processing*, EMNLP 2020, pages 8846–8863, Online. Association for Computational Linguistics.

Marco Valentino, Mokanarangan Thayaparan, and André Freitas. 2021. Unification-based Reconstruction of Multi-hop Explanations for Science Questions. In *Proceedings of the 16th Conference of the European Chapter of the Association for Computational Linguistics: Main Volume*, EACL 2021, pages 200–211, Online. Association for Computational Linguistics.

Ellen M. Voorhees. 2002. The Philosophy of Information Retrieval Evaluation. In *Evaluation of Cross-Language Information Retrieval Systems*, pages 355–370, Berlin, Heidelberg. Springer Berlin Heidelberg.

Yining Wang, Liwei Wang, Yuanzhi Li, Di He, and Tie-Yan Liu. 2013. A Theoretical Analysis of NDCG Type Ranking Measures. In *Proceedings of the 26th Annual Conference on Learning Theory*, volume 30 of *Proceedings of Machine Learning Research*, pages 25–54, Princeton, NJ, USA. PMLR.

Sarah Wiegreffe and Ana Marasović. 2021. Teach Me to Explain: A Review of Datasets for Explainable NLP.

Yuejia Xiang, Yunyan Zhang, Xiaoming Shi, Bo Liu, Wandi Xu, and Xi Chen. 2021. A Three-step Method for Multi-Hop Inference Explanation Regeneration. In *Proceedings of TextGraphs-15: Graph-based Methods for Natural Language Processing*. Association for Computational Linguistics.

Zhengnan Xie, Sebastian Thiem, Jaycie Martin, Elizabeth Wainwright, Steven Marmorstein, and Peter Jansen. 2020. WorldTree V2: A Corpus of Science-Domain Structured Explanations and Inference Patterns supporting Multi-Hop Inference. In *Proceedings of the 12th Conference on Language Resources and Evaluation*, LREC 2020, pages 5456–5473, Marseille, France. European Language Resources Association (ELRA).

Vikas Yadav, Steven Bethard, and Mihai Surdeanu. 2020. Unsupervised Alignment-based Iterative Evidence Retrieval for Multi-hop Question Answering. In *Proceedings of the 58th Annual Meeting of the Association for Computational Linguistics*, ACL 2020, pages 4514–4525, Online. Association for Computational Linguistics.

Zhilin Yang, Peng Qi, Saizheng Zhang, Yoshua Bengio, William Cohen, Ruslan Salakhutdinov, and Christopher D. Manning. 2018. HOTPOTQA: A Dataset for Diverse, Explainable Multi-hop Question Answering. In *Proceedings of the 2018 Conference on Empirical Methods in Natural Language Processing*, EMNLP 2018, pages 2369–2380, Brussels, Belgium. Association for Computational Linguistics.

# DeepBlueAI at TextGraphs 2021 Shared Task: Treating Multi-Hop Inference Explanation Regeneration as A Ranking Problem

**Chunguang Pan Bingyan Song Zhipeng Luo**
DeepBlue Technology (Shanghai) Co., Ltd
{panchg, songby, luozp}@deepblueai.com

## Abstract

This paper describes the winning system for TextGraphs 2021 shared task: Multi-hop inference explanation regeneration. Given a question and its corresponding correct answer, this task aims to select the facts that can explain why the answer is correct for that question and answering (QA) from a large knowledge base. To address this problem and accelerate training as well, our strategy includes two steps. First, fine-tuning pre-trained language models (PLMs) with triplet loss to recall top-K relevant facts for each question and answer pair. Then, adopting the same architecture to train the re-ranking model to rank the top-K candidates. To further improve the performance, we average the results from models based on different PLMs (e.g., RoBERTa) and different parameter settings to make the final predictions. The official evaluation shows that, our system can outperform the second best system by 4.93 points, which proves the effectiveness of our system. Our code has been open source, address is https://github.com/DeepBlueAI/TextGraphs-15

## 1 Introduction

Multi-hop inference is the task of doing inference by combining more than one piece of information, such as question answering (Jansen and Ustalov, 2019). The TextGraphs 2021 Shared Task on **Multi-Hop Inference Explanation Regeneration** focuses on the theme of determining relevance versus completeness in large multi-hop explanations, which asks participants to rank how likely table row sentences are to be a part of a given explanation. Concretely, given an elementary science question and its corresponding correct answer, the system need to perform the multi-hop inference and rank a set of explanatory facts that are expected to explain why the answer is correct from a large knowledge base. An example is shown in Figure 1.

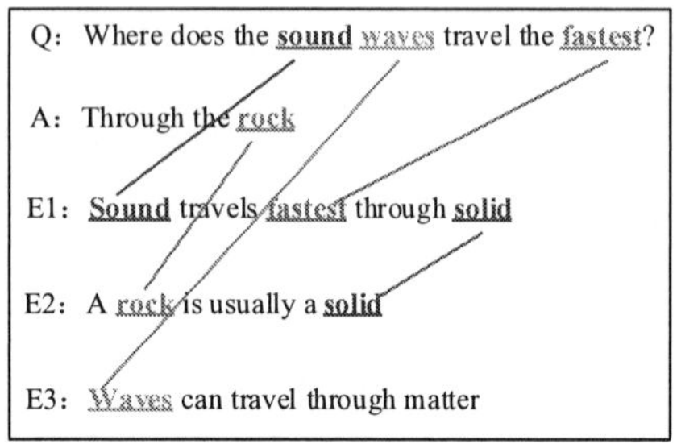


Figure 1: A multi-hop inference example which can explain why the answer is correct for the question.

A number of contemporary challenges exist in performing multi-hop inference for question answering (Thayaparan et al., 2020), including semantic drift, long inference chains, etc. Several Multi-hop inference shared tasks have been conducted in the past few years (Jansen and Ustalov, 2019, 2020), and methods based on large pre-trained language models (PLMs) such as BERT (Das et al., 2019; Chia et al., 2019), RoBERTa (Pawate et al., 2020) and ERNIE (Li et al., 2020) are proposed.

In this paper, we describe the system that we submitted to the TextGraphs 2021 shared task on Multi-Hop Inference Explanation Regeneration. There are two main parts of our system. First, we use a pre-trained language model-based method to recall the top-K relevant explanations for each question. Second, we adopt the same model architecture to re-rank the top-K candidates to do the final prediction.

When determine whether an explanation sentence is relevant to the question, the previous works (Das et al., 2019; Li et al., 2020) constructed a pair of explanations with the QA (questions with corresponding answers) sentence as the input of the PLMs. To reduce the amount of calculation and accelerate training, instead of using all the explanations from the given table, we propose to fine-tune PLMs with triplet loss (Schroff et al., 2015), a loss



*Proceedings of the Fifteenth Workshop on Graph-Based Methods for Natural Language Processing (TextGraphs-15)*, pages 166–170
June 11, 2021. 

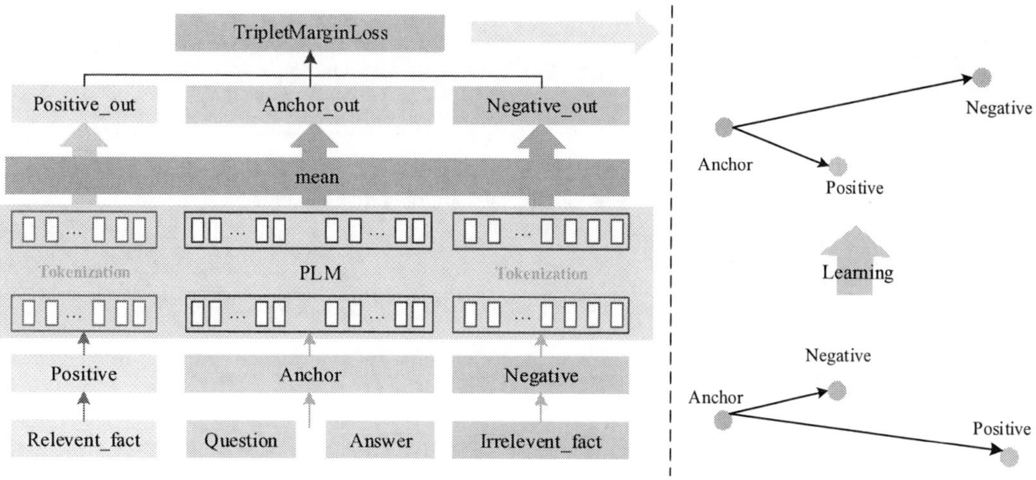


Figure 2: The architecture of the proposed model.

function where a baseline (anchor) input is compared to a positive (true) input and a negative (false) input. For choosing samples as the negative input, we design several ways which will be introduced in Section 3. Experiments on the given dataset show the effectiveness of our model and we rank first in this task.

## 2 Background

**Task Definition** The explanation regeneration task supplies models with questions, their correct answers, the gold explanation authored by human annotators, as well as a knowledge base of explanations. From this, for a given question and its correct answer, the model must select a set of explanations from the knowledge base that explain why the answer is correct.

**Dataset** The data used in this shared task contains approximately 5,100 science exam questions drawn from the AI2 Reasoning Challenge (ARC) dataset (Clark et al., 2018), together with multi-fact explanations for their correct answers extracted from the WorldTree V2.1 explanation corpus (Xie et al., 2020; Jansen et al., 2018). Different from shared task in 2020 (Jansen and Ustalov, 2020), this year's dataset has been augmented with a new set of approximately 250k pre-release expert-generated relevancy ratings. The knowledge base supporting these questions and their explanations contains approximately 9,000 facts. These facts are a combination of scientific knowledge as well as commonsense/world knowledge.

**Evaluation** As mentioned in the official evaluation procedure of TextGraphs 2021, the participating systems are evaluated using Normalized Discounted Cumulative Gain (NDCG), a common measure of ranking quality. Therefore, it inspires us to think of this task as a ranking task.

## 3 Model Architectures

Our system consists of two major components. The first part is the retrieval procedure, which utilize the PLMs fine-tuned with triplet loss to recall top-K (K>100) relevant explanations. The second part is the re-ranking procedure, which use the same model architecture to rank the top-K candidates. The model architecture is shown in Figure 2.

### 3.1 Model

Inspired by the work of Schroff et al. (2015), we adopt the triplet loss in this task. The triplet loss minimizes the distance between an anchor and a positive, and maximizes the distance between the anchor and a negative. We treat the sentences of questions with corresponding answers as the anchor, the facts annotated with high reference value as positives. Both in retrieval procedure and re-ranking procedure, we generate three different negative samples for each positive and anchor pair, which will be discussed in Section 3.3.

After constructing triplet (an anchor, a positive, a negative), we put them into the PLMs (e.g., RoBERTa) to get their representations. These PLMs first tokenize the input sentences and then output the last layer embedding of each tokens. We average each token's embedding as the final representations for the positives, anchors and negatives, which are denoted by $e_p$, $e_a$ and $e_n$ respectively. Then, the models can be fine-tuned by the triplet loss.

### 3.2 Triplet loss

After obtaining the embeddings of the triplet (an anchor ($a$), a positive ($p$) and a negative ($n$)), the triplet loss can be calculated as follow,

$$\mathcal{L}(a,p,n) = max\{d(e_a, e_p) - d(e_a, e_n) + \alpha, 0\} \quad (1)$$

$$d(x,y) = \|x - y\|_2 \quad (2)$$

$\alpha$ is a margin that is enforced between positive and negative pairs.

### 3.3 Training procedure

**Retrieval** First, we use the model introduced above to recall top-K relevant facts. In this step, for each anchor and positive pair, the negative samples are selected by three ways: 1) a sample which comes from the same table file with the positive one and does not annotated as the relevant one with the anchor; 2) a sample within the same mini-batch of positives and does not annotated as the relevant one with the anchor 3) a sample selected randomly among the facts irrelevant to the anchors.

**Re-ranking** After obtaining the top-K relevant facts, we train the re-ranking model with the same model architecture, yet use the another three different ways to select negative samples: 1) a sample within the top-K candidates but is irrelevant to the anchors; 2) a sample within top-100 candidates but irrelevant to the anchors; 3) a sample within the same mini-batch of positives but irrelevant to the anchors.

**Ensembling** Finally, to further improve the performance, we average different results from models based on different PLMs and random seeds.

## 4 Experiments

### 4.1 Parameter settings

All models are implemented based on the open source transformers library of hugging face (Wolf et al., 2020), which provides thousands of pretrained models that can be quickly download and fine-tuned on specific tasks. The PLMs we used in this task are RoBERTa (Liu et al., 2019) and ERNIE 2.0 (Sun et al., 2020). For all the experiments, we set the batch size as 48 and set 15 epochs for both retrieval and re-ranking procedure. We use the Adam optimizer and create a schedule with a learning rate that decreases linearly from the initial lr set ($1e^{-5}$) in the optimizer to 0, after a warmup period during which it increases linearly from 0 to the initial lr set in the optimizer.

| Method | NDCG |
|---|---|
| within the same mini-batch | 0.7597 |
| randomly | 0.7621 |
| **within the same file** | **0.7726** |
| all the three above | 0.771 |

Table 1: The comparison between different ways of selecting negative samples

| Methods | Recall |
|---|---|
| TF-IDF | 0.7001 |
| **Ensemble Retriever** | **0.97562** |

Table 2: The comparison between different retrieval models

### 4.2 Ablation studies

**Retrieval** Since we have design three different ways to choose the negative samples during the retrieval procedure, we did experiments on the validation set to test whether these mechanisms valid or not. From Table 1, we find the most effective way is to choose the negative samples from the same table file with the positive one. Facts in the same table file have the same pattern.

Since for each question and answer pair, there are usually more than ten annotated relevant facts, we select the top-2000 ranked facts from the retrieval phrase, and we find that the NDCG score can reach 97.56% as shown in Table 2. Besides, though the TF-IDF method can quickly score all the facts, its NDCG score is very low compared with our retriever, which proves the effectiveness of our proposed method.

**Re-ranking** To re-rank the top-K candidates, we adopt the same model architecture. We compared the results of the proposed ensemble re-ranker with the TF-IDF baseline model and the proposed ensemble retriever on the test set, as shown in Table 3. We also set different top-K for calculating NDCG@K including 100, 500, 1000, and 2000. From Table 3, we can see that after re-ranking the top-K candidates, the model performance will be improved. Besides, as the increase of K value, the growth rate of NDCG gradually slows down.

| Model | NDCG @100 | NDCG@500 | NDCG@1000 | NDCG@2000 |
|---|---|---|---|---|
| TF-IDF | 0.5011 | 0.5271 | 0.5318 | 0.5352 |
| Ensemble Retriever | 0.7635 | 0.7819 | 0.7846 | 0.7857 |
| **Ensemble Re-ranker** | 0.8027 | 0.8171 | 0.8189 | **0.8198** |

Table 3: The final results compared with different models

### 4.3 Official Ranking

We submitted the scores predicted by the re-ranking model introduced above. The official ranking is presented in Table 4. We rank first in the task, 4.9% higher than the second place, which verifies the validity of our system.

| Team | NDCG |
|---|---|
| **DeepBlueAI** | **0.8198** |
| RedDragonAI | 0.7705 |
| google-BERT | 0.7003 |
| huawei_noah | 0.6831 |
| tf-idf baseline | 0.5010 |

Table 4: Leaderboard

## 5 Conclusion

In this paper, we propose a top performing approach for the task of multi-hop inference explanation regeneration. We fine-tune pre-trained language models with the triplet loss to accelerate training and design different ways for negative sampling. The same model architecture is utilized to recall the top-K candidates from all the facts and to re-rank the top-K relevant explanations for the final prediction. Experimental results show the effectiveness of the proposed method and we win the first place for the task.

## References


Yew Ken Chia, Sam Witteveen, and Martin Andrews. 2019. Red dragon ai at textgraphs 2019 shared task: Language model assisted explanation generation. *arXiv preprint arXiv:1911.08976*.

Peter Clark, Isaac Cowhey, Oren Etzioni, Tushar Khot, Ashish Sabharwal, Carissa Schoenick, and Oyvind Tafjord. 2018. Think you have solved question answering? try arc, the ai2 reasoning challenge. *arXiv preprint arXiv:1803.05457*.

Rajarshi Das, Ameya Godbole, Manzil Zaheer, Shehzaad Dhuliawala, and Andrew McCallum. 2019. Chains-of-reasoning at textgraphs 2019 shared task: Reasoning over chains of facts for explainable multi-hop inference. In *Proceedings of the Thirteenth Workshop on Graph-Based Methods for Natural Language Processing (TextGraphs-13)*, pages 101–117.

Peter Jansen and Dmitry Ustalov. 2019. Textgraphs 2019 shared task on multi-hop inference for explanation regeneration. In *Proceedings of the Thirteenth Workshop on Graph-Based Methods for Natural Language Processing (TextGraphs-13)*, pages 63–77.

Peter Jansen and Dmitry Ustalov. 2020. TextGraphs 2020 shared task on multi-hop inference for explanation regeneration. In *Proceedings of the Graph-based Methods for Natural Language Processing (TextGraphs)*, pages 85–97, Barcelona, Spain (Online). Association for Computational Linguistics.

Peter Jansen, Elizabeth Wainwright, Steven Marmorstein, and Clayton Morrison. 2018. WorldTree: A corpus of explanation graphs for elementary science questions supporting multi-hop inference. In *Proceedings of the Eleventh International Conference on Language Resources and Evaluation (LREC 2018)*, Miyazaki, Japan. European Language Resources Association (ELRA).

Weibin Li, Yuxiang Lu, Zhengjie Huang, Weiyue Su, Jiaxiang Liu, Shikun Feng, and Yu Sun. 2020. Pgl at textgraphs 2020 shared task: Explanation regeneration using language and graph learning methods. In *Proceedings of the Graph-based Methods for Natural Language Processing (TextGraphs)*, pages 98–102.

Yinhan Liu, Myle Ott, Naman Goyal, Jingfei Du, Mandar Joshi, Danqi Chen, Omer Levy, Mike Lewis, Luke Zettlemoyer, and Veselin Stoyanov. 2019. Roberta: A robustly optimized bert pretraining approach. *arXiv preprint arXiv:1907.11692*.

Aditya Girish Pawate, Varun Madhavan, and Devansh Chandak. 2020. Chisquarex at textgraphs 2020 shared task: Leveraging pretrained language models for explanation regeneration. In *Proceedings of the Graph-based Methods for Natural Language Processing (TextGraphs)*, pages 103–108.

Florian Schroff, Dmitry Kalenichenko, and James Philbin. 2015. Facenet: A unified embedding for face recognition and clustering. In *Proceedings of the IEEE conference on computer vision and pattern recognition*, pages 815–823.

Yu Sun, Shuohuan Wang, Yukun Li, Shikun Feng, Hao Tian, Hua Wu, and Haifeng Wang. 2020. Ernie 2.0: A continual pre-training framework for language understanding. In *Proceedings of the AAAI Conference on Artificial Intelligence*, volume 34, pages 8968–8975.

Mokanarangan Thayaparan, Marco Valentino, and André Freitas. 2020. A survey on explainability in machine reading comprehension. *arXiv preprint arXiv:2010.00389*.

Thomas Wolf, Julien Chaumond, Lysandre Debut, Victor Sanh, Clement Delangue, Anthony Moi, Pierric Cistac, Morgan Funtowicz, Joe Davison, Sam Shleifer, et al. 2020. Transformers: State-of-the-art natural language processing. In *Proceedings of the 2020 Conference on Empirical Methods in Natural Language Processing: System Demonstrations*, pages 38–45.

Zhengnan Xie, Sebastian Thiem, Jaycie Martin, Elizabeth Wainwright, Steven Marmorstein, and Peter Jansen. 2020. WorldTree v2: A corpus of science-domain structured explanations and inference patterns supporting multi-hop inference. In *Proceedings of the 12th Language Resources and Evaluation Conference*, pages 5456–5473, Marseille, France. European Language Resources Association.

# A Three-step Method for Multi-Hop Inference Explanation Regeneration

**Yuejia Xiang[1], Yunyan Zhang[1], Xiaoming Shi[1], Liu Bo[2], Wandi Xu[3], Chen Xi[1*]**
[1] Tencent Jarvis Lab
[2] SCMSIT, CETC SCRXX
[3] Northeastern University
{yuejiaxiang,yunyanzhang,xiaomingshi,jasonxchen}@tencent.com
liubo69@cetc.com.cn xuwandi@stumail.neu.edu.cn

## Abstract

Multi-hop inference for explanation generation is to combine two or more facts to make an inference. The task focuses on generating explanations for elementary science questions. In the task, the relevance between the explanations and the QA pairs is of vital importance. To address the task, a three-step framework is proposed. Firstly, vector distance between two texts is utilized to recall the top-K relevant explanations for each question, reducing the calculation consumption. Then, a selection module is employed to choose those most relative facts in an autoregressive manner, giving a preliminary order for the retrieved facts. Thirdly, we adopt a re-ranking module to re-rank the retrieved candidate explanations with relevance between each fact and the QA pairs. Experimental results illustrate the effectiveness of the proposed framework with an improvement of 39.78% in NDCG over the official baseline.[1]

## 1 Introduction

Multi-hop inference for explanation generation (Jansen and Ustalov, 2020), aiming to combing two or more facts to make an inference and providing users with human-readable explanations, has shown significant potential and alluring technological value to improve medical or judicial systems. A typical application in natural language processing is **q**uestion **an**swering tasks (QA). Multi-hop explanation generation for QA aims to retrieve multiple textual facts from pre-defined candidates (typically retrieved from different books, web pages, or other documents) for a given question-answer pair. Figure 1 shows an example. The input is a QA sample and candidate facts, and the task is designed to retrieve facts $f_1, f_2, f_3$, which contribute greatly to inferring the answer.

Multi-hop explanation generation for QA suffers from a key issue: computationally prohibitive, which causes by unaffordable amount of fact combinations, especially when the number of facts required to perform an inference increases. Empirically speaking, the issue causes large drops in performance (Fried et al., 2015; Jansen et al., 2017) and limits the inference capacity (Khashabi et al., 2019). To solve the issue, previous works compute scores for facts in isolation, or by severely limiting the number of combinations of facts (Das et al., 2019; Banerjee, 2019; Chia et al., 2019). Cartuyvels et al. (2020) proposed a two-step inference algorithm for multi-hop explanation regeneration with a relevant fact recall step and an autoregressive fact selection step. In this way, the two-step algorithm prompts efficiency and accuracy.

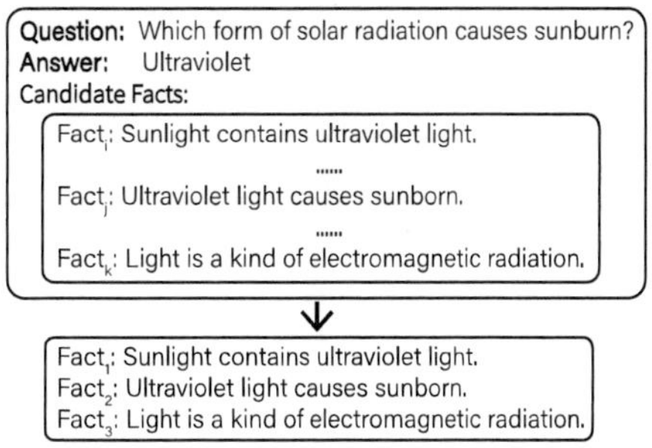


Figure 1: An example of multi-hop inference for explanation generation.

In the TextGraphs 2021 Shared Task, the relevance between the explanations and the QA pairs is of vital importance. However, the autogression selection process may hinder model's ability to recognize the relevance between each fact and QA. The main reason is that the autogression selection proceess emphasizes the relevance between QA and the retrieved facts, paying more attention on retrieved facts when there are many retrieved facts. As the example in Figure 2, the two-step algorithm fails to recognize the order of the retrieved two facts `form means kind` and `ultraviolet rays means ultraviolet light`. To ad-

* Corresponding author

[1]https://github.com/apricotxingya/tg2021task



*Proceedings of the Fifteenth Workshop on Graph-Based Methods for Natural Language Processing (TextGraphs-15)*, pages 171–175
June 11, 2021. 

dress the problem, we propose a reranking module to fine-rank the results of the two-step method with the relevance between each fact and the QA pair. Then, we propose a three-step framework to solve the task: recall, selection and reranking, aiming to iteratively recall facts, select core facts, and then rerank retrieved core facts, respectively.

Experiments on the 2021 version of the task demonstrate the effectiveness of the proposed method, which achieves improvements of 39.78% in NDCG, in comparison with the official baseline.

## 2 Method

The proposed framework is designed to predict a ranked list of facts inferring a QA sample, including three modules: a recall, selection and reranking module, as illustrated in Figure 2.

### 2.1 Recall Module

We stitch the text of Question and Answer together as $q_a$. We extract the roots of words in $q_a$ and all $e$ to reduce the number of different textual expressions caused by singular and plural tenses. For example, `cats` and `made` are modified to `cat` and `make`, respectively.

The recall module aims to iteratively recall facts with high relevance from the candidates. Formally, the recall module can be defined as a function: $f(q, a, f_1, \cdots, f_i, \cdots) : \mathbb{T}^{\mathbb{L}} \mapsto \mathbb{R}^{|C|}$, where $q$ denotes the question token sequence, $a$ denotes the answer token sequence, $f_i$ denotes the recalled facts, $\mathbb{T}$ denotes the token set, $\mathbb{L}$ denotes the length of the sequence $[q, a, f_1, \cdots, f_i, \cdots]$, and $C$ denotes the candidate set.

Specifically, we use the distances between *tf-idf* vectors to compute the distances between two texts. Let $s_i = [q_a, f_1^*, ..., f_i^*]$, where $f_i^*$ is the $i$th best candidate selected from $C_i$ by the selection module (refer to subsection 'Selection Module'). For the convenience of expression, we will write $q_a$ as $s_0$.

First, we compute the Top$k$ of $f_i$ with the smallest distance from $q_a$, forming $C_1$. Then we compute the top $K$ $f_i$ with the smallest distance from $s_1$ to form $C_2$. And so on.

### 2.2 Selection Module

We first normalize the score of each candidate fact to between 0 and 1. Since the score of $s_i$ is 0 to 6, we divide the score by 6 to complete the normalization. Then we use Bert's own binary classification model to calculate the probability size

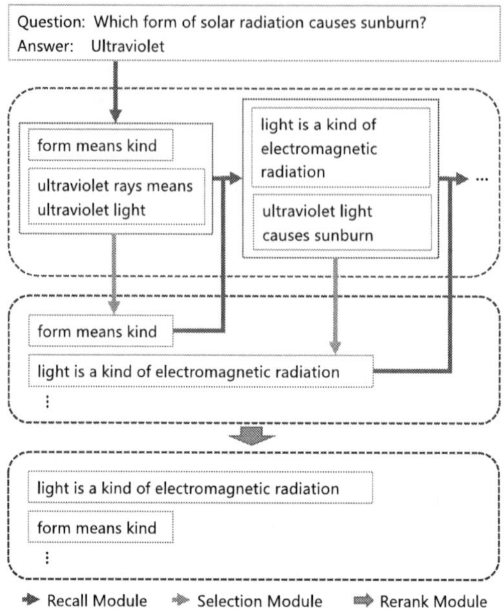


Figure 2: An overview of our method.

$P(f_i|s_{i-1}) = BERT(f_i, s_{i-1})$ of each candidate $f_i$ under $s_{i-1}$. Eventually, we will select a preferred choice with the highest probability as $f_i^*$.

In the prediction process, we keep Top$B$ candidates for each $f_i$ for iteration and treat the currently used fact in Top$B$ as $f_i^*$ in the iteration process. That is, for a $q_a$ our method will generate $B^{(m-1)} * K$ fact links of length $m$. The probability of each fact link is obtained by chain decomposition to $P(q_a, f_1, ..., f_m) = P(f_1|s_0)P(f_2|s_1)$....... Our algorithm computes only sequences of length $m < M$. We finally sort the output sequences $(f_1^{r_1}, f_2^{r_1}, ..., f_m^{r_1}, f_1^{r_2}, f_2^{r_2}, ..., f_m^{r_2}, ...)$. where $f_i^{r_j}$ denotes the $f_i$ of the fact link of sort $j$th. Then the output sequence is de-weighted by removing the non-first occurrence of the fact, to obtain the sequence O.

### 2.3 Rerank Module

The selection module hypothesizes that the predicted facts are always true and predicts the next fact given the previous facts. Such a process tends to suffer from error propagation since errors in the early modules cannot be corrected in later modules. Furthermore, one QA pair may have 20-30 relevant facts in average. The selection module may pay attention to QA at the beginning, but retrieved facts when there are many retrieved facts.

To relieve this problem, we introduce a rerank

| Parameters | Value |
|---|---|
| Learning rate | 2e-5 |
| L2 weight decay | 0.01 |
| $K$ | 50 |
| $B$ | 5 |
| $M$ | 4 |
| Epochs | 4 |

Table 1: Hyperparameters

module, which computes the relevance between the q-a pair and each fact. Unlike the selection module, rerank module does not consider the correlations between pieces of facts, which is complementary to the selection module. Inspired by Natural Language Inference(NLI) task (Williams et al., 2017; Bowman et al., 2015), we cast q-a pairs as premises and candidate facts as hypotheses and identify whether a candidate fact is related to a q-a pair. Following the standard practice for sentence-pair tasks as in BERT (Devlin et al., 2018), we concatenate the q-a pair and the candidate fact with [SEP], prepend the sequence with [CLS], and feed the input to BERT. The representation for [CLS] is fed into a sigmoid layer for a binary classifier.

We select the top $N$ candidate facts from the predicted results of the selection module and assign a score for every candidate fact according to its order. In the inference process, we calculate the probability for each candidate fact. If the probability is above a threshold, the original score of the specific candidate fact is added by a constant. After that, we rerank these candidate facts according to the updated scores. In this way, the model can obtain complementary results from both the selection module and rerank module.

# 3 Experiment

## 3.1 Data and Setting

In the 2021 version of the task, some facts are marked as deleted, duplicated, or low quality. We removed these facts, leaving 8983 facts in the end. The training dataset has 2206 data, the development dataset has 496 data, and the test dataset has 1664 data. This year, the sponsors include a very large dataset of approximately 250,000 expert-annotated relevancy ratings for facts ranked highly by baseline language models from previous years (e.g. BERT, RoBERTa).

We ran experiments on one 16GB Nvidia Tesla P100 GPU. The details of the experimental setup are shown in the table 1. The parameters not mentioned in the table use the default parameter settings of the Bert model.

| method | NDCG |
|---|---|
| Baseline | 50.10% |
| Recall+Selection | 67.89% |
| Recall+Selection+Rerank | 70.03% |

Table 2: Main Results

## 3.2 Evaluation

The evaluation uses NDCG and the organizer provides a very large dataset of approximately 250,000 expert-annotated relevancy ratings for facts ranked highly by baseline language models from previous years (e.g. BERT, RoBERTa).

## 3.3 Baseline

The shared task data distribution includes a baseline that uses a term frequency model (tf.idf) to rank how likely table row sentences are to be a part of a given explanation. The performance of this baseline on the development partition is 0.513 NDCG.[2]

## 3.4 Main Results

It can be seen from the experimental results that our method is significantly better than the baseline model. At the same time, the Rerank module brings an improvement of 2.14%. The experimental results prove that our strategy of recall module and selection module is effective, which is 17.79% higher than the baseline. The rerank module also brings performance improvements as we expected, thus the rerank module make the results more focused on question is reasonable.

## 3.5 Case Study

We show three cases in Table 3. For each case, we show the top10 facts before the rerank module and after the rerank module. We can see from these cases that after applying the recall module and the section module, most of the top10 facts are related to the question and the answer. But there will be some irrelevant facts or less relevant facts that are ranked higher. And, after applying the rerank module, The ranking of facts with high references has generally been improved.

[2] https://github.com/cognitiveailab/tg2021task

| Recall+Selection | | Recall+Selection+Rerank | |
|---|---|---|---|
| Fact (Top10) | Ref. | Fact (Top10) | Ref. |
| the amount of daylight is greatest in the summer | 6 | the amount of daylight is greatest in the summer | 6 |
| summer is a kind of season | 4 | summer is a kind of season | 4 |
| daylight hours means time during daylight | 0 | summer has the most sunlight | 6 |
| the amount of daylight is least in the winter | 2 | increase means more | 0 |
| winter is a kind of season | 2 | daylight means sunlight | 0 |
| increase means more | 0 | summer is hemisphere tilted towards the sun | 5 |
| daylight means sunlight | 0 | high is similar to increase | 0 |
| summer is hemisphere tilted towards the sun | 5 | greatest means largest; highest | 1 |
| summer has the most sunlight | 6 | receiving sunlight synonymous absorbing sunlight | 0 |
| high is similar to increase | 0 | amount of daylight means length of daylight | 0 |

(a) **Question:** *About how long does it take Earth to make one revolution around the Sun?* **Answer:** *summer.*

| Recall+Selection | | Recall+Selection+Rerank | |
|---|---|---|---|
| Fact (Top10) | Ref. | Fact (Top10) | Ref. |
| seals return the same beaches to give birth | 4 | if humans disturb animals; move to different location | 6 |
| a seal is a kind of animal | 4 | a seal is a kind of sea mammal | 4 |
| if humans disturb animals; move to different location | 6 | a seal is a kind of animal | 4 |
| a seal is a kind of sea mammal | 4 | seals return the same beaches to give birth | 4 |
| mammals give birth to live young | 0 | a mammal is a kind of animal | 2 |
| a mammal is a kind of animal | 2 | mammals give birth to live young | 0 |
| a beach is a kind of habitat; environment | 4 | a beach is a kind of location | 4 |
| a beach is a kind of location | 4 | a human is a kind of mammal | 2 |
| if something moves; something in different location | 0 | an environment is a kind of place | 2 |
| a human is a kind of mammal | 2 | an animal is a kind of living thing | 2 |

(b) **Question:** *Female seals usually return to the same beaches year after year to give birth. If they are repeatedly disturbed by humans at those beaches, how will the seals most likely respond?* **Answer:** *They will give birth at different beaches.*

| Recall+Selection | | Recall+Selection+Rerank | |
|---|---|---|---|
| Fact (Top10) | Ref. | Fact (Top10) | Ref. |
| plucking; strumming a string cause that string to vibrate | 6 | matter; molecules vibrating can cause sound | 5 |
| a violin is a kind of musical instrument | 4 | plucking; strumming a string cause that string to vibrate | 6 |
| to cause means to be responsible for | 0 | a violin is a kind of musical instrument | 4 |
| musical instruments make sound when they are played | 4 | musical instruments make sound when they are played | 4 |
| matter; molecules vibrating can cause sound | 5 | a string is a kind of object | 3 |
| a string is a part of a guitar for producing sound | 1 | to cause means to be responsible for | 0 |
| a string is a kind of object | 3 | a string is a part of a guitar for producing sound | 1 |
| a guitar is a kind of musical instrument | 0 | a musical instrument is a kind of object | 3 |
| a musical instrument is a kind of object | 3 | make means produce | 0 |
| make means produce | 0 | vibrating matter can produce sound | 5 |

(c) **Question:** *Bruce plays his violin every Friday night for the symphony. Before he plays, he plucks each string to see if his violin is in tune. Which is most responsible for the generation of sound waves from his violin?* **Answer:** *vibrations of the string.*

Table 3: Some cases in evaluation dataset.

### 3.6 Parameters in Rerank Module

Different number of parameter N in the rerank module can affect the performance to some extent, thus we report the performances using different parameter N. As shown in Table 4, the model achieves best performance with 70.03% NDCG score when N is 50. The NDCG score decreases when N is too low since the rerank module does not play its due role. Further more, a larger N is not necessary.

| K | NDCG |
|---|---|
| 5 | 67.64% |
| 20 | 69.84% |
| 30 | 70.03% |
| 50 | 69.20% |
| 100 | 68.13% |

Table 4: Experiments on parameter of K

## 4 conclusion

We proposed our approach to the shared task on "Multi-hop Inference Explanation Regeneration". Our framework consists of three modules: a recall module, a selection module and a reranking module. The recall module retrieves top-K relevant facts using the distances between *tf-idf* vectors. Then an antoregressive fact selection module is applied to predict the next fact considering the retrived facts. Finally a rerank module is applied to correct the order. The proposed framework achieved an improvement of 39.78% over the official baseline.

## References


Pratyay Banerjee. 2019. Asu at textgraphs 2019 shared task: Explanation regeneration using language models and iterative re-ranking. *ACL Workshop.*

Samuel R Bowman, Gabor Angeli, Christopher Potts, and Christopher D Manning. 2015. A large annotated corpus for learning natural language inference. *arXiv preprint arXiv:1508.05326.*

Ruben Cartuyvels, Graham Spinks, and Marie-Francine Moens. 2020. Autoregressive reasoning over chains of facts with transformers. *ACL Workshop.*

Yew Ken Chia, Sam Witteveen, and Martin Andrews. 2019. Red dragon ai at textgraphs 2019 shared task: Language model assisted explanation generation. *ACL Workshop.*

Rajarshi Das, Ameya Godbole, Manzil Zaheer, Shehzaad Dhuliawala, and Andrew McCallum. 2019. Chains-of-reasoning at textgraphs 2019 shared task: Reasoning over chains of facts for explainable multi-hop inference. In *Proceedings of the Thirteenth Workshop on Graph-Based Methods for Natural Language Processing (TextGraphs-13)*, pages 101–117.

Jacob Devlin, Ming-Wei Chang, Kenton Lee, and Kristina Toutanova. 2018. Bert: Pre-training of deep bidirectional transformers for language understanding. *arXiv preprint arXiv:1810.04805.*

Daniel Fried, Peter Jansen, Gustave Hahn-Powell, Mihai Surdeanu, and Peter Clark. 2015. Higher-order lexical semantic models for non-factoid answer reranking. *Transactions of the Association for Computational Linguistics*, 3:197–210.

Peter Jansen, Rebecca Sharp, Mihai Surdeanu, and Peter Clark. 2017. Framing qa as building and ranking intersentence answer justifications. *Computational Linguistics*, 43(2):407–449.

Peter Jansen and Dmitry Ustalov. 2020. TextGraphs 2020 Shared Task on Multi-Hop Inference for Explanation Regeneration. In *Proceedings of the Graph-based Methods for Natural Language Processing (TextGraphs)*, pages 85–97, Barcelona, Spain (Online). Association for Computational Linguistics.

Daniel Khashabi, Erfan Sadeqi Azer, Tushar Khot, Ashish Sabharwal, and Dan Roth. 2019. On the capabilities and limitations of reasoning for natural language understanding. *arXiv preprint arXiv:1901.02522.*

Adina Williams, Nikita Nangia, and Samuel R Bowman. 2017. A broad-coverage challenge corpus for sentence understanding through inference. *arXiv preprint arXiv:1704.05426.*

# Textgraphs-15 Shared Task System Description : Multi-Hop Inference Explanation Regeneration by Matching Expert Ratings


**Vivek Kalyan** *
Singapore
hello@vivekkalyan.com

**Sam Witteveen**
Red Dragon AI
Singapore
sam@reddragon.ai

**Martin Andrews** †
Red Dragon AI
Singapore
martin@reddragon.ai



## Abstract

Creating explanations for answers to science questions is a challenging task that requires multi-hop inference over a large set of fact sentences. This year, to refocus the Textgraphs Shared Task on the problem of gathering relevant statements (rather than solely finding a single 'correct path'), the WorldTree dataset was augmented with expert ratings of 'relevance' of statements to each overall explanation. Our system, which achieved second place on the Shared Task leaderboard, combines initial statement retrieval; language models trained to predict the relevance scores; and ensembling of a number of the resulting rankings. Our code implementation is made available at `https://github.com/mdda/worldtree_corpus/tree/textgraphs_2021`


## 1 Introduction

Complex question answering often requires reasoning over many evidence documents, which is known as multi-hop inference. Existing datasets such as Wikihop (Welbl et al., 2018), OpenBookQA (Mihaylov et al., 2018), QASC (Khot et al., 2020), are limited due to artificial questions and short aggregation, requiring less than 3 facts. In comparison, the TextGraphs Shared Task (Jansen and Ustalov, 2020) makes use of WorldTree V2 (Xie et al., 2020) which a large dataset of over 5,000 questions and answers, as well as detailed explanations that link them. The 'gold' explanation paths require combining an average of 6 and up to 16 facts in order to generate an full explanation for complex science questions.

The WorldTree dataset was recently supplemented with approximately 250,000 expert-annotated relevancy ratings for facts that were highly ranked by models in previous Shared Task iterations, based on the same consistent set of question and answers.

In previous years, the emphasis of the Shared Task has been on creating 'connected explanations' as completely as possible, which is difficult because of the large branching factor along an explanation path, in conjunction with semantic drift (Fried et al., 2015). In contrast, the scoring function for the 2021 Shared Task required participants to rank explanation statements according to their relevance to explaining the science situation, rather than whether they are in the single gold explanation path. Specifically, participants were required to provide ordered lists of explanation statements for each question, and the Normalized Discounted Cumulative Gain measure ('NDCG' - Burges et al., 2005) was used as a scoring function.

The main contributions of this work are:

1. We show that conventional information retrieval-based methods are still a strong baseline and use a hyperparameter-optimised version of I-BM25, an iterative retrieval method that improves inference speed and recall by emulating multi-hop retrieval.

2. We propose a simple BERT-based architecture that predicts the expert rating of each explanation statement in the context of the current question (and correct answer).

3. We ensemble language model rankings in order to increase our leaderboard score.

## 2 Models

Neural information retrieval models such as DPR (Karpukhin et al., 2020), RAG (Lewis et al., 2020), and ColBERT (Khattab and Zaharia, 2020) that assume query-document independence use a language model to generate sentence representations for the query and document separately. The advantage of this late-interaction approach is efficient

* Work done in conjunction with Red Dragon AI
† Corresponding author



*Proceedings of the Fifteenth Workshop on Graph-Based Methods for Natural Language Processing (TextGraphs-15)*, pages 176–180
June 11, 2021. ©2021 Association for Computational Linguistics

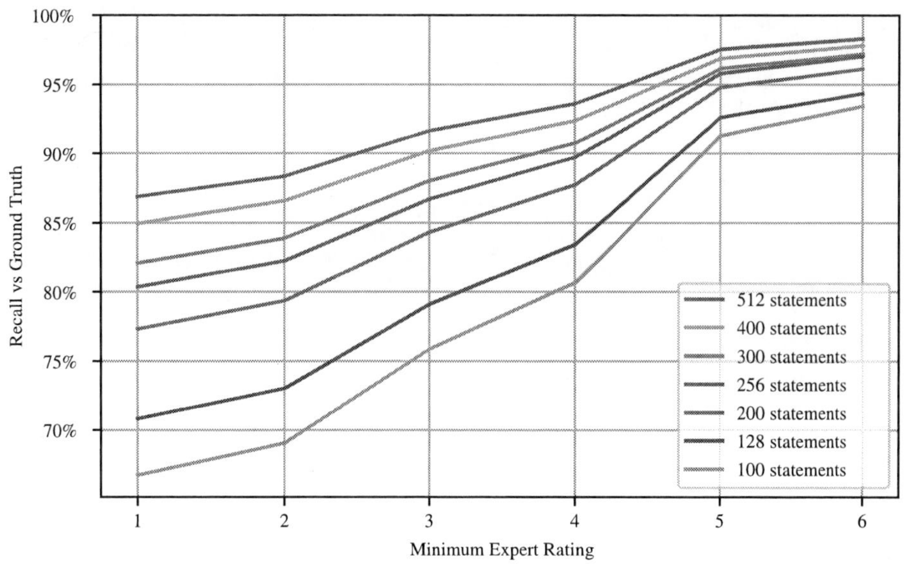


Figure 1: Recall by Rating for different numbers of statements retrieved by I-BM25 stage

inference as the sentence representations can be computed beforehand and optimized lookup methods such as FAISS (Johnson et al., 2017) exist for this purpose. However, the late-interaction compromises on deeper semantic understanding possible with language models. Early-interaction approaches such as TFR-BERT (Han et al., 2020) instead concatenate the query and document before generating a unified sentence representation. This approach is more computationally expensive but is attractive for re-ranking over a limited number of documents. To reduce this computational burden, we have a front-end to our system that retrieves a limited number of facts for later re-ranking by language models.

Overall, our final system comprised 3 distinct stages, each of which were tailored to the Shared Task : Initial retrieval, Language Models and final ensembling.

### 2.1 Iterative BM25 Retrieval

Chia et al (2019) and Chia et al (2020) showed that conventional information retrieval methods can be a strong baseline when modified to suit the multi-hop inference objective.

We adapted the iterative retrieval method (denoted 'I-BM25') from Chia et al (2020) that was shown to perform inference quickly and reduce the impact of semantic drift, resulting in a strong retrieval method for subsequent re-ranking. For pre-processing, we use spaCy (Honnibal and Montani, 2017) for tokenization, lemmatization and stop-word removal.

The I-BM25 algorithm is as follows:

1. Sparse document vectors are pre-computed for all questions and explanation candidates.

2. For each question, the closest $n$ explanation candidates by cosine proximity are selected and their vectors are aggregated by a $max$ operation. The aggregated vector is down-scaled and used to update the query vector through a $max$ operation.

3. The previous step is repeated for increasing values of $n$ until there are no candidate explanations remaining.

Included within the algorithm above are a number of hyperparameters (such as the rate of increase of $n$, and parameters of the BM25 search framework) which were previously optimised for their performance on the 2020 TextGraphs Shared Task. These were re-optimised for the 2021 version, with the goal of maximising the average recall over each category of expert score, for a given number of retrieved explanation statements. Using Figure 1, the number of retrieved statements was chosen to be 200 in the interests of balancing overall recall (93.78% of statements with scores higher than zero) with the later processing cost imposed by the length of the list of candidate statements.

| Model | Dev NDCG | Test NDCG |
|---|---|---|
| Baseline TF-IDF | 0.5130 | 0.5010 |
| I-BM25-base | 0.6669 | n/a |
| I-BM25 | 0.6785 | 0.6583 |
| I-BM25 + BERT | 0.7679 | 0.7580 |
| I-BM25 + BERT ensemble | 0.7801 | 0.7675 |
| I-BM25 + BERT + SciBERT ensemble | 0.7836 | 0.7705 |

Table 1: NDCG score comparison as evaluated locally and on the leaderboard

### 2.2 Language Models for Rating Classification/Regression

Pre-trained versions of BERT (Devlin et al., 2019) are widely adapted and fine-tuned for many downstream NLP tasks. For the Shared Task, we fine-tuned this language model to predict the Expert Rating from text sequences, where each sequence is a question (including the correct answer) and explanation pair separated by the [SEP] token, and the prediction task is a regression against the gold Expert Rating (using a Mean Square Error loss minimisation objective).

During inference, we use the 200 explanations returned by the earlier I-BM25 phase for each question, fed into BERT as a question and explanation pair. We then used the (floating point) score output by the trained BERT as a sortable value by which to rank the explanations in terms of relevancy.

### 2.3 Ensembling of Rankings

In the later stages of the competition, we decided to employ an ensemble of different models - 4 BERT models (each fine-tuned with a different seed) and a similarly fine-tuned model based on a pretrained SciBERT (Beltagy et al., 2019).

We ensembled the ranked output of each model together by simply linearly combining each rank into an aggregate.[1] More sophisticated combinations were considered, but these suffered from overfitting on the Dev set.

## 3 Experiments

Our system comprised three stages, and we present results of the experiments used to validate our choices at each stage, with the overall results being compiled in Table 1.

[1]This method was simplified since each of the re-rankings was sourced from the same I-BM25 output list

### 3.1 Retrieval

As an initial step, we focused on ensuring our retrieval model found as many relevant explanations as possible in its output list (regardless of the order), while keeping the list as short as possible. So as to measure this, we computed an "Oracle NDCG" score, the score the retrieval model would have received if it had access to an oracle and thus could return the perfect rank ordering.

| Retrieval Model | Oracle NDCG |
|---|---|
| TF-IDF | 0.7547 |
| I-BM25-base | 0.8941 |
| I-BM25 | 0.9378 |

Table 2: Oracle NDCG score on WorldTree V2 dataset

In addition to measuring the performance of the initial retrieval stage, the Oracle NDCG score also gave us the ceiling for performance of our second stage models.

### 3.2 Language Models

| Language Model | Dev NDCG |
|---|---|
| DistilBERT | 0.7353 |
| BERT | 0.7679 |
| SciBERT | 0.7541 |

Table 3: Language model comparison

While we initially tried DistilBERT (Sanh et al., 2020) - a lean version of BERT with fewer parameters - we found that BERT outperformed DistilBERT by a significant enough margin to suggest that the efficiency of DistilBERT was not a net win.

We also attempted to fine-tune RoBERTa (Liu et al., 2019) on the regression task, but were unable to achieve satisfactory results quickly enough to incorporate it into our ensembling regime.

### 3.3 Ensembling

While SciBERT performed slightly worse than other models on an individual basis, ensembling it with regular BERT models resulted in a much higher score - which suggests that its representations are well differentiated by its pretraining regime.

## 4 Negative Results

### 4.1 Two-stage representation

In addition to the straight regression models used in our final submissions, we also investigated an architecture that modelled the explanation ratings for each question/answer via a two-stage process.

The first stage was a binary indicator of whether the explanation was relevant or not (1 if it had a higher-than-zero rating, 0 if zero-rated or missing). The second stage (used during inference if the first stage signalled 'relevant'), was modelled as a distribution over the possible scores. The intuition being that some statements are 'broad, powerful concepts' (likely to score highly if relevant) whereas others are 'tiny lexical adjustments' (likely to be low-scoring if considered relevant).

Despite the intuitive appeal of modelling the statement rating process in this way, and the apparently reasonable distributions learned, this architecture did not lead to higher scores overall - though that may be due to other factors (such as running out of time to finesse the training and/or inference process).

### 4.2 Negative Sampling

While examining the types of prediction errors our initial models were making during inference, we noticed that quite a number of the incorrectly chosen explanations (from the I-BM25 stage) were lexically close to highly-rated explanation statements. This showed that there was a mismatch between frequency of zero-rated Expert Ratings in the Train set, and what would be experienced during inference. Therefore, we hypothesised that adding more negative samples would help the model discern between these similar explanations.

Two methods were tried : (i) Randomly sampling from the explanations database; and (ii) Using the retrieval model to propose other close negatives during training. Unfortunately, neither resulted in any significant improvement in scores.

## 5 Discussion

In previous versions of the Textgraphs Shared Task, the goal was essentially to obtain the single 'gold explanation' that perfectly matched an expertly crafted graph of explanation statements, with the scoring being based on a ranking metric that rewarded participants for finding these gold explanation statements. This task was challenging due to the semantic drift issue previously mentioned, and the sensitivity of the scoring to choosing the same explanation path as the original annotators.[2] Paradoxically, instead of tackling the problem with logic-oriented graph planning methods, the dominant techniques tended to rely on large language models which could maximise the ranking scores without 'understanding the bigger picture'.

The change of scoring metric in this current Shared Task, to incorporate all statements that are relevant to the question and answer, appears to target the capturing of 'bigger picture' ideas. However, this seems to have once again promoted the use of large language models, since they provide a system component that can bring the most 'common sense' into the multi-step reasoning domain, without getting tangled in the logical weeds that go into producing the gold explanations.

While the addition of the expert ratings on the explanation statements is undoubtedly positive for the Shared Task dataset, it is not clear to what extent it helps address the multi-hop nature of the challenge - on which significant progress had already been made (and will hopefully continue based on other promising directions have been identified by previous iterations of the Shared Task.)

## 6 Conclusion

Our Shared Task submissions showed that ensembles of language models trained on a regression basis to predict Expert Ratings obtain highly competitive results.

We look forward to achieving further progress on the multi-hop reasoning task in the future.

[2] In terms of extra data, supposing that a Worldtree Explanation Corpus continues to be the basis of the Textgraphs Shared Task in the future, it would be very helpful to have the structured information that resulted in the output of the Worldtree Explanation Corpus v2.1 Desk Reference, since that would allow a cleaner interpretation of the structured table data - without participants having to each independently reinvent the wheel

## References

Iz Beltagy, Kyle Lo, and Arman Cohan. 2019. SciBERT: Pretrained language model for scientific text. *arXiv preprint arXiv:1903.10676*.

Chris Burges, Tal Shaked, Erin Renshaw, Ari Lazier, Matt Deeds, Nicole Hamilton, and Greg Hullender. 2005. Learning to rank using gradient descent. In *Proceedings of the 22nd International Conference on Machine Learning*, ICML '05, page 89–96, New York, NY, USA. Association for Computing Machinery.

Yew Ken Chia, Sam Witteveen, and Martin Andrews. 2019. Red Dragon AI at TextGraphs 2019 shared task: Language model assisted explanation generation. In *Proceedings of the Thirteenth Workshop on Graph-Based Methods for Natural Language Processing (TextGraphs-13)*, pages 85–89, Hong Kong. Association for Computational Linguistics.

Yew Ken Chia, Sam Witteveen, and Martin Andrews. 2020. Red Dragon AI at TextGraphs 2020 shared task : LIT : LSTM-interleaved transformer for multi-hop explanation ranking. In *Proceedings of the Graph-based Methods for Natural Language Processing (TextGraphs)*, pages 115–120, Barcelona, Spain (Online). Association for Computational Linguistics.

Jacob Devlin, Ming-Wei Chang, Kenton Lee, and Kristina Toutanova. 2019. BERT: Pre-training of deep bidirectional transformers for language understanding. *arXiv preprint arXiv:1810.04805*.

Daniel Fried, Peter Jansen, Gustave Hahn-Powell, Mihai Surdeanu, and Peter Clark. 2015. Higher-order lexical semantic models for non-factoid answer reranking. *Transactions of the Association for Computational Linguistics*, 3:197–210.

Shuguang Han, Xuanhui Wang, Mike Bendersky, and Marc Najork. 2020. Learning-to-rank with BERT in TF-Ranking. *arXiv preprint arXiv:2004.08476*.

Matthew Honnibal and Ines Montani. 2017. spaCy 2: Natural language understanding with Bloom embeddings, convolutional neural networks and incremental parsing. To appear.

Peter Jansen and Dmitry Ustalov. 2020. TextGraphs 2020 Shared Task on Multi-Hop Inference for Explanation Regeneration. In *Proceedings of the Graph-based Methods for Natural Language Processing (TextGraphs)*, pages 85–97, Barcelona, Spain (Online). Association for Computational Linguistics.

Jeff Johnson, Matthijs Douze, and Hervé Jégou. 2017. Billion-scale similarity search with GPUs. *arXiv preprint arXiv:1702.08734*.

Vladimir Karpukhin, Barlas Oğuz, Sewon Min, Ledell Wu, Sergey Edunov, Danqi Chen, and Wen-tau Yih. 2020. Dense passage retrieval for open-domain question answering. *arXiv preprint arXiv:2004.04906*.

Omar Khattab and Matei Zaharia. 2020. ColBERT: Efficient and effective passage search via contextualized late interaction over BERT. *arXiv preprint arXiv:2004.12832*.

Tushar Khot, Peter Clark, Michal Guerquin, Peter Jansen, and Ashish Sabharwal. 2020. QASC: A dataset for question answering via sentence composition. In *AAAI*, pages 8082–8090.

Patrick Lewis, Ethan Perez, Aleksandara Piktus, Fabio Petroni, Vladimir Karpukhin, Naman Goyal, Heinrich Küttler, Mike Lewis, Wen-tau Yih, Tim Rocktäschel, et al. 2020. Retrieval-augmented generation for knowledge-intensive NLP tasks. *arXiv preprint arXiv:2005.11401*.

Yinhan Liu, Myle Ott, Naman Goyal, Jingfei Du, Mandar Joshi, Danqi Chen, Omer Levy, Mike Lewis, Luke Zettlemoyer, and Veselin Stoyanov. 2019. RoBERTa: A robustly optimized BERT pretraining approach. *arXiv preprint arXiv:1907.11692*.

Todor Mihaylov, Peter Clark, Tushar Khot, and Ashish Sabharwal. 2018. Can a suit of armor conduct electricity? A new dataset for open book question answering. *arXiv preprint arXiv:1809.02789*.

Victor Sanh, Lysandre Debut, Julien Chaumond, and Thomas Wolf. 2020. DistilBERT, a distilled version of BERT: smaller, faster, cheaper and lighter. *arXiv preprint arXiv:1910.01108*.

Johannes Welbl, Pontus Stenetorp, and Sebastian Riedel. 2018. Constructing datasets for multi-hop reading comprehension across documents. *Transactions of the Association for Computational Linguistics*, 6:287–302.

Zhengnan Xie, Sebastian Thiem, Jaycie Martin, Elizabeth Wainwright, Steven Marmorstein, and Peter Jansen. 2020. WorldTree v2: A corpus of science-domain structured explanations and inference patterns supporting multi-hop inference. In *Proceedings of the 12th Language Resources and Evaluation Conference*, pages 5456–5473, Marseille, France. European Language Resources Association.

# Author Index

**Association for Computational Linguistics**
209 N. Eighth Street
Stroudsburg, Pennsylvania 18360

CURRAN ASSOCIATES INC.
proceedings.com

ISBN 978-1-7138-9158-1

9 781713 891581